Historical Analysis
Contemporary
Approaches
to Clio's Craft

Historical Analysis
Contemporary Approaches to Clio's Craft

Richard E. Beringer
University of North Dakota

JOHN WILEY & SONS
New York Santa Barbara Chichester Brisbane Toronto

Library of Congress Cataloging in Publication Data

Beringer, Richard E   1933-
  Historical analysis.

  Includes bibliographical references.
    1. History—Methodology. 2. United States—Historiography. I. Title.
D16.B45   901'.8   77-10589
ISBN 0-471-06995-7
ISBN 0-471-06996-5 pbk.

Printed in the United States of America

10 9 8 7 6 5 4 3 2 1

To David and Jeffrey, who have methods all their own

Preface

The major purpose of this collection is to provide an elementary introduction to historical method for the average undergraduate or beginning graduate student. By historical method I do not refer to evaluation of evidence, examination of sources for bias, or any of the other multitude of necessary tasks outlined in numerous books that attempt to meet the needs of the student just beginning historical research. I mean, instead, the ways in which historical problems may be approached, and the various techniques, such as symbol analysis, reference group theory, and collective biography, that are used to organize and interpret mounds of raw data. Although traditional approaches may appear conspicuous by their absence, I do not mean to denigrate them or suggest that the basic skills needed by any historian may be ignored. But there are many handbooks and manuals that describe at tedious length one historian's encounter with spurious documents (how few students are going to find this relevant to their research!); list basic references; discuss notetaking, footnote form, and grammar; and introduce the student to problems of the objectivity and meaning of primary sources (which are very important questions indeed).

Obviously, history students must be able to assess evidence, use bibliographical aids, write well, and footnote properly. As important as these skills may be, however, there are others of equal value. A casual glance at any leading journal indicates that methods rarely used twenty or thirty years ago are commonly used today. This book, therefore, also illustrates the fact that there are many acceptable means by which historical investigation and analysis may be carried out. The major feature is a sampling of a wide range of historiographical techniques, including those employing literary criticism, psychology, sociology, and statistics. The readings and discussions are organized along a spectrum bridging the polar positions of abstract, intuitive, intellectual history, and systematic, precise, quantitative history. The first section is therefore devoted to intellectual history, including such imprecise yet highly flexible and useful concepts as the history of ideas and the *Zeitgeist*. The second section is devoted to more carefully defined yet less flexible devices contributed by psychology and sociology: developmental psychology, cognitive dissonance, informal organization, and the like. The third section deals with quantification, which is quite precise but often quite inflexible, in an effort to show how systematic measurement has been applied to history. Here collective biography, correlation and regression, and demography are among the methods illustrated. No doubt the emphasis on precision in this paragraph is misleading. While it is true that the results of quantitative studies are likely to be more precise than those of literary analysis, they are not by definition any closer to the ultimate truth that all historians aim at.

This book is also designed to illustrate something more subtle but hardly less important than methodological techniques—if, indeed, the two can be separated at all. That subtle something is historiography, the evolution of historical thought. The purpose is not to examine the history of history, the historiographical schools that have marked the development of the profession. Herodotus, Tacitus, Josephus, Froissart, Gibbon, Bancroft—these and other ancient and not so ancient classical historians are notable here solely for their absence. Instead, the goal is to explore a sample of the ways in which modern scholars interested in the past have posed their questions and answered them.

Nevertheless, the evolution of the historical profession should be obvious throughout this discussion, for methodology (how to do it) and historiography in the narrow sense (who did it and from what point of view) deal with the question basic to all historians—how to reconstruct the world we have lost. Ideas on this point have changed over the last century, the age of the professional historian.

To many historians, for example, that lost world is best captured by intellectual history, but there are some who understand this to mean the study of the history of ideas, while others see its essence as the spirit of an age, or *Zeitgeist*. Both of these historiographical points of view are included here because they also imply important conceptual differences.

Other examples of the evolution of historical writing and thinking may be found in the frequently noted transformation, occurring mostly in the last generation or so, away from rationalism to an understanding that historical events do not always appear logical because the people who created them—whether inadvertently or not—do not always behave in a fashion which most of us today would consider rational. A generation and more ago, historians tended to take historical figures, their letters, and their speeches at face value. Now insights from psychology, social psychology, and sociology indicate that this naive premise of straightforward rationality is often quite false, unbeknownst to sincere historical figures who may have thought they were behaving because of reasons which they understood. Surely the research of Sigmund Freud and Erik Erikson, whose methods are discussed here, has been most valuable on this point.

Parallel to the increased understanding of unconscious motivation is the growing conviction that historical events do not have simple and single causes. From the Progressive Era through the 1930s many leading historians held the simplistic view that they should look only at "real" causes, and real causes were almost invariably discovered to be economic; few historians illustrate this more vividly than Charles A. Beard and Orin G. Libby, who provided the basic inspiration for some of Beard's most provocative work. Both looked at the Federalist years through the eyes of economic man; to Libby, for example, the fight over ratification of the Constitution was one between commercial and agricultural interests. But Ronald Hatzenbuehler's essay indicates that the voting behavior of deliberative bodies may be marked by far more than economic motivation, often being directed by sectional and party allegiance and ideology. Similar outlooks marked the historians' interpretation of Jacksonian Democracy, a period in which political alignments were supposedly shaped by sharp distinctions between rich and poor. Lee Benson, for example, has challenged this dualism (not without opposition) with an ethnocultural approach that relies heavily on sociological theory and quantitative methodology. Such a basis of voter behavior is demonstrated here for a later period by Richard Jensen's essay, ''The Religious and Occupational Roots of Party Identification.''

As overreliance on economic factors is abandoned, economic history itself is being transformed at the same time. This is indicated by such historians as Robert Fogel and Robert Higgs, who rely on mathematical models that would have been beyond the comprehension or interest of economic historians a few decades ago. Even psychological interpretations, new in themselves, have been modified, as the essays employing Freudian and Eriksonian theory indicate significant differences in the way psychoanalytic descriptions are applied to historical issues. Thus new perceptions challenge old truths, only to be challenged in their turn by future historians with still newer approaches.

Modern historiography has thus been forced away from monocausation into acceptance of pluralism. Monolithic notions of cause and effect tend to dissolve rapidly under the penetrating influence of quantitative methods, for example. When one's independent variable explains only 40 or 50 percent of the variation in the dependent variable, one is forced, willy-nilly, to seek additional explanations; and nothing is as characteristic of the econometric approach to economic history as the concept of multiple causation—that is why the equations sometimes become so hideously complicated.

Undergraduate history students or new graduate students, for whom this collection is intended, have seldom been exposed to such a wide range of research strategies. Although they may have read the published results of different methods, the fact that they were methods, and that they incorporated differing technical processes and interpretive concepts, may never have been pointed out. Such students have thereby been deprived of much of the richness of historical study. Under these conditions it is hardly fair for instructors to complain when they receive unimaginative essays or term papers making only slight departure from straight encyclopedic narrative.

I assume that doctoral students and their instructors have already reached the higher ground. They are not likely to find much here that is new to them. Other students, I hope, will be introduced to some provocative new techniques. I do not imagine that simply reading the following selections will enable readers to employ any particular method themselves, although in three or four cases (collective biography, for example) it may suffice. It would be the exact opposite of my intentions if eager students, solely on the basis of these essays, were to try to apply Erik Erikson's model of the identity crisis to a biographical study of their favorite historical characters. Perhaps, however, eager students will be spurred to reading more about Erikson's theories (or taking elementary statistics, or enrolling in an introductory sociology course) in an effort to expand their historical understanding; the students would then have a greater appreciation of what authors are doing when the authors attribute an identity crisis to the subject of a biography. Even if the knowledge gained by these readings is never used for students' own research, it should allow them to read current historical literature with a greater degree of comprehension. Given the rapid pace of change in historical studies, this is essential. As one undergraduate said after reading a number of the following essays, ''I never knew there were so many ways to write history.'' It is this attitude I hope to develop.

But enough of the preview. To understand these somewhat cryptic remarks the student must read the book. However, please bear in mind that I do not want to make a social science out of a humanistic discipline. As I indicate quite clearly in the Introduction, history is really both, and the two need not be incompatible. Nor do I argue for ''scientific'' history (whatever that is); I do insist that all historians, using any approach or dedicated to any school of interpretation, strive for accuracy—no historian, after all, sets out determined to be wrong.

I make no pretense that these selections are comprehensive, or that a fully satisfactory choice of methods or illustrations could ever be made, but some of the more common or imaginative procedures are included. No doubt each reader would have preferred to see at least one or two other techniques, such as numismatics, simulation, or medical analysis, but it is impossible to illustrate all possible historical methods. Furthermore, each selection was chosen solely for its ability to illustrate a specific procedure with clarity and explicitness. No effort has been made to achieve balance either in time period or in subject area, for that would have defeated the purpose of the book by requiring selections to be chosen for reasons other than method.

It should not be surprising that most essays come from nineteenth-century U. S. history, the area in which I am most interested and with which I am most familiar. This should prove to be an advantage to most students for they are more likely to be informed about this area and period than any other. Profitable reading is therefore more likely to result. Selections have been abridged and footnotes have been dropped, except in a few instances where they have been inserted into the text. Reproduction here in no way implies agreement with the findings of any scholar or school of interpretation, nor enthusiastic acceptance of any particular research scheme. I have my preferences; however, what may not be so apparent is my belief that none of these tools is alone sufficient to answer the important questions, and that *research designs must usually contain elements of more than one method if they are to be successful*. It would have been easy, given the close relationship of other disciplines to historical research, to abandon history in these pages. However, I have confined my selections to the work of historians, or scholars from other fields who (for the moment) are attempting to function as historians and who have the historian in mind.

This book, then, is not a methodological cookbook, but an illustrated discussion of what historians do as they attempt to answer the questions that intrigue them. I hope, in discussion of a broad range of research designs, to fill the gaping pedagogical void created by narrowly based methods books and historiographical studies that do little more than examine one interpretive school after another with little reference to methodological concepts, especially those used by recent historians.

My goal is ambitious; like other historians my reach no doubt exceeds my grasp, and that too is one of the themes of history. I hope sympathetic students and instructors will greet the inevitable shortcomings contained here with a smile of indulgence and suggestions for future improvement.

I am obligated to a number of colleagues and friends who have read portions of the commentary and offered helpful suggestions. These scholars include W. H. Alexander, Alfred Andrea, William G. Gard, Mark S. Henry, Thomas W. Howard, Arthur P. Jacoby, Richard Jensen, Archer Jones, Norton D. Kinghorn, Ralph H. Kolstoe, Richard L. Ludtke, Edwin G. Olmstead, R. C. Raack, Lowndes F. Stephens, Robert P. Swierenga, John D. Tyler, James F. Vivian, and Jean H. Vivian. Since I am apt to be stubborn, I have not always followed the advice I have solicited; the consequent errors are my responsibility. My thanks for typing goes to Melissa R. Sogard, Dorothy L. Steiner, and Brenda L. Wiseman, whose cheerful acceptance of this dreary task is much appreciated. I especially acknowledge my wife, Luise T. Beringer, who typed and proofed most of the final manuscript. I also owe a debt to the staff of the Chester Fritz Library of the University of North Dakota, among whom the reference and interlibrary loan librarians deserve particular mention for their unfailing courtesy and frequent assistance.

Richard E. Beringer

Spring 1977

Contents

Historical Analysis
Contemporary
Approaches
to Clio's Craft

1 Introduction

The basic assumption of any book on historical method must be that historians do, in fact, have methods. The statement is not meant to be ludicrous, but we must admit that it is an assumption only. It is not a proven fact. Many monographs and articles give little hint as to the historical method employed, beyond a reasonably organized procedure for arranging notes. Historians themselves admit this to be true, but only in private moments and out of earshot of any lingering students. The notion that history has no method is shared by many in other disciplines, as Cushing Strout indicates below; but the legitimacy of their procedures has also become a gnawing source of doubt for historians themselves. Anyone who has glanced at the delightful essays compiled by L. P. Curtis, Jr., ought to be impressed by the difficulty these historians have in describing their method, and their frank confessions that their methods often developed after the research was over. One anonymous historian, who evidently did not contribute an essay, facetiously confessed to Curtis that "I am a bad person to write about methods—I have none." And another remarked of the forthcoming collection that "what we now merely suspect would be proved without question—that nobody proceeds as the research manuals say we should."[1] Some historians not only agree, but see this as a virtue. In dealing with the "intuitive" orientation of mind, Jacques Barzun demands that the historian exercise "a discerning eye and superior judgment, for there is *no method*."[2] If this is how the professionals describe their work, what may we expect of students? It is not surprising that term papers and theses (and all too many dissertations and monographs as well) appear to have been written with the most simple of methodologies: take notes until the height of the note pile equals the time available to write, and then write. D. W. Brogan put it only somewhat

---

[1]L. P. Curtis, Jr., ed., *The Historian's Workshop: Original Essays by Sixteen Historians* (New York: Alfred A. Knopf, 1970), p. xv. This fine collection provides an excellent insight into the multitude of influences that have directed historians in their careers and topic choices, as well as their research methods.
[2]Jacques Barzun, "History: The Muse and Her Doctors," *American Historical Review* 77 (February 1972):54–55.

differently when he wrote of the ''naive'' historian ''who seems to have thought, like the parish priest in *Don Quixote,* that all an historian had to do was to have patience and shuffle the cards. . . . If there were enough cards, truth would emerge.''[3] We have had enough of the shuffle of cards in this profession; students and instructors alike must plan their research carefully.

Some commentators on history and the philosophy of history frequently refer to the historical method. They do not say methods; they believe that history is *a* method, and in a sense they are right. History attempts to achieve understanding by examining a problem in its relation to time. Chronology is the key to history. But this is not a very enlightening explanation of historical methodology. We would not be satisfied with an explanation of mathematical method that said simply that mathematics deals with numbers or symbols representing numbers. We would shrug off as simplistic an explanation of the fine arts as painters painting and sculptors sculpting. To say, then, that history deals with time is true but quite misleading in its simplicity. It is also deceiving in that history is not the only discipline in which chronology plays a central role. The same is true of geology and even astronomy—but surely these are not history in the usual sense of the word.

A major theme of this collection, as its interdisciplinary nature demonstrates, is that history is really many methods. It may be that distinctions between one approach and another will sometimes appear blurred as one method fades into another closely allied to it, or as one essay uses several methods intertwined so inextricably that it becomes difficult to judge where one ends and another begins. David Donald's study of the abolitionists, for example, is important for the use of status anxiety and reference group theory, but these concepts are developed through collective biography. Knowledge is not compartmentalized; some degree of ambiguity is inevitable. Findings and procedures cannot be placed in neat methodologically labeled pigeon holes, each distinct from the others, because a single piece of historical writing frequently employs more than one approach. This methodological overlap is desirable because of the insight permitted by a variety of viewpoints. It is difficult to avoid in any case; history has by no means been exempt from the interchange of ideas between disciplines occurring most notably in the last ten or fifteen years. Most of the following essays could therefore be used to illustrate more than one lesson in historical craftsmanship. Students should not be dismayed by occasional apparent similarities between techniques—the most important distinction between articles is the methodological ''mix,'' since each essay necessarily combines attributes of varying approaches but is

---

[3]D. W. Brogan, ''The Quarrel over Charles Austin Beard and the American Constitution,'' *Economic History Review,* 2d ser. 18 (August 1965):222. Such procedures can have dire consequences. Thomas Gordon Barnes ruefully noted that his senior year in college was spent ''in surfacing and sinking in one trough after another of terror.'' It was ''the price for no prior conceptualization'' when he gathered data for his senior thesis. See Barnes, ''Largely Without Benefit of Prior Conceptualization,'' in Curtis, ed., *Historian's Workshop,* p. 140.

discussed here in terms of one particular device that it exemplifies especially well. Indeed, one of the prominent characteristics of what is sometimes called the New History is the mixture of new history, "old" history, and techniques that were once not considered to be part of historical study at all.

Oscar Handlin referred obliquely to this interdisciplinary outreach when he remarked on the "common hope of historians that others would absolve them of the necessity for original thought."[4] Surely his implication is correct; historians have borrowed more from other fields than other fields have borrowed from history—much to the detriment of some of these other fields. Cushing Strout observed, with tongue in cheek, that "from the viewpoint of methodological puritanism historians have always lived in sin, loosely cohabiting with a variety of mistresses from theology to sociology."[5] To some social scientists, historians appear to be methodologically lax—in fact, to be in a discipline that has no specific method, no discipline in the literal sense. One editor of an anthology of essays on methods of literary study asserted that "since a past can be conceived of for everything, history is everybody's sister."[6] This attitude may seem patronizing (in this specific instance it was a compliment), and some historians react most defensively. They maintain, in the face of some new quantitatively proved finding, for instance, that everyone knew it all the time. The results are ridiculed as nothing new, as if the precise degree to which a phenomenon is present were unimportant. And when the new finding contradicts the old ideas, they apathetically comfort themselves by the quite proper warning that there are important things that one cannot measure, and demand reliance on common sense. As Strout reminds us, "such common sense is only another name for ignorance and fear of the unfamiliar, an unearned and inflated professional pride that masks an anxious fear for a threatened status in an academic world in which other subjects currently have more prestige."[7] But Clio, the muse of history, is not schizophrenic. "She has many personalities," contends Rosalie L. Colie, "instructs in many different disciplines, and uses many methods of instruction. She is, in short, pluralistic."[8]

Other themes should also be noted. One, closely allied to the interdisciplinary approach, is the great difficulty encountered in attempting to explain or even to define many methods in a succinct, readily comprehended manner. Readers will doubtless find it necessary to reread an occasional paragraph or page, but this is true with any instructional material. A third theme, repeated again and again, is found in the caveats contained in most discussions. While each approach has its advantages, it also has its drawbacks. Some attention is paid to the most prominent difficulties of each method,

[4]Oscar Handlin, *The Uprooted,* 2nd ed. (Boston: Little, Brown & Co., 1973), p. 302.
[5]Cushing Strout, "Ego Psychology and the Historian," *History and Theory* 7 (1968):281.
[6]James Thorpe, "Introduction," in Thorpe, ed., *Relations of Literary Study: Essays on Interdisciplinary Contributions* (New York: Modern Language Association of America, 1967), p. xi.
[7]Strout, "Ego Psychology," p. 281.
[8]Rosalie L. Colie, "Literature and History," in Thorpe, ed., *Relations of Literary Study,* p. 23.

but there are some warnings of a general common-sense nature that ought to be underlined here. Many historians make the mistake of claiming too much for their findings. Having established an interesting point with, perhaps, a little less evidence than they ought to have, they go on to make sweeping—and sometimes impossible —claims about what they have proved. That some leading writers in a given era frequently used a certain image does not necessarily mean that perception was part of the thinking of the masses of the same time and place; that the sex ratio in a single western county was abnormally high in 1860 does not mean that it will be so in other western counties. The moral: be sure your claims do not overrun your evidence. Historians must also avoid a temptation to let their methods get out of hand. The more esoteric the researcher's procedure, the more likely it is that the tool will replace the product. When method takes precedence over thinking the results will be disastrous: then quantifiers bounce numbers back and forth with little concern for their meaning, psychohistorians reach outrageous conclusions that fly in the face of available evidence, and intellectual historians minutely dissect ideas that affected nothing because they concerned no one.

Closely allied to this difficulty is the amazing frequency with which historians of all persuasions tend to find exactly what they seek, so obviously so that findings are sometimes rendered suspect. But this is because any methodology tends to channel evidence and analysis toward a predetermined point. A broad view of the researcher's problem is necessarily precluded and some potential causal factors are emphasized at the expense of others that might be equally important. A research strategy based solely on correlation of census data is not likely to produce much insight into the intellectual or social atmosphere that enveloped the individuals involved; if the historian does draw conclusions about intellectual or social life it will only be because he or she has effectively altered his or her research design—perhaps unconsciously. On the other hand, the history of ideas approach tends to overlook behavioral determinants of historical action.

Since no one can write a perfect book, with a comprehensive view of all potential causal relationships, the remedy for this inevitable tunnel vision lies partly in the understanding of the reader and in the acknowledgment by the writer that there are facets of the topic not covered that remain to be explored by others. Recognizing this difficulty, many historians conclude by pointing out what they have had to ignore and making suggestions for future research. In either event, the problem of methods determining results is best avoided by a research design that incorporates several appropriate procedures.

Regardless of methodological preferences, any student of history is an easy prey to these assorted snares. As most of the following essays unavoidably demonstrate, highly specialized methods are best used as complements to, not replacements for, "traditional" approaches.

The apparent interdisciplinary emphasis found here may seem to abandon the idea of historian as humanist and to substitute instead the cold behaviorist. Is history becoming a behavioral or social science? The inability to define history's role may be found in the catalogues of numerous institutions of higher learning, where it is sometimes listed as a humanity and sometimes as a social science. The controversy is without end, indeed, without significance, except as evidence of a professional inferiority complex. Some think history is falling between the two pillars of social science and humanity and that it is becoming some new hybrid that is neither one nor the other. I prefer instead to think of historical study as the keystone in the arch of knowledge, bridging the gap between two frequently incompatible pillars. It would be absurd to deny that a quantifier, peering over columns of figures, is a social scientist; it would be equally fallacious to deny that an intellectual historian, searching the literature of an era for symbols that betray hitherto unknown aspects of its culture, is a humanist. But both are historians nonetheless.

In an analysis such as this oversimplification is inevitable. A neat table of contents obscures the degree to which various methods complement each other. As already indicated, some selections could have illustrated more than one method. But this introduces a new complication. It is easy to confuse method as technical or mechanical procedure with method as theoretical framework. An attempt to distinguish between the two while at the same time designing a well-organized discussion presents a serious problem. It would not be difficult, for example, to imagine a study using content analysis as one research device while placing its findings within a framework provided by the concept of symbol. This is exactly what Richard L. Merritt does in his essay.

The problem is more apparent than real. The distinction is not so much between apples and oranges as between two different apples. It should be understood explicitly that the so-called mechanical methods rest on fundamental notions of behavior and causation in history. Any historian confronting an important problem always asks questions, seeks the sources necessary to answer them, and tries to develop (consciously or unconsciously) a research design that will permit analysis of the sources in order to answer those questions. At this point all historians employ *organizing topics,* and this process is discussed at length in many conventional instructional manuals on historical methodology. But other historians go on to employ *organizing principles* as well. There is a vast difference between organizing topics and organizing principles. However, all the methods included in this book are really organizing principles. A theoretical or conceptual method is as much a tool of analysis, an organizing *principle,* as seemingly mechanical devices like collective biography or roll-call analysis. Conversely, an apparently mechanical procedure is as much an organizing principle as any theoretical framework, such as reference group theory, cognitive dissonance, or the history of ideas, which the historian may employ. Both theory and mechanics rest on fundamental understandings of human behavior. In the former case this is obvious enough, but it is also evident in the latter instance. Thus, modern study of voter behavior rests on the principle that certain identifiable personal or environmental characteristics will be highly associated with the way voters cast their ballots. The same is true of legislative behavior. In content analysis one assumes that words are often symbolic and representative of more than usual dictionary meanings, that their frequency and juxtaposition to other words carry unique, identifiable, and measurable significance. In fact the common denominator of the entire quantitative section is measurement. In the case of correlation the method is based on the premise that one can reduce to a single index figure a measure of association between two distinct phenomena, that one can go beyond adjectives such as "more" or "less" and measure (within certain limits) what a relationship may be. The technique-concept also assumes that statistical relationships can provide important clues to causation and that motivation can be inferred from numbers, regardless of what the individuals involved may have said at the time.[9] By the same token, the psychosociological and quantitative sections of this book operate under the well-established fact that people are not always motivated to act for the reasons they say they are, whether they know it or not. The psychological defense mechanism of projection is a good example of such unconscious motivation, and the essay accompanying it illustrates well the difference between the reasons people admit and their other motivations, demonstrating again that one cannot always take historical figures at face value. Drawing methodological distinctions too sharply does little more than create false impressions. Although the concept often appears to be the result of the method, actually it *is* the method.

[9]Richard Jensen, "Quantitative American Studies: The State of the Art," *American Quarterly* 26 (August 1974):226.

2 Intellectual History

Intellectual history is admired by many but understood by few. Although most historians agree that intellectual history is important, citing a few outstanding works to prove the point, a satisfactory definition is more elusive. Many students profess to be especially interested in the subject, having encountered a few striking examples of the genre that seem to bring some semblance of order to the uncertainty of human affairs, but definition is difficult for them as well. Why is this so? The skeptics look at intellectual history and look again to see if it really is there. Yes, they seem to be saying, it is important, but if there is such substantial agreement on that point why are its advocates and practitioners unable to reach a consensus on what it is?

Sometimes description must substitute for definition. Philosophers often conceive of intellectual history as the philosophy of history, or the history of ideas, or perhaps both. Literary critics may think of it as nothing more than a method of literary analysis, placing literature within its historical context. Historians see it as the history of intellectuals or of popular thought. And some simply refer to intellectual history as a method of some sort by which ideas of all kinds—cultural, economic, social, and political—are synthesized and cast into their proper historical setting. At the highest level of synthesis, advocates of intellectual history argue, it reveals the meaning and significance of what other historians have done. In this circumstance it is possible to maintain that "all history is intellectual history in some sense,"[1] for, without synthesis, what does it matter if a quantitative study measures the way legislators vote on key issues or how farmers decide to replace horses with tractors, if psychologically oriented historians believe they know the childhood bases for the quirks that determined the behavior of a Woodrow Wilson or an Adolf Hitler, or if sociologically oriented scholars discover the role played by the ancestors of Progressives or abolitionists in motivating behavior of important persons or groups?

It is the unique task of the intellectual historians to assemble the jigsaw puzzle of the

[1]John C. Greene, "Objectives and Methods in Intellectual History," *Mississippi Valley Historical Review* 54 (June 1957):59.

past from the pieces—the select, circumscribed studies—placed on the board by all sorts of scholars, including other intellectual historians. They put history in constant communication with a variety of other disciplines, including but certainly not limited to, economics, sociology, geography, law, and psychology. To understand the two generations prior to the U. S. Civil War, for example, studies of politics and war must be integrated with examinations of sectionalism, economic development, the westward movement, slavery, constitutional law, religion, literature, and popular culture. Ideally, intellectual historians operate at the level of total context; that is, they make some sense out of a jumble of disparate sources, findings, interpretations, and suggestions, which may or may not seem to be related to one another. Consequently the best intellectual historians are likely to be scholars of broader interest than most historians, having a greater knowledge in other disciplines than most historians possess.

As a branch of historical study, however, intellectual history often seems to be neglected in favor of newer, even ostentatious techniques. Once one of the dominant forces in historical thought, it sometimes appears today as a subsidiary branch of an apparently declining field of study—witness the reviewer in the popular press who snidely and naively referred to "peripheral pursuits like intellectual history" when commenting on a highly publicized work of quantitative history.[2] Nonhistorians may go on to scoff because the field is not "scientific," yet ideas can and do move people to action and register the meanings of actions already taken. Any revolution may serve as an example. What can be more important or more relevant than the study of thoughts such as these? All history is indeed intellectual history, at least in part, because all people are influenced by their intellectual environment—as are the historians who analyze and write about them. This influence is inescapable. It is one of the reasons why pure objectivity in history is impossible, for who can evade their surroundings?

Just as there are many kinds of thought, so too there are numerous ways to study them. One scholar separates the history of philosophy from intellectual history on the ground that the former "involves a discontinuous series of connected events," while the latter deals with phenomena that are "continuously present throughout the time-span" under study.[3] The distinction seems a moot one at best. Some scholars divide the field into intellectual history proper and the history of ideas, which are presumably distinct. Others, supposedly to avoid confusion, use the terms interchangeably.[4] Perhaps it would be more helpful to think of intellectual history as a series of overlapping subdisciplines ranging along a spectrum from history at the most ethereal and abstract levels to the history of popular thought and culture. At the former extreme the historian "comes close to being a philosopher, or at least a historian of philosophy,"

---

[2] *Time,* June 17, 1974, p. 99.

[3] Maurice Mandelbaum, "The History of Ideas, Intellectual History, and the History of Philosophy," *History and Theory,* Beiheft 5 (1965):60–61.

[4] Rush Welter, "The History of Ideas in America: An Essay in Redefinition," *Journal of American History* 51 (March 1965):599–601n2.

while at the other "he comes close to being a social historian, or just a plain historian, concerned with the daily lives of human beings."[5] Not surprisingly, the claim has been made that intellectual history "embraces not only theology, philosophy, the natural and social sciences, but also belles-lettres, the fine arts, and popular literature of all sorts."[6]

Intellectual history might best be described in terms of two approaches, one internal and humanist, the other external and oriented toward the social sciences. Between them are divided, with no particular neatness, the various subdisciplines that comprise the field.[7] The divisions are arbitrary but they nevertheless facilitate the organization of the materials of intellectual history along the spectrum from pure abstraction to practical application. In the internal context, where the humanist is likely to feel at home, intellectual history is the study, through time, of ideas per se without regard to their social origins or implications.[8] We may discover here the relationship of ideas not only to other ideas but also to the history of philosophy and literature, as well as the history of intellectuals themselves—"pristine" ideas, H. Stuart Hughes calls them, in a slightly different context.[9] This internal view (idea to idea) is necessarily highly subjective and tends to deal more with individual imagination than collective creation. To the workaday historian, this orientation may seem somewhat sterile and to smack of elitism, the ivory tower, and academic detachment, which is exactly its attraction to many scholars. This value judgment is not intended to deny that intrinsically the ideas may be every bit as vital as in any other area of scholarship; but because inquiry into pure abstraction is unlikely to examine the effect of intellectuals upon their world, it may seem divorced from meaningful social reality. Thus the external context of intellectual history possesses greater social relevance. It involves the examination of ideas as related to events, and may stress "the content of popular beliefs, sociological and ideological modes of analysis, description rather than close study of public opinion."[10] Practitioners of the external context (idea to action) approximate the behaviorism of the social scientist, who is less concerned with individual cases than with groups, and who attempts to generalize his findings into rules.

No form of intellectual history is likely to employ entirely one extreme or the other; each contains both internal and external elements. But literary analysis tends to be

---

[5]Crane Brinton, *Ideas and Men: The Story of Western Thought* (New York: Prentice-Hall, 1950), p. 9.
[6]Franklin L. Baumer, "Intellectual History and Its Problems," *Journal of Modern History* 21 (September 1949):191.
[7]For discussion of the dichotomy between humanist and social science orientations see John Higham, "Intellectual History and Its Neighbors," in Higham, *Writing American History: Essays on Modern Scholarship* (Bloomington: Indiana University Press, 1970), pp. 27–40, especially p. 33.
[8]Welter, "History of Ideas in America," p. 599.
[9]H. Stuart Hughes, *Consciousness and Society: The Reorientation of European Social Thought, 1890–1930* (New York: Alfred A. Knopf, 1958), p. 11, as referred to in Welter, "History of Ideas in America," p. 602.
[10]Welter, "History of Ideas in America," pp. 599–600.

more internal than external in approach. One has only to think of long, dreary essays on what T. S. Eliot (or Hawthorne, or Milton) "was really trying to say" to provide illustration. Literally, of course, literary analysis is the basis of any research in written records, yet the phrase customarily implies something close to the internal context (idea to idea) rather than the external context (idea to action).

Similarly, the study of symbol and image usually falls within the internal context: what is the meaning of the white whale in *Moby Dick,* or the rural arcadia (the Garden) in American culture? On the other hand, symbol and image may also be found in popular thought, as illustrated by the log cabin in Henry Nash Smith's article, "The West As an Image of the American Past." In the last century the Union was both a geographical entity and a symbol of nationalism, freedom, democracy, and republicanism that was so potent, so firmly fixed in the mass mind that several hundred thousand men died to preserve it—while several hundred thousand others died to rend it. Normally, however, a symbol or image is less pervasive in daily life. When Leo Marx discusses the Garden in American thought some pages ahead, he deals with a mental image not in the forefront of the popular mind, a symbol not nearly as conscious as that of the Union a century ago. And yet that Garden has been a very real formative agent of American culture.

Intellectual history as the history of ideas is best illustrated by Arthur O. Lovejoy, who tried to trace the development of "unit-ideas." The term implies an orientation applicable to both the internal and external contexts of intellectual history. Indeed this approach to intellectual history has moved far enough across the spectrum that it truly reflects polar opposites; its objective may be either the pristine ideas of intellectuals or the popular ideas of the public. Scholars who equate all of intellectual history with the history of ideas contend that the major role of intellectual historians is to outline the intellectual assumptions of an age and to explain the transformations in those assumptions from one age to another. In practice this technique (which is no longer as popular as formerly) often glosses over the history of any given epoch in favor of monolithic, all-inclusive ideas; like threads in a suit, ideas supposedly move back and forth while remaining much the same, unmodified by time or place. Lovejoy himself "tended to deal with his unit-ideas as if they were fairly stable and hard, indestructible, like Greek atoms."[11]

As with the unit-idea concept, the *Zeitgeist* study may employ both internal and external contexts. To some historians, John Higham for example, the explanation and description of the *Zeitgeist,* or spirit of an age, is the primary objective of the intellectual historian. This endeavor is actually the sum and substance of the specialty, he feels, because it "estimates the changing level of intellectual achievement; relates thinking to behavior; and defines the patterns of feeling and opinion which, on the most

---

[11]Rosalie L. Colie, "Literature and History," in James Thorpe, ed., *Relations of Literary Study: Essays on Interdisciplinary Contributions* (New York: Modern Language Association of America, 1967), p. 18.

extended scale, make up the spirit of an age or of a people."[12] The *Zeitgeist* historian examines similar expressions of the same idea, but Rosalie Colie identifies the seductive fallacy: thoughts are not necessarily related just because they coincide in time. Nor does the presence of one "spirit of the time" preclude the presence of another. There may be several *Zeitgeister,* and they may or may not be related. The historian who attempts to delineate the spirit of an age must be aware that there may well be more "spirits" than he discovers. At the same time, the *Zeitgeist* concept is frequently so nebulous that it is easy to conjure up one that does not exist at all. A telltale wisp of evidence cited to prove the existence of a spirit of an age actually may prove no more than an intellectual or cultural trend, perhaps only an anomaly. For that reason some historians deny that such a thing as the *Zeitgeist* exists. But again Colie points out that sometimes ideas really are in the air;[13] one would not want to attempt a synthesis of the intellectual origins of the American Revolution that ignored the impact of Newtonian physics and the social contract.

The unit-idea and *Zeitgeist* are often placed within the internal approach to intellectual history, but they are far enough removed from the philosophy of history or literary criticism that they may involve the relationship between thought and consequent deed, which characterizes the external context. For example, E. M. W. Tillyard's *The Elizabethan World Picture*[14] examines some of the unit-ideas that created the spirit of the Elizabethan age, and suggests that ideas were in the air and that they did affect the thinking, writing, and routine behavior of all Elizabethans—not merely the intellectuals. In short, if Tillyard is correct, he perceived the interaction of ideas and everyday behavior that characterizes the external context. While Tillyard's argument is open to criticism,[15] he went beyond examination of ideas for their own sake (internal context). He reminded us that, in a sense, the greatest thoughts of an age are also among the most commonplace—indeed, that is what makes them great: "Raleigh's remarks on the glories of creation and on death, Shakespeare's on the state of man in the world seem to be utterly their own, as if compounded of their very lifeblood; [but] divested of their literary form they are the common property of every third-rate mind of the age."[16] The thoughts of a multitude of third-rate minds help to create a true *Zeitgeist.*

The external context of intellectual history, where the social science-oriented historian is most likely to be concerned, therefore involves the interaction of ideas and their consequent events and verges on social and cultural history. To Crane Brinton the

---

[12]John Higham, "American Intellectual History: A Critical Appraisal," *American Quarterly* 13 (Supplement, Summer 1961):221, and Higham, "The Study of American Intellectual History," in Higham, *Writing American History,* p. 48.

[13]Colie, "Literature and History," pp. 18–19.

[14]E. M. W. Tillyard, *The Elizabethan World Picture* (New York: Random House, n.d.). Originally published in London by Chatto and Windus in 1943.

[15]See Colie, "Literature and History," p. 19.

[16]Tillyard, *Elizabethan World Picture,* p. 108.

primary task of the intellectual historian is to establish *"the relations between the ideas of the philosophers, the intellectuals, the thinkers, and the actual way of living of the millions who carry the task of civilization."* Brinton, who would have us avoid the purely internal context of intellectual history, calls upon historians to ignore "abstract ideas that breed more abstract ideas." Ideas are to be studied wherever they are found, whether absurd or sensible, as long as they relate to humanity's total existence.[17] Although Brinton's external view emphasizes the practical results of thought, intellectuals are still central because it is their thoughts that are being examined.

But there are further possibilities. If intellectual history is expanded to include the history of people—all people—as they think, then it need not be confined to the thought of intellectuals. The formula stories that abound in popular fiction, such as westerns and mysteries, with their familiar and highly predictable plots, are good examples of how the feelings and sentiments, hopes and fears, of the great mass of humanity become grist for the mill of the intellectual historian. In a word, popular culture enters the external context. Frederick Lewis Allen's essay illustrating the *Zeitgeist* approach is also an exposition of the popular culture of the 1920s, and, in the quantitative section, Richard L. Merritt's use of content analysis is also intellectual history because it examines popular culture. In sum, intellectual history "concentrates on experiences occurring inside men's heads," and "includes Little Orphan Annie as well as Adam Smith . . . the comics as well as . . . the philosophers."[18] The quality of the intellectual process, if it could ever be measured, is not really relevant: "Lack of intellectual content," as Rosalie Colie perceptively observes, "is also data for the intellectual historian."[19] And, we might add, it is the rule more often than the exception. Mr. Everyman is necessarily preoccupied with the practical problems of day-to-day living and has little time for the rarified thoughts or deep philosophical ponderings of historians who favor a strict internal context.

The distinction between internal (idea to idea) and external (idea to action) orientations nevertheless seems arbitrary. Both concepts apply to the history of ideas, the *Zeitgeist,* and, under some conditions, even to literary analysis, including the study of image, metaphor, and symbol. In an effort to close the gap between the two orientations, Rush Welter emphasizes that although a scholar may devote an entire lifetime to the study of a single idea without seeking its effect, still "the very step of making the inquiry would seem to imply that the idea was important beyond itself."[20] The external context thus takes precedence over the internal context; certainly no intellectual historian ever pursued his studies convinced beforehand that his subject never had any

[17]Brinton, *Ideas and Men*, p. 7, emphasis in original.
[18]John G. Cawelti, *Adventure, Mystery, and Romance: Formula Stories as Art and Popular Culture* (Chicago: The University of Chicago Press, 1976); Higham, "Intellectual History and Its Neighbors," pp. 29, 30.
[19]Colie, "Literature and History," p. 25.
[20]Welter, "History of Ideas in America," p. 608.

importance beyond itself, and never would. That would be an exercise in futility.

In addition to the internal versus external contexts of intellectual history that these selections display, they also illustrate a difference between technique and concept that may appear greater than necessary. All four of the following examples of intellectual history are based on important underlying assumptions, as the ensuing pages should reveal. However, the last two methods, history of ideas and the *Zeitgeist*, go beyond method per se. Both are also comprehensive statements on the entirety of intellectual history in a way that is not true of literary analysis or the use of images, metaphors, and symbols. Both attempt to model the function and importance of intellectual history, and have at one time or another been used virtually as synonyms for the field. For our purposes, however, they may be considered methodological tools as well, based like other methods on important notions of how one may view and structure the history of human thought and action. In this sense the two are not mutually exclusive, and the use of the *Zeitgeist* need not preclude the investigator from employing the history of ideas approach—or any other historical method.

Any historian is convinced that his or her subject is important before studying it, or else he or she would pass on to some other topic. And that is the danger. Having come so far, it is easy—too easy—for the historian to arrive at a long-dormant conclusion. No student is exempt, though some are more careful than others. This leads to the common-sense warning, amplified in the following pages, that the intellectual historian may tend to find the wellsprings of historical action in the intellectual realm, or at least within the bounds of popular culture, denying (for example) the role of unconscious motivation that the psychohistorian may assign. The student of intellectual history must be careful to make allowances accordingly, for often this unbalance lies more in the eye of the reader than in the pen of the writer. An intellectual history of anything must not be expected to be more than the writer intended it to be; it is never fair to criticize authors for the books they did not choose to write.

Superficial intellectual history is easy to dash off. Solid, exhaustive analyses of intellectual life or the consequences of mass thought are more difficult, perhaps because ideas are so elusive. It is sometimes difficult to determine just what intellectual historians are attempting to do, and, sometimes bewildered, they also puzzle long over their problems, awaiting a sudden flash of insight that will lay bare a scheme of analysis. John William Ward illustrates this experience in a personal account of how he wrote his widely acclaimed *Andrew Jackson: Symbol for an Age.* Ward frankly admits that he did not write the book he originally conceived. His problem, commonplace for intellectual historians in general, was to fathom the thoughts and feelings of an inarticulate mass of people who left little record of their ideas. He worked hard on this mystery without being sure of what he was seeking, and confesses that his "book evolved in a distinctly haphazard fashion, the result finally of personal accident, chance encounters, and casual suggestion.'' (Many historians, regardless of their method, have had similar experiences. It is Ward's success that is unusual.) After visiting the great libraries and accumulating ''an enormous and ungovernable mass of notes I had no idea what to do with,'' Ward had to admit that he was at the '' 'shuffle, cut, and deal' stage of scholarship.''

He then recounts the crucial point at which the design of the book became crystal clear:

> I had collected some eulogies on the death of Andrew Jackson from newspapers. Then I came upon Benjamin Dusenbery's printed collection of twenty-five of them. I dutifully took the book home and spent an evening reading those declamatory tributes, taking still more notes, of course. The next day remains the clearest memory I have of the composition of the book. Seated in a dusty carrel in the University of Minnesota Library, listlessly reading what must be one of the dullest testaments of a political leader in American history, Van Buren's cautious reminiscences, in a passage which had nothing much of interest in it, I came to the word ''civilization.'' With it, the design of the entire book was given to me, ''given'' in the sense that I was the passive recipient of a detailed plan and outline. After those months of stumbling in the dark, it was as if my unconscious mind had worked the whole thing out and laid it before my conscious eye. I remember pushing Van Buren to one side and hastily, for fear I would lose it, scribbling for hours a detailed outline of the plan of the book I was yet to write, an outline which stood up remarkably well, with only one major and a few minor, particular changes. . . .
>
> What I realized suddenly was that all the eulogies I had read, however different their anecdotes, however different their emphases, could be gathered under three major headings, the headings which now provide the three divisions of the book: ''Nature, Providence, and Will.''[21]

So vague is Ward's description of his experience, and so fortuitous was the inspiration that finally revealed the meaning in his material, that one is at a loss to describe his method. Sitting in a library carrel, shuffling notes, and waiting for a flash of inspiration is not a well-planned strategy for writing history; Ward himself has referred elsewhere to ''the methodological innocence of most practicing historians.''[22] His account suggests the amorphous quality of some historical methods. It also indicates why intellec-

---

[21]John William Ward, ''Looking Backward: *Andrew Jackson: Symbol for an Age,*'' in L. P. Curtis, Jr., ed., *The Historian's Workshop: Original Essays by Sixteen Historians* (New York: Alfred A. Knopf, 1970), pp. 207–213. The extended quotation is from pp. 212–213. Copyright 1970 Alfred A. Knopf, Inc. I thank the publisher for permission to quote this material.

[22]John William Ward, ''Generalizations Upon Generalizations,'' *American Quarterly* 15 (Fall 1963):465.

tual history is so difficult to define and to write. The average historian, faced with Ward's purpose and pile of notes, would eventually have produced a dreary dissertation on "Historical Symbolism as Illustrated by Perceptions of Andrew Jackson." The key to Ward's success, and that of other intellectual historians, is insight. Surely insight (literally, sudden perception or intuition) is as important—perhaps more important—in intellectual history as in any other portion of Clio's realm. Even after reading Ward's own account the student cannot be sure what his method was, beyond "cut and shuffle," although some of the material below should clarify the matter somewhat. Yet the result was undeniably brilliant. Having immersed himself in his subject, the author pondered what he knew until he discerned the unifying theme.

Some historians will point to this as a problem. Saturating oneself in the "facts" provides no assurance either that the facts have been mastered or that an accurate cross section of thought has been examined. The conscientious historian must anticipate these problems and plan a research design to circumvent them. The description of Ward's experience does not seem satisfactory; possibly the method of intellectual history does not always lend itself to clear description. The analogy frequently employed to compare writing intellectual history to nailing jelly to a wall is not inappropriate. Intellectual history is not something created out of nothing, but it does require the delicate skill of a fine artist to write.

A fully satisfactory definition or description of intellectual history is impossible. For the present purpose, however, we shall assume that somehow it always involves the transmission of the thought of the past, usually by means of literature or the arts. That literature or art may or may not be "great" or "intellectual"; it may include not only philosophy, theology, and epic poetry, but also sermons, debates, tracts, stump speeches, pictures, cartoons, barrackroom ballads, and even graffiti—whatever preserves a record of human thought. A more-or-less operational label might simply designate intellectual history as the study and analysis, in the dimension of time, of what happens when men and women from all walks of life think.

The following selections present four approaches to intellectual history: literary analysis; image, metaphor, and symbol; the history of ideas; and the *Zeitgeist*. As stated previously, the methods overlap. The first selection uses symbolism, while all of them obviously use literary analysis in some form. Note, also, the interdisciplinary nature of these selections, since they not only deal with literature, history, and philosophy, but also psychology, political science, anthropology, and popular culture.

chapter one

Literary Analysis

Literary analysis is the basic historical method and the common denominator of all historical inquiry, no matter what other methods may be employed. Simply stated, it involves reading source material and deriving evidence from that material to be used in supporting a point of view or thesis. The quantifier, looking up figures, may be using literary analysis. The same applies to a legal historian, who carefully checks cases and precedents, or a psychohistorian, who examines the papers of a historical figure, reading between the lines to determine motives, relationships, and childhood traumas. Ordinarily, however, the term refers specifically to the study of literature—poetry, novels, short stories, essays, and the like. It is usually assumed that the literature in question will be ''serious,'' and the methods used to deal with it will probably be those of the literary critic.

Although this approach is characteristic of philosophers and English professors, it is also the method used as a rule by students of intellectual history. Examination of the literature of an era is one of the most promising ways to understand that era, and the ideas presented in that literature may be explicated for their own sake, their relation to other ideas, their influence on the actions of men and women, or their role in shaping a culture, as is the case with this selection by Leo Marx.

The basic assumption on which such research rests must be that literary evidence can and should be taken seriously. Although it would not suffice to base a study of the law of entail on the novels of Jane Austen, the practical effects of that law on British gentry, their younger sons, their anxious daughters, and their fearful widows are perhaps more vividly portrayed in Austen's *Pride and Prejudice* than in any other single source. Here fiction provides a clear view of social stresses and relationships that would be difficult to obtain in any other way. To illustrate further, casual conversations in eighteenth-century Virginia are lost forever, even though much of the literature of the period survives. The pages may be foxed, the binding broken, and the print faded, but the words are exactly the same as when colonials wrote, printed, and read them. Although election practices of that time and place have been subjected to historical scrutiny, most notably in Charles S. Sydnor's *Gentlemen Freeholders*,[1] the most vivid portrayal of the electoral customs of the era still comes not from the pen of a twentieth-century historian but from a contemporary playwright. About 1770, Robert Munford wrote a play titled *The Candidates; or, the Humours of a Virginia Election,* which contains a wealth of information about electioneering and politics in Virginia just prior to the Revolution. Complete with the allegorical names typical of the literature of the period, it includes the stock stereotypes of the colonial gentleman and drunken country bumpkin. Even the allegorical names are revealing—this is their purpose—since Munford presented us with such characters as Sir John Toddy, his agent Guzzle, and Wou'dbe, the hopeful but not very tactful candidate. (The hero's name, as one might guess, is Worthy.) As Sydnor pointed out, if Munford's play were the sole trace of evidence about Virginia electioneering, we would be in a quandary about what to make of it. But since its profiles are supported by other evidence, including disputed election cases and personal letters from many Virginia candidates, the basic picture appears to be faithful to the reality it purports to portray, even if it is somewhat overdrawn.[2]

That the theme in *The Candidates* can be found in other documents as well brings to mind the most obvious but often ignored caveat about the use of literary sources, and thus literary analysis. Such sources are not necessarily representative or accurate. No matter how well the analysis is done, if a literary source is not representative the results will not be worth the effort (unless one's goals extend no further than that single source). A good illustration of the problem is found in the writings of William Shakespeare. His history is often incorrect, and the inferences that are sometimes drawn from his plays may be quite misleading. It is commonplace to refer to the young age at which girls married in Elizabethan England, and *Romeo and Juliet,* with its fourteen-year-old heroine, immediately comes to mind as an instance. But, as Peter Laslett has demonstrated (and this point is to be examined more fully in another section), here the proof of literature is no proof at all. In Shakespeare's time marriage at age fourteen was extremely rare; indeed, given the later age of physical maturity, it is highly improbable that many girls would marry that early. The average age of brides was a full ten years older than that of precocious Juliet, meaning that today's brides are younger, not older, than those in Elizabethan England.[3]

A second, and equally important, problem is that literary analysis may fail to reveal the dynamics of growth in an idea, mood, or trend. All historical evidence has a chronological tag—its date—that cannot be ignored. Frequently, studies of an ex-

---

[1]Charles S. Sydnor, *Gentlemen Freeholders: Political Practices in Washington's Virginia* (Chapel Hill: University of North Carolina Press for the Institute of Early American History and Culture, 1952), later republished as *American Revolutionaries in the Making: Political Practices in Washington's Virginia* (New York: Collier Books, 1962).

[2]Ibid., pp. 149–50.

[3]Peter Laslett, *The World We Have Lost* (New York: Charles Scribner's Sons, 1965), pp. 81–84.

tended time span (e.g., the 1920s or the colonial era) fail to take this into account. To mix in one pot literary (or other) evidence from 1921 and 1929 without providing any chronological reference will tend to obscure some very real differences between the two points in time. Obviously, the more protracted the span under consideration the more serious the problem becomes. A study of thought in colonial America that indiscriminately quotes sermons from the 1650s alongside sermons from the 1750s will inevitably miss much of the significance of the time element. Ideas change, usually slowly, but change and the process by which it occurs cannot be ignored. Like all other sources, literary evidence must be evaluated carefully with attention to detail.

This is the case not only with such obvious uses of literary evidence as those already cited, but also with the more sophisticated literary analysis like that practiced by Leo Marx. Here it is not the surface incidents that are of major interest, but, rather, major themes that may or may not have been underlined consciously by their creators. Marx provides a good example when he observes that simply because Emerson, Thoreau, Hawthorne, or Melville actually wrote little about the Industrial Revolution, it does not follow that their work did not involve that process as a major theme; thus Marx's purpose is to demonstrate how changes wrought by the advent of machines have helped to shape American literature. This approach necessitates a deft touch, a finesse. Artists do not "respond to history . . . by making history their manifest subject," as Marx points out (p. 21). Therefore one must always delve beneath surface appearances in order to determine not only an author's true, conscious intent, but his unconscious intent as well, "to look through and behind documents to grasp a man's thought."[4] For the intellectual historian, these subtle and unconscious messages may sometimes be the most important part of the literature. They are, in fact, indicators of a covert culture Marx discussed elsewhere (to be dealt with later under the heading, "Image, Metaphor, and Symbol").

All this implies a very close and important relationship between literature and history. Blending the two disciplines cannot be left solely to literary scholars, who often lack historical training and are sometimes wholly innocent of historical interest. Twentieth-century students of literature have frequently avoided the historical dimension of their work. Every bit as aloof as philosophers, literary scholars in departments of literature have written their brand of intellectual history primarily from an internal context. The result has been adaptation of the discipline to the requirements of literary criticism.[5] Although this antihistorical bias may now be dying out, if the melding of literature and history is ever to occur it may well have to be accomplished by historians who study literature rather than by literary scholars who study history. And to anyone who recognizes the validity of any historical research, it is important that careful

---

[4]John Higham, "The Study of American Intellectual History," in Higham, *Writing American History: Essays on Modern Scholarship* (Bloomington: Indiana University Press, 1970), p. 68.
[5]Higham, "Intellectual History and Its Neighbors," in Higham, *Writing American History*, p. 35.

examination of literary sources be undertaken to provide ever-increasing evidence of how people thought in earlier ages, and thus how they differ from us, their descendants. For history prior to the twentieth century—before new dimensions in the transmission of thought were opened by the development of radio and television—the *and* written record is the principal means that Western civilization possesses of transmitting thought and culture with any consistent accuracy. *was thro' mouth — Folk tales.*

On the surface, the historian's method in literary analysis is simple enough: read the literature; note the themes; discuss them; support conclusions by examples. But thousands of dreary monographs and articles warn that this is not so easy to accomplish. One scholar suggested that those engaged in literary analysis arrive at their method as they proceed, a practice that is altogether too frequent in both the scholar's discipline (English) and history. Perhaps the key to the historical study of literature lies in the basic questions raised by Rosalie Colie, who contends that, since no work of art exists for itself alone, "then one is willy-nilly committed to consider its 'history,' or, as I prefer to say, its histories." "What," she goes on to ask, "is the relation of that work [of art] to its creator, its audience, its genre, its time, its place, its particular language? What can be said about this work of art in relation to its fellows, to the taste of its time, and to the history of style or styles?"[6] All of Colie's questions seek to determine the impact of the work of art upon other things. True, the arrows of influence radiate from literature. But arrows of influence also converge in literature, which may be passively shaped by outside pressures. The historian who analyzes literature may also add other queries, including the vital questions of the impact of great events and movements on authors and their eras—questions that may be answered by literary clues even when the authors did not specifically write about their times.

In the following article Leo Marx notes one such instance in the writings of Nathaniel Hawthorne. Although Hawthorne did not write specifically about the impact of the Industrial Revolution, Marx demonstrates, nevertheless, that a connection exists between industrialization and the short story, "Ethan Brand." Using the internal context of intellectual history, examining the interrelation of ideas, Marx places the story in the context of the early nineteenth century; it is this time element that makes the article not merely a literary study but a historical study as well. Colie puts it more precisely: "Literary history depends upon an assumption of relative chronology—that the time when a thing was written has something to do with its nature."[7] Perhaps this observation ought to be turned around; for the historian engaged in literary analysis the nature of a work of art has something to do with the time it was written.

The use of literature as a historical source has been insufficiently exploited by

---

[6]Rosalie L. Colie, "Literature and History," in James Thorpe, ed., *Relations of Literary Study: Essays on Interdisciplinary Contributions* (New York: Modern Language Association of America, 1967), p. 1.
[7]Ibid., p. 9.

literary critics and scholars generally. If literature is to be taken seriously as historical evidence, it must be by historians like Leo Marx who have expanded their consciousness to the point of seeing the opportunities that other disciplines provide and are sufficiently deft to use them.[8]

The Machine in the Garden
Leo Marx

> . . . *the artist must employ the symbols in use in his day and nation to convey his enlarged sense to his fellow-men.*
>
> Ralph Waldo Emerson

The response of American writers to industrialism has been a typical and, in many respects, a distinguishing feature of our culture. The Industrial Revolution, of course, was international, but certain aspects of the process were intensified in this country. Here, for one thing, the Revolution was delayed, and when it began it was abrupt, thorough, and dramatic. During a decisive phase of that transition, our first significant literary generation, that of Hawthorne and Emerson, came to maturity. Hence it may be said that our literature, virtually from the beginning, has embodied the experience of a people crossing the line which sets off the era of machine production from the rest of human history. As Emerson said, speaking of the century as the ''age of tools,'' so many inventions had been added in his time that life seemed ''almost made over new.'' This essay demonstrates one of the ways in which a sense of the transformation of life by the machine has contributed to the temper of our literature. The emphasis is upon the years before 1860, because the themes and images with which our major writers then responded to the onset of the Machine Age have provided us with a continuing source of meaning.

Some will justifiably object, however, that very little of the work of Emerson, Thoreau, Hawthorne, or Melville actually was *about* the Industrial Revolution. But this fact hardly disposes of the inquiry; indeed, one appeal of the subject is precisely the need to meet this objection. For among the many arid notions which have beset inquiries into the relations between literature and society, perhaps the most barren has been the assumption that artists respond to history chiefly by making history their manifest subject. As if one might adequately gauge the imaginative impact of atomic

Leo Marx, ''The Machine in the Garden,'' *The New England Quarterly,* XXIX (March 1956), 27–30, 33–42. Copyright © 1956 by *The New England Quarterly*. Reprinted with deletion of notes and abridgment by permission of the author and publisher.

[8]John V. Fleming, ''Historians and the Evidence of Literature,'' *Journal of Interdisciplinary History* 4 (Summer 1973), provides further discussion of the use of literature as historical evidence.

power by seeking out direct allusions to it in recent literature. Our historical scholars do not sufficiently distinguish between the setting of a literary work (it may be institutional, geographical, or historical) and its subject-matter or theme. A poem set in a factory need be no more about industrialism than *Hamlet* about living in castles. Not that the setting is without significance. But the first obligation of the scholar, like any other reader of literature, is to know what the work is about. Only then may he proceed to his special business of elucidating the relevance of the theme to the experience of the age.

But here a difficulty arises: the theme itself cannot be said to "belong" to the age. It is centuries old. The Promethean theme, for example, belongs to no single time or place; history periodically renews man's sense of the perils attendant upon the conquest of nature. This obvious fact lends force to the view, tacit postulate of much recent criticism, that what we value in art derives from (and resides in) a realm beyond time, or, for that matter, society. Yet because the scholar grants his inability to account for the genesis of themes, he need not entertain a denial of history. True, he should not speak, for example, of *the* literature of industrialism, as if there were serious works whose controlling insights originate in a single, specific historical setting. But he has every reason to assume that certain themes and conventions, though they derive from the remote past, may have had a peculiar relevance to an age suddenly aware that machines were making life over new. That, in any case, is what seems to have happened in the age of Emerson and Melville. Because our writers seldom employed industrial settings until late in the century we have thought that only then did the prospect of a mechanized America affect their vision of life. My view is that an awareness of the Machine Revolution has been vital to our literature since the eighteen thirties.

But what of a man like Hawthorne, whom we still regard as the "pure" artist, and whose work apparently bears little relation to the Industrial Revolution of his age? In his case it is necessary to demonstrate the importance for his work of matters about which he wrote virtually nothing. Here is "Ethan Brand," a characteristic story developed from an idea Hawthorne recorded in 1843: "The search of an investigator for the Unpardonable Sin;—he at last finds it in his own heart and practice." The theme manifestly has nothing to do with industrialization. On the contrary, it is traditional; we correctly associate it with the Faust myth. Nevertheless, some facts about the genesis of the tale are suggestive. For its physical details, including characters and landscape, Hawthorne drew upon notes he had made during a Berkshire vacation in 1838. At that time several new factories were in operation along the mountain streams near North Adams. He was struck by the sight of machinery in the green hills; he took elaborate notes, and conceived the idea of a malignant steam engine which attacked and killed its human attendants. But he did nothing with that idea, or with any of his other observations upon the industrialization of the Berkshires. And the fact remains that nowhere, in "Ethan Brand" or the notebooks, do we find any explicit evidence of a direct link between Hawthorne's awareness of the new power and this fable of the quest for knowledge of absolute evil.

Nevertheless this connection can, I believe, be established. What enables us to establish it is the discovery of a body of imagery through which the age repeatedly expressed its response to the Industrial Revolution. This "imagery of technology" is decisively present in "Ethan Brand". . . . ·

In 1838, five years before Hawthorne had formulated the moral germ of "Ethan Brand," he had been struck by an actual sight of this change in American society. "And taking a turn in the road," he wrote, "behold these factories. . . . And perhaps the wild scenery is all around the very site of the factory and mingles its impression strangely with those opposite ones." Here was history made visible. What most impressed Hawthorne was a "sort of picturesqueness in finding these factories, supremely artificial establishments, in the midst of such wild scenery." Nevertheless, ten years later, when Hawthorne so thoroughly mined this Berkshire notebook for "Ethan Brand," he passed over these impressions. The factories do not appear in the story. Nor is there any overt allusion to industrialization. To speculate about the reasons for this "omission" would take us far afield. Whatever the reason, the important fact is not that "Ethan Brand" contains no mention of the factories themselves, but that the ideas and emotions they suggested to Hawthorne are central to the story.

A sense of loss, anxiety, and dislocation hangs over the world of "Ethan Brand." The mood is located in the landscape. At the outset we hear that the countryside is filled with "relics of antiquity." What caused this melancholy situation becomes apparent when Hawthorne describes the people of the region. Brand has returned from his quest. Word is sent to the village, and a crowd climbs the mountain to hear his tale. From among them Hawthorne singles out several men: the stage-agent, recently deprived of his vocation; an old-fashioned country doctor, his useful days gone by; and a man who has lost a hand (emblem of craftsmanship?) in the "devilish grip of a steam-engine." He is now a "fragment of a human being." Like the Wandering Jew and the forlorn old man who searches for his lost daughter (said to have been a victim of Ethan's experimental bent), all are derelicts. They are victims of the fires of change. Like the monomaniac hero himself, all suffer a sense of not belonging.

This intense feeling of "unrelatedness" to nature and society has often been ascribed to the very historical forces which Hawthorne had observed in 1838. Discussing the intellectual climate of that era, Emerson once remarked that young men then had been born with knives in their brains. This condition was a result, he said, of the pervasive "war between intellect and affection." He called it "detachment," and found it reflected everywhere in the age: in Kant, Goethe's *Faust,* and in the consequences of the new capitalist power. "Instead of the social existence which all shared," he wrote, "was now separation." Whatever we choose to call it—"detachment" or "alienation" (Karl Marx), or "anomie" (Emile Durkheim) or "dissociation of sensibility" (T.S. Eliot)—this is the malaise from which Ethan suffered. Though there are important differences of emphasis, each of these terms refers to the state of mind of an individual cut off from a realm of experience said to be an indispensable source of life's meaning. The source may vary, but it is significant that the responsible agent, or *separator,* so to speak, is invariably identified with science or industrial technology. In this sense Hawthorne's major theme was as vividly contemporary as it was traditional. He gave us the classic American account of the anguish of detachment.

The knife in Ethan's brain was a "cold philosophical curiosity" which led to a "separation of the intellect from the heart." Now it is of the utmost significance that this scientific obsession is said to have literally emanated from the fire. There was a legend about Ethan's having been accustomed "to evoke a fiend from the hot furnace." Together they spent many nights by the fire evolving the idea of the quest. But the fiend always retreated through the "iron door" of the kiln with the first glimmer of sunlight. Here we discover how Hawthorne's earlier impressions of industrialization have been transmuted in the creative process. Here is the conduit through which thought and emotion flow to the work from the artist's experience of his age. In this case the symbolic contrast between fire and sun serves the purpose. It blends a traditional convention (we think of Milton's Hell) and immediate experience; it provides the symbolic frame for the entire story. "Ethan Brand" begins at sundown and ends at dawn. During the long night the action centers upon the kiln or "furnace" which replaces the sun as source of warmth, light, and (indirectly) sustenance. The fire in the kiln is at once the symbolic source of evil and of the energy necessary to make nature's raw materials useful to man. Moreover, it can be shown that the very words and phrases used to describe this fire are used elsewhere, by Hawthorne, in direct reference to industrialization. In the magazines of the day fire was repeatedly identified with the new machine power. Hence fire, whatever its traditional connotations, is here an emblem, or fragment of an emblem, of the nascent industrial order. The new America was being forged by fire.

But if fire cripples men and devastates the landscape in "Ethan Brand," the sun finally dispels anxiety and evil, restoring man's solidarity with nature. When Ethan dies, his body burned to a brand by the satanic flames which had possessed his soul, the fire goes out and the ravaged landscape disappears. In its stead we see a golden vision of the self-contained New England village. The sun is just coming up. The hills swell gently about the town, as if resting "peacefully in the hollow of the great hand of Providence." In pointed contrast to the murky atmosphere of Ethan's Walpurgisnacht, there is no smoke anywhere. The sun allows perfect clarity of perception. Every house is "distinctly visible." At the center of this pastoral tableau the spires of the churches catch the first rays of the sun. Now the countryside is invested with all the order and serenity and permanence which the fire had banished. This harmony between man and nature is then projected beyond time in the vision of a stepladder of clouds on which it seemed that (from such a social order?) "mortal man might thus ascend into heavenly regions." Finally, though he had already hinted that stage coaches were obsolete, Hawthorne introduces one into this eighteenth-century New England version of the Garden of Eden.

Beneath the surface of "Ethan Brand" we thus find many of the ideas and emotions aroused by the Machine's sudden entrance into the Garden. But this is not to say that the story is *about* industrialization. It is about the consequences of breaking the magic chain of humanity. That is the manifest theme and, like the symbols through which it is developed, the theme is traditional. His apprehension of the tradition permits Hawthorne to discover meanings in contemporary facts. On the other hand, the capacity of this theme and these images to excite the imagination must also be ascribed to their vivid relevance to life in modern America. This story, in short, is an amalgam of tradition, which supplies the theme, and experience, which presents the occasion, and imagery common to both.

But it may be said that, after all, this is merely one short story. The fact remains, however, that the same, or related, images may be traced outward from this story to Hawthorne's other work, the work of his contemporaries, the work of many later writers, and the society at large.

It is revealing, for example, that Hawthorne so often described his villains as alchemists, thereby associating them with fire and smoke. We recall that Aylmer, the scientist in "The Birthmark," made a point of building his laboratory underground to avoid sunlight. Or consider Rappaccini, whose experiments perverted the Garden itself. His flowers were evil because of their "artificialness indicating . . . the production . . . no longer of God's making, but the monstrous offspring of man's depraved fancy. . . ." From Hamilton's "Report on Manufactures" in 1791 until today, American thinking about industrialism, in and out of literature, has been tangled in the invidious distinction between "artificial" and "natural" production. These adjectives, like so much of American political rhetoric, along with Hawthorne's theme of isolation, are a characteristic legacy of agrarian experience. They are expressions of our native tradition of pastoral, with its glorification of the Garden and its consequent identification of science and technology with evil. To Hawthorne's contemporaries, Emerson, Thoreau, and Whitman, the sun also represented the primal source of redemption. "The sun rose clear," Thoreau tells us at the beginning of *Walden*; though he notes that the smoke of the train momentarily obscures its rays, the book ends with a passionate affirmation of the possibility of renewed access, as in "Ethan Brand," to its redeeming light: "The sun is but a morning star."

In *Moby-Dick,* published three years after "Ethan Brand," the identical motif emerges as a controlling element of tragedy. The "Try-Works," a crucial chapter in Ishmael's progressive renunciation of Ahab's quest, is quite literally constructed out of the symbols of "Ethan Brand." Again it is night, and vision is limited to the lurid light of a "kiln" or "furnace." Fire again is a means of production, rendering the whale's fat, and again it is also the source of alienation. Ishmael, at the helm, controls the ship's fate. Like Ethan he momentarily succumbs to the enchantment of fire, and so nearly fulfills Ahab's destructive destiny. But he recovers his sanity in time, and tells us: "Look not too long in the face of the fire, O Man! . . . believe not the *artificial fire* when its redness makes all things look ghastly. Tomorrow, in the *natural sun,* the skies will be bright; those who glared like devils in the forking flames, the more will show in far other, at least gentler relief; the glorious, golden, glad sun, the only true lamp—all others but liars!"

From this passage we may trace lines of iconological continuity to the heart of Melville's meaning. When the *Pequod* sailed both Ahab and Ishmael suffered the pain of "detachment." But if the voyage merely reinforced Ahab's worship of the power of fire, it provoked in Ishmael a reaffirmation of the Garden. Ahab again and again expressed his aspiration in images of fire and iron, cogs and wheels, automata, and manufactured men. He had his "humanities," and at times was tempted by thoughts of "green land," but Ahab could not finally renounce the chase. In *Moby-Dick* space is the sea—a sea repeatedly depicted in images of the American landscape. The conquest of the whale was a type of our fated conquest of nature itself. But in the end Ishmael in effect renounced the fiery quest. He was cured and saved. His rediscovery of that pastoral accommodation to the mystery of growth and fertility was as vital to his salvation as it had been to the myth of the Garden. The close identity of the great democratic God and the God of the Garden was a central facet of Melville's apocalyptic insight.

His was also a tragic insight. Ahab and Ishmael, representing irreconcilable conceptions of America's destiny, as indeed of all human experience, were equally incapable of saving the *Pequod*. From Melville to Faulkner our writers have provided a desperate recognition of this truth: of the attributes necessary for survival, the Ahabs alone have been endowed with the power, and the Ishmaels with the perception. Ishmael was saved. But like one of Job's messengers, he was saved to warn us of greater disasters in store for worshippers of fire. In this way imagery associated with the Machine's entrance into the Garden has served to join native experience and inherited wisdom.

chapter two
Image, Metaphor, and Symbol

in lecture notes.

One of the most important uses of intellectual history is to determine the relationship between people's images, metaphors, and symbols and their thoughts or actions. Since thought and action are cultural attributes (Stone Age tribesmen on another continent do not think and act in the same way as the average North American in identical situations), images, metaphors, symbols, and even individual words have an important cultural content that can provide clues as to the nature of that culture. These terms once again require some definitions.

By culture we mean those social values and behavioral patterns characteristic of a society, nation, tribe, ethnic group, or the like, that will be handed down to and understood by future generations, whether the transmission process be conscious or unconscious. It includes, but is not limited to, the way of life, customs, worldview, and mode of adaptation to the environment. *In the Fens.*

Since intellectual history usually analyzes images, metaphors, and symbols as they appear in literary sources, we shall accept definitions derived from literary criticism, although they may seem murky and thus not entirely acceptable to historians. (Even literary critics draw much the same conclusion; one confesses that if he were required to give a brief definition of metaphor he would be at a loss to do so—and then goes on to write an essay about metaphor.[1] When literary critics have trouble defining literary terms historians should not complain when they also encounter difficulty.) Thus an image is "a literal and concrete representation of a sensory experience or of an object that can be known by one or more of the senses," a direct reference to something that actually exists.[2] In contrast, a symbol suggests a further meaning, one more profound and on a deeper level than the literal meaning suggests.[3] A metaphor is similar to an

---

[1] L. C. Knights, "*King Lear* as Metaphor," in Bernice Slote, ed., *Myth and Symbol: Critical Approaches and Applications* (Lincoln: University of Nebraska Press, 1963), p. 21.

[2] C. Hugh Holman, William Flint Thrall, and Addison Hibbard, eds., *A Handbook to Literature,* 3rd ed. (Indianapolis: The Odyssey Press, 1972), p. 263.

[3] Ibid., p. 519.

give as . from notes!

image or symbol, except that it implies an analogy between two essentially dissimilar objects in order to compare the familiar and the unfamiliar. The device usually moves from a readily comprehended, familiar image to something "perhaps vaguer, more problematic, or more strange."[4] While marking their differences, however, it is also important to note that these three figures of speech have an important property in common. Each goes beyond the literal meaning of the words or phrases used, indicating a degree of double entendre, and creating a conscious meaning that would not otherwise be found and that is clear to the members of the culture that produced them. For each we could repeat what L. C. Knights says of metaphor: "Fixed meanings are modified or destroyed, and a new apprehension—or ... a new direction of awareness—takes place."[5] Thus the purpose of these forms of expression is to explain abstract ideas in a more explicit way than would otherwise be possible.

Perhaps definition will be clarified by examples. Since an image is a concrete representation of reality, "the blood-red sea" brings to mind a large body of reddish water. A symbol is an abstraction beyond literal meaning; "to bear one's cross" produces a mental picture of a person in anguish rather than of a man carrying a cross. Metaphors call to mind analogous events; in this article Henry Nash Smith castigates the use of biological metaphors in history, referring specifically to the germ theory. Here "germ" is an image that conveys the metaphor. It is not a symbol because it suggests no deeper meaning. Instead, it is intended to suggest a direct analogy between the growth of institutions and of living things—both institutions and plants are said to germinate and grow. An army may be a ponderous machine (metaphor); here machine is the image that provides the vehicle of the metaphor. An army might also be the focal point of nationalism (symbol).

The role of symbol in society was stressed by Carl G. Jung, whose ideas influenced both literary critics and historians. His explanations are more abstract than those of the literary critics, sometimes approaching the mystical. Jung, who rejected Freud's far-reaching theories of sex and developed instead his own theory of psychoanalysis, thought of symbol as something that could not be expressed directly, something for which words did not even exist. A "word or an image is symbolic when it implies something more than its obvious and immediate meaning," something that may not even be susceptible to definition and comprehension. They may be used either consciously or unconsciously.[6] To illustrate, the log cabin to which Smith refers is an image that must "express value-judgments that everyone is expected to endorse. A symbol of this kind ... suggests to the members of the social group a special conception of themselves ..." (p. 33). The American citizenry is the "we" to whom the image (which has become a symbol) is aimed. Presumably all of us will interpret that log cabin in the same way and will therefore react in the same way, accepting the

---

[4] Philip Wheelwright, *Metaphor and Reality* (Bloomington: Indiana University Press, 1962), pp. 72–73.
[5] Knights, "*King Lear* as Metaphor," p. 23.
[6] Carl G. Jung, "Approaching the Unconscious," in Jung, ed., *Man and His Symbols* (Garden City, N. Y.: Doubleday and Co., 1964), pp. 20–21. This was Jung's last work, and was an effort to make his ideas comprehensible to the general reader (pp. 10–11).

conception of America that the log cabin implies. John William Ward, whose masterly *Andrew Jackson: Symbol for an Age* was mentioned earlier, points out that because abstractions are usually poor means of persuasion, a culture creates symbols as a way of transforming them into a concrete reality. The historical reality behind the symbols may be lacking—were the log cabin pioneers really so strong and resourceful?—but the symbol carries its meaning nevertheless.[7]

The higher abstraction of the symbol is so common that it is widely found outside of literature and fine arts, at the popular, even practical, level of daily use. The Founding Fathers stand for integrity and wisdom; Teapot Dome and Watergate for corruption (the former is a specific geological formation in Wyoming, the latter is the terminus of the Chesapeake and Ohio Canal); the pyramids mean the ages; the olive branch symbolizes peace; and of special interest to college professors are the three golden balls indicating the location of a pawnshop. Occasionally the meaning of a symbol may not be agreed on, as in the case of carpetbagger. But no mature American, North or South, conceives of one simply as a person who carries baggage that appears to be made of carpeting. And the symbol may be so far divorced from reality that it has no logical relationship to it. Is it logical that justice is blind? Would it not be more reassuring to believe that "justice" can see what she is doing?

Analysis of images, metaphors, and symbols is not a mere mechanical device, for it demands a subtle and thorough familiarity with the sources and the society that produced them. Earlier we mentioned the concept of culture, including in its definition the requirement that it be transmitted from one generation to the next and the contingency that this transmission may be unconscious. These essential characteristics have enabled intellectual historians to develop a technique for understanding the past that utilizes the images, metaphors, and symbols common to the era. Since the culture tends to remain constant, changing only slowly, its figures of speech can be understood readily by historians subsequently reared in that culture, for authors or artists necessarily share the words and symbols they employ with other, even future, members of their society. Thus all readers of this book, functioning for the moment as intellectual historians, understand something of the religious symbolism of the cross, even though the symbol is many centuries old. But to someone wholly ignorant of the Western world the symbol may convey no meaning whatever. The cross is an excellent example of what we may call overt culture, that is, it is openly acknowledged by the members of that society.

Conversely, there is also covert culture—"traits of culture rarely acknowledged by those who possess them" that are "seriously inconsistent with other parts of culture and so get driven underground."[8] This underground culture is unconscious. It consists of those social values and behavioral patterns that we do not ordinarily acknowledge.

---

[7] John William Ward, *Andrew Jackson: Symbol for an Age* (New York: Oxford University Press, 1962 [originally published 1955]), pp. 173, 208.

[8] Bernard Bowran, Leo Marx, and Arnold Rose, "Literature and Covert Culture," *American Quarterly* 9 (Winter 1957): 377–86, quotes from pp. 377–78. Much of the following discussion is based on this article.

Sometimes perceptive artists detect these and insert them in their work. It then befalls the intellectual historian to explain them to a later generation, just as Leo Marx explains the "imagery of technology" in Hawthorne's "Ethan Brand" or as Smith analyzes the metaphor of the germ theory. On other occasions, as when analyzing popular literature and art or serious literature and art containing unintended messages, historians are faced with a more difficult task. Then they must detect the unconscious use of these literary devices in an attempt to reveal unconscious values and behavior patterns, such as Smith has done with the log cabin symbol. How is this done? Since the popular artist does not knowingly reveal this hidden culture, popular literature (and pictorial art) "may be studied for what it *betrays* as well as what it *depicts*. In other words, it may be approached as a projection of covert culture," the projection taking place by means of image, metaphor, or symbol. A cliché or isolated reference is of little interest in this connection. What is important is the repeated use of related figures of speech "*in varying language* to describe similar phenomena." The covert aspect derives "from the impulse to adhere (simultaneously) to logically incompatible values."[9] For example, Smith believes that Frederick Jackson Turner implied personal agreement with the metaphor of the germ theory of history, even if he did not choose to emphasize it. In so doing, Turner (and, by extension, the legion of historians and popular writers and artists of his culture who absorbed his ideas) revealed a covert oversimplification of American history, since the identification of the frontier image with American democracy was so incompatible with other parts of our culture that, to quote Smith, it "gives us no framework for considering the consequences of technological development, or the imposing fact of urbanization" (p. 37).

Images, metaphors, and symbols may be suggestive, but only if the historian isolates them. There must be a willingness to penetrate the façade of literature or pictorial art, a willingness to inquire what the work of art says—or does not say—that is not readily apparent and an urge "to look through and behind documents to grasp a man's thought."[10] In this way we may sometimes capture meanings that contemporaries expressed subconsciously or inadvertently—meanings that reveal the assumptions on which people thought and acted. This attempt to read between the lines is likely to succeed only if historians are products of or closely familiar with the society that prompted the work they examine. By definition, image, metaphor, and symbol are culture bound and are often created unconsciously (Hemingway is supposed to have said that the best symbols are those that come by accident). Twentieth-century Americans are likely to have more success understanding the symbols of eighteenth-century America than they are of another culture in their own time.

Furthermore, and this may seem a strange reminder for historians, we must not look at symbol analysis as a static process, divorced from the time dimension. Images are

---

[9] Ibid., pp. 380, 381, 385.

[10] John Higham, "The Study of American Intellectual History," in Higham, *Writing American History: Essays on Modern Scholarship* (Bloomington: Indiana University Press, 1970), p. 68.

created, developed into symbols, accepted, and forgotten, and this historic process should form a part of the examination of any extended study. John William Ward criticizes his major work on this very point. The analysis did not take the time element into account, all evidence being treated as if it bore the same date. This was a deliberate, calculated decision, but Ward confesses surprise that his strategy has not been attacked for its failure to capture something of the chronological movement that is the basis of history.[11]

Another danger lurks within this very promising historical method: avoid the implication that a causal connection exists between the image, metaphor, or symbol, and what other people thought or did, unless there are sound reasons for making the assertion. Note that Smith does make the connection between the metaphor of the germ theory and the resulting oversimplification of history, though some students might find this part of his essay somewhat weak. Simply because the cause-to-effect relationship seems logical and plausible does not prove that such a relationship existed.

There are further cautions to be observed: be wary of symbolic interpretation unless you are well grounded in your sources, for here as elsewhere the consequence of failure to heed this warning will be results so limited by method that they become meaningless. Indeed, this entire selection may be viewed as Henry Nash Smith's warning against uncritical acceptance and heavy-handed use of images, metaphors, and symbols. Another problem is that these devices are easily found where they do not exist; many writers have been mortified to learn that readers find in their works symbols that are less literary devices than figments of some critic's imagination. Sometimes, of course, writers project their symbols unconsciously, but other times they project none at all. Novelist Vladimir Nabokov remarks that "the notion of symbol itself has always been abhorrent to me. . . . The symbolism racket in the schools," he goes on to say, "attracts computerized minds but destroys plain intelligence as well as poetical sense. It bleaches the soul. It numbs all capacity to enjoy the fun and enchantment of art."[12] The lesson is clear: an aspiring historian who is committed to find symbolism will, unfortunately, find it in the most unlikely places whether it is there or not.

In the following article, Henry Nash Smith examines the log cabin and the agricultural frontier as images in the American experience. They are more than images, however, for they have been imbued with symbolic content and stand for the democratic way of life. In academic dress the log cabin becomes the frontier thesis of Frederick Jackson Turner, which, by its acceptance of the metaphor of the germ theory of history, has, according to Smith, cut Americans off from vital parts of their past, those portions that the metaphor was unable to explain. As is the case with other selections in this collection, Smith's work could have been used to illustrate more than one method.

[11] John William Ward, "Looking Backward: *Andrew Jackson: Symbol for an Age*," in L. P. Curtis, Jr., ed., *The Historian's Workshop: Original Essays by Sixteen Historians* (New York: Alfred A. Knopf, 1970), pp. 217–18. Ward was a student in Smith's seminar.

[12] Vladimir Nabokov, *Strong Opinions* (New York: McGraw-Hill Book Co., 1973), pp. 304–305.

Obviously he used literary analysis, but it is less obvious that he is dealing with the history of ideas, both the symbol of the log cabin and the metaphor of the germ theory being potentially part of a discussion of basic unit-ideas. The emphasis on culture also indicates the interdisciplinary aspects of the article.

This discussion tends to emphasize the internal context of intellectual history, since the metaphor of the germ theory of history is the major topic. As such, it underlines the relation of thought to other thoughts, of the assumptions taught in the seminars of Herbert Baxter Adams to the thought of Frederick Jackson Turner. In its brief discussion of the log cabin symbol, however, the article illustrates the external context, for it examines the relationship between thought and the beliefs of a large number of American citizens; in short, it deals briefly with popular culture.

The West as an Image of the American Past
Henry Nash Smith

During the past three days our discussion of the influence of the West on American ideas and institutions has emphasized economic, social, and political history, and has inevitably involved frequent references to the greatest historian of the West, Frederick Jackson Turner. I shall come back to Turner before I am through, but at the outset I should like to turn aside from the usual areas of historical inquiry to consider the influence of the West on American thought at the level of unsystematic popular ideology.

I shall use as a starting point a cartoon by Edmund Duffy which recently appeared in the *Saturday Evening Post* [January 20, 1951]. The cartoon depicts an American civilian scowling through his spectacles across the Pacific at a sinister Asiatic figure in military uniform which is peering above the Far Eastern horizon beneath a cloud of smoke labeled "Aggression." At the feet of the American, on land labeled "U. S.," stands a log cabin from whose chimney issues a smaller cloud of smoke labeled "Freedom."

This cartoon seems to me to embody several familiar doctrines of contemporary American ideology. The United States is identified with a log cabin, and the cabin is represented as the source of the abstract value Freedom. The American, who is rolling up his sleeve in defiance of the foreign enemy, is wearing the clothing of an urban officeworker, yet his roots, so to speak, are not defined by the skyline of a city or the smokestacks of a factory but by the conventional symbol of the agricultural frontier. We are asked to accept the proposition that the meaning of our society is implicit in the

"The West as an Image of the American Past," by Henry Nash Smith in *The University of Kansas City Review*, Vol. XVIII, No. 1, pp. 29–40 (autumn 1951). Copyrighted © 1951 by the University of Kansas City. Reprinted with deletion of notes and abridgment by permission of the author and *New Letters* (formerly *The University of Kansas City Review*).

cabin, or, in other words, that the essence of our institutions and our way of life is the frontier experience.

By the side of this cartoon, which refers to the early agricultural West, the West just within the frontier, I should like to place an image which comes down to us from the Wild West beyond the agricultural frontier: the image of the cowboy. This figure is such a familiar part of our mythology that it needs no description. During the year 1950, there were sold in this country 214 million copies of paper-backed "pocket books." The largest category of these, a miscellaneous group called in the publishing trade simply "novels," made up 32 per cent of the total. The second largest category was that of "mysteries." The third largest class was "Westerns," novels about cowboys, which made up 18 per cent of the total. The Westerns far outranked the third specific category, that of "love novels," which accounted for only seven per cent of total sales.

The log cabin and the cowboy are symbols which every member of American society, regardless of education or social level, recognizes at once. Anthropologists call such symbols "cultural images." Many, perhaps most cultural images, like the two I have mentioned, are regarded as versions of actual historical events or situations, and they are the principal form in which knowledge of the past is really current in the society. The cultural images thus define the sense of the past which is common to the members of our culture. The experience of sharing these images is one of the major forces making for social cohesion, because the images express value-judgments that everyone is expected to endorse. A symbol of this kind does much more than convey a simple declarative statement concerning the past. It exerts a power of attraction. It suggests to the members of the social group a special conception of themselves, and tends to impose on them very definite notions of what is good and what is desirable in social policy.

The cartoon I have described illustrates the tendency of cultural images to impose judgments of value. The cartoonist wishes to recommend a national policy in the present crisis, and at the same time to arouse in his audience a feeling of strength. To this end he emphasizes the brawny muscles of the forearm which is revealed as the American rolls up his sleeve, and invokes a feeling of group solidarity by implying that all of us have a common past, a tradition, which is defined by the log cabin. He evidently assumes that the symbols he uses will be intelligible to a wide audience.

The cultural image of the cowboy is quite different from that of the log cabin: the cowboy is emphatically not a farmer. Yet this image too suggests to Americans a certain conception of themselves and embodies value judgments. Although the cowboy is a relatively recent addition to the roster of American folk heroes, he is heir to an imposing body of emotion associated with the Manifest Destiny of the United States in the Far West. The novelist Frank Norris, for example, was one among many observers who believed that the conquest of the high plains and mountain ranges beyond the Mississippi was an achievement of epic proportions, a phase of our history deserving commemoration in a literary masterpiece comparable to the great epics of the past.

> The Trojan War [wrote Norris in the 1890's] left to posterity the charac-
> ter of Hector; the wars with the Saracens gave us Roland; the folklore of
> Iceland produced Grettir; the Scotch border poetry brought forth the Doug-
> las; the Spanish epic the Cid. But the American epic, just as heroic, just as
> elemental, just as important and as picturesque, will fade into history,
> leaving behind no finer type, no nobler hero than Buffalo Bill.

In Norris's imagination, the cowboy was "the Hector of our ignored Iliad," and he suggested what lineaments this hero should be given if the unwritten epic were ever composed. The cowboy was not a lawbreaker, as the dime novels had portrayed him, "but a lawmaker; a fighter, it is true, as is always the case with epic figures, but a fighter for peace, a calm, grave, strong man who hated the lawbreaker as the hound hates the wolf." Mounted on his faithful horse, the hero faced his enemies with tranquil courage, and "fear was not in him even at the end. For such a man as this could die no quiet death in a land where law went no further than the statute books and life lay in the crook of my neighbor's forefinger." "He is of all the world-types the one distinctive to us—peculiar, particular, and unique."

The epic which Norris called for has not been written and it almost certainly never will be, for reasons which are evident in Norris's own essay. The attitudes embodied in the passage I have just quoted are not epic, except as Hollywood uses the term. They are melodramatic and sentimental, and the cowboy as a cultural image has continued to lead his vigorous and exciting existence at a subliterary level of melodramatic stereotypes. . . .

This kind of identification with the image of the cowboy has little or no social significance. The cowboy is an exotic figure. He belongs to a world which has always seemed half unreal because it is so far removed from the everyday life led by the bulk of our people. He is outside society. The cowboy of popular imagination is the product of a literary and subliterary development proceeding from James Fenimore Cooper's character Leatherstocking, who fled from civilization to live alone in the wilderness. Thus the Wild Western hero does not seem to have direct relevance to organized community life. He is not "serious." It is true that when we identify with this image we revert to a childish level, and do so only at the expense of virtually ceasing to think at all. In such day-dreaming we achieve an illusion of integration which is too easily bought. It is not valid for any situation which involves problems that cannot be solved by hard riding and close shooting. But precisely because the cowboy is an exotic figure, we are under no temptation to generalize the cultural image in which he figures; we do not for a moment imagine that it embodies a complete account of American experience.

The cultural image of the agricultural frontier, on the other hand, has a very different status. As Mr. Duffy's cartoon illustrates, the American of the present day can be invited to identify with it at a level of the highest seriousness, as a means of defining a position and perhaps even formulating national policy in a time of the most appalling crisis. I suggest that this difference is due to the fact that the frontier farmer called to mind by the symbol of the log cabin was inside, not outside the agricultural frontier; he was a part of society, and he can be made to seem the spiritual ancestor of the American of the present day.

Let me try to state more fully the propositions about American society and character, past and present, which seem to be involved in the identification of twentieth-century urban America with a frontier past. If I seem to be reading too much into a single cartoon (although I do not think I am), then let me phrase the question in a conditional mode: What would be the consequences for our society if this cultural image were generally accepted as having the status given it by the cartoonist? What meaning for the present is contained in the notion that the frontier, the agricultural West embodies the only "usable past" of our society?

I state this idea in an extreme form in order to bring out more clearly the issue which I think it raises. We are discussing a tendency which is perhaps nowhere carried to its logical extreme, but I believe the tendency can be observed at more than one level of contemporary American thought. I venture to suggest that the crude generalizations implied in Mr. Duffy's cartoon are a kind of parody of Turner's Frontier Hypothesis: a statement in vulgarized terms of ideas which Turner advanced as a general interpretation of American history, and which during the past half-century have achieved wide currency both in historical research and in the textbooks used in colleges and secondary schools. The relation between the cultural image and the historical theory is a difficult matter to analyze. Turner's thought was of course much more subtle and various than the *Post* cartoon, and I certainly do not propose to hold him directly responsible for the development of the cultural image. The materials of it are at least a hundred years older than Turner's formulation of his hypothesis, and its currency demonstrates that it gives expression to impulses and attitudes far broader than the work of any single man. One can find ideas about the West in Thomas Jefferson that are almost as relevant to the cartoon as is Turner's essay on "The Significance of the Frontier in American History." Nevertheless, these ideas seem to me to have come down into the twentieth century largely through the channel of Turner's persuasive statement of the case for the dominant importance of the Western frontier in our history.

Turner's 1893 essay contains a number of assertions that the frontier experience has been central in American development, that it is indeed "the really American part of our history." The most famous sentence in the essay asserts that "The existence of an area of free land, its continuous recession, and the advance of American settlement westward, explain American development." The character of the frontiersman, in the same essay, is declared to be the source of basic American attitudes. On this point I ask your indulgence for a long quotation. The passage is one that has often been reproduced:

> From the conditions of frontier life came intellectual traits of profound importance. The works of travelers along each frontier from colonial days onward describe certain common traits, and these traits have, while softening down, still persisted as survivals in the place of their origin, even when

a higher social organization succeeded. The result is that to the frontier the American intellect owes its striking characteristics. That coarseness and strength combined with acuteness and inquisitiveness; that practical, inventive turn of mind, quick to find expedients; that masterful grasp of material things, lacking in the artistic but powerful to effect great ends; that restless, nervous energy; that dominant individualism, working for good and evil, and with all that buoyancy and exuberance which comes with freedom —these are traits of the frontier, or traits called out elsewhere because of the existence of the frontier. Since the days when the fleet of Columbus sailed into the waters of the New World, America has been another name for opportunity, and the people of the United States have taken their tone from the incessant expansion which has not only been open but has even been forced upon them.

The condensed character-sketch of the frontiersman contained in this memorable passage is consistently maintained in Turner's work, as Professor George W. Pierson has shown through a careful compilation of Turner's numerous references to the subject. Mr. Pierson further demonstrates that the transformation of institutions brought about by the frontier was in Turner's opinion the result of a transformation in the character of the people who underwent the frontier experience. The focus of the Frontier Hypothesis is, in other words, the character of the people involved; the symbol of the log cabin calls our attention to a human type, the frontier farmer.

I should like also to emphasize Turner's explicit generalization of the frontier influence. The advance of settlement "explains American development." The American intellect, in general, owes to the conditions of frontier life its striking characteristics. Turner provides us with a detailed portrait of the American type which he regards as the product of our common historical experience. Although he occasionally points out that the frontiersman's individualism led to evil as well as to good, these reservations are overshadowed in popular understanding of the Frontier Hypothesis (and apparently often forgotten by Turner himself) because frontier individualism is hardly to be distinguished from frontier democracy. And frontier democracy is identified with American democracy. The image of the frontier farmer thus acquires an almost sacrosanct status as the source of the highest value of our society.

Interpreted in this fashion, the image seems to me seriously misleading. The most striking feature of it is what it leaves out. Pointless as the observation may seem, I remind you that the world of Western frontier farmers does not comprehend Boston and New York and Philadelphia and Charleston, and this omission takes on great significance if the frontier image is made the key to American history. Furthermore, as has often been pointed out, it does not provide an adequate basis for taking account of the enormous contribution of Europe to our development. (In this regard, incidentally, I think Turner's own work is hardly more useful than the simplified interpretations of it in popular thought. The metaphor of "germs" which Turner employs to define the European contribution to American history provides but a meager vehicle for the transit of Occidental culture to the New World, and implies further that significant European influence ended with the act of planting these germs in new soil.) The image of the frontier gives us no framework for considering the consequences of technological development, or the imposing fact of urbanization. If we take it at all literally, the image makes it difficult to explain how Benjamin Franklin can be regarded as a truly American figure; or Jonathan Edwards, or Hawthorne, or Melville; or Willard Gibbs, or Henry Adams, or William Faulkner. To take the log cabin in the clearing as the absolute American fact is to label as "un-American" a range of experiences and attitudes which are indispensable to the realization of our full stature as human beings: the sense of guilt and of evil; even the experience of doubt and despair; all subtlety and depth in the consideration of ideas, or in art; indeed, the sense of the past itself, the whole range of historic time and its embodiment in tradition, including all historical scholarship.

An image of man and of society lacking these dimensions is grossly oversimplified, and oversimplified in a dogmatic and systematic fashion. It is primitive, and the affirmation of the image as an account either of the American past or of the American present is a species of primitivism. The image of the agricultural frontier is as anti-intellectual as is that of the Wild West, but it has implications for present social policy that are lacking in the splendid make-believe of the cowboy cult.

The vagaries of popular ideology which lead to the notion that we are now about to defend a log cabin against Asiatic aggression, however devious, are familiar enough to demand no analysis for this audience. But the continued currency of the cultural image of the frontier in its academic form, that of the Turner Hypothesis, seems to me more puzzling. I shall conclude therefore with an effort to understand why this image has attained such wide currency in the world of scholarship; and to notice what seem to me to be some of the consequences of the hypothesis for the study and teaching of American history.

We must recognize at the outset that Turner's thesis was a great deal more satisfactory than the two principal conceptions of American history against which he was protesting—the excessive emphasis on the slavery controversy and the version of the "germ theory" which Herbert B. Adams was propagating in the graduate history seminar at Johns Hopkins. The hypothesis explains a great deal of American history which these prevalent theories left unaccounted for. Turner's vital and charming personality, his unparalleled gifts as a teacher, and his eloquence are bound to have increased the influence which his views exerted. Beyond these factors are certain broader and more conjectural possibilities which may well have furthered the acceptance of his doctrines. His original paper was read at one of the learned meetings sponsored by the Chicago World's Fair of 1893, which was widely recognized at the time as a formal proclamation that the Middle West had reached cultural maturity and must henceforth be taken into account in the world of art and ideas as well as in the world of business and politics. Turner's interpretation of American history from a Middle Western point of view was an appropriate accompaniment to the general assertion of the new importance of the region.

The fact that Turner's influence seems to have increased very rapidly after about 1920 is likewise suggestive in relation to the general development of American thought. This was the period when the revolt against the Genteel Tradition reached its climax, when the Young Intellectuals were proclaiming the liberation of American literature and thought from the dominance of conservative critics in the tradition of the New England Brahmins. Turner's reinterpretation of American history was highly destructive of the earlier tendency to view our history, especially our intellectual development, as having its focus along the Atlantic seaboard or even more narrowly within a thirty-mile radius of the Harvard Yard. Many critics and writers who ordinarily paid little attention to academic historical scholarship found Turner a useful weapon in the all-out campaign against ''Puritanism'' and the outworn ''ideality'' of nineteenth-century official artistic theory.

For professional historians around the turn of the twentieth century Turner's methods and doctrines had a further attraction: they were emphatically ''scientific'' in the sense that they emphasized demonstrable causes and effects in the historical process. Like other scientific historians, Turner sought to explain historical events as the necessary outcome of uniform principles having a close resemblance to the laws which had been discovered and formulated by nineteenth-century natural science. His assumptions are on the whole biological: his work belongs to the general movement of Social Darwinism.

It will be recalled that the Turner hypothesis affirms the decisive influence of the frontier on American *development*. In the second paragraph of the famous 1893 paper Turner remarks, ''All peoples show development; the germ theory of politics has been sufficiently emphasized''—sufficiently, perhaps a little too much, but the implication is plain that the historian has no quarrel with the underlying metaphor of the germ theory. He clearly regarded society as an organism which had undergone an evolution comparable to the evolution which Darwinian theory ascribed to biological organisms. ''Behind institutions, behind constitutional forms and modifications,'' Turner asserts, ''lie the vital forces that call these organs into life and shape them to meet changing conditions.'' And again:

> Limiting our attention to the Atlantic coast, we have the familiar phenomenon of the evolution of institutions in a limited area, such as the rise of representative government; the differentiation of simple colonial governments into complex organs; the progress from primitive industrial society, without division of labor, up to manufacturing civilization. But we have in addition to this a recurrence of the process of evolution in each western area reached in the process of expansion.

Yet again, the historian remarks: ''Our early history is the study of European germs developing in an American environment.'' To mention only one further example, he finds a striking analogy to describe the development of transportation routes within the United States: ''It is like the steady growth of a complex nervous system for the originally simple, inert continent.''

The general impression left by these metaphors is of changes and adaptations taking place at a very rudimentary level. Consciousness apparently plays no part in them. The germs and organs mentioned seem to be devoid of the power of thought, and even the central nervous system in the last quotation is viewed at an embryonic stage of development.

Such biological metaphors pose a delicate problem of interpretation. At one semantic level they are indispensable parts of our vocabulary. Although the term "evolution" is much less common now in historical writing than it was only a couple of decades ago, synonyms with similar denotation but less nineteenth-century coloring are still in current use. Professor Ralph Gabriel writes cautiously of *The Course of American Democratic Thought,* but Professor Merle Curti calls his impressive book *The Growth of American Thought,* and Professors Morrison and Commager call their masterly survey *The Growth of the American Republic.* And we can hardly talk about history at all without using the term "development."

The difference between the terms "growth" and "development," on the one hand, and "evolution" on the other seems slight, but I believe it is significant. What "evolution" conveys that is not conveyed by its apparent synonyms is precisely the elaborate biological overtones which Turner makes explicit in his comparisons of institutions to organs and of transportation routes to a nervous system. We have less confidence now in the validity of the biological metaphors if they are at all insisted upon, if any real weight is put on them. We feel the need for caution; we have an impulse to keep clearly in mind that the metaphor is only a rhetorical aid to discourse, not an assertion of identity that can be made good through empirical demonstration.

To state this point in somewhat different language, Turner evidently took for granted certain propositions about the process of history which almost no one would venture to defend at the present time without drastic qualifications and reservations. Two of these propositions are as follows:

(1) The course of history is strictly comparable to biological evolution; that is, it is determined by an interaction of organisms and their physical environment at a preconscious level.

(2) The course of history follows a uniform pattern. It invariably exhibits an evolution of institutions from simple and undifferentiated forms to complex and highly differentiated forms. This evolution proceeds through easily recognizable social stages, the character of which is determined by the type of economic organization prevalent in each.

Of these two propositions, the second bears on its face the marks of its origin in eighteenth-century social theory; the first is to be identified historically with the later nineteenth century, with the climate of post-Darwinian social theory, especially that of Herbert Spencer.

I do not mean to fall into a genetic fallacy by imagining that the validity of theories can be tested by inquiring into their origins. Nevertheless, it is not irrelevant to call attention to the difference between the intellectual climates in which these two important components of the Turner Hypothesis originated, and the intellectual climate of the present day. The theory can be translated from the one to the other only if suitable revisions can be made in the "dated" portions of it.

Nor do I intend to discuss the question whether the Turner theory can be revised in such a fashion as to make it a satisfactory instrument for guiding historical research in the present. Instead, I should like merely to comment on what seem to me serious shortcomings of the theory as it has been applied in practice. Since I have elsewhere suggested the handicaps which the historian of the West incurs when he adopts the theory of civilization and uniform social stages, I shall refer here primarily to the proposition that the course of history is determined by the interaction of organisms with a physical environment.

If one is prepared to undertake a philosophical task comparable to that of John Dewey he can perhaps construct an evolutionary theory that takes into account the full range of man's intellectual and cultural activities. Possessing such a theory, one might conceivably find himself in a position to deal with the inner life of the American people, their ideas and systems of thought, their arts and sciences, in a word the life of the mind, without passing beyond the limits imposed by the original image of organisms and environment. But in practice American historians under the influence of Turner have not developed such a philosophy. I can convey my meaning best by introducing a metaphor myself, and saying that a great deal of American history has been written as if the Logos, the incarnate Word, had played no part in American society of the past or present. The biological metaphor has provided a framework within which it has proved possible to record overt behavior on a vast scale and to find economic explanations for selected portions of American experience, especially to analyze political events with great and convincing subtlety. But the metaphor has had a constant tendency to confine attention to those aspects of the past which it could explain, and to foster the assumption that other aspects of American experience, those not readily accounted for by reference to the processes of adaptation to environment, are not significant, or at any rate not susceptible to orderly and systematic study, and therefore not appropriate objects of the historian's concern.

This contention can be dramatized by an exaggeration: we have had a great deal of decerebrate history. As a consequence, there is a drastic and deplorable dissimilarity of outlook between most professional students of American history and most students of American literature, art, religion, and ideas. The historian has taken it for granted that there is no real reason why he should concern himself with art and philosophy; and the student of literature has frequently considered himself not obliged to pay serious attention to history. The literary critic and literary historian has thereby cut himself off from a full understanding of American literature, because he has fallen into the error of assuming that it has been produced and read in a social vacuum. He has become a victim of the genteel fallacy, the malady of the highbrow. But the historian has suffered as much by his tendency to the opposite extreme of anti-intellectualism, by his infection with the malady of the lowbrow. I do not suggest that the Turner Hypothesis as it has been interpreted (or perhaps misinterpreted) by historians is the only anti-intellectual force that has been brought to bear on the American mind during the first half of the twentieth century, but I believe that much of its influence on historical scholarship has been unfortunate. You will perceive by now what answer I would give to the question I raised earlier this evening concerning the consequences which would follow from accepting the image of the frontiersman and the log cabin as the primary facts of the American past. Used in this fashion, the image cuts us off from vital and necessary portions of our history, especially from the more subtle adventures in speculation and in art on which Americans have embarked. The literary scholars, whom I suppose I represent on this occasion, have their own serious shortcomings to atone for, but I believe that many American historians have been led by the general tendency of Turner's writings to accept a far too rudimentary conception of human nature as their guiding principle. And if the historians themselves do not actively resist such an oversimplification of the American past, we need not be surprised if popular ideology turns the cultural image of the frontier West to the ends illustrated by Mr. Duffy's cartoon.

chapter three

History of Ideas

"It is the special glory of history," wrote Allan Nevins, "that it touches the realm of ideas at more points than almost any other study." He went on to observe that history is necessarily in contact with and influenced by all of the great ideas of any civilization that create the uniqueness of any age.[1] Thus ideas are prime movers of history. H. G. Wells went so far as to assert that the history of ideas was the essence of human history. This is a deliberate contradiction of the great man theory, which holds that major events are likely to be caused by important leaders, usually politicians or generals, with a cleric or merchant occasionally thrown in. Such people do contribute to history, but they are more likely to be products of history, specifically of certain historic ideas. Indeed, some would argue that the history of man is "almost entirely a history of ideas, [and] that these are the engines that chiefly determine the direction of human movement."[2] If politicians become important, it is primarily because they succeed in convincing others that their ideas are important. Yet it is quite unlikely that their ideas will be entirely original. Instead, the ideas will probably be extensions or logical implications of earlier thoughts, marking that individual as part of an intellectual chain in which the first links were forged generations before and the last ones will not be added for generations to come. Ideas almost have a life of their own, it seems. Generals fight because of political ideas, churchmen institutionalize religious ideas, and businessmen operate within an intellectual tradition that may encourage one form of economic activity and discourage another.

Our time is as much influenced by key ideas and their evolutionary change as any other. Concepts such as progress, equality, predestination, justification by faith, free enterprise, and nationalism are so powerful that people have not only been ready to kill but even to die in their name. The power of ideas must never be underestimated. At no

---

[1] Allan Nevins, *The Gateway to History,* revised ed. (Garden City: Doubleday and Co., 1962), p. 299.
[2] Robert Jones Shafer et al., eds., *A Guide to Historical Method* (Homewood, Ill.: The Dorsey Press, 1969), p. 19.

time was this more apparent than during the bicentennial of the American Revolution, when the ideas responsible for the event were reexamined by historians and reaffirmed by politicians and citizens. Because ideas do affect our daily lives their history is fundamental to understanding of oneself and one's past.

The history of ideas is no less murky a term than intellectual history. Frequently used as a synonym for intellectual history yet often used to denote something quite different from the rest of intellectual history, it sometimes carries a regrettable imprecision in meaning. The usage here will be that popularized by Arthur O. Lovejoy, for whom it meant "something at once more specific and less restricted than the history of philosophy," which in his time tended to dominate intellectual history. He was interested in breaking up "individual systems" into their components, called "unit-ideas," which he saw "in the collective thought of large groups of persons, not merely in the doctrines or opinions of a small number of profound thinkers or eminent writers." The history of ideas was not the same as the history of intellectuals or the history of philosophy, though these were part of it. He belittled those who paid attention only to an idea in "philosophical full dress," disregarding "its ulterior workings in the minds of the non-philosophic world." The most impressive traces of such ideas were to be found in art and literature, but it was art and literature that were subject to wide exposure.[3] Obviously unit-ideas could be found, as Rosalie Colie indicated, as readily among minor writers as anywhere else.[4] In this sense Lovejoy would have agreed that the history of ideas was part of both the internal and external concepts of intellectual history, to employ the modern terminology.

So influential was Lovejoy's interpretation and method that it is sometimes confused with the entire field of intellectual history. In spite of this confusion, the history of ideas, like all of intellectual history, has developed a disciplinary rigor that is often strong enough to overcome occasional laxity in method—which is a warning to the unwary that serious and subtle thinking is an absolute requirement in order to evade the several possible pitfalls of this technique. One of these is the tendency to judge an idea by the type of literature in which it is found. Just because traces of a concept are found in "good" literature does not make the idea any more inherently valid or representative of its age. Indeed, given the reading tastes of many people, it might possibly prove just the opposite. Ideas found scribbled on walls or in cheap pulp magazines may be far more important than those found in the literature or art that satisfies avant-garde or even generally accepted critical standards of the day. At the same time the historian of ideas must avoid the temptation to think automatically of a newly encountered idea as a reflection of the larger world outside the work of art in which it appears. Usually this will be the case, but even then the incorporation of the idea will frequently be uncon-

[3] Arthur O. Lovejoy, *The Great Chain of Being: A Study of the History of an Idea* (Cambridge, Mass.: Harvard University Press, 1936), pp. 3, 17, 19.

[4] Rosalie L. Colie, "Literature and History," in James Thorpe, ed., *Relations of Literary Study: Essays on Interdisciplinary Contributions* (New York: Modern Language Association of America, 1967), p. 25.

scious. Not all writers seize on the ideas in their environment for exploitation. The possibility always exists that a thinker might be saying something original, or nearly so, or something that has not been repeated for some time. Perhaps the Biblical injunction that "there is nothing new under the sun" should be set alongside this warning to counteract it. Even so, some ideas are fresh enough to constitute something of a break with previous thought and one should not be too eager to expect unit-ideas where they do not exist. Lovejoy himself, writes George Watson, from the viewpoint of a literary historian, seems to have overlooked the chance that some thought was unique and failed to give due credit to originality (though it is certainly difficult to know when a thought is truly unique). This failure, says Watson (in a thinly veiled reference to Lovejoy's *The Great Chain of Being*), results in "an obsession with intellectual daisy-chains, with the ways in which 'unit-ideas' have been handed down" that may well obscure the freshness of an original intellect. Watson warns the historian of ideas that if his discipline is really "concerned with thought itself, it cannot content itself with minor problems concerning the ways in which thought has been transmitted from mind to mind." To concentrate on these small problems, thinks Watson, is to trivialize the history of ideas.[5]

A far more serious problem than trivialization is that of compartmentalization. Although it may circumscribe results, the unit-idea technique is beguilingly attractive. It is therefore subject to one of the prime occupational hazards of intellectual history: the tendency—even the driving urge—which scholars possess to classify, rank, and label ideas, compartmentalizing them into neat intellectual packages which may happen to fit their equally neat intellectual categories. This makes it easy to attribute to groups or individuals a clarity of thought they may never have enjoyed and an ideological distinctiveness that may hide common denominators in the intellectual assumptions of opponents. Only recently, for example, has it become clear that Loyalists and Patriots often agreed about the potentially oppressive nature of English rule in the years immediately prior to the American Revolution, and justified their opposing loyalties by drawing upon the same intellectual background. In the same way, prior to the U. S. Civil War Northerners generally shared the racist attitudes of the Southerners with whom they were soon at war.

The reader should determine the degree to which H. Trevor Colbourn has evaded these snares. Whatever the judgment, however, Colbourn cannot be accused of trivializing the history of ideas. The whig interpretation of history, so eagerly grasped by Thomas Jefferson, is hardly minor thought, and it turned out to be a justification for a major revolution. Some of the writers familiar to Jefferson are of little significance today; what is important is their ideas and their effect on a leading revolutionary figure. Colbourn thus illustrated the tendency of the history of ideas to possess the attributes of both the internal and external approaches to intellectual history. Obviously the author

[5]George Watson, *The Study of Literature* (London: Allen Lane The Penquin Press, 1969), pp. 199–203.

is not unduly concerned with, again to repeat Crane Brinton, "abstract ideas that breed more abstract ideas."[6] The relationship is not simply between one thought and another. But, though the goal is to study the influence of thought on action (which is characteristic of the external context of intellectual history), it is not the response of the multitude that is under scrutiny, as was the case with Henry Nash Smith's examination of the symbol of the log cabin. Instead, it is the action of a single man—an elitist, an intellectual, and an aristocrat—who was hardly one of the masses. Yet the result of Jefferson's thought, and the ideas he incorporated into his own philosophy, was action—action that had a profound worldwide impact lasting into and beyond our own time. Motivated by the whig interpretation of history, Jefferson and his contemporaries were moved to action that allowed his ideas, and the ideas on which he relied, to become part of the intellectual baggage of most citizens of the country he helped to create—and of millions of other people throughout the world as well. For citizens of the United States there could be no more relevant example of the history of ideas.

Thomas Jefferson's Use of the Past
H. Trevor Colbourn

. . . History books played a vital role in instructing and informing Jefferson, and they supply a fascinating picture of what he thought happened in the past, explaining much of the practical application he was to make of a particular interpretation of history. It is not to be suggested that the books Jefferson read supplied his motivation. The dangers of implying such causation are painfully obvious, and the most that can be claimed is that the character of Jefferson's reading habits, his peculiar preferences and comments on them, can and do inform powerfully on his own thinking. Carl Becker judged astutely when he declared that "Generally speaking, men are influenced by books which clarify their own thought, which express their own motives well, or which suggest to them ideas which their minds are already predisposed to accept."

To understand the peculiarities of Jefferson's historical vision, it should be remembered that history had not only been subject to the vagaries of intellectual vogue but was also under fierce political pressures. There had developed, in short, two principal views of English history; the one, usually the more accurate by modern scholastic standards, can be called the tory interpretation—although not in any party sense; the other is reasonably familiar as the whig interpretation, although it too existed long before a formal Whig party and continued long after Whig politicians opportunistically

---

[6] Crane Brinton, *Ideas and Men: The Story of Western Thought* (New York: Prentice-Hall, 1950), p. 7.

H. Trevor Colbourn, "Thomas Jefferson's Use of the Past," *William and Mary Quarterly*, 3d. ser., XV (January 1958), 58–70. Copyright © 1958 by the Institute of Early American History and Culture. Reprinted with deletion of notes and abridgment by permission of the author and the *William and Mary Quarterly*, in which it first appeared.

lost interest in it. The historical whigs were writers seeking to support parliamentary claims upon the royal prerogatives by exalting the antiquity of parliament and by asserting that their political ambitions had solid foundation in ancient customs. They presented an idealized version of an Anglo-Saxon democracy, which they usually found overturned by Norman treachery and feudalism. The tory historians instead \ preferred to see the parliamentary claims as without any ancient source, and viewed Anglo-Saxon England as feudalistic, but lacking in Norman stability and order.

The overwhelming majority of the historians and legal authorities Jefferson consulted were of the whig persuasion—the lawyers inducted into the whig historical ranks by way of their inherent concern for the English common law with its emphasis on the past and its reverence for precedents. And the more history Jefferson read, the more whigs he inevitably encountered because of their sheer productivity and weight of numbers. Among the fifty more important authors studied by Jefferson, only two substantially denied the whig interpretation.

Young Jefferson's first introduction to whig history probably came when he dipped into the two folio volumes of Rapin's *History of England* included in the small library collected by his father, Peter Jefferson. Rapin was a good whig who presented a clear picture of the essential foundation of the whig interpretation, namely the myth of Saxon democracy. In reading Rapin, Jefferson learned that the Saxons who invaded and populated England much resembled the "antient *Germans,* as described by Tacitus," and brought with them their habits of Germanic democracy, thus establishing an elective monarchy and annual parliaments in Anglo-Saxon England. Even the tory historian David Hume, whose heresies so distressed Jefferson, was inclined to concede a tendency towards an elective monarchy in Saxon England. For Hume, however, this explained the consequent "intemperance, riot and disorder" that marked the pre-Conquest period.

The source for most historians when writing on Anglo-Saxon England was Tacitus' *Germania.* Perhaps this fact was further impressed on Jefferson by the recommendation found in Blackstone's *Commentaries.* Blackstone, whom Jefferson admired save for differences on contemporary politics, had noted that a well-trained lawyer should look to the originals of the Law, which "should be traced to their fountains as well as our distance will permit; to the customs of the Britons and Germans, as recorded by Caesar and Tacitus; to the codes of the northern nations on the continent, and more especially to those of our own Saxon princes . . . but above all, to that inexhaustible reservoir of feudal antiquities and learning, the feudal law." Jefferson certainly gave Tacitus his undying affection and attention, and as a lawyer carefully pursued Blackstone's injunction to study feudal law with diligence. Both subjects of study led him more surely to the whig historical viewpoint.

Tacitus became one of the books that Jefferson most widely recommended: any inquiring law student would receive Jefferson's suggestion to look to Tacitus as "the first writer in the world without exception," since his work was "compounded of history and morality of which we have no other exception." Jefferson also took the extraordinary step of having two sets of his favorite translation collated with the Latin text—the second being a replacement for that sold to Congress in 1815. The translation was indeed special, being prepared by the ardent whig pamphleteer, Thomas Gordon, who adorned his text with highly moralistic "Discourses" denouncing tyranny. Gordon was probably as fascinated with the message proclaimed by Tacitus as was Jefferson, for it was a clear description of a Germanic democracy in the northern woods of Europe, of a race which elected their monarchs and which lived "in a state of chastity well secured, corrupted by no seducing shews and public diversions, by no irritations from banqueting." The fundamental of this idealized Germanic existence was an allodial land tenure, holding land in fee simple without the military and labor obligations associated with feudalism.

Under the legal tutelage of George Wythe, Jefferson studied the origins and development of feudalism with great care, examining the views of a host of authorities such as Sir Henry Spelman, Sir John Dalrymple, Francis Sullivan, Roger Acherley, Lord Kames, and, of course, one of the early contributors to some aspects of the whig interpretation, Sir Edward Coke. Particularly detailed on the precise character of feudalism was Spelman, one of the greatest of the antiquarians, whose *De Terminis Juridicis* was extensively transcribed by Jefferson into his legal commonplace book. Spelman asserted bluntly that "The feudal laws was introduced into England at and shortly after the Conquest." And Jefferson also noted Spelman's comment on the Norman invasion: "After this all things resounded with the feudal oppressions, which, in the time of the Saxons had never been heard of." Dalrymple, whose *Feudal Property* Jefferson studied closely for information on land tenures, also supplied notes on how William the Bastard converted all the allodial lands into feudal holdings and began the right of primogeniture.

Many whigs found it hard that the democratic Saxons should have been vanquished by a Norman tyrant, and Jefferson discovered various explanations in the books he favored. Henry Care's *English Liberties* held that William was in reality no conqueror, since "he pretended a right to the Kingdom, and was admitted by the Compact, and did take an Oath to observe the Laws and Customs." The truth was, added Care, "he did not perform that Oath so as he ought to have done," and the Normans "made frequent encroachments upon the Liberties of their People." As Roger Acherley commented, the Normans had "dashed in pieces the orginal Constitution." Jefferson also found anti-Popery writers quick to point out that "William the first obtained the crown of England by favor of the clergy," for the Pope had blessed the Norman invasion. Only after the Conquest, explained one valued whig, did "civil and religious tyranny walk hand in hand, two monsters till then unknown in England."

Interesting and inspiring as the Saxon myth undoubtedly was, Jefferson found the story of the English struggle to end feudal tyranny and regain Saxon liberties equally fascinating. The first historical marker of the struggle to regain these ancient liberties came in the thirteenth century, with Magna Carta, which Jefferson later described as "the earliest statute . . . the text of which has come down to us in an authentic form." No royal gift, the Great Charter was for the whig historians an affirmation of the Saxon common law, ratified by people who were reclaiming their liberties, privileges, and birthright. Sir Edward Coke probably set the pattern for Jefferson's historical thought here, with his original popularization of the Charter as a democratic document in *The Second Part of the Institutes.* Coke's credulous acceptance of dubious authorities, like the *Modus Tenendi Parliamentum* and the *Mirrour of Justices,* was followed by other writers who cited Coke for their source. It is clear that the epigram "history never repeats itself, but historians always repeat each other" enjoys a rather frightening relevance to this development of the whig interpretation. Roger Acherley pronounced the Charter a renewal of "the Original Contract," since King John merely agreed to observe what were ancient customs, and most of the historians studied by Jefferson agreed with Coke that the Charter was "no new declaration."

Subsequent English history, as portrayed by Jefferson's most valued sources, saw frequent monarchical encroachments on ancient rights. Even in the reign of Elizabeth I, Jefferson discovered, when Parliament made "frequent attempts to extend their Privileges," the Queen forgot her Saxon history and callously nipped such claims in the bud. But the really critical period, from Jefferson's perspective, was the seventeenth century with its abortive Puritan Revolution, and the unrealized hopes raised by the Glorious Revolution of 1688.

One of Jefferson's preferred authorities on this period was Catharine Macaulay—that "incomparable female historian," as a fellow whig called her—whose complete eight-volume *History of England* Jefferson purchased and also had included in the University of Virginia library. Mrs. Macaulay showed England as preserving a steady course towards slavery and public ruin, only partly relieved by the unsuccessful revolutions of 1642 and 1688. She denounced Cromwell and his standing army as an unhappy contrast with the free Saxon militia of the past, and she noted how little improvement had been brought with the final expulsion of the Stuarts. Most whigs agreed that Parliament in 1688 had not been seeking anything new, but "their ancient *Rights* and *Priviledges,"* as Sir Robert Atkyns described them. However, the ambitious politicians, once in power, lost sight of the rights of the people. They stopped the Glorious Revolution almost where it should have begun—converting the government, Jefferson read in his much-used *Historical Essay on the English Constitution,* "into a fixed and standing aristocracy."

Against this background, Jefferson's view of eighteenth-century England reflected the real dismay of whig observers who had seen the efforts to restore Saxon liberties miscarry at the apparent height of success. The seeming failure of England to reinstitute the happy system of her ancestors played an important part in Jefferson's decision to institutionalize such a system in the Saxon settlements in the New World. For in such publications as *Cato's Letters,* Jefferson found examples of whig endeavor to arouse Englishmen over their fast-receding rights, and he found sermons on the present canker of luxury and corruption. Bolingbroke, for obvious personal political ends, had joined in the critical chorus in denouncing Sir Robert Walpole as the "archcorrupter." James Burgh, a firm favorite of Jefferson, supported this verdict when he wrote in 1774 that "The Stuarts meant a tyranny by one; the Walpolians, an aristocracy, which is worst." Others, like the author of the *Historical Essay,* explained to an interested Jefferson how an unrepresentative and corrupted Parliament faced the farce of an election only every seven years, instead of annually as in ancient Saxon times. The present dangers were self-evident to any alert whig observer, and a comment by the radical Granville Sharp had a particular pertinence for American readers on the eve of their revolution: legislation without popular participation and consent, wrote Sharp, was "INIQUITOUS, and therefore unlawful. . . ."

For Jefferson, the problems leading to the American Revolution provided the occasion for a classic demonstration of his combined eighteenth-century optimism and his historical consciousness. His best revolutionary writing came in 1774, his *Summary View of the Rights of British America.* Here is Jefferson's most cogent and sustained examination of the American present, and what he thought should be the future. Here was the first graphic illustration of the political use Jefferson made of his careful reading of the past, and specifically the past of his English forefathers. Behaving more like an archaeologist than a revolutionary, Jefferson revealed an identification of the good with the ancestral rather than with the rational. He was unquestionably optimistic about the future but quite historical in his approach to the present.

Looking at American rights, Jefferson insisted from the outset on an historical context that far antedated the seventeenth-century settlements in North America. He went back to "our Saxon ancestors" who "left their native wilds and woods in the North of Europe, [and] had possessed themselves of the island of Britain. . . ." These forefathers, he observed, had enjoyed the right of departing their native land to establish new societies in the New world that was England. To the new habitat, the transplanted Saxons had carried their free customs and political democracy, and, Jefferson noted, there was never any question of their being subject to any form of allegiance or control by the mother country from which they had emigrated. In any case, these fine Saxon forefathers would have had "too firm a feeling of the rights derived to them from their ancestors to bow down the sovereignty of their state before such visionary pretentions." Concluding this line of argument, Jefferson declared pointedly that "no circumstance has occurred to distinguish materially the British from the Saxon emigration." If the Saxons could migrate freely from Germany to England, then their descendants could move with equal liberty to North America.

If the *Summary View* was a fine Jeffersonian vehicle for historical argument, it was no less useful for a closely allied legal approach to colonial problems, and Jefferson gave considerable attention to the issue of land tenure in America. Like the bulk of the historians he had read so carefully, Jefferson believed that in Saxon England, "feudal holdings were certainly altogether unknown, and very few if any had been introduced at the time of the Norman conquest." His Saxon ancestors had held their lands and personal property "in absolute dominion, disencumbered with any superior, answering nearly to the nature of those possessions which the Feudalists term Allodial. . . ." The responsibility for the unhappy change in England, Jefferson placed squarely upon "William the Norman" just as had such scholars as Spelman and Dalrymple. Rather laboring the point, Jefferson summed up: "Feudal holdings were, therefore, but the exceptions out of the Saxons laws of possession, under which all lands were held in absolute right." Feudalism was thus an alien, Norman thing, established only by conquest. And since Englishmen in America were no conquered people, their lands were surrendered neither to the Normans nor to their successors. The ancient Saxons had made their settlements at their own expense, with no aid from their mother country, and thus no obligation; and so it had been with the descendants of these Saxons in the seventeenth century when they came to America. In both cases, argued Jefferson, "For themselves they fought, for themselves they conquered, and for themselves alone they have a right to hold." Jefferson's acceptance and exposition of the Anglo-Saxon myth in his *Summary View* is in a real sense an acceptance, both proper and predictable for the eighteenth century, of an historical realization of Locke's first compact-founded society.

The seeming weakness of Jefferson's appeal to whig history lay in the fact of current American submission to the British Crown, a weakness reminiscent of general whig embarrassment at the fact of the Norman Conquest. The ancient Saxons had not indulged their Germanic forefathers so generously as to consider themselves dependent upon them politically, but Jefferson went on to explain that the early American colonists, who, as he later pointed out, were "laborers, not lawyers," had "thought proper to adopt that system of laws under which they had hitherto lived in the mother country, and to continue their union with her by submitting themselves" to a common monarch. The monarchy then, was the "central link connecting the several parts of the empire thus newly multiplied." Unfortunately, the history of that empire from almost its very inception was replete with examples of invasions, by Crown and by Parliament, of the rights acquired with the "lives, the labors and the fortunes of individual adventurers. . . ."

The list of examples of British iniquities included by Jefferson was long indeed, and plainly intended to prove continuous effort on the part of Crown and Parliament to reduce America to a new form of feudal slavery. Stuart tyranny he described as followed by an unrepresentative Parliament controlling a totally unrepresented America. And the measure of parliamentary tyranny now approached a climax with the recent Coercive Acts, which breached the right of Englishmen under Magna Carta to be tried by their peers of their vicinage.

Jefferson's message in the *Summary View* was plain for all to understand: the rights of British America were extensive, and with a solid historical foundation. The colonists, in resisting British tyranny, were standing for their rights as transplanted Englishmen, "expatriated men" entitled to the liberties now sadly forgotten in the mother country. If England had insufficient regard for her noble Saxon heritage, then Jefferson was determined that America should avoid the weakening disease of corruption and luxury, by separation if necessary. Clearly George III would not be permitted the role of another William the Norman and fasten a similar tyranny upon the Saxon emigrant in America.

Here then was an historical justification of revolution, a justification powerfully influenced by the colonial concern for legitimacy and by Jefferson's personal legal training. Yet Jefferson was not merely revealing an historical conservatism; he was not looking to the past from fear of the future. After all, the past he expounded and believed in was an historic example of how a particular democratic Saxon system had been conquered and had declined. Jefferson rather used the past as Bolingbroke prescribed—"philosophy teaching by examples"—as an illustration of dangers to be avoided, and democratic delights to be recaptured. Jefferson accepted the possibility of decline as normal—hence his famous suggestion for bloody fertility rites about the tree of liberty—but he was imbued with sufficient eighteenth-century optimism to believe that an awakened historical consciousness would be adequate in warning of encroachments of tyranny in all its predictable forms.

It is in this historical context that Jefferson's later career should be studied. His constant aim in politics was to avoid the political pitfalls into which England had evidently fallen, to establish a democracy which would not fall prey to petty ambition and political corruption, and to restore the ancient Saxon principles of polity. Naturally Jefferson worked hard to sweep away all vestiges of feudalism in America; and primogeniture, entail, quitrents, and even the established church fell before the Jeffersonian crusade. To Edmund Pendleton he wrote in August 1776, "Are we not better for what we have hitherto abolished of the feudal system? Has not every restitution of the ancient Saxon laws had happy effects? Is it not better that we return at once into that happy system of our ancestors, the wisest and most perfect ever yet devised by the wit of man. . .?"

Jefferson's whig history gave him an outlook which made for a strangely reactionary revoluntary: a man who wanted change, but not innovation, a man who wished to advance to the political perfection of an earlier age. He was practical enough to realize, however, that his newly re-created Saxon democracy could only survive if its citizens were suitably informed of their precious heritage, and their reason thus adequately armed for battle. To this end Jefferson was to work patiently for the establishment of a university close to Monticello where young Virginians would be exposed to a sound whig education, with reliable antidotes like John Baxter's notorious *New and Impartial History* to combat the tory heresies of David Hume.

The persistent and enduring affection for whig history that is evident in Jefferson suggests a consistency in his thought and action yet to be fully explored. But it is already clear that the whig historical approach had much that was attractive to Jefferson, although his receptivity probably varied with political necessity. Certainly it is more than pleasant to think of one's forefathers as exponents of democracy and liberty, and it was a comfort to subscribers to the Saxon myth to know that there had existed a political utopia in Saxon England. In fact the basis of whig history was largely this pre-Norman utopia, where there had been no menace from a standing army, no society organized for war on a feudal basis, and where land was owned outright in allodial holdings. This Saxon society, Jefferson learned, had been a society of law, unplagued by a shackling established church, a society governed originally by an elective monarchy and a popular assembly meeting in that original of parliaments, the annual Saxon *witenagemot.*

This was the encouraging and sometimes inspiring view presented Jefferson from the books he studied most carefully, books which contributed to his peculiar historical optimism, his belief in the "happy system" of his Saxon ancestors, his staunch faith that the past could be successfully adapted to the future in America. As he came increasingly to see the uniqueness of the United States by merit of its size and its unexploited land, history came to lack the immediate pertinence previously evident. He never needed history as desperately as when he had sought revolutionary direction, but he was never dominated by it; history lent him an understanding of his political and economic problems, it supplied a reassuringly empirical basis for argument.

It was Jefferson's ability to learn from and employ history for the present and future that contributed to his historical optimism. While he might repeat the historians he studied and admired, he did not see why history should repeat itself, and he did not subscribe to any cyclic theory which would deny man's perfectability. The past for Thomas Jefferson was by no means the past seen by modern scholarship. What matters is that he was governed by what he believed happened in the days of his Saxon ancestors, and that he was optimistic enough to believe that this early version of democracy would be re-established on an enduring basis in America.

chapter four

The *Zeitgeist*

The fourth type of intellectual history illustrated here is the *Zeitgeist* approach, or the effort to capture the spirit of an age. When placed on the internal-external spectrum, it falls somewhere in the middle, and may be used to illustrate both the internal (idea to idea) and external (idea to action) contexts of intellectual history.

The term may be utilized simply as a label for historical periodization, implying that a certain dominating idea characterizes an entire era (the Age of Revolution or the Age of the Common Man, for example), but the usual application is more sophisticated. It is actually a theoretical framework intended, in the words of Israeli philosopher Nathan Rotenstreich, "to define the characteristic spirit of a historical era taken in its totality and bearing the mark of a preponderant feature which dominated its intellectual, political, and social trends"; the concept is also used to denote the boundaries of an age that limit and channel the development of thought and culture.[1] As the *Zeitgeist* changes, society undergoes a parallel transformation, although perhaps not immediately. In the present selection the *Zeitgeist* might be oriented toward a scientific world view, but the development of thought and culture may lag behind, at least on a popular level.

The *Zeitgeist* concept was attractive to nineteenth-century historians who wallowed in emotion and thought it a positive approach to fathom their feelings and project their own convictions onto the historical characters they wrote about. This was considered necessary to complete the picture of an age, for the *Zeitgeist* "would always elude the fact-monger." Enthusiasm and emotion thus substituted for scholarship, or were at least placed equal to it.[2] This obviously abused the whole concept by giving strong support to notions of historical inevitability. Seeking the comfort of certainty, some historians even today may attempt to satisfy their needs by adopting an attitude of

---

[1]Nathan Rotenstreich, "Zeitgeist," in Philip P. Wiener et al., eds., *Dictionary of the History of Ideas: Studies of Selected Pivotal Ideas,* 5 vols. (New York: Charles Scribner's Sons, 1968–1974), 4:535–37.
[2]George H. Callcott, *History in the United States 1800–1860: Its Practice and Purpose* (Baltimore: The Johns Hopkins Press, 1970), pp. 147–50 (quote is from p. 149).

absolute certainty about the past, a condition supposedly achieved by putting oneself in tune with the *Zeitgeist* of one's own era. The result is a narrow, deterministic view of history in which eras and ideas become equivalents, and inevitable trends are discovered and projected into either the past or future (it works both ways). "The *Zeitgeist* may seem to be victoriously sweeping along to the outcome known to the historian," concluded Pieter Geyl, who observes that the scholar would perform far better if he paid attention instead to "the abundant fullness and . . . infinite complexity" of history. The *Zeitgeist* historian, Geyl feared, examines only those ideas that survived and triumphed, thereby neglecting defeated, alternative possibilities which may yet prove significant.[3] Indeed, this use of the *Zeitgeist* makes the concept appear less a distinct idea than a vague mood. The pitfall is frequently found in the writing of presentist historians, who thrust the present into the past in such manner that, regardless of which dusty corner of history they look into, they find roots, early manifestations, or parallel circumstances to any current concern. Utilized with caution by intellectual historians who understand its limitations, however, the *Zeitgeist* concept is a helpful and valid way to structure historical research.

Another major detriment to the effective use of the *Zeitgeist* in writing intellectual history is simply that it is too easy to link as one the slightly differing examples of similar ideas. The *Zeitgeist* may become little more than an excuse to take any phenomenon and exaggerate its importance until it contains the spirit of the age, or at least a major component thereof. The result is distortion of history by gross generalization. Seeking the great synthesis, the scholar is altogether too likely to find common elements that may not really exist. "The skeptic," says Rosalie L. Colie, "cuts all connectives, the *Zeitgeister* insists upon connecting everything."[4]

This technique is also abused by the frequent and usually unspoken assumption of uniqueness. Indeed, as historians once employed the term it did refer to *the* spirit of an age, at least in a given culture or geographical area. The *Oxford English Dictionary* defines it as "the spirit or genius which marks the thought or feeling of a period or age." Such a narrow definition is obsolete. The difficulty, says Colie, is that there may be more than one *Zeitgeist* at any given time; the presence of one does not preclude the existence of another. Surely it would be absurd to deny that in the nineteenth century there was an entirely different *Zeitgeist* underlying the thought and actions of American or Canadian frontiersmen, on the one hand, and the Indians with whom they clashed, on the other. And surely the spirit of the age in Paris or Vienna was quite different from that felt in the black belt of Mississippi or the commercial establishments of New York. *Zeitgeist* exists and it can be a useful concept. But the scholar must be aware that there may be more than a single spirit of the time in a given period, place, or culture.

[3] Pieter Geyl, *Use and Abuse of History* (New Haven: Yale University Press, 1955), pp. 67–68, 80.
[4] Rosalie L. Colie, "Literature and History," in James Thorpe, ed., *Relations of Literary Study: Essays on Interdisciplinary Contributions* (New York: Modern Language Association of America, 1967), pp. 18–19.

It will be readily apparent that the application of this nebulous concept to any period or place might well bring together ideas and activities that the present-day mind would find quite unrelated. An early nineteenth-century American periodical, *The Spirit of the Times; a Chronicle of the Turf, Agriculture, Field Sports, Literature and the Stage,* provides a good example in its coverage as in its title. To its editor, the *Zeitgeist* of his era was to be found in the leisure-time activities of its well-to-do citizens, including amusements in a variety of sports and literature. One present-day historian characterizes this newspaper as "a bible of the subliterature," which printed and preserved many of the tall tales for which the West was already famous. Not only did this paper give expression to the *Zeitgeist*; it also portrayed an important segment of the popular culture of the time.[5] This proposition leads to the conclusion that popular culture may possibly be the key ingredient in the spirit of the time. The thought of intellectuals may have no important role in the *Zeitgeist* until it has been popularized and bowdlerized, and in the process transformed into something embarrassing to its originators. Freudian ideas were part of the *Zeitgeist* in Western countries in the 1930s and 1940s, but were often quite distorted, just as Darwin's ideas were distorted by the advocates of Social Darwinism, and Christian doctrine was perverted to support chattel slavery.

This supports the contention that the *Zeitgeist* method is a concept frequently employed by the intellectual historian, and so it is. However, it is important to observe that nowadays the technique is generally adopted unconsciously. The word *Zeitgeist* was once used frequently. Today, in history at least, one seldom reads it yet frequently encounters the method. Determination of the spirit of the time remains a major preoccupation of intellectual history. Nowhere is this more the case than in the study of popular culture. Indeed, the essence of the current emphasis on the study of popular culture is the hope of recovering the *Zeitgeist* of an earlier era.

Clearly historians must agree with Crane Brinton that the description of the spirit of an age, or *Zeitgeist*, is "one of the most difficult tasks" the intellectual historian is compelled to face. To Brinton, the *Zeitgeist* was "a total impression made by a huge number of details that *somehow* fit together."[6] The vague nature of the method is demonstrated by Brinton's adverbial use of "somehow"; that it is also closely related to popular culture may be demonstrated further by the fact that this notion, which we so strongly associate with intellectual history, is mentioned in the *International Encyclopedia of the Social Sciences* under the heading of Fashion. According to Herbert G. Blumer's article in the *Encyclopedia,* the key seems to be change. Fashion, or what is frequently no more than fad, intrudes into those parts of social life which undergo frequent change, whether style of dress, ideology, or the fine arts. One temporarily

[5] See Daniel J. Boorstin, *The Americans: The National Experience* (New York: Random House, 1965), p. 334.
[6] Crane Brinton, *Ideas and Men: The Story of Western Thought* (New York: Prentice-Hall, 1950), p. 55, emphasis mine.

acceptable form is replaced by another, and it by a third, in a never-ending process, as a form of "collective judgment of what is proper and correct shifts in response to the direction of sensitivity and taste." The essential aspect of fashion is modernity, the urge to be up to date at all times. The responsiveness of fashion to this urge, thinks Blumer, "seems to be the chief factor in the formation of a 'spirit of the times' or *Zeitgeist*."[7]

It was suggested earlier that popular culture is one of the legitimate domains of intellectual history. The following selection further illustrates the impossibility of neat categorization of intellectual history by using a technique placed at the middle of the internal-external spectrum to illuminate a facet of popular culture, even though popular culture itself is an extreme example of the external context. To Frederick Lewis Allen there was indeed such a thing as *Zeitgeist*, and he both assumed it (in his emphasis on a spirit of scientific skepticism as characteristic of the 1920s) and explored it. For Allen, it was more than science that permeated the age. There was also the development of a new ingredient in popular culture, under the influence of the mass media (itself a creature of both science and culture). "The national mind," wrote Allen, "had become as never before an instrument upon which a few men could play. And . . . [they] were learning . . . to play upon it in a new way—to concentrate upon *one tune at a time*."[8] This single-minded emphasis of the press and radio on whatever tune was current (Allen calls it ballyhoo) produced a public generally ignorant of truly significant events, while devoting attention to a series of superficial fads. These included such frivolous diversions as cross word puzzle books and such thrilling affairs as murder trials and football (which have been deleted from Allen's chapter on "The Ballyhoo Years"), in addition to the Floyd Collins tragedy, the Scopes trial, the Dempsey-Tunney fights, Rudolph Valentino's funeral, and the exploits of Charles A. Lindbergh. Indeed, Allen would characterize the *Zeitgeist* of the 1920s as one of superficiality, as the image makers presented to the public one excitement after another.

The *Zeitgeist* of the 1920s did not last. The age of ballyhoo may have been killed off, as Allen suggests, by public awareness of its technique, or perhaps by the onset of the depression of the 1930s. Yet if ballyhoo was no longer the characteristic of the time, it continues to exist and the image makers continue to ply their trade. Nor is scientific skepticism absent from our technical era. Surely Allen detected not one *Zeitgeist*, but several. Perhaps the uniqueness of any period and any popular culture is

---

[7]Herbert G. Blumer, "Fashion," in David S. Sills, ed., *International Encyclopedia of the Social Sciences*, 17 vols. (n.p.: Crowell Collier and Macmillan, 1968), 5:342–43.

[8]Frederick Lewis Allen, *Only Yesterday: An Informal History of the Nineteen-Twenties* (New York: Harper and Brothers Publishers, 1931), p. 189. This passage has been deleted from the selection below.

determined by its particular and peculiar combination of, and interaction with, the spirits of the age that composed it.

The Ballyhoo Years
Frederick Lewis Allen

All nations, in all eras of history, are swept from time to time by waves of contagious excitement over fads or fashions or dramatic public issues. But the size and frequency of these waves is highly variable, as is the nature of the events which set them in motion. One of the striking characteristics of the era of Coolidge Prosperity was the unparalleled rapidity and unanimity with which millions of men and women turned their attention, their talk, and their emotional interest upon a series of tremendous trifles—a heavyweight boxing-match, a murder trial, a new automobile model, a transatlantic flight. . . .

It was now possible in the United States for more people to enjoy the same good show at the same time than in any other land on earth or at any previous time in history. Mass production was not confined to automobiles; there was mass production in news and ideas as well. For the system of easy nation-wide communication which had long since made the literate and prosperous American people a nation of faddists was rapidly becoming more widely extended, more centralized, and more effective than ever before. . . .

. . . Syndicate managers and writers, advertisers, press agents, radio broadcasters, all were aware that mention of the leading event of the day, whatever it might be, was the key to public interest. The result was that when something happened which promised to appeal to the popular mind, one had it hurled at one in huge headlines, waded through page after page of syndicated discussion of it, heard about it on the radio, was reminded of it again and again in the outpourings of publicity-seeking orators and preachers, saw pictures of it in the Sunday papers and in the movies, and (unless one was a perverse individualist) enjoyed the sensation of vibrating to the same chord which thrilled a vast populace. . . .

It was the tragedy of Floyd Collins, perhaps, which gave the clearest indication up to that time of the unanimity with which the American people could become excited over a quite unimportant event if only it were dramatic enough.

Floyd Collins was an obscure young Kentuckian who had been exploring an underground passage five miles from Mammoth Cave, with no more heroic purpose than

Frederick Lewis Allen, "The Ballyhoo Years," Chapter VIII in *Only Yesterday: An Informal History of the Nineteen-Twenties* (New York: Harper & Brothers Publishers, 1931). Abridged from pp. 186–190, 193–195, 199–206, 209–210, 212–213, 216–221 ONLY YESTERDAY by Frederick Lewis Allen Copyright © 1931 by Frederick Lewis Allen; renewed 1959 by Agnes Rogers Allen By permission of Harper & Row, Publishers, Inc.

that of finding something which might attract lucrative tourists. Some 125 feet from daylight he was caught by a cave-in which pinned his foot under a huge rock. So narrow and steep was the passage that those who tried to dig him out had to hitch along on their stomachs in cold slime and water and pass back from hand to hand the earth and rocks that they pried loose with hammers and blow-torches. Only a few people might have heard of Collins's predicament if W. B. Miller of the *Louisville Courier-Journal* had not been slight of stature, daring, and an able reporter. Miller wormed his way down the slippery, tortuous passageway to interview Collins, became engrossed in the efforts to rescue the man, described them in vivid dispatches—and to his amazement found that the entire country was turning to watch the struggle. Collins's plight contained those elements of dramatic suspense and individual conflict with fate which make a great news story, and every city editor, day after day, planted it on page one. When Miller arrived at Sand Cave he had found only three men at the entrance, warming themselves at a fire and wondering, without excitement, how soon their friend would extricate himself. A fortnight later there was a city of a hundred or more tents there and the milling crowds had to be restrained by barbed-wire barriers and State troops with drawn bayonets; and on February 17, 1925, even the *New York Times* gave a three-column page-one headline to the news of the dénouement:

FIND FLOYD COLLINS DEAD IN CAVE TRAP ON 18TH DAY; LIFELESS AT LEAST 24 HOURS; FOOT MUST BE AMPUTATED TO GET BODY OUT

Within a month, as Charles Merz later reminded the readers of the *New Republic,* there was a cave-in in a North Carolina mine in which 71 men were caught and 53 actually lost. It attracted no great notice. It was "just a mine disaster." Yet for more than two weeks the plight of a single commonplace prospector for tourists riveted the attention of the nation on Sand Cave, Kentucky. It was an exciting show to watch, and the dispensers of news were learning to turn their spotlights upon one show at a time.

Even the Collins thriller, however, was as nothing beside the spectacle which was offered a few months later when John Thomas Scopes was tried at Dayton, Tennessee, for teaching the doctrine of evolution in the Central High School.

The Scopes case had genuine significance. It dramatized one of the most momentous struggles of the age—the conflict between religion and science. Yet even this trial, so diligently and noisily was it ballyhooed, took on some of the aspects of a circus. . . .

So powerful was the invasion of scientific ideas and of the scientific habit of reliance upon proved facts that the Protestant churches—which numbered in their membership five out of every eight adult church members in the United States—were broken into two warring camps. Those who believed in the letter of the Bible and refused to accept any teaching, even of science, which seemed to conflict with it, began in 1921 to call themselves Fundamentalists. The Modernists (or Liberals), on the other hand, tried to reconcile their beliefs with scientific thought; to throw overboard what was out of date, to retain what was essential and intellectually respectable, and generally to mediate between Christianity and the skeptical spirit of the age.

The position of the Fundamentalists seemed almost hopeless. The tide of all rational thought in a rational age seemed to be running against them. But they were numerous, and at least there was no doubt about where they stood. Particularly in the South they controlled the big Protestant denominations. And they fought strenuously. They forced the liberal Doctor Fosdick out of the pulpit of a Presbyterian church and back into his own Baptist fold, and even caused him to be tried for heresy (though there was no churchman in America more influential than he). They introduced into the legislatures of nearly half the states of the Union bills designed to forbid the teaching of the doctrine of evolution; in Texas, Louisiana, Arkansas, and South Carolina they pushed such bills through one house of the legislature only to fail in the other; and in Tennessee, Oklahoma, and Mississippi they actually succeeded in writing their anachronistic wishes into law.

The Modernists had the *Zeitgeist* on their side, but they were not united. Their interpretations of God—as the first cause, as absolute energy, as idealized reality, as a righteous will working in creation, as the ideal and goal toward which all that is highest and best is moving—were confusingly various and ambiguous. Some of these interpretations offered little to satisfy the worshiper: one New England clergyman said that when he thought of God he thought of "a sort of oblong blur." And the Modernists threw overboard so many doctrines in which the bulk of American Protestants had grown up believing (such as the Virgin birth, the resurrection of the body, and the Atonement) that they seemed to many to have no religious cargo left except a nebulous faith, a general benevolence, and a disposition to assure everyone that he was really just as religious as they. Gone for them, as Walter Lippmann said, was "that deep, compulsive, organic faith in an external fact which is the essence of religion for all but that very small minority who can live within themselves in mystical communion or by the power of their understanding." The Modernists, furthermore, had not only Fundamentalism to battle with, but another adversary, the skeptic nourished on outlines of science; and the sermons of more than one Modernist leader gave the impression that Modernism, trying to meet the skeptic's arguments without resorting to the argument from authority, was being forced against its will to whittle down its creed to almost nothing at all.

All through the decade the three-sided conflict reverberated. It reached its climax in the Scopes case in the summer of 1925.

The Tennessee legislature, dominated by Fundamentalists, passed a bill providing that "it shall be unlawful for any teacher in any of the universities, normals and all other public schools of the State, which are supported in whole or in part by the public school funds of the State, to teach any theory that denies the story of the Divine creation of man as taught in the Bible, and to teach instead that man has descended from a lower order of animals."

This law had no sooner been placed upon the books than a little group of men in the sleepy town of Dayton, Tennessee, decided to put it to the test. George Rappelyea, a mining engineer, was drinking lemon phosphates in Robinson's drug store with John Thomas Scopes, a likeable young man of twenty-four who taught biology at the Central High School, and two or three others. Rappelyea proposed that Scopes should allow himself to be caught red-handed in the act of teaching the theory of evolution to an innocent child, and Scopes—half serious, half in joke—agreed. Their motives were apparently mixed; it was characteristic of the times that (according to so friendly a narrator of the incident as Arthur Garfield Hays) Rappelyea declared that their action would put Dayton on the map. At all events, the illegal deed was shortly perpetrated and Scopes was arrested. William Jennings Bryan forthwith volunteered his services to the prosecution; Rappelyea wired the Civil Liberties Union in New York and secured for Scopes the legal assistance of Clarence Darrow, Dudley Field Malone, and Arthur Garfield Hays; the trial was set for July, 1925, and Dayton suddenly discovered that it was to be put on the map with a vengeance.

There was something to be said for the right of the people to decide what should be taught in their tax-supported schools, even if what they decided upon was ridiculous. But the issue of the Scopes case, as the great mass of newspaper readers saw it, was nothing so abstruse as the rights of taxpayers versus academic freedom. In the eyes of the public, the trial was a battle between Fundamentalism on the one hand and twentieth-century skepticism (assisted by Modernism) on the other. . . .

. . . The atmosphere of Dayton was not simply that of rural piety. Hot-dog venders and lemonade venders set up their stalls along the streets as if it were circus day. Booksellers hawked volumes on biology. Over a hundred newspaper men poured into the town. The Western Union installed twenty-two telegraph operators in a room off a grocery store. In the courtroom itself, as the trial impended, reporters and camera men crowded alongside grim-faced Tennessee countrymen; there was a buzz of talk, a shuffle of feet, a ticking of telegraph instruments, an air of suspense like that of a first-night performance at the theater. Judge, defendant, and counsel were stripped to their shirt sleeves—Bryan in a pongee shirt turned in at the neck, Darrow with lavender suspenders, Judge Raulston with galluses of a more sober judicial hue—yet fashion was not wholly absent: the news was flashed over the wires to the whole country that the judge's daughters, as they entered the courtroom with him, wore rolled stockings like any metropolitan flapper's. Court was opened with a pious prayer—and motion-picture operators climbed upon tables and chairs to photograph the leading participants in the trial from every possible angle. The evidence ranged all the way from the admission of fourteen-year-old Howard Morgan that Scopes had told him about evolution and that it hadn't hurt him any, to the estimate of a zoölogist that life had begun something like six hundred million years ago (an assertion which caused gasps and titters of disbelief from the rustics in the audience). And meanwhile two million words were being telegraphed out of Dayton, the trial was being broadcast by the *Chicago Tribune*'s station WGN, the Dreamland Circus at Coney Island offered "Zip" to the Scopes defense as a "missing link," cable companies were reporting enormous increases in transatlantic cable tolls, and news agencies in London were being besieged with requests for more copy from Switzerland, Italy, Germany, Russia, China, and Japan. Ballyhoo had come to Dayton.

It was a bitter trial. Attorney-General Stewart of Tennessee cried out against the insidious doctrine which was "undermining the faith of Tennessee's children and robbing them of their chance of eternal life." Bryan charged Darrow with having only one purpose, "to slur at the Bible." Darrow spoke of Bryan's "fool religion." Yet again and again the scene verged on farce. The climax—both of bitterness and of farce—came on the afternoon of July 20th, when on the spur of the moment Hays asked that the defense be permitted to put Bryan on the stand as an expert on the Bible, and Bryan consented.

So great was the crowd that afternoon that the judge had decided to move the court outdoors, to a platform built against the courthouse under the maple trees. Benches were set out before it. The reporters sat on the benches, on the ground, anywhere, and scribbled their stories. On the outskirts of the seated crowd a throng stood in the hot sunlight which streamed down through the trees. And on the platform sat the shirt-sleeved Clarence Darrow, a Bible on his knee, and put the Fundamentalist champion through one of the strangest examinations which ever took place in a court of law.

He asked Bryan about Jonah and the whale, Joshua and the Sun, where Cain got his wife, the date of the Flood, the significance of the Tower of Babel. Bryan affirmed his belief that the world was created in 4004 B.C. and the Flood occurred in or about 2348 B.C.; that Eve was literally made out of Adam's rib; that the Tower of Babel was responsible for the diversity of languages in the world; and that a "big fish" had swallowed Jonah. When Darrow asked him if he had ever discovered where Cain got his wife, Bryan answered: "No, sir; I leave the agnostics to hunt for her." When Darrow inquired, "Do you say you do not believe that there were any civilizations on this earth that reach back beyond five thousand years?" Bryan stoutly replied, "I am not satisfied by any evidence I have seen." Tempers were getting frazzled by the strain and the heat; once Darrow declared that his purpose in examining Bryan was "to show up Fundamentalism . . . to prevent bigots and ignoramuses from controlling the educational system of the United States," and Bryan jumped up, his face purple, and shook his fist at Darrow, crying, "To protect the word of God against the greatest atheist and agnostic in the United States!" . . .

On the morning of July 21st Judge Raulston mercifully refused to let the ordeal of Bryan continue and expunged the testimony of the previous afternoon. Scopes's lawyers had been unable to get any of their scientific evidence before the jury, and now they saw that their only chance of making the sort of defense they had planned for lay in giving up the case and bringing it before the Tennessee Supreme Court on appeal. Scopes was promptly found guilty and fined one hundred dollars. The State Supreme Court later upheld the anti-evolution law but freed Scopes on a technicality, thus preventing further appeal.

Theoretically, Fundamentalism had won, for the law stood. Yet really Fundamentalism had lost. Legislators might go on passing anti-evolution laws, and in the hinterlands the pious might still keep their religion locked in a science-proof compartment of their minds; but civilized opinion everywhere had regarded the Dayton trial with amazement and amusement, and the slow drift away from Fundamentalist certainty continued.

The reporters, the movie men, the syndicate writers, the telegraph operators shook the dust of Dayton from their feet. This monkey trial had been a good show for the front pages, but maybe it was a little too highbrow in its implications. What next? . . . How about a good clean fight without any biology in it? . . .

The public mania for vicarious participation in sport reached its climax in the two Dempsey-Tunney fights, the first at Philadelphia in September, 1926, the second at Chicago a year later. Prize-fighting, once outlawed, had become so respectable in American eyes that gentlefolk crowded into the ringside seats and a clergyman on Long Island had to postpone a meeting of his vestrymen so that they might listen in on one of the big bouts. The newspapers covered acres of paper for weeks beforehand with gossip and prognostications from the training-camps; public interest was whipped up by such devices as signed articles—widely syndicated—in which the contestants berated each other (both sets of articles, in one case, being written by the same "ghost"), and even a paper so traditionally conservative in its treatment of sports as the *New York Times* announced the result of a major bout with three streamer headlines running all the way across its front page. One hundred and thirty thousand people watched Tunney outbox a weary Dempsey at Philadelphia and paid nearly two million dollars for the privilege; one hundred and forty-five thousand people watched the return match at Chicago and the receipts reached the incredible sum of $2,600,000. Compare that sum with the trifling $452,000 taken in when Dempsey gained his title from Willard in 1919 and you have a measure of what had happened in a few years. So enormous was the amphitheater at Chicago that two-thirds of the people in the outermost seats did not know who had won when the fight was over. Nor was the audience limited to the throng in Chicago, for millions more—forty millions, the radio people claimed—heard the breathless story of it, blow by blow, over the radio. During the seventh round—when Tunney fell and the referee, by delaying the beginning of his count until Dempsey had reached his corner, gave Tunney some thirteen seconds to recover—five Americans dropped dead of heart failure at their radios. Five other deaths were attributed to the excitement of hearing the radio story of the fight. . . .

. . . [In August 1926] there was a striking demonstration of what astute press-agentry could do to make a national sensation. A young man named Rudolph Alfonzo Raffaele Pierre Filibert Guglielmi di Valentina d'Antonguolla died in New York at the age of thirty-one. The love-making of Rudolph Valentino (as he had understandably preferred to call himself) had quickened the pulses of innumerable motion-picture addicts; with his sideburns and his passionate air, "the sheik" had set the standard for masculine sex appeal. But his lying in state in an undertaker's establishment on Broadway would hardly have attracted a crowd which stretched through eleven blocks if his manager had not arranged the scenes of grief with uncanny skill, and if Harry C.

Klemfuss, the undertaker's press agent, had not provided the newspapers with every-thing they could desire—such as photographs, distributed in advance, of the chamber where the actor's body would lie, and posed photographs of the funeral cortège. . . . With such practical assistance, the press gave itself to the affair so whole-heartedly that mobs rioted about the undertaker's and scores of people were injured. Sweet are the uses of publicity: Valentino had been heavily in debt when he died, but his posthumous films, according to his manager's subsequent testimony, turned the debt into a $600,000 balance to the credit of his estate. High-minded citizens regretted that the death of Charles William Eliot, which occurred at about the same time, occasioned no such spectacular lamentations. But the president emeritus of Harvard had had no professional talent to put over his funeral in a big way. . . .

A great many people . . . regarded with dismay the depths to which the public taste seemed to have fallen. Surely a change must come, they thought. This carnival of commercialized degradation could not continue.

The change came—suddenly.

The owner of the Brevoort and Lafayette Hotels in New York, Raymond Orteig, had offered—way back in 1919—a prize of $25,000 for the first non-stop flight between New York and Paris. . . . [In May 1927] three planes were waiting for favorable weather conditions to hop off from Roosevelt Field, just outside New York, in quest of this prize: the *Columbia,* which was to be piloted by Clarence Chamberlin and Lloyd Bertaud; the *America,* with Lieutenant-Commander Byrd of North Pole fame in command; and the *Spirit of St. Louis,* which had abruptly arrived from the Pacific coast with a lone young man named Charles A. Lindbergh at the controls. There was no telling which of the three planes would get off first, but clearly the public favorite was the young man from the West. He was modest, he seemed to know his business, there was something particularly daring about his idea of making the perilous journey alone, and he was as attractive-looking a youngster as ever had faced a camera man. The reporters—to his annoyance—called him ''Lucky Lindy'' and the ''Flying Fool.'' The spotlight of publicity was upon him. Not yet, however, was he a god. . . .

Then something very like a miracle took place.

No sooner had the word been flashed along the wires that Lindbergh had started than the whole population of the country became united in the exaltation of a common emotion. Young and old, rich and poor, farmer and stockbroker, Fundamentalist and skeptic, highbrow and lowbrow, all with one accord fastened their hopes upon the young man in the *Spirit of St. Louis.* To give a single instance of the intensity of their mood: at the Yankee Stadium in New York, where the Maloney-Sharkey fight was held on the evening of the 20th, forty thousand hard-boiled boxing fans rose as one man and stood with bared heads in impressive silence when the announcer asked them to pray for Lindbergh. The next day came the successive reports of Lindbergh's success—he had reached the Irish coast, he was crossing over England, he was over the Channel, he had landed at Le Bourget to be enthusiastically mobbed by a vast crowd of Frenchmen—and the American people went almost mad with joy and relief. And when the reports of Lindbergh's first few days in Paris showed that he was behaving with charming modesty and courtesy, millions of his countrymen took him to their hearts as they had taken no other human being in living memory.

Every record for mass excitement and mass enthusiasm in the age of ballyhoo was smashed during the next few weeks. Nothing seemed to matter, either to the newspapers or to the people who read them, but Lindbergh and his story. On the day the flight was completed the *Washington Star* sold 16,000 extra copies, the *St. Louis Post-Dispatch* 40,000, the *New York Evening World* 114,000. The huge headlines which described Lindbergh's triumphal progress from day to day in newspapers from Maine to Oregon showed how thorough was public agreement with the somewhat extravagant dictum of the *Evening World* that Lindbergh had performed "the greatest feat of a solitary man in the records of the human race." Upon his return to the United States, a single Sunday issue of a single paper contained one hundred columns of text and pictures devoted to him. Nobody appeared to question the fitness of President Coolidge's action in sending a cruiser of the United States navy to bring this young private citizen and his plane back from France. He was greeted in Washington at a vast open-air gathering at which the President made—according to Charles Merz—"the longest and most impressive address since his annual message to Congress." The Western Union having provided form messages for telegrams of congratulations to Lindbergh on his arrival, 55,000 of them were sent to him—and were loaded on a truck and trundled after him in the parade through Washington. One telegram, from Minneapolis, was signed with 17,500 names and made up a scroll 520 feet long, under which ten messenger boys staggered. After the public welcome in New York, the Street Cleaning Department gathered up 1,800 tons of paper which had been torn up and thrown out of windows of office buildings to make a snowstorm of greeting—1,800 tons as against a mere 155 tons swept up after the premature Armistice celebration of November 7, 1918!

Lindbergh was commissioned Colonel, and received the Distinguished Flying Cross, the Congressional Medal of Honor, and so many foreign decorations and honorary memberships that to repeat the list would be a weary task. He was offered two and a half million dollars for a tour of the world by air, and $700,000 to appear in the films; his signature was sold for $1,600; a Texas town was named for him, a thirteen-hundred-foot Lindbergh tower was proposed for the city of Chicago, "the largest dinner ever tendered to an individual in modern history" was consumed in his honor, and a staggering number of streets, schools, restaurants, and corporations sought to share the glory of his name.

Nor was there any noticeable group of dissenters from all this hullabaloo. Whatever else people might disagree about, they joined in praise of him.

To appreciate how extraordinary was this universal outpouring of admiration and love—for the word love is hardly too strong—one must remind oneself of two or three facts.

Lindbergh's flight was not the first crossing of the Atlantic by air. Alcock and Brown had flown direct from Newfoundland to Ireland in 1919. That same year the

N-C 4, with five men aboard, had crossed by way of the Azores, and the British dirigible R-34 had flown from Scotland to Long Island with 31 men aboard, and then had turned about and made a return flight to England. The German dirigible ZR-3 (later known as the *Los Angeles*) had flown from Friedrichshafen to Lakehurst, New Jersey, in 1924 with 32 people aboard. Two Round-the-World American army planes had crossed the North Atlantic by way of Iceland, Greenland, and Newfoundland in 1924. The novelty of Lindbergh's flight lay only in the fact that he went all the way from New York to Paris instead of jumping off from Newfoundland, that he reached his precise objective, and that he went alone.

Furthermore, there was little practical advantage in such an exploit. It brought about a boom in aviation, to be sure, but a not altogether healthy one, and it led many a flyer to hop off blindly for foreign shores in emulation of Lindbergh and be drowned. Looking back on the event after a lapse of years, and stripping it of its emotional connotations, one sees it simply as a daring stunt flight—the longest up to that time—by a man who did not claim to be anything but a stunt flyer. Why, then, this idolization of Lindbergh?

The explanation is simple. A disillusioned nation fed on cheap heroics and scandal and crime was revolting against the low estimate of human nature which it had allowed itself to entertain. For years the American people had been spiritually starved. They had seen their early ideals and illusions and hopes one by one worn away by the corrosive influence of events and ideas—by the disappointing aftermath of the war, by scientific doctrines and psychological theories which undermined their religion and ridiculed their sentimental notions, by the spectacle of graft in politics and crime on the city streets, and finally by their recent newspaper diet of smut and murder. Romance, chivalry, and self-dedication had been debunked; the heroes of history had been shown to have feet of clay, and the saints of history had been revealed as people with queer complexes. There was the god of business to worship—but a suspicion lingered that he was made of brass. Ballyhoo had given the public contemporary heroes to bow down before—but these contemporary heroes, with their fat profits from moving-picture contracts and ghost-written syndicated articles, were not wholly convincing. Something that people needed, if they were to live at peace with themselves and with the world, was missing from their lives. And all at once Lindbergh provided it. Romance, chivalry, self-dedication—here they were, embodied in a modern Galahad for a generation which had foresworn Galahads. Lindbergh did not accept the moving-picture offers that came his way, he did not sell testimonials, did not boast, did not get himself involved in scandal, conducted himself with unerring taste—and was handsome and brave withal. The machinery of ballyhoo was ready and waiting to lift him where every eye could see him. Is it any wonder that the public's reception of him took on the aspects of a vast religious revival? . . .

③ Psychosociological History

The coupling of psychological, social psychological, and sociological approaches to the study of history is based on their common involvement—on an individual or group basis—with the human mind. Each examines phenomena that, because they concern human behavior (how people think, feel, and react), lie outside the realm of physical science and, for the most part, biological science as well. In an earlier age these disciplines might have been considered part of the study of man's soul. Despite this thread of kinship, however, there are important differences.

In the broadest sense psychology is the science of individual behavior, but it is a discipline broken up into a number of schools of thought. A generation or so ago, one could point to a dichotomy created by psychoanalytic and behavioral orientations; there are other theoretical positions among psychologists today (Rogerian and humanistic, for example), but since these have been little noticed by psychohistorians we will confine our attention to the psychoanalytic and behavioral schools, and to the rather large proportion of psychologists who are eclectic and do not align themselves with any particular theoretical position.

Psychoanalytic theory, both as a form of therapy and as a theory of personality, represents one of the most influential psychological orientations and is the one that has received the most attention from historians—although increasing attention is likely to be paid to behavioral psychology. A major difference between these two branches of psychology lies in the assumptions they use in therapy. Adherents of psychoanalytic theories, such as those of Sigmund Freud and Erik Erikson, believe that emotional problems are the result of basic underlying disturbance in the personality. This approach is sometimes referred to as depth psychology, because it goes beyond an examination of surface symptoms only and seeks instead to treat the personality in its full depth—although the term is used rather imprecisely here, since followers of theoreticians like Harry Stack Sullivan also use a depth approach but may not identify themselves as psychoanalytic. To psychoanalysts, the whole personality, including the unconscious, must be subjected to therapy. If it is not, permanent cure for mental disability is unlikely. It is apparent that psychoanalysis is a long and painstaking task; patients may have to spend years before treatment is completed.

In contrast, behaviorally oriented psychologists hold that psychological disorders may often be treated without such drastic recourse. People receive stimuli and respond accordingly. Thus they are about what they seem to be; all behavior is really nothing more than learned habits—that is, the association of responses with stimuli. Emotional problems, then, are the product of undesirable habits, and may be cured simply by changing those habits. Probing deeply into the psyche—or the past—for unconscious motives, buried memories, infant traumas, and the like, is irrelevant and unnecessary. Therapy focuses on observable behavior (habits) and institutes changes at that level. Treatment techniques are therefore likely to be less probing than those that a psychoanalytically oriented therapist might suggest, and may take only a few weeks to complete. Less interested than psychoanalysts in comprehensive theories that explain the entire personality, behaviorists might examine more limited—but still important—aspects of behavior, including defense mechanisms (like projection) and cognition. Treatment techniques similarly focus on more limited objectives, such as anxiety reduction, and may include systematic desensitization, biofeedback, hypnosis, aversive conditioning, and modeling.

Eclectics, however, are just what the name implies. Using psychoanalytic theories in one instance, behavioral theories in another, and on other occasions techniques derived from still other orientations, they employ whatever therapeutic tools seem most likely to be of aid in any given instance. Their objectives are also variable, sometimes probing deeply and other times treating surface symptoms only.

Psychoanalysts, behaviorists, and eclectics share the common goal of understanding individual personality and behavior, with a view toward helping persons who have mental health problems. They also share a division into two other psychological camps, which are determined by modes of practice: clinicians (i.e., practitioners) and academicians (teachers and researchers). Clinicians may be eclectic, or they may be aligned with psychoanalytic, behavioral, or some other theoretical position, as may academicians; among the latter, however, the number who are exclusively psychoanalytic in orientation is relatively small.

Social psychologists and sociologists, on the other hand, are not involved in the study or treatment of individual pathology; although they may deal with any number of problems of deviant behavior, their goal is to understand the behavioral complexities of groups, individuals in groups, and institutions—not in an attempt to provide individual therapy but to increase their understanding of the world around them. Individuals depressed to the point of suicide might go to a psychoanalyst or behavioral psychologist for help; they would be ill-advised if they made an appointment with a social psychologist or sociologist. Social psychology is the overlapping portion of psychology and sociology that treats individual behavior within a social context, while the sociologist examines the relationship of individuals to each other, often within small groups and institutions. Sometimes the sociologist studies the dynamics of groups and institutions per se, whether formally organized (the church, the nation, the army), informally organized (cliques, street-corner gangs, poker parties), or unorganized social aggregations (young mothers, middle-aged bankers, the unemployed, the handicapped).

The members of these disciplines—psychoanalytic scholars, behaviorists, social psychologists, and sociologists—are somewhat like intellectual historians in that they attempt to explore the mind. They do not, however, seek unit-ideas or popular symbols, as intellectual historians might do, although these may possibly be part of the outcome of their research. The concepts of class and status, for example, are a part of the history of ideas, but the social psychologist or sociologist who deals with them usually is not concerned with their historical dimensions. Instead, the goal is more presentist, in an attempt to understand current behavior.

However, once a theory of individual or group behavior has been developed, regardless of disciplinary origin or label, the insights achieved may be applied to the study of the past. Indeed, as the following selections attempt to show, some exceedingly rich and rewarding ideas have been developed through the interdisciplinary melding of historical and psychological research. For example, Erik Erikson, one of today's leading psychoanalytic theorists, points out that "the psychoanalytic method is essentially a historical method. Even where it focuses on medical data, it interprets them as a function of past experience."[1]

The attempt to divide psychosociological aspects of history into neat, compartmentalized segments fails, of course. Just as various types of intellectual history meld one into the other, so do these approaches. In their study of Woodrow Wilson, for example, Sigmund Freud and William C. Bullitt constantly label their work a psychological study; Freud specifically pointed out that they used psychoanalytic methods and hypotheses because psychoanalysis is really psychology.[2] And the sociologists and psychologists constantly cite not only each other, but the psychoanalysts as well. The psychological defense mechanisms, such as projection, regression, repression, and reaction formation, which were originally formulated by Freud, are accepted by most psychologists, many of whom reject other aspects of Freudian theory; one of the early formulators of the sociological concept of reference group theory did so in a book entitled *The Psychology of Status;*[3] social psychologist Richard Centers defines the sociological concept of class as "a *psychological* phenomenon in the fullest sense of the term";[4] and Fred Weinstein and Gerald M. Platt attempt to use psychoanalytic theory to study social change in a book entitled *Psychoanalytic Sociology.*[5] Interdisciplinary cross fertilization thus makes precise dividing lines impossible to define.

Nevertheless these psychosocial approaches to history may be placed on a spectrum from psychoanalytic at one extreme to sociological at the other, from individual to group study, from intuitive to precise, and (to use words in a popular sense, implying a

[1] Erik H. Erikson, *Childhood and Society,* 2nd ed. (New York: W. W. Norton and Co., 1963), p. 16.

[2] Sigmund Freud and William C. Bullitt, *Thomas Woodrow Wilson: Twenty-eighth President of the United States: A Psychological Study* (Boston: Houghton Mifflin Co., 1967), p. xiv.

[3] Herbert H. Hyman, *The Psychology of Status,* Archives of Psychology, No. 269 (New York: n. p., 1942).

[4] Richard Centers, *The Psychology of Social Classes: A Study of Class Consciousness* (Princeton: Princeton University Press, 1949), p. 27.

[5] Fred Weinstein and Gerald M. Platt, *Psychoanalytic Sociology: An Essay on the Interpretation of Historical Data and the Phenomena of Collective Behavior* (Baltimore: The Johns Hopkins University Press, 1973).

contrast that does not necessarily exist), from "humanistic" to "scientific." At the psychoanalytic, individual, intuitive, and humanistic end, the methods are closely related to those of intellectual history; Freud was as preoccupied with symbols and Greek myths as any literary historian, and the whole concept of psychoanalysis could be made part of a fascinating study in the history of ideas.[6] At the sociological, group, precise, and scientific end of the spectrum, however, we approach the quantitative techniques used not only by academic psychologists, social psychologists, and sociologists, but also by political scientists, economists, geographers, and (within the last ten years) historians of all varieties.

The application of psychosociological theories and techniques may not always be appropriate or well conceived, to be sure. It is difficult to interpret past events in terms of hypotheses and conjectures obtained from live patients on the couch (in psychoanalysis), rats in a maze or individuals undergoing behavior modification (behavioral psychology), or questionnaires on group attitudes (sociology). Historical figures and events seldom leave enough records suitable for psychosociological research. For this reason, and because of their timidity to use a method with which they are unfamiliar, until very recent years historians have been extremely hesitant to use the insights of these other disciplines. Psychoanalysis serves as a good illustration; "so much that goes on in 'treatment,' " says Robert Coles, a psychiatrist, "is mysterious, intangible, elusive; one hesitates to apply to politics concepts already of very circumscribed or indeterminate value."[7] As a therapy, psychoanalysis necessitates an interaction between therapist and patient. The goal is to change the patient, not the somewhat passive analyst. As a theory, however, it is applied by a psychohistorian to a subject who is inaccessible or even dead. The analytic process, therefore, works itself out within the historian-therapist, who interacts with passive sources. This is quite a change of roles. Patients are not available to report their growing understanding of themselves; lacking this essential feedback, scholar-analysts are necessarily at a great disadvantage in the use of their method. Having in mind this limitation, and the difficulty of obtaining empirical proof to support logical conclusions derived from psychoanalytic theory, one scholar has questioned whether or not historians using psychoanalytic methodology are "writing historical fiction and not history." It is not surprising that it is only within the last decade or so that many serious attempts have been made to apply psychoanalytic theory to history, and two studies by Erik Erikson, *Gandhi's Truth* and *Young Man Luther*, serve as excellent examples of the potentials of this historical method.[8]

[6]The entire issue of *The Psychoanalytic Review* 60 (Summer 1973), for example, is devoted to literary classics. It includes such articles as "Identity Crisis in a Midsummer Nightmare: Comedy as Terror in Disguise," "Adler, Oedipus, and the Tyranny of Weakness," and "Coal as an Erotic Symbol."

[7]Robert Coles, "Shrinking History—Part Two," *New York Review of Books* 20 (March 8, 1973):27.

[8]Beatrice Cowper Green, "Comment and Controversy," *AHA Newsletter* 14 (October 1976):5–6; Erik H. Erikson, *Gandhi's Truth: On the Origins of Militant Nonviolence* (New York: W. W. Norton and Co., 1969) and *Young Man Luther: A Study in Psychoanalysis and History* (New York: W. W. Norton and Co., 1958).

Some other applications of psychological insight to history have been somewhat dubious. Meyer A. Zeligs' *Friendship and Fratricide: An Analysis of Whittaker Chambers and Alger Hiss,*[9] was poorly received. One reviewer accused the author of accepting the testimony of one antagonist without question while automatically dismissing the testimony of the other except to support a preconceived opinion. The bias was so extreme, thought the reviewer, that Zeligs' work "should not be taken as an example of psychoanalytic method. The misuse of psychoanalysis here exceeds anything I have read in wild applications of Freud's concepts to biography and history."[10] A milder example is Bruce Mazlish's *In Search of Nixon,* which received better, although mixed, reviews. One reviewer noted the sparse source material and concluded that the book was nevertheless a valuable contribution to psychohistory despite its limitations.[11] But an academic psychologist to whom I showed the study wrote me that he "read it and was horrified. This kind of thing is of value neither to History or to Psychology." Whatever the merit of these particular criticisms, it is obvious that psychohistorical inquiry must be conducted with extreme caution. Even Freud had his knuckles rapped when he ventured into psychohistory, as we shall soon see.

Despite obvious pitfalls, such as those mentioned by Coles a few paragraphs previously, recent psychohistory (including psychobiography) is especially attracted to contemporary figures. No doubt this is partially due to the increasingly presentist orientation of Clio's Craftsmen. At the same time, contemporaries are often available for the historian to interview, or at least their acquaintances are; this, plus the tendency of modern figures to write memoirs, hold press conferences, and the like, provides evidence that is more susceptible to psychological uses than the stilted speeches and apologias written by the departed statesmen of a prior century.

One of the most interesting studies of the past few years, therefore, is Doris Kearns' *Lyndon Johnson and the American Dream.* Kearns had become acquainted with the President while she worked as a White House Fellow, and after Johnson left Washington she agreed to help him with his memoirs. Their working relationship became close; he confessed that she reminded the former President of his dead mother, but, says Kearns, "it is more likely that he talked to me simply because I was there, present, as he moved, knowingly, terrified, toward death." Kearns' psychological analysis is subtle and restrained. But she suggests that Johnson was strongly influenced by inner tensions created by "his mother's demands for intellectual achievement and his father's notions of manly pride." Thus he learned to avoid confrontation and achieved consensus, for to choose his father could cause him to lose the love of his mother; to choose his mother could endanger his male identity. Although she is not a therapist, Kearns used psychological knowledge to make maximum effectiveness of the materials

[9]Meyer A. Zeligs, *Friendship and Fratricide: An Analysis of Whittaker Chambers and Alger Hiss* (New York: Viking Press, 1967).

[10]Meyer Schapiro, "Dangerous Acquaintances," *New York Review of Books* 8 (February 23, 1967):5, 6.

[11]Bruce Mazlish, *In Search of Nixon: A Psychohistorical Inquiry* (New York: Basic Books, 1972); *New York Times Book Review,* June 4, 1972, pp. 37–38.

Johnson provided in their long discussions, and she bolsters her credibility by acknowledging the assistance provided by Erik Erikson and the Group for Applied Psychoanalysis.[12]

One of the popular figures for psychohistorical inquiry is Adolph Hitler; among the most provocative studies are Robert G. L. Waite, "Adolph Hitler's Anti-Semitism: A Study in History and Psychoanalysis," and Rudolph Binion's *Hitler Among the Germans*. Waite contends that Hitler projected his own fears and guilts onto Jews, including inadequacy, incest, and sexual perversion, while Binion sees Hitler's success as stemming from "his having coordinated his private traumatic fury with the national traumatic need." Of special interest, perhaps, is Walter C. Langer, *The Mind of Adolph Hitler,* a publication of a secret intelligence report written by psychiatrist Langer during World War II. Although Langer's book has been much criticized, it was significant because it was a practical application of psychoanalytic method in a historical context; with the sources available, Langer attempted to use psychoanalytic theory in an effort to predict Hitler's future behavior.[13]

Another popular object of psychohistory is King George III. In his own time he was judged insane, and various historical postmortem diagnoses have been made of the precise nature of his malady. In the words of Ida Macalpine and Richard Hunter, "Textbook concepts of psychopathology were applied to him and a man riddled with weaknesses, conflicts and unfulfilled desires conjured up on fashionable psychological theory—not on evidence or fact." The results, say Macalpine and Hunter, were "psychiatry by defamation, if not character assassination." The authors diagnose the king's illness as porphyria, a hereditary disease of the metabolism that may have mental side effects. The diagnosis of porphyria is so difficult that other researchers may be forgiven their conclusions, for even today victims of this illness are sometimes admitted to mental hospitals for treatment.[14] It is only fair to add that if the reviews of this book are any indicator historians are more impressed than physicians. One reviewer accepted many of the authors' findings, but contended that George III was nevertheless a victim of mental illness since the outbreaks of porphyria tended to occur

---

[12]Doris Kearns, *Lyndon Johnson and the American Dream* (New York: Harper & Row, 1976), pp. 18, 367, 370, 373. A visitor to the LBJ ranch recalled that on one occasion when Kearns left the room "the former President said to her, 'You remind me of my mother.' As the door closed behind her, Johnson turned to me and added, 'My mother had a weight problem, too.'" *Time,* November 18, 1974, p. 59. The key that lends trustworthiness to Kearns' account, however, is that she was closely and personally acquainted with her subject, which is necessarily most infrequent in psychohistory. Whether she meant to or not, Kearns functioned almost like a therapist.

[13]Robert G. L. Waite, "Adolph Hitler's Anti-Semitism: A Study in History and Psychoanalysis," in Benjamin B. Wolman, ed., *The Psychoanalytic Interpretation of History* (New York: Basic Books, 1971), pp. 203–207; Rudolph Binion, *Hitler Among the Germans* (New York: Elsevier, 1976), p. 127; Walter C. Langer, *The Mind of Adolph Hitler: The Secret Wartime Report* (New York: Basic Books, 1972). Erikson, "The Legend of Hitler's Childhood," *Childhood and Society,* Chapter IX, is also of interest.

[14]Ida Macalpine and Richard Hunter, *George III and the Mad-Business* (New York: Pantheon Books, 1969), pp. 360, 173–74.

during periods of stress. The problem thus becomes more subtle when the confusion is supposedly cleared away, as psychology blends into medical history.[15]

The use of psychology, including psychoanalytic theory, is thus a very tenuous thing in history. It may easily degenerate into a simple case of what David Donald has termed "psychiatric name-calling," as historians increasingly tend "to label—without research and without clinical knowledge—men they dislike as psychotic, paranoid, and the like." "Psychoanalysis," Donald reminds us, "is not a substitute for historical research."[16] John E. Mack, a psychiatrist, agrees, deprecating the use of psychoanalysis "to reduce important or creative persons to psychosexual banality." Mack also underlines one of the major problems with psychohistory, finding it appalling that psychohistorical analyses are often made on the basis of material too slight to allow reliable psychoanalytic insight.[17]

The current fad of bandying about psychological terms without careful attention to their proper and precise meanings has an additional consequence in the dilution of their meaning or, as it is sometimes described, word inflation. Feebleminded was a descriptive term for those later called retarded, and more recently called mentally handicapped; the original term is now used only as an insult. Hysteria once referred to a specific nervous disorder but was soon applied to any unhealthy emotional outbreak; today it may simply be used as a term of scorn. Even the more modern "identity crisis" has been emasculated. Erik Erikson's label applies, strictly speaking, to the crisis reached at a specific stage of ego development. But the term has been used so generally that its original meaning is being lost.

No matter how well done, no matter how carefully the language is employed, some educated readers might reject the various psychological approaches to history because they feel the basic assumptions of such methods automatically stack the deck. The psychological study of social movements, says Norman Pollack, "imposes a static model" on society "because it requires a standard or reference point by which to judge what is or is not irrational." Behavior that does not conform to this standard thus becomes irrational by definition, "with the result that the analysis is biased in favor of the status quo." Deviations are then more likely to be examined than their causes.[18] Psychological approaches may also be attacked for their tendency to claim too much. A relatively new journal, originally called *History of Childhood Quarterly,* was sub-

---

[15]*Psychoanalytic Quarterly* 41 (July 1972):444–50. The reviewer was Bernard C. Meyer, a psychiatrist. See Edwin A. Weinstein, "Woodrow Wilson's Neurological Illness," *Journal of American History* 57 (September 1970):324–51, for an excellent example of the combination of medicine and psychology in historical methodology.

[16]See Donald's review of Wolman, *The Psychoanalytic Interpretation of History,* in the *Journal of Southern History* 38 (February 1972):111–12.

[17]John E. Mack, "Psychoanalysis and Historical Biography," *Journal of the American Psychoanalytic Association* 19 (January 1971):154, 155.

[18]Norman Pollack, "Hofstadter on Populism: A Critique of 'The Age of Reform,' " *Journal of Southern History* 26 (November 1960):495–96.

titled *The Journal of Psychohistory,* as if the two were necessarily equated and the only way to study the history of childhood was through psychology. The first issue even claimed for childhood history the status of a separate discipline. In a later issue of that journal one psychohistorian went so far as to assert that "the how and the why [of history] are *never* to be found 'out there' in the realm of social relationships, contemporary institutions, or political and economic structures," a contention that is, at best, a gross exaggeration. Still other historians attack psychohistory because it lacks concreteness. It uses concepts derived from nineteenth- and twentieth-century Western Europe and America, and applies them to individuals in other times and places, as if the concepts were universal—which has not yet been proved. Nor is it, as we shall see, a unified theory; instead, it is a mixture created by the contributions of a host of psychoanalytic and behavioral theorists who vary in their emphasis; one may stress the unconscious, while another may place primary importance on a conscious, adult ego. The difference is basic, but it is a rare psychohistorian who explains his theoretical assumptions to his readers.[19]

Psychohistory is also open to attack for its use of evidence. In his study of Hitler, Walter C. Langer concludes that Hitler "must have discovered his parents during intercourse." From the less than certain "must have" Langer jumps to the conclusion that Hitler "*was* [not, 'might have been'] indignant at his father for what he considered to be a brutal assault upon his mother," and "*was* indignant with his mother because she submitted." This experience was supposedly relived symbolically, and thus "played an important part in shaping his future destinies."[20] A resultant behavior is used to conjure evidence, which itself is used to verify the behavior. But the real question is whether this event took place, not how it might have shaped Hitler, if it actually occurred. Did little Adolph peep in at the wrong moment or not? Langer can provide no objective answer; he has become the captive of his technique.

This last paragraph demonstrates the danger of historical compartmentalization. The concept that provides the methodological framework has all but prohibited acceptance of other evidence or even the formulation of other vital questions. This is the sort of thing Pollack objected to in the study of Populists in the United States. Some scholars contend that this danger is more pronounced with psychohistorical procedures than others, although it is certainly a difficulty that warrants precautions regardless of approach.

There are other reasons, too, why historians have shied away from psychohistory.

---

[19]Lloyd deMause, "The History of Childhood: The Basis for Psychohistory," *History of Childhood Quarterly* 1 (Summer 1973):2; Paul Monaco, "Psychohistory: Independence or Integration?" *History of Childhood Quarterly* 3 (Summer 1975):127 (emphasis mine); Clifford S. Griffin, "Oedipus Hex," *Reviews in American History* 4 (September 1976):310–11. An advertisement for the *History of Childhood Quarterly* quoted the rather expansive claim that "Psychohistory isn't a division of history; its [sic] a replacement for sociology—the first new discipline in the social sciences in the 20th century." The revision of the title in 1976 to *The Journal of Psychohistory: A Quarterly Journal of Childhood and Psychohistory* seems to reflect a more moderate viewpoint. Griffin's article reviews the first three volumes of the *History of Childhood Quarterly.*

[20]Langer, *Mind of Adolph Hitler,* p. 151, emphasis mine.

There is the suspicion that Oedipus complexes and oral and anal stages are somewhat ridiculous.[21] Some historians no doubt agree with Vladimir Nabokov's assessment of "the Freudian racket" as nothing but a "jumbo thingum of polished wood with a polished hole in the middle which doesn't represent anything except the gaping face of the Philistine."[22] Other scholars may find odd the paradox that historians become more interested in Freud at the very time psychiatrists become less interested. Still others do not see the relevance of psychology to lectures on revolutionary loyalism or the Second Bank of the United States. Some may simply be resisting that which they do not understand, as people in all callings are prone to do, contending (often in error) that psychological approaches to history are useless because they cannot be empirically verified.

Although psychoanalytic concepts are increasingly used in historical study, there has been far less application of less comprehensive psychological theories. The many references to the developmental psychology of Freud and Erikson in recent historical literature are not matched by references to more restricted uses of psychological insight. There are only a few essays, such as that by David Brion Davis, which attempt to understand historical currents through the use of projection or some other defense mechanism. And there are almost no historical studies that utilize the results of psychological laboratory research—historian Richard L. Schoenwald was able to cite only R. C. Raack's article, which is reproduced in chapter nine. Such findings, which fit into the category of academic psychology, are nevertheless more likely to be used in the future. The death or increasing age of most of the leading psychoanalytic theoreticians, and the increasing use of quick and inexpensive types of therapy, probably means that psychology will continue its abandonment of the psychoanalytic approach; then psychoanalysis is likely to become so abstruse that it will be of interest only to an initiated intellectual elite. One might therefore expect research such as that of Raack to become both more common and more important.[23]

---

[21] For example, in a footnote deleted from R. C. Raack's selection, below, the following passage is quoted from Rudolph Binion, *Frau Lou, Nietzsche's Wayward Disciple* (Princeton: Princeton University Press, 1968), p. 6: "Little Lelia was wretched amidst plenty as only a human being can be. Her trouble was psychic growing pains which fortunately can, and unfortunately must, be traced to their crude source. This was a craving for her father excited by excretion and attended by darkling visions of reentering his bowel-womb to repossess his penis." Now really. "Since psychoanalysis has become a religion, its more dogmatic devotees have been pushing the master's errors to ever new heights of absurdity;" some of them, says Stanislav Andreski, "are plainly mad"! *Social Sciences as Sorcery* (New York: St. Martin's Press, 1972), p. 138.

[22] Vladimir Nabokov, *Strong Opinions* (New York: McGraw-Hill, 1973), p. 116.

[23] Monaco, "Psychohistory: Independence or Integration," p. 130; Richard L. Schoenwald, "Using Psychology in History: A Review Essay," *Historical Methods Newsletter* 7 (December 1973):16–17. In his famous call for use of psychological techniques in history, William L. Langer contended that "academic psychology . . . , so far as I can detect, has little bearing on historical problems." See "The Next Assignment," *American Historical Review* 63 (January 1958):284. Gordon W. Allport discusses and compares a wide range of psychological techniques in *Letters from Jenny* (New York: Harcourt, Brace, and World, 1965), in which he applies each of several theories in turn to the interpretation of a series of letters written by a rather unhappy and maladjusted lady in the last decade of her life. The same techniques and assumptions used to analyze these letters may be employed to study the correspondence of historical figures.

Historical studies using sociological concepts are more numerous than those using academic psychology, although these have sometimes been so subtle that historians have not understood the sociological implications of what they wrote and read. The multivolume *History of American Life* series, for example, was an attempt to come to terms with social history. To Richard Hofstadter the effort was not particularly successful because "historians were trying to write a kind of sociological history without having any sociological ideas." Although this tends to confuse the two genres (surely sociological theory is not always necessary to write good social history), the point is well taken. "If history was to be more sociological" (and, we might add, more psychological, more precise, or more quantitative), wrote Hofstadter, "it must also have more ideas and a better sense of method."[24] To illustrate, the existence of an "establishment" in the Confederate States of America during the Civil War has frequently been noted, but it was not until Thomas Lawrence Connelly and Archer Jones wrote *The Politics of Command* (included below) that this elementary observation was fitted into the sociological notion of the informal organization so as to enhance greatly our understanding of the decision-making process in the Confederate Army. So too, while the concept of class has been employed in historical analysis for some time, it was not until the last decade or so that historians—usually with some sociological or other interdisciplinary training—began to apply rigid, objective definitions and tests to large population groups so that the class structure and mobility of a previous era may be understood in more than impressionistic terms.[25]

Sociological methods also have their critics, however. Polish-born sociologist Stanislav Andreski, for example, makes a delightful attack on all social sciences (including sociology) for, among other things, hiding behind smoke screens of jargon, obscured simplification of the obvious, quantification, and ideology.[26] More appropriate is the criticism of Carl Bridenbaugh who contends that history is losing its sense of the importance of particular human beings. This warning cannot apply to psychohistory, which usually applies its insights on the individual level. But it most certainly applies to sociological history, which, by definition, is concerned with groups. "We discourse learnedly," grumbles Bridenbaugh, "of peasants in the mass, as a class, as though each one did not possess an individuality." Thus historians "retreat to politics" and enlist in the "cult of the contemporary," leaving other kinds of history to the social scientists, who "deal in statistics, with units and trends, hoping to deduce laws of society" while their systematic work shows little historical sense and no chronology.[27] Such criticisms are embarrassing because they are often well deserved.

[24]Richard Hofstadter, "History and Sociology in the United States," in Seymour Martin Lipset and Richard Hofstadter, eds., *Sociology and History: Methods* (New York: Basic Books, 1968), pp. 8–9.

[25]For excellent examples of this type of work see Stephan Thernstrom, *Poverty and Progress: Social Mobility in a Nineteenth Century City* (Cambridge: Harvard University Press, 1964), and Peter R. Knights, *The Plain People of Boston, 1830–1860: A Study in City Growth* (New York: Oxford University Press, 1971).

[26]Andreski, *Social Sciences as Sorcery.*

[27]Carl Bridenbaugh, "The Great Mutation," *American Historical Review* 68 (January 1963):323–25.

To illustrate sociological theories as applied to history, therefore, works by historians have been chosen. A historian can maintain the feeling of history and chronology without having to jettison the intellectual rigor of systematic inquiry that is not, Bridenbaugh to the contrary, a vice—it is a prime virtue of any scholar.

Other historians may join Jacques Barzun in complaining that, like psychological methods of historical study, sociological methods are dominated by a scientific spirit distinct (as if it could be) from what is more properly called history, which is supposedly more intuitive than scientific.[28] If by drawing this philosophical line Barzun means to say that the scientifically oriented historian attempts to achieve a methodological precision that is alien to the intellectual or traditional narrative historian, he may be right. Some historians would agree with David S. Landes and Charles Tilly, who characterize this dichotomy as that between system and art, between historian as social scientist and historian as humanist—although again the division seems artificial and unnecessary.[29]

A more important dichotomy is that created by the ways in which sociology and history may be combined. On one hand, there are those who use history as a means of testing sociological theory or providing examples across time. Scholars who join the two disciplines in this way are likely to consider themselves sociologists. On the other hand, the situation may be reversed. Sociological study is not the end in itself; instead, it facilitates historical analysis, as is the case with the selections included below. Such an approach uses sociological means to reach historical ends and is adopted by scholars who think of themselves as historians rather than sociologists.

As the following selections reveal, today's historians must be more scientific than their predecessors, but no less literary. It is no longer sufficient to gather the facts in chronological order and write about them in minimal grammatical style. Some sort of unifying concept must often be added if history is to rise above antiquarianism. Seymour Martin Lipset's explanation of the use of sociological models in history— even when the models are somewhat vague—may be applied as well to other interdisciplinary approaches. Simply to use sociological procedures and notions "does not turn the historian into a systematizing social scientist. Rather, these offer him sets of categories with which to order historical materials and possibly enhance the power of his interpretive or causal explanations."[30] Such organizing principles as status and reference group, for example, may give hints of significance to otherwise meaningless data, or might direct research along more precise lines than otherwise—much as any well-constructed hypothesis will do. However, researchers must avoid the temptation to let the sociological theory structure their initial search for evidence. When theory

[28]Jacques Barzun, "History: The Muse and Her Doctors," *American Historical Review* 77 (February 1972):54.

[29]David S. Landes and Charles Tilly, eds., *History As Social Science* (Englewood Cliffs, N.J.: Prentice-Hall, 1971), pp. 10–11.

[30]Seymour Martin Lipset, "History and Sociology: Some Methodological Considerations," in Lipset and Hofstadter, eds., *Sociology and History*, p. 23.

governs data, the outcome, at least in historical inquiry, is likely to be a severe distortion of objective reality. Results are those that are expected, for overusing a theory transforms research into a self-fulfilling prophecy. Or as J. H. Hexter somewhat strongly declares, "a historian who cuts his historical suit to fit the cloth of any other social science will find himself more skimpily clad in a garment less likely to protect him from the chill of ignorance and vacuity."[31]

The following selections, like those preceding, illustrate the attempt of historians to achieve precision and accuracy. These goals are not the exclusive domain of quantitative history; they are part and parcel of every historical method. Although accuracy may seem more obvious in sociological history, it is also a characteristic of, for example, psychohistorians who carefully apply psychoanalytic theory to their material. Indeed, the development of that theory was part of an effort to achieve reliable, consistent, and accurate interpretation of the events that shape personality. Psychosociological methods, however, often have a third goal that cannot be claimed for intellectual history: the search for prediction.

Usually prediction is only subtly implied in historical writing. But one thing most historians do, unless they confine themselves to straight narrative, is make generalizations. An author may assert that a revolutionary army (and, by implication, some other revolutionary armies as well) needed only to maintain its existence in order to achieve its goals; another may claim that a new nation with vast unsettled lands tended to develop unique institutions. A third may point to the electoral process in a certain democracy and contend that great changes occurred as the franchise was expanded. Each of these statements implies a generalization that can be tested on a larger scale. More than that, such generalizations may be predictive in nature even though the investigator may not have intended that they be so. There is no better way to test a generalization than to check its applicability to analogous events, and there is no requirement that all the other events must have taken place in the past. In such a way psychoanalytic theory developed, basing its generalizations on numerous individual observations until the generalizations were so firmly established that they became predictive devices. Though one may be amused by some of the claims of psychoanalysis, one is brought up short by the fact that Walter C. Langer did predict the suicide of Adolph Hitler, and that Bruce Mazlish implied (and thus predicted) that Richard M. Nixon would become involved in crisis in an effort to enhance his feelings of adequacy, that he would use " 'crisis as a weapon, as a tactic' and will so create and use it in the future when 'tactics' call for it." Indeed, he would do more. Nixon would even "*create* crises, as a means of testing himself and assuring himself greater public support." Remembering President Nixon's resignation, did we see a prediction come true?[32]

[31] J. H. Hexter, *Doing History* (Bloomington: Indiana University Press, 1971), p. 116.
[32] Mazlish, *In Search of Nixon,* pp. 86, 92, 127. Mazlish claims only very limited predictive powers for psychohistory (see pp. 161–65), yet the tenor of his work is predictive. In one instance he notes the confirmation by new evidence of what had formerly been merely a guess (p. 101).

Perhaps in these two particular instances the scholars were as lucky as they were skillful in the application of their method. But one of history's great shortcomings has been its failure to explain that which seems irrational; relying on logic, we have too often accepted explanations that rejected apparently irrational behavior, attempting instead to explain away such evidence as inaccurate, biased, or otherwise questionable. One of the most important contributions of the psychosocial methodologies is to provide the potential insights needed to understand certain types of behavior not otherwise understandable. What Bruce Mazlish claims for psychohistory may with equal justice be asserted about sociologically oriented approaches to history. Each "seeks to reorient history, toward an understanding of the unconscious emotions underlying the overt actions of human beings as they perform on the stage of history. It claims that traditional history hitherto has mistaken the tip of the iceberg for the great hulking mass of motives, 'irrational' rather than rational, that exist beneath the surface of events."[33] It would be extremely foolish to ignore the claims of such techniques.

[33]Bruce Mazlish, "On Teaching History," *AHA Newsletter* 14 (April 1976):7.

chapter five
Freudian Personality Theory

Sigmund Freud's theory of personality developed over a period of many years and was modified by the lessons of his experience. It is not necessary to trace this evolution here. By 1932, when the book from which the following selection is taken was for all practical purposes finished, Freud's theories were substantially complete. Few alterations were made in the seven years of life remaining to him.

Freud's model of personality features three elements, the id, the ego, and the superego. The id denotes the instincts (sex, hunger, and aggression, for example), which are unlearned motivators of the psychological activities of the personality. The id's aim is to reduce tension by immediate satisfaction of instinctual desires. Since tensions are unpleasant, their reduction is pleasurable; hence the id is supposedly characterized by pleasure seeking. However, the id cannot achieve its goals alone; it must be aided by a second element, the ego, which controls the personality's contacts with the real world. The ego forces the tension-reducing efforts of the id into appropriate channels in order to insure that adjustment to reality is made in a suitable way with some acceptance of whatever inevitable frustrations may be involved. One must eat the proper food, for example, and to obtain it one must learn what is proper and one must accept some unavoidable but frustrating delay. It is the ego that guides the id by learning, through the development of memory and perception, what food is; when the ego is properly developed the normal child will not attempt to eat his or her rattle or teddy bear. Freud's third element is the superego, which functions as the moral ruler of the personality. It imposes on the child a code of behavior that is learned from the parents, and seeks to direct the child and its id in ways that will secure parental approval. The superego attempts to make the personality attain perfection by opposing many of the instinctual impulses of the id and insuring that the ego does its work in a moral way. The effectiveness of the superego depends on its ability to deliver positive and negative rewards. If an individual acts—or even thinks—in a manner that violates the ideals of the superego, he or she will be punished. If the transgression is serious enough, the consequent retribution may include not only feelings of inadequacy, shame, and guilt, but also physical maladies, such as stomach pains and headaches, or even accidental injury.

The personality needs energy to function, and this psychic energy comes from the instincts, which reside in the id. The energy of the life instincts (there are also, said Freud, death instincts), including sex, is called libido. This libido is distributed to the ego and superego by the process of identification. In reference to the ego, identification is the frustrating process of learning how to match a mental image with its duplicate in the real world. For the superego, identification is the attempt of the child to match (or identify) its behavior with that desired by the idolized, powerful parents. If the superego has more than its share of psychic energy, the personality will value rectitude above all and will be bogged down in a morass of moralistic considerations; the ego will therefore be hindered in performing its role as an effective intermediary between the id and the real world.

If this theory has merit, it is plausible that the son of an orthodox Presbyterian minister, as Woodrow Wilson was, might adopt to an unusual extent the values of his idealized and seemingly powerful father. He might unconsciously identify his father with God the Father, thus identifying himself with Christ, the Son of God the Father. In addition, it could possibly explain why Wilson might behave passively toward his father, for rebellion against such a father would be rebellion against God, which the superego could not condone. Thus the natural tendency of a male to react passively to the influence of other men (which Freud thought was basic) would be reinforced and an almost total submission to the father's will would not be unlikely.

Passivity toward the father and thus the eager acceptance of the father's ideals could also be explained, according to Freud, by the Oedipus complex. That is, the little boy, having developed sexual feelings for his mother, fears his competitor—his father, who (compared to the boy) is omnipotent. Fearing that his father may castrate him because of his desire for his mother, he gives up that desire. He subordinates himself to the father and identifies with him, the degree of identification varying according to the intensity of this Oedipal conflict. Under some conditions he may even identify with his mother—making his normal bisexuality even more feminine—and play the passive family role Freud expected her to play.[1]

---

[1] The most important of Freud's work for understanding the ideas discussed in this selection is *The Ego and the Id*, which was originally published in 1923 and which has been reprinted frequently. I used the version edited by James Strachey, published in *The Standard Edition of the Complete Psychological Works of Sigmund Freud*, 24 vols. (London: The Hogarth Press and the Institute of Psycho-Analysis, 1953–1966), 19. Since Freud's work is so voluminous, with major ideas often repeated in somewhat variant form throughout his publications, any attempt at brief summarization must also rely on compendiums published by later authors. For example, see Calvin S. Hall, *A Primer of Freudian Psychology* (New York: The World Publishing Company, 1954); Hans H. Strupp, *An Introduction to Freud and Modern Psychoanalysis* (Woodbury, N.Y.: Barron's Educational Series, 1967); and Calvin S. Hall and Gardner Lindzey, *Theories of Personality,* 2nd ed. (New York: Wiley, 1970). For this selection, the discussion of Freud's theories in Chapter I of Sigmund Freud and William C. Bullitt, *Thomas Woodrow Wilson, Twenty-eighth President of the United States: A Psychological Study* (Boston: Houghton Mifflin Co., 1967), which some students may wish to read, would perhaps have been more appropriate. Because of the controversy surrounding the book, however, I have not used it. Although it appears generally consistent with Freudian theory, it is remarkably ponderous and mechanistic, suggesting the possibility that it may not have been written by Freud alone.

Because of limitations of space, this discussion of Freud's ideas errs greatly due to drastic oversimplification and omission of points that do not facilitate understanding of the following selection. Perhaps they are not worth extensive discussion in any event. Most psychohistorians today nod and tip their hats to Freud; but it is Erik Erikson they embrace. Freud is, to quote one psychologist, "passé," and his subtle, yet heavyhanded, literal, mechanical qualities are repugnant to today's sophisticated scholars. His mechanistic approach seems to have caused Freud to restrict his horizons by frequent use of metaphors from physical science (just as Henry Nash Smith contended that the direction of historical study was channeled by the biological metaphor of the germ theory). The idea that the amount of psychic energy in a personality remains constant, for example, is reminiscent of preatomic physics, with its dictum that mass or energy can be neither created nor destroyed. That this energy should be redistributed from the id to charge the ego and superego, and that it should be shunted from one of these three components of personality to another on the basis of what seems like user demand, reminds one of a sort of psychic power grid with switches to be flipped according to the temporary energy needs of any segment of the grid. The psychoanalyst becomes a psychic electrician.

Freud's theories have been subject to extensive criticism, the merits of which are beyond the scope of this book. The important thing for those of us who are interested in historical methodology is that psychoanalytic theory opens new doors to the interpretation of individual motivation. Perhaps Woodrow Wilson behaved as he did because of his sincere, unshakable faith in the institutions he supported, and his genuine disappointment when the individuals he loved let him down. But why did he have such unshakable faith? Why did he rely on the love of certain individuals? How did he choose those persons to love, and why did he detect betrayal in some of them—some of whom certainly did not betray him? There is no definite answer to these questions, but in one way or another they must be confronted. They are basic to history.

The book from which the following selection is taken, *Thomas Woodrow Wilson, Twenty-eighth President of the United States: A Psychological Study,* apparently was originally conceived about 1930. By 1932 it was virtually complete, but the authors disagreed on some last-minute revisions. In 1938 they reached full accord on the text, but decided not to publish while Wilson's widow still lived. She died in 1961, and the book was published in 1967.[2]

The reader should be aware that, like all other interpreters of history, the authors were not always unbiased in their opinions. In an undated introduction Freud wrote that he was unsympathetic to Wilson as the American president entered into European affairs, a sentiment that became more pronounced as Wilson's influence on Europe increased.[3] Freud also states that he developed an overwhelming pity for Wilson. One must recall, however, that Freud was Austrian, and that the Austrian Empire was

---

[2]Freud and Bullitt, *Woodrow Wilson.* See Bullitt's "Foreword," pp. v–viii.
[3]Ibid., p. xi.

dismembered as a result of World War I, the fragmentation being confirmed by a treaty that Wilson signed that did not possess the compensations of justice Wilson had promised. Bullitt too had possible bias. A member of the American delegation at the Versailles Conference in 1919 (later ambassador to Russia and, on the eve of World War II, France), he felt Wilson had acquiesced in the infliction of new injustices upon the world by disastrous compromises involving the status of China's Shantung province, the Danzig corridor, the Saar, and various other questions. Bullitt wrote Wilson that the President could have avoided compromise if he had fought for his principles; he did not, thought Bullitt, who consequently resigned his position.[4]

Many readers have therefore suspected that both authors lacked objectivity and for this reason, as well as the way in which psychoanalytic theory was used, the book was severely criticized when it was published. One historian referred to it as a "silly and even pathetic collaboration" that produced an "alleged biography."[5] Cushing Strout thought it a disaster, a work of "character assassination," and hoped it would not discredit the attempt to combine history and psychoanalytic theory. Strout thought Erik Erikson's theory of development was more promising than the Freudian approach. Erikson himself also deplored the book and speculated that much, perhaps all of it, was written by Bullitt, except for Freud's introduction and possibly the second chapter. Geoffrey Gorer agreed with other reviewers. The book was a "distasteful essay in posthumous denigration" having little historical value. He speculated that Freud's work underlay only the first three chapters at most.[6]

One sometimes feels, however, that the psychohistorian critics protest too much. Freud is honored as the founder of psychoanalysis; one who reads a work supposedly coauthored by him that appears to be poorly done is thus faced with a choice. Either he must admit that the great man seriously blundered, or he can rationalize on the ground that Freud did not do much of the work and that the book was really Bullitt's. The latter preserves not only Freud's reputation, but also avoids possible suspicion about the logic behind all of his work. However, Bullitt said that the book was an "amalgam for which we were both responsible," and Freud wrote that "for the analytic part we are both equally responsible; it has been written by us working together."[7]

The critics make some good points. The book is often vague as to chronology and causation, and its organization is lacking as it hops about both in time and subject. Loosely written, it is a chronicle of Wilson's failures with few mentions of his successes—surely they too contributed to his state of mind. (This point as well as any other illustrates how methodological preconceptions may shape conclusions.) The study is not put into the context of its time, and many of its conclusions are not based

---

[4]Ibid., pp. 271–72.

[5]Robin W. Winks, ed., *The Historian as Detective: Essays on Evidence* (New York: Harper & Row, 1969), p. 347.

[6]Strout's review is in the *Journal of American History* 54 (June 1967): 183–84; those of Erikson and Gorer are reprinted in the *International Journal of Psycho-Analysis* 48 (July 1967): 462–70.

[7]Freud and Bullitt, *Wilson,* pp. vii, xiv.

on sufficient fact. The latter criticism, however, could be made by any skeptic about almost any piece of psychohistory. To readers who may not have been convinced of the practicality of applying psychoanalytical concepts to history, or who do not accept the basic tenets of psychoanalytic theory, speculation on the basis of doubtful fact may appear to be the essence of psychohistory. While empirical evidence in history is often hard to come by with any method, it may sometimes seem impossible with this one—although that fact does not necessarily preclude the validity of the method.

Bear in mind that this selection was written during the early 1930s and approved for publication in 1938. As such it must be considered a document from the 1930s, not from the 1960s when it was finally published. If it had appeared thirty years earlier, it would doubtless have had a better reception. At the very least, the book is an interesting curiosity. If it tells us little about Wilson and little more about Freud, it may nevertheless tell us something about Bullitt and a great deal about the state of psychohistory on the eve of World War II.

Thomas Woodrow Wilson . . . A Psychological Study
Sigmund Freud and William C. Bullitt

Before we consider Wilson as a youth and man we must complete our examination of his desires when he was a child, and we have not yet considered his passivity to his father. We trust that during our discussion of this element in Wilson's nature the reader will remember that his own character, and the character of every other man, is as firmly rooted in bisexuality as was Wilson's character. Nearly all men have learned to contemplate the physical elements in the human body without shame. To call attention to the presence of oxygen and hydrogen in the body of a man no longer causes excitement; but not all men have yet learned to look calmly at the psychic elements of human nature. To mention the bisexual nature of man still seems somewhat scandalous to the ill-educated. Yet bisexuality is a fact of human nature which, in itself, should arouse no more emotion than the fact that fifty-nine percent of the body consists of water. If human beings were not bisexual, they would not be human beings. To be born bisexual is as normal as to be born with two eyes. A male or a female without the element of bisexuality would be as inhuman as a Cyclops. Just as an artist may employ the same paints to produce either a beautiful picture or an ugly picture, so the Ego may combine the original masculinity and femininity of a man to compose either a beautiful character or an ugly character. To judge the final product, whether picture or character,

Sigmund Freud and William C. Bullitt, *Thomas Woodrow Wilson: Twenty-eighth President of the United States: A Psychological Study,* Chapter III (Boston: Houghton Mifflin Company, 1967). Copyright © 1966 by Sigmund Freud Copyright Ltd. and William C. Bullitt. Reprinted by permission of the Publisher Houghton Mifflin Company.

is legitimate. To condemn the elements is absurd. Masculinity may be employed to produce the heroism of Leonidas or the act of a murderer. There is everything to praise and blame in the results the Ego produces with original masculinity and femininity, but there is nothing praiseworthy or blameworthy in the mere existence of these elements. They exist. That is all. When Margaret Fuller, "high priestess of New England transcendentalism," declared, "I accept the universe," Carlyle remarked, "By God, she'd better." Like the universe, the bisexuality of mankind has to be accepted.

The outlets employed by Wilson's Ego for his passivity to his father were all outlets approved by his Super-Ego. His chief outlet was through direct submission to the will of his father. He did what his father wanted him to do and did not do what his father did not want him to do. He accepted his father's thoughts without question and his father's leadership with adoration. He submitted every problem of his life to his father. In Mr. Ray Stannard Baker's words: "Until after he was forty years old, Woodrow Wilson never made an important decision of any kind without first seeking his father's advice." He depended on his father financially until he was twenty-nine years old. His father wished him to be a good moral Presbyterian. He became one. His father wished him to become a specialist in words and a speaker. He became one.

Throughout Wilson's life much of his libido found outlet by way of speech-making. His excessive interest in making speeches would be surprising if it were not obvious that he found in the performance outlet not only for passivity to his father but also through identification, for activity toward his father. When he spoke, he was doing what his father wished him to do; but he was also by identification becoming his father. The Reverend Joseph Ruggles Wilson was, after all, essentially a speaker. Thus speechmaking gave expression to Thomas Woodrow Wilson's two strongest desires.

A portion of Wilson's passivity to his father found outlet through direct submission to his father; but the submission which, in his unconscious, he desired to make was far more profound and specific than the submission he was able to make in life. He therefore sought more ways in which to submit. He found an outlet, fully approved by his Super-Ego, through submission to the God who represented his father. All his life he enjoyed daily acts of submission to that God: morning prayers, evening prayers, grace before each meal and Bible reading each day. Moreover, so great was his need to submit to his God that never in his life could he allow himself to entertain religious doubt. To have doubted would have been to cut off an outlet which he needed for his passivity. "God is the source of strength to every man and only by prayer can he keep himself close to the Father of his spirit," he said. Twice, at least, he remarked: "I believe in Divine Providence. If I did not I would go crazy." Inasmuch as he made this remark about himself one need not feel that it is indecent to agree with him. So considerable a portion of his passivity to his father found outlet through his daily submissions to the God who represented his father that he might have found it impossible to discover another adequate and acceptable outlet. If he had not been able to make his daily submissions to God, he might indeed have taken refuge in paranoia and developed a "persecution mania"; he might have become not the occupant of the White House but the inmate of an asylum.

Another outlet for Wilson's passivity to his father was through a mother identification. We do not know enough about Wilson to make any estimate of the relative importance of his mother identification. We know only that he had a mother identification. In spite of his conscious wish to be like his father, Wilson resembled his mother not only in physique but in character. He had not only her thin weak body but also her severity, shyness and aloofness. He often felt like his mother, and he knew it. His remark to Dudley Field Malone is striking: "When I feel badly, sour and gloomy and everything seems wrong, then I know that my mother's character is uppermost in me. But when life seems gay and fine and splendid, then I know that the part of my father which is in me is in the ascendance." He usually felt "badly, sour and gloomy."

Were Wilson alive and would he submit to psychoanalysis, we would doubtless find that mother identification played a momentous part in his life. As it is, we must content ourselves with noting that we shall find evidence of mother identification when we consider the later stages of his life. Available evidence permits us to say merely that he, like all other men, had a mother identification and through it a portion of his passivity to his father found outlet.

Another vital tie with regard to which we have almost no evidence is his relationship to his brother Joseph. When Joseph Ruggles Wilson, Jr., was born, Thomas Woodrow Wilson was ten years old. Therefore, in spite of the fact that his development was retarded, it seems certain that he had passed the most important stages of his psychic development before the birth of this little brother. Nearly all children by the end of their sixth year have achieved some sort of a reconciliation of the conflicts of the Oedipus complex and have entered a period of sexual latency which usually lasts until adolescence. In consequence, most boys who are ten years old at the time of the birth of a younger brother find it comparatively easy to accept the intruder. Normally, the elder brother in his unconscious becomes father to the younger brother and also identifies himself with the younger brother, so that in the relationship he plays father to himself: to the elder brother, the younger brother represents himself as a small child. Through the passivity of his little brother (himself as a small child) to himself (representing his father) he obtains an outlet for his own passivity to his own father.

There is invariably present also an element of hostility. The younger brother is a rival for the love of the father and mother; and the birth of the younger brother, as we have already pointed out, gives rise to a feeling of "betrayal." Usually neither the hostility to the younger brother nor the sense of betrayal is pronounced in the case of a normal boy who has passed into the period of latency before the birth of his younger brother. If the elder brother has reached the age of ten before the birth of the younger brother, he ordinarily finds it easy to adopt a fatherly attitude toward the infant in the manner we have described and either preserves this attitude throughout life or follows the pattern of this relationship in his friendships with smaller and younger men who represent his brother.

We have no evidence as to Tommy Wilson's emotions at the time of the birth of his brother Joe, and we know little about their future relations. We know that Thomas

Woodrow Wilson at one time taught his little brother as his father had taught him, that he helped his brother in various ways, that he wrote, "I love my brother passionately," that he refused, when President, to appoint his brother to a postmastership or to allow his brother to be made Secretary to the Senate. Our information is so scanty that we should be glad to pass over this relationship without attempting to discuss it; but we must mention the probability that Joe Wilson played a far larger part in the emotional life of Thomas Woodrow Wilson than either realized.

In later life Thomas Woodrow Wilson always needed to have at least one affectionate relationship with a younger and physically smaller man, preferably blond. In these friendships Wilson clearly played the part of his own father and his friend represented himself as a boy. The pattern for these relationships probably was established by the emotions aroused in the ten-year-old Tommy Wilson by the birth of the infant Joe. We have noted that normally the elder brother identifies himself with the younger brother and plays father to himself and in addition that a sense of hostility, distrust and betrayal may accompany the affectionate emotions. Wilson's intense friendships were characterized by just such manifestations. He loved John Grier Hibben and Colonel House intensely so long as they preserved the obedient little brother attitude toward him. He finally concluded that each had betrayed him and cast each into the outer darkness as a Judas. We have seen that this paranoid sense of betrayal springs always from passivity to the father, and that it is often connected with the birth of a younger brother. We must, therefore, mention the probability that the birth of Joe Wilson inaugurated two important characteristics of his brother Thomas Woodrow Wilson. First, Joe's birth may have marked the beginning of his inclination to establish friendships in which he played father to a younger and smaller man who represented himself. Second it may have established his inclination to protect himself from his passivity by a paranoid mechanism. Briefly, his little brother Joe may have been the original much-loved betrayer who was followed many years later in his unconscious by Hibben and House. The original emotion involved was, of course, Tommy Wilson's passivity to his own father; but it seems to have reached his friends by way of his brother Joe. It is noteworthy that the most unjustified distrust of Wilson's life—his distrust of his White House Secretary, the faithful Joseph P. Tumulty—was directed toward a younger, smaller blond male named Joe. Joe Tumulty, to Wilson's unconscious, may well have represented Joe Wilson. The actions of a human being are often determined by far more absurd identifications than this.

When one considers Wilson's later relations with his brother Joe, Hibben, House, Tumulty and others, one is driven to conclude that the birth of the infant Joe Wilson must have aroused far stronger emotions in the ten-year-old Tommy Wilson than are usual in a child of that age confronted by an infant brother. His over-violent reaction was no doubt produced by the magnitude of his passivity to his father which made it inevitable that he should regard with excessive hostility a brother who ousted him from his unique position as the only begotten son of his father. It seems clear that at the age of ten Wilson's passivity to his father was still his dominant desire and that a portion of this current of libido, accompanied by much hostility and a paranoid sense of betrayal, charged his relationship to his brother Joe.

Another outlet for Wilson's passivity to his father was his identification of himself with Jesus Christ. This identification probably was established in his early childhood as a correlative to his identification of his father with God; but it seems not to have accumulated a large charge of libido until his adolescence. We shall, therefore, for the moment postpone discussion of it.

We have now glanced at the distribution of Wilson's libido in his childhood. We have observed that his love of self was ample; that his father, not his mother, was his chief emotional object; that his relations with women promised to be normal and commonplace; that a part of his activity toward his father had been repressed and a part had produced an exalted Super-Ego; and that his passivity to his father was his dominant emotion and required many outlets, among which were submission to his father and to God and identification with his mother and with his brother Joe. Before we consider Wilson's youth, adolescence and adult life let us for a moment look at the child as a whole.

Thomas Woodrow Wilson was a rather pathetic little boy, a child to whom one cannot refuse sympathy. He was weak, sickly and nervous, retarded in his development, his eyesight was defective and he suffered constantly from indigestion and headaches. That he should have been nervous is not extraordinary. Nervousness is the visible sign of an inner conflict which the Ego has been unable to solve. And, aside from all minor conflicts which may have harassed him, there was plenty of cause for nervousness in the conflict between his Super-Ego which commanded that he should be all masculinity, God Himself, and his passivity to his father which demanded that he should submit to his father in all ways even to the point of becoming all femininity. Thus his early relationship to his father doomed him to expect of himself all his life more than his body or mind could give. The nervousness and discontent which marked his life were early established. For this reason he compels our pity.

Yet it must also be recognized that he was in many ways favored by fate. His sisters and cousins had led him to an easy transfer of his libido from his mother to women outside the immediate family so that he was on his way to a normal sexual life. Moreover, his nature was admirably fitted to the civilization and class into which he was born.

The Lollard tradition of the British non-conformist middle class transferred to America, in which he was brought up, produced an atmosphere in which it was difficult for a man whose masculinity exceeded his femininity to flourish, except economically; but one well suited to women and to men whose femininity exceeded their masculinity. The "Thou shalt not!" of Lollardry is intolerable to a masculine man but congenial to women.

A more masculine boy than Tommy Wilson would have felt hostility to the *mores* of the family and community in which the Minister's son was reared; but he felt no impulse to revolt. His masculinity was feeble. His Ego-Ideal was not hostile to the ideals of his family or his community. The problems of his life arose not from conflicts with his environment but from conflicts within his own nature. He would have had to face those conflicts if he had been brought up in the comparative freedom of European civilization. The screen of rationalizations which allowed him to live all his life without facing his passivity to his father would have fallen early on the continent of Europe. He was fortunate to have been born in a nation which was protected from reality during the nineteenth century by inherited devotion to the ideals of Wyclif, Calvin and Wesley.

chapter six

Eriksonian Developmental Theory

The theory of psychoanalysis that is most widely accepted today, at least by those who use it as an historical method, is that of Erik Erikson. Erikson accepts much of Freud's theory (in fact he calls himself a Freudian), but he modifies and expands it to include a wider role for the ego, the culture in which the child lives, and the continuing development of the personality after childhood.

To Freud, the personality develops in psychosexual stages. The earliest is the oral phase, which is more critical than those that follow because the child is especially susceptible to influence. In this phase the child is loved, warmed, caressed, and fed by the mother; little is required of the child, but much is required of the parents, who usually fulfill their obligations toward the little one quite promptly. As the child grows older the parents begin to make demands, most notably in the matter of the child's bowels. As toilet training starts the child enters the anal phase, in which the outside world imposes its authority, inhibiting and prescribing behavior. This is soon followed by a phallic, or Oedipal, stage in which the child tends to explore his or her genital organs and develops sexual desires for the parent of the opposite sex; this development is different for boys and girls, but for both it is a period when they learn that desires cannot always be filled and that they often have to delay gratification. The conclusion of these three pregenital phases, which—since they may overlap—are not individually distinct, marks the start of the period of latency. Before developing further, the child, who is by now seven or eight years of age, seems to have suspended psychosexual development, although he or she is still learning the vital social skills that will be needed in the future. The child comes to know other adults and thus begins to leave parental influence, a process that is accelerated as the youngster, no longer a child, enters the genital phase of the early teens. Freud said little about further development.[1]

---

[1]Freud's outline of development appears with variations throughout his work. An early formulation is included in the second and third of the *Three Essays on the Theory of Sexuality,* written in 1905, and again in lectures XX and XXI of the *Introductory Lectures on Psycho-Analysis* (1915–1917). Freud's modified ideas about the little girl's experience with the Oedipus complex are found in *Female Sexuality* (1931). One of his

Ego psychology and developmental psychology, for which Erikson is known, consider the growth of an individual to be a series of positive efforts on the part of the ego to surmount crises encountered at each of several stages of ego development. These efforts are parallel to Freud's psychosexual phases of development and are sometimes called psychosocial or psychosensual phases. The most basic difference between Freud's and Erikson's stages is that where Freud concentrates on childhood only, Erikson sees ego development as a lifelong process of interaction between individuals and the world around them. Erikson does agree with Freud that the child is father to the man, but would go on to add that the man is father to the older man.

Freud's system seems excessively deterministic. He thought the decisive formative period was over by the end of the Oedipal phase; by then the nature of the adult was set. In Erikson's theory, however, personality growth and interaction with the total society continues throughout life, culminating in advanced age, when individuals fully accept both themselves and the inevitable fate of their "one and only life cycle." One sometimes has the feeling that among historians, Erikson's theories are more acceptable not because they are a closer approximation to truth than those of Freud (which they might well be), but because they allow greater flexibility of interpretation and are more comforting.

Erikson's model is a theoretical framework consisting of a series of eight stages of growth, each of which has its own crisis. As with Freud, these periods are not neatly divided, one from another; the line of separation is hazy, and an individual may be in more than one stage at a time. At each point, the healthy personality overcomes the crisis, adds a new ego quality and new inner strength, and moves on to the next challenge. Failure to overcome the crisis checks emotional growth. "A lasting ego identity," says Erikson, "cannot be completed without a promise of fulfillment which from the dominant image of adulthood reaches down into the baby's beginnings and which, by the tangible evidence of social health, creates at every step of childhood and adolescence an accruing sense of ego strength."[2] In the first stage, which roughly corresponds to Freud's oral stage, the baby must establish *basic trust* as he "takes in" the society that surrounds him—not only by eating (here the mother plays the key role) but also by the senses of sight, hearing, and touch, as they develop. In this stage infants face several critical junctures. In their attempt to incorporate and explore more and more of the world they perceive, they come to realize that they are distinct individuals, and, as they grow older, they must face the shattering knowledge that the

---

last statements about psychosexual development is found in Chapter III of *An Outline of Psychoanalysis* (1938). See James Strachey, ed., *The Standard Edition of the Complete Psychological Works of Sigmund Freud,* 24 vols. (London: The Hogarth Press and the Institute of Psycho-Analysis, 1953–1966), 7, 16, 21, and 23. See also Calvin S. Hall, *A Primer of Freudian Psychology* (New York: The World Publishing Company, 1954), and Hans H. Strupp, *An Introduction to Freud and Modern Psychoanalysis* (Woodbury, N. Y.: Barron's Educational Series, 1967).

[2]Erik H. Erikson, *Childhood and Society,* 2nd ed. (New York: W. W. Norton and Co., 1963), pp. 245–46.

mother cannot devote all her time to them and that they are accordingly losing, in a sense, the one other person who has meaning for them. Thus there is the potential to develop a sense of *mistrust;* if the ego is to develop in a healthy manner, the crisis of mistrust must be overcome by a sense of trust so that the child can meet the challenge of the next period of growth.

By the second and third years of life little children are in the second stage of development, comparable to Freud's anal stage, as they gain an ever-increasing sense of *autonomy;* this is related to physical maturity, as children learn to use their own muscles including, not in the least, those that control elimination. If youngsters' efforts to achieve autonomy are blocked, they will have a sense of impotence, of inability to control even their own bodies and their functions; they will develop *doubt* and a sense of *shame.* To protect them at this crisis, children must be assured that the basic trust already developed will not be lost simply because they want to become more autonomous. If checked at this point, they may continue their attempts at self-expression, even though they may have to pay the price of shame for acting contrary to their parents' wishes. But children must not overextend themselves either, for if they do the price is failure, and failure also creates doubt and shame.

At the age of four or five children enter the third phase of growth, as they seek to develop a sense of *initiative.* They are, now, good learners, willing to undertake obligations and to promise performance. But their early, fumbling attempts to be what their parents are lead inevitably to failure, creating a sense of inadequacy. For both boys and girls this feeling is intensified by the knowledge that they will not be able to possess the parent of the opposite sex (hence the correspondence of this phase to Freud's Oedipal stage). These desires create a feeling of *guilt,* which is accompanied by a growth of the conscience. To alleviate guilt, which is the crisis of the stage of initiative, children must be assured that their worth is equal to that of their parents. Despite their many failures they will eventually be the equal of their parents in all respects.

The next stage of childhood development, according to Erikson, occurs in the early school years, as the successfully maturing child develops a sense of *industry.* They desire to enter into the adult world, and to learn, create, work, and be useful. Even play tasks, if successfully accomplished, lead to a feeling of mastery. But children are vulnerable to failure, which may create in them a feeling of *inadequacy.* Somewhat parallel to Freud's period of latency, the stage of initiative sees the abandonment of sexual desires directed toward parents. This is a critical time; tasks undertaken under the influence of the sense of industry often require help, and the child thus learns cooperation.

As childhood comes to an end, youths enter the vital stage in which they search for *ego identity,* meaning their social roles—the niches that they will fill as adults. Youths seek a sense of belonging and of knowing that their existence is meaningful for others. Like other stages, this one has its crisis—the widely talked about identity crisis or *identity diffusion.* Most frequently this occurs when young people are uncertain of their future occupations. It is then that they may seek identity by joining a mass movement or social clique and may display an intolerance of those who are in some way different. This behavior is a defense against identity diffusion, which is usually an inability to make a decision about their lifetime occupations that is satisfactory to the youths. Seeking some sort of solution to identity diffusion, young people may overidentify with hero figures and leaders; this compensation helps to explain the appeal that totalitarian ideology may have for the youth, who is "eager to be affirmed by his peers, and is ready to be confirmed by rituals, creeds, and programs."[3] Another characteristic of this stage of growth is a moratorium, "a span of time after they [youth] have ceased being children, but before their deeds and works count toward a future identity."[4] Today the moratorium may be the college years or an enlistment in the army; for Martin Luther, argues Erikson, it was spent in a monastery. Erikson suggests that his own moratorium occurred during his years as a wandering artist, after he left art school and before he began psychoanalytic training.[5] Fawn Brodie surmises that Thomas Jefferson's five years' study of law was his moratorium,[6] while Cushing Strout suggests that for William James it was a long trip to Europe for study and relaxation.

We must use the term identity quite carefully. It does not necessarily refer to a conscious sense. In most cases, as Erikson uses the word, "An increasing sense of identity . . . is experienced preconsciously as a sense of psychosocial well-being. Its most obvious concomitants are a feeling of being at home in one's body, a sense of 'knowing where one is going,' and an inner assuredness of anticipated recognition from those who count." Furthermore, identity is not something that one gets and keeps. "Like a 'good conscience,'" says Erikson, "it is constantly lost and regained." It is something that is developed through an entire life, growing out of the "selective repudiation and mutual assimilation of childhood identifications, and their absorption in a new configuration."[7] One problem is that, in recent years, young people (and adults, too) have been altogether too conscious of the concept of identity.

---

[3]Ibid., pp. 262–63. Cushing Strout, "Ego Psychology and the Historian," *History and Theory* 7 (1968): 296–97, points out that Erikson has applied the concept of identity to groups as well as to individuals, thereby detaching it, for some purposes, from his theory of the life cycle.

[4]Erik H. Erikson, *Young Man Luther: A Study in Psychoanalysis and History* (New York: W. W. Norton and Co., 1962 [originally published 1958]), p. 43.

[5]Erik H. Erikson, *Life History and the Historical Moment* (New York: W. W. Norton and Co., 1975), pp. 28–29.

[6]Fawn M. Brodie, *Thomas Jefferson: An Intimate History* (New York: Bantam Books, 1974), p. 62.

[7]Erik H. Erikson, *Identity and the Life Cycle*, which forms the entire first issue of *Psychological Issues* 1 (1959):118, 113. He explains the term further in *Life History and the Historical Moment*, pp. 18–21. Perhaps one reason for Erikson's emphasis on the identity crisis is that he suffered from one himself, as he points out. For example, he grew up not knowing his real father, a Jew to his schoolmates but a gentile to Jews (*Life History and the Historical Moment*, pp. 26–32). Is the identity crisis therefore an experience, which, having had it himself, Erikson projects on everyone else whether it is there or not? Or having suffered identity confusion, did he thereby gain the insight necessary to generalize and interpret an experience that is part of the normal life cycle?

When, as Erikson points out with embarrassment, newspapers talk of an identity crisis in Africa or in the glass industry in Pittsburgh, the real meaning of the term has been lost. (Perhaps the height of this semantic dilution came when a student group at a major university announced that it would hold an identity crisis at a future meeting.) Furthermore, the term has become so popular that it influences the behavior it attempts to describe. Erikson poses the question of whether "some of our youth [would] act so openly confused and confusing if they did not *know* they were *supposed* to have an identity crisis?"[8]

The last three phases of the developmental model are those of adulthood; although Erikson places more emphasis on the adult period than Freud, for our purposes we may be brief. First comes a period of *intimacy,* which is only possible after the youth has established a sense of identity. Seeking to join his or her identity with that of another individual, the young person seeks a mate. If the quest is successful the young adult enters the phase of *generativity.* This primarily means a desire to have children and to guide them as they face the crises of their life cycle, although the drives involved may be applied to creativity or altruism instead of parenthood. The last developmental stage is the achievement of *ego integrity,* that is, the full acceptance of one's self and one's inevitable fate. The "one and only life cycle" is understood "as something that had to be and that, by necessity, permitted of no substitutions"; resignation and wisdom mark the realization "that an individual life is the accidental coincidence of but one life cycle with but one segment of history."[9]

It was suggested before that psychoanalytic theory might be helpful in solving problems of individual motivation. Freud played the premier role in bringing this to the attention of the general public, but Erikson, building on Freud's ideas, has provided a more thought-provoking model for understanding the sources of behavior. Everyone has "hangups," to use the modern slang terminology. What are they? Where do they come from? Most important, how do they effect behavior? Studies of leaders or of other outstanding individuals must take these questions into account. The past effects us all, and our own intimate yesterdays help to determine what we shall be tomorrow. It is in this connection that the Eriksonian developmental model has become a basic historical method. It is comprehensive and internally consistent yet sufficiently flexible to be applicable to a wide variety of behavioral phenomena.

Therein lies both its lure and its danger for the historian. Flexible theories are so easily misapplied that they may become worse than useless except in practiced hands.

[8] Erik H. Erikson, *Identity, Youth and Crisis* (New York: W. W. Norton and Co., 1968), pp. 15–16, 18–19. Note the use of the term in regard to the concept of reference group, p. 167.

[9] Erikson, *Childhood and Society,* p. 268. For Erikson's basic ideas see *Identity and the Life Cycle* and *Childhood and Society,* which were originally published in 1959 and 1950, respectively. They are amplified in his other works, notably *Young Man Luther.* Erikson has applied his psychoanalytic developmental model not only to Luther but also, in book-length form, to Gandhi and Thomas Jefferson (*Gandhi's Truth: On the Origins of Militant Nonviolence* [New York: W. W. Norton and Co., 1969] and *Dimensions of a New Identity: The 1973 Jefferson Lectures in the Humanities* [New York: W. W. Norton and Co., 1974]).

It is altogether too easy to make glib generalizations about someone's identity crisis or moratorium. The separation between one stage and another in the development of personality is vague and the concept of eight stages seems rather mechanical. It has not been proved in any event; it remains only a widely accepted hypothesis. Such theories are open to conjecture, and for Freud and even for Erikson one may also question whether the theories pay too little attention to deeply searing, traumatic events in adult life. Perhaps the "determinative prior experience," as Rudolph Binion puts it, need not have been in childhood or even in the adolescent years, since "to live through a catastrophe anew is routine in the emotional life of individuals."[10] The "new experience," Binion suggests, "is unconsciously taken to be the old one even while consciously the connections between them go unnoticed. . . ."[11] In any event, the Eriksonian model, especially the emphasis on the identity crisis, has been widely accepted when used with proper caution.

In the following article by Cushing Strout, note the application of Erikson's ideas to William James. The words autonomy and identity recur, with the latter being the central point around which the article revolves. The characteristics of the identity phase and the crisis of diffusion are recounted: "the ideological turmoil, a psychic 'moratorium' or postponement, an over-commitment to a wrong choice, a harking back in the identity-crisis to the shame and doubt of an earlier stage of emotional development, a perfectionist conscience that inhibits helpful apprenticeships, and the

---

[10]Rudolph Binion, "Repeat Performance: A Psychohistorical Study of Leopold III and Belgian Neutrality," *History and Theory* 8 (1969):213–59; Binion, "Hitler Looks East," *History of Childhood Quarterly* 3 (Summer 1975):99. In the former article Binion examines the origins of Leopold's neutrality policy prior to World War II, concluding that it arose out of his "felt need to repeat a prior experience while modifying its outcome." The "determinative prior experience" was in 1935 when his queen was killed in an automobile accident while he was driving ("Repeat Performance," pp. 245–46). "In the back of his mind, his realm stood for his sometime Queen" (p. 249). "Here, then, is a clear-cut, solid example of how, even in history, great effects can follow from small causes: of how *la grande histoire* can follow from *la petite histoire*. And yet our professional histories are generally written as if all big events followed from other big events" (p. 256).

[11]Binion, *Hitler Among the Germans* (New York: Elsevier, 1976), p. xii. This model and its application may be difficult for some readers to accept. As Binion warns (p. xiii), "reader hold tight." Supposedly Adolph Hitler adopted the German *Volk* as a substitute for his beloved mother. "To his unconscious mind the summons to revive and avenge Germany came as a summons to revive and avenge his dying mother." He came to terms with the trauma of her death by reliving it. "The point of reliving a traumatic experience seems to be to will, to control, to master it after having been overcome by it the first time, and to inure oneself to it so that it will 'pass' after all." In the destruction of the Jews "Hitler repeated his mother's terminal [cancer] treatment—applied it to Germany, that is—while also taking it out on Bloch [his mother's physician, a Jew] alias the Jew." He also contended that Hitler did not think of the intended conquest of Russia as conquest at all, but rather reconquest of land gained by Ludendorff's eastern victories of 1917–1918. *Hitler Among the Germans*, pp. xi, xii, 20, 21, 34.

expression of over-identification with troublesome parental figures."[12] James followed his father even to becoming "a pathetic parody" of him, "a crippled philosopher without a job" (p. 105). Self-punishing guilt and psychosomatic illness were finally overcome and a sense of identity achieved as James came to terms with his father after the latter's death; then he gradually turned away from science and toward philosophy, which had attracted him so strongly when he was a young man.

William James and the Twice-Born Sick Soul
Cushing Strout

. . . James's own struggle for forming a personal identity and finding his proper vocation was acute. His growth to greatness was precarious and painful, vulnerable to chronic debility, depression, and distress. James's theory of the great man has one conspicuous weakness: It does not cover himself. There is more to the great man than favorable social conditions, the spontaneous variations of genetics, or what James called the "seething caldron of ideas" in the "highest order of minds." He believed that the "genesis [of ideas] is sudden and, as it were, spontaneous," but 'ne history of his own development is a refutation of any such sudden spontaneity. Spontaneity was in his case a hard-won achievement of a personality threatened by imminent disorganization. What James needed to round out his theory of the great man was an ordered way of talking about the inner history of the great man's relation to himself and to the significant others in his family.

In this sense, the great man is made, in part, by that intimate society, filled with resounding echoes of the world in the significant speech, gesture, and silence of parents and siblings, which he in turn remakes by his appearance in it. If he is truly great, he conspires with circumstance to turn his private conflicts into public issues with relevance for others. He learns to speak not only to his family and his society but, in principle, to all men. Paradoxically, he might even learn to speak to all men just because on certain matters he cannot speak openly to his family. The sign of that inability would be a kind of sickness, a bafflement of development, referring to the unspeakable. For such individuals, as Erik H. Erikson has taught us in *Young Man Luther,* the identity crisis of early manhood may be a period in which endangered youths, "although suffering and deviating dangerously through what appears to be a prolonged adolescence, eventually come to contribute an original bit to an emerging

---

[12]Strout, "Ego Psychology and the Historian," p. 285. This article describes and explains the writing of the following essay. Erikson also found William James to be the victim of identity confusion. His discussion is found in *Identity, Youth and Crisis,* pp. 150–55, 204–207.

Cushing Strout, "William James and the Twice-Born Sick Soul," *Daedalus* 97 (Summer 1968), 1063–1074, 1076–1077, abridged, notes deleted. Copyright © 1968 by the American Academy of Arts and Sciences. Reprinted by permission of *Daedalus,* Journal of the American Academy of Arts and Sciences, Boston, Massachusetts. Summer 1968, *Philosophers and Kings: Studies in Leadership.*

style of life: the very danger which they have sensed has forced them to mobilize capacities to see and say, to dream and plan, to design and construct, in new ways.'' Erickson suggests that ''born leaders seem to fear only more consciously what in some form everybody fears in the depths of his inner life; and they convincingly claim to have an answer.'' The conscious fear that James grappled with was the apprehension that scientific determinism, what he called ''medical materialism,'' would leave no meaningful space for the human will. That fear was closely connected with his fears as a member of the James family. I propose to analyze that linkage in narrative form, trying to do justice to the relevant claims of psychoanalysis, history, and philosophy. . . .

William James first decided to become a painter. As a boy he had shown a spontaneous interest in drawing, and with his first real youthful friend shared a hope of becoming an artist. Unfortunately, in 1859 his father whisked young William off to Europe, away from his friend and from William Morris Hunt's studio at Newport. The father explained to a friend:

> Newport did not give the boys what they required exactly, and we didn't relish their separation from us. Willy especially felt, we thought, a little too much attraction to painting—as I suppose from the contiguity to Mr. Hunt; let us break that up, we said, at all events. I hoped that his career would be a scientific one . . . and to give up this hope without a struggle, and allow him to tumble down into a mere painter, was impossible.

In the end, the elder James relented because his son pleaded, very respectfully and humbly, that his life ''would be embittered'' if he were not allowed to try painting. The father need not have worried; the son himself echoed his father's judgment by declaring before entering Hunt's studio: ''There is nothing on earth more deplorable than a bad artist.'' For a conscientious boy who much admired his father, this venture in vocation must have engendered a bad conscience. Within the year he had abandoned art school though he kept up his drawing for several years. In 1872, he was to confess that he ''regretted extremely'' letting it die out. Meanwhile, the Civil War was a call to action, and in 1861 both William and Henry sought to enlist in the Union Army. Once again their father had other plans: ''I have had a firm grasp upon the coat tails of my Willy and Harry, who both vituperate me beyond measure because I won't let them go.'' Both boys soon developed illnesses that incapacitated them for service anyway, and it was the younger brothers, Wilkinson and Robinson, the forgotten Jameses, who with father's blessing joined the army.

In 1861, William dutifully gave his father a plan of his future life: to study chemistry, anatomy, and medicine as preparation for spending several years with Louis Agassiz in natural history. The plan was shaped to his father's hopes for him. That fall William entered the Lawrence Scientific School in Cambridge as a student of chemistry. ''Relentless Chemistry claims its hapless victim,'' he wryly wrote to a friend. As his teacher later recalled, nervous illness began to interfere with his work at this point.

In 1863, he entered medical school where Jeffries Wyman taught, a man for whom James had a "a filial feeling," perhaps because Wyman was also an excellent draftsman. The next year, under the spell of the "godlike" charm of Louis Agassiz, William went to Brazil as part of an exploring and collecting expedition. There he caught varioloid, a mild form of smallpox, and spent over two despondent weeks in the hospital, resting his eyes and rethinking his future. His experience convinced him that he hated collecting and was "cut out for a speculative rather than an active life." Having recovered the use of his eyes and having lost his respect for Agassiz's pretensions to omniscience, he joyfully returned home with a new resolution: "When I get home I'm going to study philosophy all my days."

Privately James read philosophy voraciously, but publicly he resumed his medical studies and undertook a brief internship at the Massachusetts General Hospital. His comments on the medical profession, excepting surgery, were always contemptuous, convicting it of "much humbug." Nevertheless, his disenchantment with Agassiz and natural history forced him to consider medicine as a possible career unless he were to abandon the scientific bent of his education. In retrospect, the Brazil expedition gave him a "feeling of loneliness and intellectual and moral deadness." In the fall and winter of 1866, he complained of digestive disorders, eye troubles, acute depression, and weakness of the back. His symptoms are characteristic of hypochondriasis, and in psychosomatic illness unconscious imitation often plays a part in the selection of discomforts. He revived those symptoms which he had felt in Brazil, and he now also spoke, in revealing language, of a "delightful disease" in the back "which has so long made Harry so interesting." Henry had developed this symptom from a trival accident incurred while he was trying to put out a fire in 1861. When his father was thirteen, he had sustained under similar circumstances an injury that led to a leg amputation and two years in bed. William's back and eye trouble provided him with an excuse for not practicing medicine. Shortly before taking his exams for the medical degree in 1869, he wrote his brother: "I am perfectly contented that the power which gave me these faculties should recall them partially or totally when and in what order it sees fit. I don't think I should give a single damn now if I were struck blind." In the winter of 1866, he felt himself on the "continual verge of suicide" and sometime during these years he was paralyzed in panic fear by the image of a greenish, withdrawn epileptic idiot whom he had seen in an asylum. *"That shape am I,* I felt, potentially," he confessed, and for months he dreaded being alone in the dark.

What did this paralyzing recollection mean? As a medical student he might easily have read the well-known work by the English doctor William Acton, *The Functions and Disorders of the Reproductive Organs.* Steven Marcus has pointed out in *The Other Victorians* that Acton's book is a classic statement of Victorian attitudes toward sex; indeed, one of Acton's themes is the moral need to break willfully the habit of introspection in order to ward off the temptation of masturbation, luridly imagined as a threat to sanity. Acton points up his moral by a description of inmates of an insane asylum: "The pale complexion, the emaciated form, the slouching gait, the clammy palm, the glassy or leaden eye, and the averted gaze, indicate the lunatic victim to this vice.'' This image resembles James's memory of the epileptic patient, and in the late 1860's he was unsuccessfully courting Fanny Dixwell, whom his friend Oliver Wendell Holmes, Jr., married in 1872. James was thirty-six when he married, and no doubt sexual frustration had plagued him, but his vocational problem persisted after 1878. That hideous figure, we may speculate, objectified not only the self-punishing guilt in his own symptoms, but also his fear of being trapped in a medical career which seemed to be his only option after his disillusionment with natural history. Neither Wyman nor Agassiz had shaken his belief that his father was, as James had written in Brazil, ''the *wisest* of all men'' he had ever known. And his father was a metaphysician—not a physician.

James defined his dilemma to a despondent friend: ''I am about as little fitted by nature to be a worker in science of any sort as anyone can be, and yet . . . my only ideal of life is a scientific life.'' His whole program, outlined to his father in 1861, had collapsed along with his health and spirits. In submitting his prospectus, he had prophesied wryly that the last stage would be ''death, death, death with inflation and plethora of knowledge.'' That jest had come symbolically true, as if he had unconsciously feared the worst in the pursuit of his scientific career. In 1867 he sailed for Europe, which served him as a psychic moratorium from commitment. Subjecting himself to the tortures of the baths and galvanic remedies, he felt ashamed not to be earning money like his brothers. He found solace in the theater, art galleries, music, novels, and glimpses of pretty *frauleins,* while he read philosophy and dutifully attended university lectures on physiology. After passing his medical exams for the degree in 1869, he wrote a sketch of his philosophical gropings which put his own pain at the center of things: ''Three quantities to determine. (1) how much pain I'll stand; (2) how much other's pain I'll inflict (by existing); (3) how much other's pain I'll 'accept,' without ceasing to take pleasure in their existence.'' To a friend he confessed: ''I am poisoned with Utilitarian venom, and sometimes when I despair of ever doing anything, say: Why not step out into the green darkness?' '' Similarly greenish in hue was his image of the idiotic, epileptic patient, huddled in the corner of his cell. To stick to his chosen path would be, in short, a kind of suicide. He could not find himself in medicine nor the acting self in medical materialism's picture of the world.

By 1872 James had discovered a desperately needed sense of initiative in the French philosopher Renouvier's arguments for free will. He also passed up an opportunity ''to strike at Harvard College'' for a subprofessorship of philosophy, accepting instead an appointment there to teach physiology. ''Philosophy I will nevertheless regard as my vocation and never let slip a chance to do a stroke at it,'' he confided to his diary. Reluctant to accept a reappointment in physiology because he had such ''arrears of lost time'' in ''the line of mental science,'' he nevertheless acquiesced on psychological grounds: ''Philosophy as a *business* is not normal for most men, and not for me.'' Philosophic doubt was too unnerving because he was not yet prepared to make that much of a bid for autonomy: ''My strongest moral and intellectual craving,'' he confessed, "is for some stable reality to lean upon." In 1874, thirteen years after the onset of his psychosomatic troubles, his mother complained: "Whenever he speaks of himself he says he is no better. This I cannot believe to be the true state of the case, but his temperament is a morbidly hopeless one, and with this he has to contend all the time, as well as with his physical disability."

In the year of his marriage in 1878 he signed a contract to write the *Principles of Psychology*. He spent twelve years on the book, delivering it at last like a man relieved of a kidney stone. "Seriously," he wrote an admiring reader, "your determination to read that fatal book is the one flaw in an otherwise noble nature. I wish that I had never written it." As Perry notes, "he never afterwards produced any considerable article or book on the standard problems of psychology." Not until the late-1890's, however, did he cut himself free of the laboratory work which he had always disliked; he advised a fellow-sufferer to study philosophy with a good conscience because the best thing a man can work at "is usually the thing he does most spontaneously." Not until 1899 could he write:

> I have surrended all psychological teaching to Munsterberg and his assistant and the thought of psycho-physical experimentation and altogether of brass-instrument and algebraic formula psychology fills me with horror. All my future activity will probably be metaphysical—that is, if I have any future activity, which I sometimes doubt. The Gifford Lectures . . . are a fine opportunity were I only able to meet it.

At the age of fifty-seven James was at last prepared, with some trepidation, to give his full attention to those philosophical issues which had defined his ambition at the age of twenty-three. Suffering from a valvular lesion of the heart, he then spent six years trying to resign from Harvard. Four years after his resignation he died, convinced that his philosophy was "too much like an arch built only on one side." Nearly all his major philosophical work, as Perry points out, began when he thought his professional career was finished.

The basic clue to understanding James's search for a vocation is provided by Erikson's remark in *Young Man Luther* that it is usually a parent, who has "selected this one child, because of an inner affinity paired with an insurmountable outer distance, as the particular child who must *justify the parent*," that by an "all-pervasive presence and brutal decisiveness of judgment" precipitates the child into "a fatal struggle for his own identity." If in contemporary America that parent would usually be the mother, in Victorian America it would have been the father. It is significant that James's vivid memory of the shape in the asylum closely resembles a similar experience his father suffered in 1844 when he felt "an insane and abject terror" before "some damned shape squatting invisible" to him within his room "and raying out from his fetid personality influences fatal to life." Henry James, senior, had written Emerson one or two years earlier to seek help:

> What shall I do? Shall I get me a little nook in the country and communicate with my *living* kind, not my talking kind—by life only—a word, may be, of *that* communication, a fit word, once a year? Or shall I follow some commoner method, learn science and bring myself first into men's respect, that thus I may the better speak to them? I confess this last theory seems rank with earthliness—to belong to days forever past.

Son of a rich Calvinist merchant, William's father had been cut off without a legacy because of his worldly tastes and heretical opinions. He had temporarily fled college to work as a proofreader, made an abortive attempt to please his father by studing law, and revolted against the Presbyterian orthodoxy of Princeton Theological Seminary to become an original, if obscure and eccentric, theologian. Having broken his father's will, he was able by his inheritance to devote himself entirely to his writings and to his remarkable family, whom he shuttled constantly about in America and Europe. In 1846 he was rescued from the "endless task of conciliating a stony-hearted Deity"—*his* father's Calvanist God—by a conversion to Swedenborg, as William would be rescued from propitiating the deterministic god of medical materialism by conversion to the philosophy of Renouvier and the idea of free will.

"The children were constantly with their parents and with each other," as William's son later described his father's childhood, "and they continued all their lives to be united by much stronger attachments than usually exist between members of one family." The elder James refused to send his sons to college out of contempt for a gentleman's conventional education. Depositing them briefly with a succession of instructors, he involved his sons mainly with his own spirited intellectual and moral reactions to the world. In his eldest son he must have seen an opportunity to realize his own forsaken alternative of trying to "learn science" and bring himself "into men's respect." A visionary advocate of freedom and spontaneous love, he was also a fierce polemicist. In the family circle as with strangers, the elder James spoke his mind with trenchant, witty, and brusque decisiveness. "What a passion your father has in writing and talking his religion!" exclaimed Oliver Wendell Holmes, Jr., a toughminded skeptic. "Almost he persuadeth me to be a Swedenborgian." For William, his father was a vivid, perpetual presence. After his father's death in 1882, the forty-year-old son made a significant confession:

> It is singular how I'm learning every day now how the thought of his comment on my experience has hitherto formed an integral part of my daily consciousness, without my having realized it at all. I interrupt myself incessantly now in the old habit of imagining what he will say when I tell him this or that thing I have seen or heard.

His father was still an inner court of tribunal for him long after that is normally the case.

In this family it was easy for William to resolve his feelings and thoughts about his father because his mother had a soft spot for Henry, who was known in the family as "the Angel." Father himself, after his wife's death in 1881, felt that he had "fallen heir to all dear mother's fondness'' for Henry, who had "cost us the least trouble, and given us always the most delight.'' William, the oldest brother, had reason to be envious of Henry, who first achieved literary fame and financial independence. William's ''hypochondriacal condition''—as his family called it—involved a set of highly charged elements: his career choice, his attraction to philosophy, but fear of embracing it; his dislike of practical scientific work, whether as collector, medical student, or laboratory psychologist; and his need to become financially independent. His father was closely linked to all these issues, and because Henry was obviously the mother's favorite, it was especially important for William to feel that he was in good standing with his father.

The sickness in this family gives deeper meaning to Perry's innocent remark about the James household that "the region of family life was not empty, but was charged with palpable and active forces.'' There is a strong hint of suppressed hostility in Alice James's confession that in her hysteria she sometimes felt "a violent inclination'' to throw herself out of the window or "knock . . . off the head of the benignant Pater, as he sat, with his silver locks, writing at the table.'' The same point could be made of the benign father's remark to Emerson that he "wished sometimes the lightning would strike his wife and children out of existence, and he should suffer no more from loving them.'' As the head of a religion with only one member, the father's life had something of the smell of futility about it, and his son felt uneasy about the prophet's role. "Certainly there is something disheartening in the position of an esoteric philosopher,'' he wrote in a letter he did not want shown to his father. Although he followed his father's wish for a scientific career, the son could not but be aware that his father believed that science was ultimately inferior to metaphysics and religion. During his depressed years in Europe, he received from his father a nineteen-page letter of ontological speculation which boasted: "I am sure I have something better to tell you than you will be able to learn from all Germany—at least all scientific Germany. So urge me hard to your own profit.'' Ambivalently attracted and repelled by both science and philosophy—an ambivalence connected with his feelings about his father's wishes, attitudes, and example—the son found his path hard to see clearly. He could not follow both his father's example and his advice—yet he tried to do both. The "sicker'' he became, the more guilt he felt for prolonging his financial dependence. In his worst years, he made himself a pathetic parody of his father—a crippled philosopher without a job. "The crisis in such a young man's life,'' as Erikson has noted, "may be reached exactly when he half-realizes that he is fatally overcommitted to what he is not.'' James made that discovery in medical school.

These emotional issues were linked to intellectual conflicts, for young men need ideological convictions to support their growing identity. During his period of invalidism, William wrote his brother Henry that their father was "a religious genius,'' but unfortunately his "absence of *intellectual* sympathies of any sort'' made it hard to respond to "the positive side of him.'' William James found himself in late adolescence "tending strongly to an empiristic view of life.'' Unlike his father, he was willing to believe that "God is dead or at least irrelevant, ditto everything pertaining to the 'Beyond,' " but the consequences left him full of doubt. The problem was "to get at something absolute without going out of your own skin!" During his depression years, he was "going slowly" through his father's books; though he was impressed with their "definite residuum" of "great and original ideas," he could not find in them an explanation of his own torments. "For what purpose we are thus tormented I know not," he wrote his suffering brother in 1869. "I don't see that Father's philosophy explains it any more than anyone else's." He could not bring himself into so much sympathy "with the total process of the universe as heartily to assent to the evil that seems inherent in its details." He refused to "blink the evil out of sight, and gloss it over. It's as real as the good, and if it is denied, good must be denied too. It must be accepted and hated, and resisted while there's breath in our bodies." Like his father's peculiar blend of Swedenborg and Calvin, scientific determinism seemed to make these evils inevitable too—on physiological grounds. In April 1870, he finished reading Renouvier's essay on freedom and made his first act of positive belief: "My first act of free will shall be to believe in free will."

James found a solution to the problem of determinism by sustaining a thought "*because I choose to* when I might have other thoughts." If he could not yet choose his vocation, he could validate choice in principle, and that freedom was enough to defend the moral power to fight evil. Erikson has relevantly observed that an aggravated identity crisis tends to generate a state of mind in which actual commitment is minimized, while an inner feeling of retaining the power of decision is maximized; at such a time, a person attempts to rebuild the shaky identifications of childhood, as if he wanted to be born again. The general problem of determinism for William gained personal force from its association with his medical-scientific training and his need to find autonomy as a person. This issue was also intimately related to his involvement with his father. In his diary for 1868 the son noted: "My old trouble and the root of antinomianism in general seems to be a dissatisfaction with anything less than grace." He acknowledged that his antinomian tendency was partly derived from the example of his father, who always made "moralism the target of his hottest attack, and pitted religion and it against each other as enemies of whom one must die utterly, if the other is to live in genuine form." The elder James routinely condemned moralists as prigs who believed that their good works entitled them to salvation. His "amiable ferocity was," as Perry well puts it, "an exercise in contempt for selfhood, on his own part and in behalf of others." This contempt was an unrecognized threat to a conscientious boy struggling to find his own sense of self and to be responsive to his father's attitudes. The elder James believed that men fell from grace individually, but could be saved collectively in a redeemed socialized society. His son, however, needed an individual salvation not only through faith, but also in works. To translate this theological idiom, he needed to believe that there was point and purpose to some particular work of his own with social meaning. He would finally save himself through his writing, finding courage in Carlyle's gospel of work, forgetting complaint and rapture alike in "the vision of certain works to be done . . . for the leaving of them undone is perdition." To his father's antinomianism, he would oppose an Arminian emphasis on work, a moral equivalent for "the strenuous life" idealized in his period by Roosevelt, Holmes, and the naturalistic novelists London, Norris, and Dreiser.

The connection between the intellectual and emotional development of William James can be followed in the growth of his work and the betterment of his health, as he successfully, but slowly came to terms with his father's teachings and example. Four days before his father died in 1882, the son wrote him from Europe: "All my intellectual life I derive from you. . . . What my debt to you is goes beyond all my power of estimating—so early, so penetrating and so constant has been the influence." And he concluded this great and touching letter with final benediction: "Good-night, my sacred old Father! If I don't see you again—Farewell! a blessed farewell!" At the age of forty, the son would also very slowly bid farewell to his scientific career and gradually move from psychology toward those deep interests he shared with his father in religion and metaphysics. As he abandoned his image of himself as a scientist, he learned to yield to his spontaneous interest in philosophy, which had been born in his crisis of health and career in Brazil. He would increasingly see himself as well enough in body and strong enough in ego to become a philosopher by vocation, assimilating and rejecting aspects of his father's personality in a new configuration. . . .

Having settled his intellectual accounts with his father, he was now prepared to devote himself to philosophy, writing freely "without feeling in the least degree fatigued." But he had only a few years left. "I live in apprehension lest the Avenger should cut me off," he wrote in 1906, "before I get my message out. It is an aesthetic tragedy to have a bridge begun and stopped in the middle of an arch." James died with his "somewhat systematic" book unfinished. He had been able to assure Royce in 1877 that "a young man might rightfully devote himself to philosophy if he chose," an assurance James found so very difficult to achieve for himself. From a psychoanalytic point of view, the resolution of critical emotional issues in infancy "will determine whether an individual is apt to be dominated by a sense of autonomy, or by a sense of shame and doubt," and the way in which adults meet the child's shame and doubt "determines much of a man's future ability to combine an unimpaired will with ready self-discipline, rebellion with responsiblity." Significantly, the father's crisis happened when the son was two years old, struggling to form his first sense of will. His later development illustrates the psychoanalytic point that "the neurotic ego has, by definition, fallen prey to overidentification and to faulty identifications with disturbed parents." The historian must add that while the elder Henry James had made the son's struggle for identity particularly difficult, he had also made the resolution of that struggle particularly fruitful. His influence largely determined the kinds of problems that would be central for his son's intellectual development. That influence delayed the son's maturity, but it also enriched it by giving him that double focus on science and religion and that note of authenticity in dealing with the issues of freedom and determinism which stamped his work as vividly original. The father must also have engendered the son's charming tolerance of cranks and vigorous scorn for prigs of all kinds. William James had selectively assimilated and rejected what his father meant to him in a struggle of fifty years' duration. . . .

chapter seven

Role Theory, Significant Others, and Analogy

Few historians have made more striking use of personality theory than has Stanley Elkins. Using role psychology and the interpersonal theory of Harry Stack Sullivan, Elkins attempted to offer an explanation for the "Sambo stereotype" that so pervades contemporary accounts of the American slave system. "The typical plantation slave," wrote Elkins, "was docile but irresponsible, loyal but lazy, humble but chronically given to lying and stealing; his behavior was full of infantile silliness and his talk inflated with childish exaggeration. His relationship with his master was one of utter dependence and childlike attachment."[1] Acting on the assumption that slaves existed who actually filled this stereotyped role, Elkins sought the reasons for such behavior. His explanation was that personality can be molded so as to force individuals to behave in childish ways; to prove the point he drew an analogy between the plantation and the Nazi concentration camp. Like slaves, camp inmates did not rebel and they often lacked hatred of their captors; sometimes they even imitated the ways of the SS guards. How is this to be explained?

Elkins turned to the theories of Harry Stack Sullivan, a psychiatrist who thought his discipline overlapped that of the social psychologist. To Sullivan, the study of interpersonal relations called for the use of field theory, meaning "that which can be studied is the pattern of processes which characterize the interaction of personalities in particular recurrent situations or fields which 'include' the observer."[2] Since any single personality is part of the interaction of many personalities, one can only study this interaction. Individuals really do not exist alone, nor is their behavior created in a vacuum. Accordingly, interpersonal theory attempts to isolate the crucial determinant of human behavior—the way in which other people want an individual to behave.

These people are *significant others*, that is, their expectations are important enough to induce behavior. Parents expect children not to spill their milk, and usually the

---

[1]Stanley M. Elkins, *Slavery: A Problem in American Institutional and Intellectual Life,* 3rd ed. rev. (Chicago: The University of Chicago Press, 1976), p. 82.
[2]Harry Stack Sullivan, *The Interpersonal Theory of Psychiatry* (New York: W. W. Norton and Co., 1953), p. 368.

children do not. The master probably expected slaves to be docile and lazy (though he hoped the latter would not be true); therefore, implies Elkins, they were docile and lazy. For the infant, thought Sullivan, the mother is the significant other who counts most. As children grow, they develop a "self system" or "self dynamism," which (along with the tension and anxiety generated by fear of parental disapproval and punishment) guides their conduct. It is not events but people that matter.[3]

Role psychology, as Elkins indicates, supplements the theory of significant others. Individuals' behavior tends to be a compromise among the many roles that those powerful enough or significant enough to affect their lives wish them to play. Roles help people know what others expect of them; they mediate between individuals and the groups they confront. They inform people of the demands and taboos to which they are expected to conform; in turn demands and taboos assure them that if they follow those roles the behavior of others toward them will be reasonably predictable. In short, there is a kind of security in knowing one's place and acting accordingly, even if that place be prisoner or slave. The roles are not created by individuals; roles are imposed on them, although they may have the opportunity to manipulate others' expectations and thus vary their roles. But if manipulation fails individuals have no choice. They must bend or break; failing to play the prescribed role, they must expect to be eliminated from the group. On the plantation or in the concentration camp, says Elkins, this could mean death.

Confusion is added by the fact that people play multiple roles. Each significant other, to use Sullivan's term, might have a different expectation of one's behavior and these expectations may be in conflict. Thus the slave may actually have had to play the cooperative companion for fellow slaves, the irresponsible but capable field hand for the overseer, the husband for his mate, and the happy, irresponsible, docile Sambo for the master.[4]

Another technique Elkins employs in this selection is analogy, which is an examination of one object or area with a view toward learning more about another. It is, says Elkins, "a kind of extended metaphor. It brings together two situations, each of which—however dissimilar they may be otherwise—contains mechanisms that are

---

[3]Harry Stack Sullivan, *Conceptions of Modern Psychiatry,* 2nd ed. (New York: W. W. Norton and Co., 1953), especially pp. 16–29, 46, 77. Even if an individual commits suicide, it "is to be understood on the basis not of the particular 'objective' events which bring about the circumstance . . . ; it is to be understood on the basis of the experience which is the foundation of the self system, the organization of experience reflected to one from the significant people around one—which determines the personal characteristics of those events" (p. 24). See also Sol L. Garfield, *Clinical Psychology: The Study of Personality and Behavior* (Chicago: Aldine Publishing Company, 1974), pp. 42–43; and Calvin S. Hall and Gardner Lindzey, *Theories of Personality,* 2nd ed. (New York: Wiley, 1970), pp. 137–57.

[4]For general discussion of role psychology, see Eugene L. Hartley and Ruth E. Hartley, *Fundamentals of Social Psychology* (New York: Alfred A. Knopf, 1961), Chapters XVI (cited by Elkins) and XVII, especially pp. 518–35.

metaphorically comparable and analytically interchangeable."[5] Elkins uses a literal analogy when he points out the similarities between the plantation and the concentration camp, examines the dynamics of personality change among camp prisoners, and suggests that similar dynamics operated on the slave to produce the infantile behavior that was supposed to be characteristic of the Sambo personality.[6]

Because he did not find the Sambo stereotype in Latin American slavery, Elkins concluded that it must have been created by something unique in the American experience. Using some of the studies by and of former German concentration camp prisoners, which showed "that infantile personality features could be induced in a relatively short time among large numbers of adult human beings coming from very diverse backgrounds," he proceeded to study the problem of adjustment to absolute power, such as that held by the slave owner or camp guard.[7] This analogy implied that the same mechanism that produced a docile prisoner could produce a docile slave.

When originally published, in 1959, Elkins' *Slavery* was received with misgivings. The contention that, because of the way in which slavery damaged personality development, Sambo might actually have existed brought an initial censure that has been repeated frequently in the years since. For example, historian Harvey Wish liked the interdisciplinary approach but thought it doubtful that Sambo existed. The average slave was more likely to be rebellious than Elkins thought, for minority groups have had to learn to adapt to the expectations of the majority with which they are associated.[8] Wish believed that the docile appearance was a façade created by slaves to appease their masters. This is the crux of the argument and a major point that must determine the reader's acceptance or rejection of Elkins' thesis of the applicability of role theory. Granted there were roles; were they adopted consciously to mask conscious attitudes? Or were they adopted unconsciously (i.e., internalized) so that the victims cooperated in the molding of their personalities without being fully aware of what they were doing? Was the role a case of dissembling or was it a genuine acceptance of imposed standards of behavior?

To social psychologist Robert A. Gordon the argument about the Sambo stereotype was both convincing and restrained, and he thought the parallel between the behavioral evidence and the historical evidence was astonishing. Adopting sociologist Robert K. Merton's concept of the status-set,[9] Gordon suggested that it may affect personality.

---

[5]Elkins, *Slavery*, p. 305.

[6]Historian Robin W. Winks calls this "the single best example of arguing by analogy yet seen in American historiography." Winks, ed., *The Historian As Detective: Essays on Evidence* (New York: Harper & Row, 1969), p. 492.

[7]Elkins, *Slavery*, pp. 82–89. Quote is from p. 88.

[8]Review by Harvey Wish in the *Mississippi Valley Historical Review* 47 (September 1960):319–20.

[9]Robert K. Merton, *Social Theory and Social Structure*, 3rd ed. (New York: The Free Press, 1968), pp. 423–24, 434–35. The "status-set" is simply the complex of various statuses of a given individual, which, because everyone does not have the same status-set, provides a "basic form of interdependence between the institutions and subsystems of a society" (p. 435).

"Confinement from birth within a narrow status-set," for example, "restricts opportunities to learn and canalizes gratification toward residual sources which are likely to be infantile."[10] Shorn of jargon, this means simply that if children do not have the opportunity to learn adolescent or adult behaviors, they will continue to behave as children.

Elkins apparently did not expect his analogy to be received without criticism, judging from the somewhat defensive manner in which it is presented, and his expectation was certainly justified. In the first place, he seems to have assumed that Sambo was the dominant personality type among slaves. But if the Sambo role had been internalized, wrote Mary Agnes Lewis, then the cruel punishments used against recalcitrant slaves would not have been necessary at all;[11] if Sambo were real, the underlying theme of brutality in slavery would not have been present and the camp analogy would be irrelevant.

Perhaps the most effective attack on the concentration camp parallel was that the institutions under study were too dissimilar, primarily in the degree to which they were closed systems. Here Elkins may have been the captive of his technique, for the differences between concentration camp and plantation may be so great that they prohibit meaningful comparison. That slavery was highly oppressive is not contradicted; but restricted as it was, the institution provided more elbow room to its victims than the Nazi camp provided for its prisoners. Sambo, says Earl E. Thorpe, was merely "the side of his personality which the Negro chose to present to the white man," for "most bondsmen never internalized many of the planters' values." Furthermore, in the camp hard work was the prerequisite for avoiding the gas chamber, yet many a slave temporarily avoided his assigned tasks by feigning illness or running away—forms of resistance that would have meant instant death in the Nazi system. Thorpe reminds the reader that slave women nursed white children, that slaves produced music of great beauty, and that at the moment of ultimate defeat in 1865, the Confederacy proposed to arm its slaves—hardly things the Nazis did with their camp inmates.[12]

The best refutation of the closed-system analogy was that of George M. Fredrickson and Christopher Lasch, who not only denied the applicability of the concentration

---

[10]Robert A. Gordon, "Slavery and the Comparative Study of Social Structure," *American Journal of Sociology* 66 (September 1960):184–86. See also the review by Arnold A. Sio in the *American Sociological Review* 25 (October 1960):757–59. Sio also has no apparent quarrel with Elkins' use of the various theories of personality.

[11]Mary Agnes Lewis, "Slavery and Personality," in Ann J. Lane, ed., *The Debate Over Slavery: Stanley Elkins and His Critics* (Urbana: University of Illinois Press, 1971), p. 81. Many of these and other criticisms actually fall into two categories of argument. Elkins himself, as he indicates in the third edition of *Slavery* (Chapter VI), emphasized the damage done to black personality. Other arguments, which are implied criticisms of Elkins, underline the positive achievements of slave resistance and black culture.

[12]Earl E. Thorpe, "Chattel Slavery and Concentration Camps," in Lane, *Debate Over Slavery*, pp. 27, 37–40.

camp parallel but substituted one of their own. Expressly underlining the necessity of this device in order to comprehend the meaning of slavery, the authors proposed instead the analogy of the penitentiary. Like the slave system, the penitentiary does not allow absolute authority to guards and in both the functioning of the system depends on rewards, punishments, and compromises.[13]

The controversy continues; indeed there have been few more controversial books published in American history in the last generation. Though attacked by many leading historians, it has been the focal point of numerous discussions of slavery since its original publication. Perhaps the major attraction that historians had, and still have, for *Slavery* is its interdisciplinary methodology. Subject to extreme criticism, Elkins' book must nevertheless be counted a success—in spite of scholarship which has successfully disputed Elkins on a number of points. Eugene D. Genovese, one of Elkins' most severe and knowledgeable critics, acknowledged that Elkins had "raised the study of Southern slavery to a far higher level than ever before . . . at a moment when the subject seemed about to be drowned in a sea of moral indignation." Elkins also illustrated the use of psychology in history and this, thinks Genovese, was one of his greatest accomplishments. Even so, Genovese distrusts Elkins' psychology. He thinks the theory of significant others is misapplied because Elkins overestimated the amount of power the master possessed, and points out that the overseer, the master's wife, and other slaves also affected a slave's behavior.[14]

Elkins' arguments are indeed open to criticism but his methods are nevertheless imaginative and potentially useful tools of interpretation for other historians. For instance, John W. Blassingame included the theories Elkins used—theories of role and significant others—in his own study of slavery; he came to different conclusions, believing that Sambo was only one of the personality types found among slaves.[15] These interdisciplinary techniques might be applied to other historical situations as well. No doubt role theory might facilitate understanding of certain phases of nineteenth-century labor relations while the concept of significant others surely should be applied to the study of childhood and the family in the historical context—and, of course, both phenomena operate among us and our contemporaries today, helping to shape our daily lives and future history just as they molded the actions of the historical figures we may study.

---

[13]George M. Fredrickson and Christopher Lasch, "Resistance to Slavery," ibid., pp. 223–44. Elkins himself admits this to be one of the most instructive suggestions he has received. See Elkins, *Slavery,* p. 246.

[14]Eugene D. Genovese, "Rebelliousness and Docility in the Negro Slave: A Critique of the Elkins Thesis," in Lane, *Debate Over Slavery,* pp. 73, 66–67.

[15]John W. Blassingame, *The Slave Community: Plantation Life in the Antebellum South* (New York: Oxford University Press, 1972). For comparison of Elkins and Blassingame, see William Issel, "History, Social Science, and Ideology: Elkins and Blassingame on Ante-Bellum American Slavery," *The History Teacher* 9 (November 1975):56–72.

This selection attempts to explain the behavior of the victims of concentration camp and plantation. The "first theory" examined is that of Freud, which Elkins thinks insufficient and which has been deleted from this presentation. The author then turns to Sullivan's interpersonal theory, the "second theoretical scheme" of personality mentioned on p. 119. Elkins suggests how the expectations of the concentration camp SS guards might have induced certain behavior patterns, or roles, among prisoners (this may be nothing more than common sense; people who hold guns automatically become significant others). Significant others and role psychology are obviously far less philosophical and more behavioral than the Freudian or Eriksonian theories discussed earlier. Yet it is interesting to note that Cushing Strout, in his Eriksonian discussion of William James, also referred to significant others (p. 99).

As the selection begins, Elkins has just observed that "something very profound" would be required to destroy an individual's cultural attachments and thereby produce "a society of helpless dependents" such as that alleged to have existed on the plantation.[16]

Slavery and Personality
Stanley M. Elkins

. . . We may suppose that every African who became a slave underwent an experience whose crude psychic impact must have been staggering and whose consequences superseded anything that had ever previously happened to him. Some effort should therefore be made to picture the series of shocks which must have accompanied the principal events of that enslavement.

The majority of slaves appear to have been taken in native wars, which meant that no one—neither persons of high rank nor warriors of prowess—was guaranteed against capture and enslavement. Great numbers were caught in surprise attacks upon their villages, and since the tribes acting as middlemen for the trade had come to depend on regular supplies of captives in order to maintain that function, the distinction between wars and raiding expeditions tended to be very dim. The first shock, in an experience destined to endure many months and to leave its survivors irrevocably changed, was thus the shock of capture. It is an effort to remember that while enslavement occurred in Africa every day, to the individual it occurred just once.

The second shock—the long march to the sea—drew out the nightmare for many weeks. Under the glaring sun, through the steaming jungle, they were driven along like

[16]Elkins, *Slavery*, p. 98.

Stanley M. Elkins, *Slavery: A Problem in American Institutional and Intellectual Life*, 3rd ed., rev. (Chicago: The University of Chicago Press, 1976) pp. 98–102, 104–108, 111–113, 119–120, 122–123, 125–126, 128–130.© 1959, 1968, 1976 by The University of Chicago. All rights reserved. Third Edition Published 1976 by The University of Chicago Press. Reprinted with deletion of notes and abridgment by permission of The University of Chicago Press and the author.

beasts tied together by their necks; day after day, eight or more hours at a time, they would stagger barefoot over thorny underbrush, dried reeds, and stones. Hardship, thirst, brutalities, and near starvation penetrated the experience of each exhausted man and woman who reached the coast. One traveler tells of seeing hundreds of bleaching skeletons strewn along one of the slave caravan routes. But then the man who must interest us is the man who survived—he who underwent the entire experience, of which this was only the beginning.

The next shock, aside from the fresh physical torments which accompanied it, was the sale to the European slavers. After being crowded into pens near the trading stations and kept there overnight, sometimes for days, the slaves were brought out for examination. Those rejected would be abandoned to starvation; the remaining ones —those who had been bought—were branded, given numbers inscribed on leaden tags, and herded on shipboard.

The episode that followed—almost too protracted and stupefying to be called a mere "shock"—was the dread Middle Passage, brutalizing to any man, black or white, ever to be involved with it. The holds, packed with squirming and suffocating humanity, became stinking infernos of filth and pestilence. Stories of disease, death, and cruelty on the terrible two-month voyage abound in the testimony which did much toward ending the British slave trade forever.

The final shock in the process of enslavement came with the Negro's introduction to the West Indies. Bryan Edwards, describing the arrival of a slave ship, writes of how in times of labor scarcity crowds of people would come scrambling aboard, manhandling the slaves and throwing them into panic. The Jamaica legislature eventually "corrected the enormity" by enacting that the sales be held on shore. Edwards felt a certain mortification at seeing the Negroes exposed naked in public, similar to that felt by the trader Degrandpré at seeing them examined back at the African factories. Yet here they did not seem to care. "They display . . . very few signs of lamentation for their past or of apprehension for their future condition; but . . . commonly express great eagerness to be sold." The "seasoning" process which followed completed the series of steps whereby the African Negro became a slave.

The mortality had been very high. One-third of the numbers first taken, out of a total of perhaps fifteen million, had died on the march and at the trading stations; another third died during the Middle Passage and the seasoning. Since a majority of the African-born slaves who came to the North American plantations did not come directly but were imported through the British West Indies, one may assume that the typical slave underwent an experience something like that just outlined. This was the man —one in three—who had come through it all and lived and was about to enter our "closed system." What would he be like if he survived and adjusted to that?

Actually, a great deal had happened to him already. Much of his past had been annihilated; nearly every prior connection had been severed. Not that he had really "forgotten" all these things—his family and kinship arrangements, his language, the tribal religion, the taboos, the name he had once borne, and so on—but none of it any longer carried much meaning. The old values, the sanctions, the standards, already unreal, could no longer furnish him guides for conduct, for adjusting to the expectations of a complete new life. Where then was he to look for new standards, new cues—who would furnish them now? He could now look to none but his master, the one man to whom the system had committed his entire being: the man upon whose will depended his food, his shelter, his sexual connections, whatever moral instruction he might be offered, whatever "success" was possible within the system, his very security—in short, everything. . . .

Introducing . . . certain elements of the German concentration-camp experience involves the risky business of trying to balance two necessities—emphasizing both the vast dissimilarities of the two regimes and the essentially limited purpose for which they are being brought together, and at the same time justifying the use of the analogy in the first place. The point is perhaps best made by insisting on an order of classification. The American plantation was not even in the metaphorical sense a "concentration camp"; nor was it even "like" a concentration camp, to the extent that any standards comparable to those governing the camps might be imputed to any sector of American society, at any time; but it should at least be permissible to turn the thing around—to speak of the concentration camp as a special and highly perverted instance of human slavery. Doing so, moreover, should actually be of some assistance in the strategy, now universally sanctioned, of demonstrating how little the products and consequences of slavery ever had to do with race. The only mass experience that Western people have had within recorded history comparable in any way with Negro slavery was undergone in the nether world of Nazism. The concentration camp was not only a perverted slave system; it was also—what is less obvious but even more to the point—a perverted patriarchy. . . .

The concentration camps and everything that took place in them were veiled in the utmost isolation and secrecy. Of course complete secrecy was impossible, and a continuing stream of rumors circulated among the population. At the same time so repellent was the nature of these stories that in their enormity they transcended the experience of nearly everyone who heard them; in self-protection it was somehow necessary to persuade oneself that they could not really be true. The results, therefore, contained elements of the diabolical. The undenied existence of the camps cast a shadow of nameless dread over the entire population; on the other hand the *individual* who actually became a prisoner in one of them was in most cases devastated with fright and utterly demoralized to discover that what was happening to *him* was not less, but rather far more terrible than anything he had imagined. The shock sequence of "procurement," therefore, together with the initial phases of the prisoner's introduction to camp life, is not without significance in assessing some of the psychic effects upon those who survived as long-term inmates.

The arrest was typically made at night, preferably late; this was standing Gestapo policy, designed to heighten the element of shock, terror, and unreality surrounding the arrest. After a day or so in the police jail came the next major shock, that of being transported to the camp itself. "This transportation into the camp, and the 'initiation' into it," writes Bruno Bettelheim (an ex-inmate of Dachau and Buchenwald), "is often the first torture which the prisoner has ever experienced and is, as a rule, physically and psychologically the worst torture to which he will ever be exposed." It involved a planned series of brutalities inflicted by guards making repeated rounds through the train over a twelve- to thirty-six hour period during which the prisoner was prevented from resting. If transported in cattle cars instead of passenger cars, the prisoners were sealed in, under conditions not dissimilar to those of the Middle Passage. Upon their arrival—if the camp was one in which mass exterminations were carried out—there might be sham ceremonies designed to reassure temporarily the exhausted prisoners, which meant that the fresh terrors in the offing would then strike them with redoubled impact. An SS officer might deliver an address, or a band might be playing popular tunes, and it would be in such a setting that the initial "selection" was made. The newcomers would file past an SS doctor who indicated, with a motion of the forefinger, whether they were to go to the left or to the right. To one side went those considered capable of heavy labor; to the other would go wide categories of "undesirables"; those in the latter group were being condemned to the gas chambers. Those who remained would undergo the formalities of "registration," full of indignities, which culminated in the marking of each prisoner with a number.

There were certain physical and psychological strains of camp life, especially debilitating in the early stages, which should be classed with the introductory shock sequence. There was a state of chronic hunger whose pressures were unusually effective in detaching prior scruples of all kinds; even the sexual instincts no longer functioned in the face of the drive for food. The man who at his pleasure could bestow or withhold food thus wielded, for that reason alone, abnormal power. Another strain at first was the demand for absolute obedience, the slightest deviation from which brought savage punishments. The prisoner had to ask permission—by no means granted as a matter of course—even to defecate. The power of the SS guard, as the prisoner was hourly reminded, was that of life and death over his body. A more exquisite form of pressure lay in the fact that the prisoner had never a moment of solitude: he no longer had a private existence; it was no longer possible, in any imaginable sense, for him to be an "individual."

Another factor having deep disintegrative effects upon the prisoner was the prospect of a limitless future in the camp. In the immediate sense this meant that he could no longer make plans for the future. But there would eventually be a subtler meaning: it made the break with the outside world a *real* break; in time the "real" life would become the life of the camp, the outside world an abstraction. Had it been a limited detention, whose end could be calculated, one's outside relationships—one's roles, one's very "personality"—might temporarily have been laid aside, to be reclaimed more or less intact at the end of the term. Here, however, the prisoner was faced with the apparent impossibility of his old roles or even his old personality ever having any future at all; it became more and more difficult to imagine himself resuming them. It was this that underlay the "egalitarianism" of the camps; old statuses had lost their meaning. A final strain, which must have been particularly acute for the newcomer, was the omnipresent threat of death and the very unpredictable suddenness with which death might strike. Quite aside from the periodic gas-chamber selections, the guards in their sports and caprices were at liberty to kill any prisoner any time. . . .

The most immediate aspect of the old inmates' behavior which struck . . . observers was its *childlike* quality. "The prisoners developed types of behavior which are characteristic of infancy or early youth. Some of these behaviors developed slowly, others were immediately imposed on the prisoners and developed only in intensity as time went on." Such infantile behavior took innumerable forms. The inmates' sexual impotence brought about a disappearance of sexuality in their talk; instead, excretory functions occupied them endlessly. They lost many of the customary inhibitions as to soiling their beds and their persons. Their humor was shot with silliness and they giggled like children when one of them would expel wind. Their relationships were highly unstable. "Prisoners would, like early adolescents, fight one another tooth and nail . . . only to become close friends within a few minutes." Dishonesty became chronic. "Now they suddenly appeared to be pathological liars, to be unable to restrain themselves, to be unable to make objective evaluation, etc." "In hundreds of ways," writes Colaço Belmonte, "the soldier, and to an even greater extent the prisoner of war, is given to understand that he is a child. . . . Then dishonesty, mendacity, egotistic actions in order to obtain more food or to get out of scrapes reach full development, and theft becomes a veritable affliction of camp life." This was all true, according to Elie Cohen, in the concentration camp as well. Benedikt Kautsky observed such things in his own behavior: "I myself can declare that often I saw myself as I used to be in my school days, when by sly dodges and clever pretexts we avoided being found out, or could 'organize' something." Bruno Bettelheim remarks on the extravagance of the stories told by the prisoners to one another. "They were boastful, telling tales about what they had accomplished in their former lives, or how they succeeded in cheating foremen or guards, and how they sabotaged the work. Like children they felt not at all set back or ashamed when it became known that they had lied about their prowess."

This development of childlike behavior in the old inmates was the counterpart of something even more striking that was happening to them: *"Only very few of the prisoners escaped a more or less intensive identification with the SS."* As Mr. Bettelheim puts it: "A prisoner had reached the final stage of adjustment to the camp situation when he had changed his personality so as to accept as his own the values of the Gestapo." The Bettelheim study furnishes a catalogue of examples. The old prisoners came to share the attitude of the SS toward the "unfit" prisoners; newcomers who behaved badly in the labor groups or who could not withstand the strain became a liability for the others, who were often instrumental in getting rid of them. Many old prisoners actually imitated the SS; they would sew and mend their uniforms in such a way as to make them look more like those of the SS—even though they risked punishment for it. "When asked why they did it, they admitted that they loved to look like . . . the guards." Some took great enjoyment in the fact that during roll call "they really had stood well at attention." There were cases of nonsensical rules, made by the guards, which the older prisoners would continue to observe and try to force on the others long after the SS had forgotten them. Even the most abstract ideals of the SS, such as their intense German nationalism and anti-Semitism, were often absorbed by the old inmates—a phenomenon observed among the politically well-educated and even among the Jews themselves. The final quintessence of all this was seen in the "Kapo"—the prisoner who had been placed in a supervisory position over his fellow inmates. These creatures, many of them professional criminals, not only behaved with slavish servility to the SS, but the way in which they often outdid the SS in sheer brutality became one of the most durable features of the concentration-camp legend.

To all these men, reduced to complete and childish dependence upon their masters, the SS had actually become a father-symbol. "The SS man was all-powerful in the camp, he was the lord and master of the prisoner's life. As a cruel father he could, without fear of punishment, even kill the prisoner and as a gentle father he could scatter largesse and afford the prisoner his protection." The result, admits Dr. Cohen, was that "for all of us the SS was a father image. . . ." The closed system, in short, had become a kind of grotesque patriarchy. . . .

A second theoretical scheme [of personality] is better prepared for crisis and more closely geared to social environment than the Freudian adaptation indicated above, and it may consequently be more suitable for accommodating not only the concentration-camp experience but also the more general problem of plantation slave personality. This is the "interpersonal theory" developed by the late Harry Stack Sullivan. One may view this body of work as the response to a peculiarly American set of needs. The system of Freud, so aptly designed for a European society the stability of whose institutional and status relationships could always to a large extent be taken for granted, turns out to be less clearly adapted to the culture of the United States. The American psychiatrist has had to deal with individuals in a culture where the diffuse, shifting, and often uncertain quality of such relationships has always been more pronounced than in Europe. He has come to appreciate the extent to which these relationships actually support the individual's psychic balance—the full extent, that is, to which the self is "social" in its nature. Thus a psychology whose terms are flexible enough to permit altering social relationships to make actual differences in character structure would be a psychology especially promising for dealing with the present problem.

Sullivan's great contribution was to offer a concept whereby the really critical determinants of personality might be isolated for purposes of observation. Out of the hopelessly immense totality of "influences" which in one way or another go to make up the personality, or "self," Sullivan designated one—the estimations and expectations of others—as the one promising to unlock the most secrets. He then made a second elimination: the *majority* of "others" in one's existence may for theoretical purposes be neglected; what counts is who the *significant* others are. Here, "significant others'' may be understood very crudely to mean those individuals who hold, or seem to hold, the keys to security in one's own personal situation, whatever its nature. Now as to the psychic processes whereby these ''significant others'' become an actual part of the personality, it may be said that the very sense of ''self'' first emerges in connection with anxiety about the attitudes of the most important persons in one's life (initially, the mother, father, and their surrogates—persons of more or less absolute authority), and automatic attempts are set in motion to adjust to these attitudes. In this way their approval, their disapproval, their estimates and appraisals, and indeed a whole range of their expectations become as it were internalized, and are reflected in one's very character. Of course as one ''grows up,'' one acquires more and more significant others whose attitudes are diffuse and may indeed compete, and thus ''significance,'' in Sullivan's sense, becomes subtler and less easy to define. The personality exfoliates; it takes on traits of distinction and, as we say, ''individuality.'' The impact of particular significant others is less dramatic than in early life. But the pattern is a continuing one; new significant others do still appear, and theoretically it is conceivable that even in mature life the personality might be visibly affected by the arrival of such a one—supposing that this new significant other were vested with sufficient authority and power. In any event there are possibilities for fluidity and actual change inherent in this concept which earlier schemes have lacked. . . .

Consider the camp prisoner—not the one who fell by the wayside but the one who was eventually to survive; consider the ways in which he was forced to adjust to the one significant other which he now had—the SS guard, who held absolute dominion over every aspect of his life. The very shock of his introduction was perfectly designed to dramatize this fact; he was brutally maltreated (''as by a cruel father''); the shadow of resistance would bring instant death. Daily life in the camp, with its fear and tensions, taught over and over the lesson of absolute power. It prepared the personality for a drastic shift in standards. It crushed whatever anxieties might have been drawn from prior standards; such standards had become meaningless. It focused the prisoner's attention constantly on the moods, attitudes, and standards of the only man who mattered. A truly childlike situation was thus created: utter and abject dependency on one, or on a rigidly limited few, significant others. All the conditions which in normal life would give the individual leeway—which allowed him to defend himself against a new and hostile significant other, no matter how powerful—were absent in the camp. No competition of significant others was possible; the prisoner's comrades for practical purposes were helpless to assist him. He had no degree of independence, no lines to the outside, in any matter. Everything, every vital concern, focused on the SS: food, warmth, security, freedom from pain, all depended on the omnipotent significant other, all had to be worked out within the closed system. Nowhere was there a shred of privacy; everything one did was subject to SS supervision. The pressure was never absent. It is thus no wonder that the prisoners should become ''as children.'' It is no wonder that their obedience became unquestioning, that they did not revolt, that they could not ''hate'' their masters. Their masters' attitudes had become *internalized* as a part of their very selves; those attitudes and standards now dominated all others that they had. They had, indeed, been "changed."

There still exists a third conceptual framework within which these phenomena may be considered. It is to be found in the growing field of "role psychology." This psychology is not at all incompatible with interpersonal theory; the two might easily be fitted into the same system. But it might be strategically desirable, for several reasons, to segregate them for purposes of discussion. One such reason is the extraordinary degree to which role psychology shifts the focus of attention upon the individual's cultural and institutional environment rather than upon his "self." At the same time it gives us a manageable concept—that of "role"—for mediating between the two. As a mechanism, the role enables us to isolate the unique contribution of culture and institutions toward maintaining the psychic balance of the individual. In it, we see formalized for the individual a range of choices in models of behavior and expression, each with its particular style, quality, and attributes. The relationship between the "role" and the "self," though not yet clear, is intimate; it is at least possible at certain levels of inquiry to look upon the individual as the variable and upon the roles extended him as the stable factor. . . .

What sorts of things might this explain? It might illuminate the process whereby the child develops his personality in terms not only of the roles which his parents offer him but of those which he "picks up" elsewhere and tries on. It could show how society, in its coercive character, lays down patterns of behavior with which it expects the individual to comply. It suggests the way in which society, now turning its benevolent face to the individual, tenders him alternatives and defines for him the style appropriate to their fulfilment. It provides us with a further term for the definition of personality itself: there appears an extent to which we can say that personality is actually made up of the roles which the individual plays. And here, once more assuming "change" to be possible, we have in certain ways the least cumbersome terms for plotting its course.

The application of the model to the concentration camp should be simple and obvious. What was expected of the man entering the role of camp prisoner was laid down for him upon arrival:

> Here you are not in a penitentiary or prison but in a place of instruction. Order and discipline are here the highest law. If you ever want to see freedom again, you must submit to a severe training. . . . But woe to those who do not obey our iron discipline. Our methods are thorough! Here there is no compromise and no mercy. The slightest resistance will be ruthlessly suppressed. Here we sweep with an iron broom! . . .

The impact of this role, coinciding as it does in a hundred ways with that of the child, has already been observed. Its rewards were brutally simple—life rather than death; its punishments were automatic. By the survivors it was—it had to be—a role *well played*. . . .

Both [slavery and the concentration camp] were closed systems from which all standards based on prior connections had been effectively detached. A working adjustment to either system required a childlike conformity, a limited choice of "significant others." Cruelty per se cannot be considered the primary key to this; of far greater importance was the simple "closedness" of the system, in which all lines of authority descended from the master and in which alternative social bases that might have supported alternative standards were systematically suppressed. The individual, consequently, for his very psychic security, had to picture his master in some way as the "good father," even when, as in the concentration camp, it made no sense at all. But why should it not have made sense for many a simple plantation Negro whose master did exhibit, in all the ways that could be expected, the features of the good father who was really "good"? If the concentration camp could produce in two or three years the results that it did, one wonders how much more pervasive must have been those attitudes, expectations, and values which had, certainly, their benevolent side and which were accepted and transmitted over generations. . . .

chapter eight

Projection

According to Freud, instincts sometimes lead to attempts to fulfill desires that the world would disapprove. To illustrate, individuals who have been unfaithful to their spouses, or who have repressed impulses to be unfaithful, may deny that they have faced the temptation to wander. Despite denial, the temptation may be so strong that the ego defends itself by means of projection. That is, the ego may circumvent tensions caused by the temptation to be unfaithful by attributing the forbidden desire to the spouse instead. The tables are then turned. Instead of feeling guilty because of adulterous urges, the individuals can feel hurt because they think the spouses have such longings and that, far from being the sinner, they are the ones sinned against—they point out to themselves that the partner to whom faith is owed also has such desires. The partners may indeed have these impulses; the cleverness of the projection is that the minds that employ it "let themselves be guided by their knowledge of the unconscious, and displace to the unconscious minds of others the attention which they have withdrawn from their own."[1]

In more general use, projection is the result of internal thoughts or desires that produce sufficiently great psychological discomfort to force their victim to defend himself by treating them as if they came not from within, but from without.[2] For example, a homosexual may unconsciously think that he loves another man. This must be denied and may be further defended against via the mechanism of reaction formation, which distorts an impulse by claiming its opposite. "I do not *love* him—I *hate* him." Since this statement must also be denied, " 'I hate him' [internal stimulus] becomes transformed by *projection* into another one: '*He hates* (persecutes) *me* [external stimulus], which will justify me in hating him.' " People may also use projection

---

[1] Freud discusses this specific instance of projection in *Some Neurotic Mechanisms in Jealousy, Paranoia, and Homosexuality,* in James Strachey, ed., *The Standard Edition of the Complete Psychological Works of Sigmund Freud,* 24 vols. (London: The Hogarth Press and the Institute of Psycho-Analysis, 1953–1966), 18:221–32, see especially pp. 224, 226.

[2] Freud, *Beyond the Pleasure Principle,* ibid., p. 29.

to accept their own urges. It is easier to deal with one's own feelings when one is convinced that others harbor the same desires. A thief will be more comfortable when he projects his actions on others, and believes that most people are as dishonest as he is.[3]

Projection is thus an excellent illustration of people's capacity for fooling themselves, for unconscious motivations replace finely spun arguments stated for public and even for personal consumption. How often have crusaders challenged in the outside world something they unconsciously feared in themselves, and how frequently have anxious individuals been unable to recognize the significance of their own behavior while castigating similar behavior by others? During the U. S. Civil War Southerners talked of freedom and maintained that the Union would place them into the bonds of slavery while at the same time they fought to keep the chains firmly riveted around the wrists of black Southerners. The mechanism of projection is not confined to neurotics or individuals of suspect stability. It operates in each of us—and in the historical figures we may study.

Projection is only one of the defense mechanisms of the ego; among the others are repression (where a threatening recollection or desire is forced out of a person's consciousness—or denied—in order to avoid the anxiety or fear it creates), reaction formation (in which a personality trait is hidden by transforming it into its opposite —aggressive, hostile behavior may be replaced by meekness), regression (when an individual retreats to an earlier stage of development, as the child who acts like a baby when he realizes his new baby sister has come to stay), or sublimation (the neutralization of an instinct by adopting a more socially accepted form of behavior, such as artistic or philanthropic activity).[4]

Most of these defense mechanisms were originally theorized by Sigmund Freud and Anna Freud, his daughter, but we do not have to buy the whole Freudian package.[5] That is, the validity of the concept of the defense mechanism of projection does not depend on accepting Freud's description of paranoia. Many psychologists who do not accept Freud's theories as anything more than early, somewhat mistaken, attempts to understand the human mind fully accept the existence of the various defense mechanisms on a descriptive level; indeed their existence has been demonstrated by experimental evidence. If the mechanisms are so widely accepted, they should be

---

[3]Freud, *Psycho-Analytic Notes on an Autobiographical Account of a Case of Paranoia (Dementia Paranoides)*, ibid., 12:63. See also p. 66, where Freud describes projection as the suppression of an internal perception so that the content, now distorted, is received as an external perception.

[4]See Calvin S. Hall, *A Primer of Freudian Psychology* (New York: The World Publishing Company, 1954), pp. 85–97; and Hans H. Strupp, *An Introduction to Freud and Modern Psychoanalysis* (Woodbury, N. Y.: Barron's Educational Series, 1967), pp. 47–54. Elementary texts in psychology sometimes add other types of behavior to the list of defense mechanisms, among them compensation, displacement, and rationalization.

[5]Anna Freud, *The Ego and the Mechanisms of Defense* (London: The Hogarth Press and the Institute of Psycho-Analysis, 1937).

prime devices for understanding psychological forces behind events in the past. As a matter of fact, this has seldom been done consciously and effectively, no doubt because of the basic problem with all psychohistory: it is impossible to get departed historical figures on the analyst's couch, and living historical personages have shown no inclination to come forward voluntarily. The material for such studies is therefore insufficient, although there is every reason to use these mechanisms in the study of a single individual where the historical record is unusually full. Applying any of these defenses to groups, or even the majority of a nation's population, is much more difficult.

However, this is exactly what David Brion Davis has done in the following selection. The article's thesis seems to be established. The skill with which Davis has applied the theory tends to seduce the reader into believing it. Such applications should not be taken too seriously without additional proof; the value of this approach in application to groups is that it is able to suggest important hypotheses for future study. Here Davis makes an interesting suggestion about the role of repressed sexual desires in mid-nineteenth-century America. It is not subject to absolute proof, any more than most historical hypotheses. But it does provide a provocative and potentially useful way to look at Americans undergoing the impact of industrialization, rapid urban growth, and changing sexual roles.[6]

However, note that the uncritical application of the concept of projection to a historical problem could create untenable, automatic assumptions of innocence or guilt—here that sexual desires were in fact repressed and that the victimized groups were not guilty of what their accusers contended. In this instance, the assumptions are reasonable enough; convents were not houses of prostitution and priests were not attempting to undermine the Republic. But to say that A projects his feelings on B, does not necessarily mean that B does not have the feelings that are attributed to him. Using the example at the beginning of this chapter, when spouses project their adulterous urges on their mates, it will often be the case that one of them will have the same adulterous urges and may even project them on the other. Thus, projection, like beauty, is in the mind of the beholder. And when groups are examined, as in Davis' essay, we must also remember that we dare not generalize the hypothesis to infer the motivations of any particular individual.

Davis' essay illustrates the mechanism of projection well. Fearing their own sexual desires, fearing their own fanaticism, fearing their own intolerance, nineteenth-century

---

[6]For two other interesting uses of projection, see D. A. Hartman, ''The Psychological Point of View in History: Some Phases of the Slavery Struggle,'' *Journal of Abnormal Psychology and Social Psychology* 17 (October-December, 1922):261–73, which uses both rationalization and projection in order to comprehend the Southern defense of slavery, and Robert G. L. Waite, ''Adolf Hitler's Anti-Semitism: A Study in History and Psychoanalysis,'' in Benjamin B. Wolman, ed., *The Psychoanalytic Interpretation of History* (New York: Basic Books, 1971), especially pp. 202–216, which makes a plausible case for the contention that Hitler's belief that Jews were sexually perverted was a projection of his own sexual perversions.

nativists allegedly projected these fears on groups that seemed suspicious because they "demanded unlimited allegiance as a condition of membership and excluded certain activities from the gaze of a curious public" (p. 129).[7] As one of Freud's interpreters put it, "A person who is afraid of his own aggressive and sexual impulses obtains some relief for his anxiety by attributing aggressiveness and sexuality to other people."[8] It reminds one of the Biblical story (Matthew 7:4) of the mote and the beam: "how wilt thou say to thy brother, Let me pull out the mote out of thine eye; and, behold, a beam is in thine own eye?" In addition to projection, note Davis' frequent reference to other psychosociological concepts, including repression and status anxiety.

Sexuality is especially important in this discussion, and, if Davis is correct, we may suppose that there was much unrelieved sexual tension in mid-nineteenth-century America. Although Catholics, with convents and priestly celibacy, and Mormons, who practiced polygamy, were prime targets for the projection of such tensions, Masons were also involved. This is more difficult to understand, since Masons conformed to the sexual patterns of the general population. But they did have an aura of secrecy such as the kind that surrounded Catholics and Mormons; Davis points out the sexual connection in a footnote that has been deleted for the purposes of this presentation: Masons were sometimes criticized because they did not admit women to membership and because their oath to respect the chastity of the wives, daughters, and sisters of other members did not include the chastity of all women. To nativists, the implication was obvious. If one swore to protect the honor only of some women, did that not specifically sanction advances toward other women? Like Catholics and Mormons, Masons were also considered potentially violent and this violence was all the more believable because in 1826 William Morgan, once involved in the Masonic order, disappeared, allegedly murdered to prevent him from revealing the order's secrets.

Some Themes of Counter-Subversion: An Analysis of Anti-Masonic, Anti-Catholic, and Anti-Mormon Literature
David Brion Davis

During the second quarter of the nineteenth century, when danger of foreign invasion appeared increasingly remote, Americans were told by various respected leaders that

[7] Note that Davis' use of the term nativist, which ordinarily refers only to opponents of immigration, includes anti-Catholics as well as opponents of Masons and Mormons.

[8] Hall, *Primer of Freudian Psychology*, p.89.

David Brion Davis, "Some Themes of Counter-Subversion: An Analysis of Anti-Masonic, Anti-Catholic, and Anti-Mormon Literature," *Mississippi Valley Historical Review,* XLVII (September 1960), 205, 208–221, 223–224. Copyright © 1960 by the Mississippi Valley Historical Association. Reprinted with deletion of notes and abridgment by permission of the author and *The Journal of American History* (formerly *Mississippi Valley Historical Review,* in which it was originally published).

Freemasons had infiltrated the government and had seized control of the courts, that Mormons were undermining political and economic freedom in the West, and that Roman Catholic priests, receiving instructions from Rome, had made frightening progress in a plot to subject the nation to popish despotism. This fear of internal subversion was channeled into a number of powerful counter movements which attracted wide public support. The literature produced by these movements evoked images of a great American enemy that closely resembled traditional European stereotypes of conspiracy and subversion. In Europe, however, the idea of subversion implied a threat to the established order—to the king, the church, or the ruling aristocracy—rather than to ideals or a way of life. If free Americans borrowed their images of subversion from frightened kings and uneasy aristocrats, these images had to be shaped and blended to fit American conditions. The movements would have to come from the people, and the themes of counter-subversion would be likely to reflect their fears, prejudices, hopes, and perhaps even unconscious desires. . . .

If Masons, Catholics, and Mormons bore little resemblance to one another in actuality, as imagined enemies they merged into a nearly common stereotype. Behind specious professions of philanthropy or religious sentiment, nativists discerned a group of unscrupulous leaders plotting to subvert the American social order. Though rank-and-file members were not individually evil, they were blinded and corrupted by a persuasive ideology that justified treason and gross immorality in the interest of the subversive group. Trapped in the meshes of a machine-like organization, deluded by a false sense of loyalty and moral obligation, these dupes followed orders like professional soldiers and labored unknowingly to abolish free society, to enslave their fellow men, and to overthrow divine principles of law and justice. Should an occasional member free himself from bondage to superstition and fraudulent authority, he could still be disciplined by the threat of death or dreadful tortures. There were no limits to the ambitious designs of leaders equipped with such organizations. According to nativist prophets, they chose to subvert American society because control of America meant control of the world's destiny.

Some of these beliefs were common in earlier and later European interpretations of conspiracy. American images of Masonic, Catholic, and Mormon subversion were no doubt a compound of traditional myths concerning Jacobite agents, scheming Jesuits, and fanatical heretics, and of dark legends involving the Holy Vehm and Rosicrucians. What distinguished the stereotypes of Mason, Catholic, and Mormon was the way in which they were seen to embody those traits that were precise antitheses of American ideals. The subversive group was essentially an inverted image of Jacksonian democracy and the cult of the common man; as such it not only challenged the dominant values but stimulated those suppressed needs and yearnings that are unfulfilled in a mobile, rootless, and individualistic society. It was therefore both frightening and fascinating.

It is well known that expansion and material progress in the Jacksonian era evoked a fervid optimism and that nationalists became intoxicated with visions of America's millennial glory. The simultaneous growth of prosperity and social democracy seemed to prove that Providence would bless a nation that allowed her citizens maximum liberty. When each individual was left free to pursue happiness in his own way, unhampered by the tyranny of custom or special privilege, justice and well-being would inevitably emerge. But if a doctrine of laissez-faire individualism seemed to promise material expansion and prosperity, it also raised disturbing problems. As one early anti-Mormon writer expressed it: What was to prevent liberty and popular sovereignty from sweeping away "the old landmarks of Christendom, and the glorious old common law of our fathers"? How was the individual to preserve a sense of continuity with the past, or identify himself with a given cause or tradition? What, indeed, was to insure a common loyalty and a fundamental unity among the people?

Such questions acquired a special urgency as economic growth intensified mobility, destroyed old ways of life, and transformed traditional symbols of status and prestige. Though most Americans took pride in their material progress, they also expressed a yearning for reassurance and security, for unity in some cause transcending individual self-interest. This need for meaningful group activity was filled in part by religious revivals, reform movements, and a proliferation of fraternal orders and associations. In politics Americans tended to assume the posture of what Marvin Meyers has termed "venturesome conservatives," mitigating their acquisitive impulses by an appeal for unity against extraneous forces that allegedly threatened a noble heritage of republican ideals. Without abandoning a belief in progress through laissez-faire individualism, the Jacksonians achieved a sense of unity and righteousness by styling themselves as restorers of tradition. Perhaps no theme is so evident in the Jacksonian era as the strained attempt to provide America with a glorious heritage and a noble destiny. With only a loose and often ephemeral attachment to places and institutions, many Americans felt a compelling need to articulate their loyalties, to prove their faith, and to demonstrate their allegiance to certain ideals and institutions. By so doing they acquired a sense of self-identity and personal direction in an otherwise rootless and shifting environment. . . .

Few men questioned traditional beliefs in freedom of conscience and the right of association. Yet what was to prevent "all the errors and worn out theories of the Old World, of schisms in the early Church, the monkish age and the rationalistic period," from flourishing in such salubrious air? Nativists often praised the work of benevolent societies, but they were disturbed by the thought that monstrous conspiracies might also "show kindness and patriotism, when it is necessary for their better concealment; and oftentimes do much good for the sole purpose of getting a better opportunity to do evil." When confronted by so many sects and associations, how was the patriot to distinguish the loyal from the disloyal? It was clear that mere disagreement over theology or economic policy was invalid as a test, since honest men disputed over the significance of baptism or the wisdom of protective tariffs. But neither could one rely on expressions of allegiance to common democratic principles, since subversives would cunningly profess to believe in freedom and toleration of dissent as long as they remained a powerless minority.

As nativists studied this troubling question, they discovered that most groups and denominations claimed only a partial loyalty from their members, freely subordinating themselves to the higher and more abstract demands of the Constitution, Christianity, and American public opinion. Moreover, they openly exposed their objects and activities to public scrutiny and exercised little discrimination in enlisting members. Some groups, however, dominated a larger portion of their members' lives, demanded unlimited allegiance as a condition of membership, and exluded certain activities from the gaze of a curious public.

Of all governments, said Richard Rush, ours was the one with most to fear from secret societies, since popular sovereignty by its very nature required perfect freedom of public inquiry and judgment. In a virtuous republic why should anyone fear publicity or desire to conceal activities, unless those activities were somehow contrary to the public interest? When no one could be quite sure what the public interest was, and when no one could take for granted a secure and well-defined place in the social order, it was most difficult to acknowledge legitimate spheres of privacy. Most Americans of the Jacksonian era appeared willing to tolerate diversity and even eccentricity, but when they saw themselves excluded and even barred from witnessing certain proceedings, they imagined a "Mystic power" conspiring to enslave them. . . .

The distinguishing mark of Masonic, Catholic, and Mormon conspiracies was a secrecy that cloaked the members' unconditional loyalty to an autonomous body. Since the organizations had corrupted the private moral judgment of their members, Americans could not rely on the ordinary forces of progress to spread truth and enlightenment among their ranks. Yet the affairs of such organizations were not outside the jurisdiction of democratic government, for no body politic could be asked to tolerate a power that was designed to destroy it. Once the true nature of subversive groups was thoroughly understood, the alternatives were as clear as life and death. How could democracy and Catholicism coexist when, as Edward Beecher warned, "The systems are diametrically opposed: one must and will exterminate the other"? Because Freemasons had so deeply penetrated state and national governments, only drastic remedies could restore the nation to its democratic purity. And later, Americans faced an "irrepressible conflict" with Mormonism, for it was said that either free institutions or Mormon despotism must ultimately annihilate the other.

We may well ask why nativists magnified the division between unpopular minorities and the American public, so that Masons, Catholics, and Mormons seemed so menacing that they could not be accorded the usual rights and privileges of a free society. Obviously the literature of counter-subversion reflected concrete rivalries and conflicts of interest between competing groups, but it is important to note that the subversive bore no racial or ethnic stigma and was not even accused of inherent depravity. Since group membership was a matter of intellectual and emotional loyalty, no *physical* barrier prevented a Mason, Catholic, or Mormon from apostatizing and joining the dominant in-group, providing always that he escaped assassination from his previous masters. This suggests that counter-subversion was more than a rationale for group rivalry and was related to the general problem of ideological unity and diversity in a free society. When a "system of delusion" insulated members of a group from the unifying and disciplining force of public opinion, there was no authority to command an allegiance to common principles. This was why oaths of loyalty assumed great importance for nativists. Though the ex-Catholic William Hogan stated repeatedly that Jesuit spies respected no oaths except those to the Church, he inconsistently told Masons and Odd Fellows that they could prevent infiltration by requiring new members to swear they were not Catholics. It was precisely the absence of distinguishing outward traits that made the enemy so dangerous, and true loyalty so difficult to prove.

When the images of different enemies conform to a similar pattern, it is highly probable that this pattern reflects important tensions within a given culture. The themes of nativist literature suggest that its authors simplified problems of personal insecurity and adjustment to bewildering social change by trying to unite Americans of diverse political, religious, and economic interests against a common enemy. Just as revivalists sought to stimulate Christian fellowship by awakening men to the horrors of sin, so nativists used apocalyptic images to ignite human passions, destroy selfish indifference, and join patriots in a cohesive brotherhood. Such themes were only faintly secularized. When God saw his "lov'd Columbia" imperiled by the hideous monster of Freemasonry, He realized that only a martyr's blood could rouse the hearts of the people and save them from bondage to the Prince of Darkness. By having God will Morgan's death, this anti-Mason showed he was more concerned with national virtue and unity than with Freemasonry, which was only a providential instrument for testing republican strength.

Similarly, for the anti-Catholic "this brilliant new world" was once "young and beautiful; it abounded in all the luxuries of nature; it promised all that was desirable to man." But the Roman Church, seeing "these irresistible temptations, thirsting with avarice and yearning for the reestablishment of her falling greatness, soon commenced pouring in among its unsuspecting people hoardes of Jesuits and other friars." If Americans were to continue their narrow pursuit of self-interest, oblivious to the "Popish colleges, and nunneries, and monastic institutions," indifferent to manifold signs of corruption and decay, how could the nation expect "that the moral breezes of heaven should breathe upon her, and restore to her again that strong and healthy constitution, which her ancestors have left to her sons"? The theme of an Adamic fall from paradise was horrifying, but it was used to inspire determined action and thus unity. If Methodists were "criminally indifferent" to the Mormon question, and if "avaricious merchants, soulless corporations, and a subsidized press" ignored Mormon iniquities, there was all the more reason that the *"will of the people* must prevail."

Without explicitly rejecting the philosophy of laissez-faire individualism, with its toleration of dissent and innovation, nativist literature conveyed a sense of common dedication to a noble cause and sacred tradition. Though the nation had begun with the blessings of God and with the noblest institutions known to man, the people had somehow become selfish and complacent, divided by petty disputes, and insensitive to signs of danger. In his sermons attacking such self-interest, such indifference to public concerns, and such a lack of devotion to common ideals and sentiments, the nativist revealed the true source of his anguish. Indeed, he seemed at times to recognize an almost beneficent side to subversive organizations, since they joined the nation in a glorious crusade and thus kept it from moral and social disintegration.

The exposure of subversion was a means of promoting unity, but it also served to clarify national values and provide the individual ego with a sense of high moral sanction and imputed righteousness. Nativists identified themselves repeatedly with a strangely incoherent tradition in which images of Pilgrims, Minute Men, Founding Fathers, and true Christians appeared in a confusing montage. Opposed to this heritage of stability and perfect integrity, to this society founded on the highest principles of divine and natural law, were organizations formed by the grossest frauds and impostures, and based on the wickedest impulses of human nature. Bitterly refuting Masonic claims to ancient tradition and Christian sanction, anti-Masons charged that the Order was of recent origin, that it was shaped by Jews, Jesuits, and French atheists as an engine for spreading infidelity, and that it was employed by kings and aristocrats to undermine republican institutions. If the illustrious Franklin and Washington had been duped by Masonry, this only proved how treacherous was its appeal and how subtly persuasive were its pretensions. Though the Catholic Church had an undeniable claim to tradition, nativists argued that it had originated in stupendous frauds and forgeries "in comparison with which the forgeries of Mormonism are completely thrown into the shade." Yet anti-Mormons saw an even more sinister conspiracy based on the "shrewd cunning" of Joseph Smith, who convinced gullible souls that he conversed with angels and received direct revelations from the Lord.

By emphasizing the fraudulent character of their opponents' claims, nativists sought to establish the legitimacy and just authority of American institutions. Masonic rituals, Roman Catholic sacraments, and Morman revelations were preposterous hoaxes used to delude naïve or superstitious minds; but public schools, a free press, and jury trials were eternally valid prerequisites for a free and virtuous society.

Moreover, the finest values of an enlightened nation stood out in bold relief when contrasted with the corrupting tendencies of subversive groups. Perversion of the sexual instinct seemed inevitably to accompany religious error. Deprived of the tender affections of normal married love, shut off from the elevating sentiments of fatherhood, Catholic priests looked on woman only as insensitive objects for the gratification of their frustrated desires. In similar fashion polygamy struck at the heart of a morality based on the inspiring influence of woman's affections: "It renders man coarse, tyrannical, brutal, and heartless. It deals death to all sentiments of true manhood. It enslaves and ruins woman. It crucifies every God-given feeling of her nature." Some anti-Mormons concluded that plural marriage could only have been established among foreigners who had never learned to respect women. But the more common explanation was that the false ideology of Mormonism had deadened the moral sense and liberated man's wild sexual impulse from the normal restraints of civilization. Such degradation of women and corruption of man served to highlight the importance of democratic marriage, a respect for women, and careful cultivation of the finer sensibilities.

But if nativist literature was a medium for articulating common values and exhorting individuals to transcend self-interest and join in a dedicated union against evil, it also performed a more subtle function. Why, we may ask, did nativist literature dwell so persistently on themes of brutal sadism and sexual immorality? Why did its authors describe sin in such minute details, endowing even the worst offenses of their enemies with a certain fascinating appeal?

Freemasons, it was said, could commit any crime and indulge any passion when "upon the square," and Catholics and Mormons were even less inhibited by internal moral restraints. Nativists expressed horror over this freedom from conscience and conventional morality, but they could not conceal a throbbing note of envy. What was it like to be a member of a cohesive brotherhood that casually abrogated the laws of God and man, enforcing unity and obedience with dark and mysterious powers? As nativists speculated on this question, they projected their own fears and desires into a fantasy of licentious orgies and fearful punishments.

Such a projection of forbidden desires can be seen in the exaggeration of the stereotyped enemy's powers, which made him appear at times as a virtual superman. Catholic and Mormon leaders, never hindered by conscience or respect for traditional morality, were curiously superior to ordinary Americans in cunning, in exercising power over others, and especially in captivating gullible women. It was an ancient theme of anti-Catholic literature that friars and priests were somehow more potent and sexually attractive than married laymen, and were thus astonishingly successful at seducing supposedly virtuous wives. Americans were cautioned repeatedly that no priest recognized Protestant marriages as valid, and might consider any wife legitimate prey. Furthermore, priests had access to the pornographic teachings of Dens and Liguori, sinister names that aroused the curiosity of anti-Catholics, and hence learned subtle techniques of seduction perfected over the centuries. Speaking with the authority of an ex-priest, William Hogan described the shocking result: "I have seen husbands unsuspiciously and hospitably entertaining the very priest who seduced their wives in the confessional, and was the parent of some of the children who sat at the same table with them, each of the wives unconscious of the other's guilt, and the husbands of both, not even suspecting them." Such blatant immorality was horrifying, but everyone was apparently happy in this domestic scene, and we may suspect that the image was not entirely repugnant to husbands who, despite their respect for the Lord's Commandments, occasionally coveted their neighbors' wives.

The literature of counter-subversion could also embody the somewhat different projective fantasies of women. Ann Eliza Young dramatized her seduction by the Prophet Brigham, whose almost superhuman powers enchanted her and paralyzed her will. Though she submitted finally only because her parents were in danger of being ruined by the Church, she clearly indicated that it was an exciting privilege to be pursued by a Great Man. When Anti-Mormons claimed that Joseph Smith and other prominent Saints knew the mysteries of Animal Magnetism, or were endowed with the highest degree of ''amativeness'' in their phrenological makeup, this did not detract from their covert appeal. In a ridiculous fantasy written by Maria Ward, such alluring qualities were extended even to Mormon women. Many bold-hearted girls could doubtless identify themselves with Anna Bradish, a fearless Amazon of a creature, who rode like a man, killed without compunction, and had no pity for weak women who failed to look out for themselves. Tall, elegant, and ''intellectual,'' Anna was attractive enough to arouse the insatiable desires of Brigham Young, though she ultimately rejected him and renounced Mormonism.

While nativists affirmed their faith in Protestant monogamy, they obviously took pleasure in imagining the variety of sexual experience supposedly available to their enemies. By picturing themselves exposed to similar temptations, they assumed they could know how priests and Mormons actually sinned. Imagine, said innumerable anti-Catholic writers, a beautiful young woman kneeling before an ardent young priest in a deserted room. As she confesses, he leans over, looking into her eyes, until their heads are nearly touching. Day after day she reveals to him her innermost secrets, secrets she would not think of unveiling to her parents, her dearest friends, or even her suitor. By skillful questioning the priest fills her mind with immodest and even sensual ideas, ''until this wretch has worked up her passions to a tension almost snapping, and then becomes his easy prey.'' How could any man resist such provocative temptations, and how could any girl's virtue withstand such a test?

We should recall that this literature was written in a period of increasing anxiety and uncertainty over sexual values and the proper role of woman. As ministers and journalists pointed with alarm at the spread of prostitution, the incidence of divorce, and the lax and hypocritical morality of the growing cities, a discussion of licentious subversives offered a convenient means for the projection of guilt as well as desire. The sins of individuals, or of the nation as a whole, could be pushed off upon the shoulders of the enemy and there punished in righteous anger.

Specific instances of such projection are not difficult to find. John C. Bennett, whom the Mormons expelled from the Church as a result of his flagrant sexual immorality, invented the fantasy of ''The Mormon Seraglio'' which persisted in later anti-Mormon writings. According to Bennett, the Mormons maintained secret orders of beautiful prostitutes who were mostly reserved for various officials of the Church. He claimed, moreover, that any wife refusing to accept polygamy might be forced to join the lowest order and thus become available to any Mormon who desired her.

Another example of projection can be seen in the letters of a young lieutenant who stopped in Utah in 1854 on his way to California. Convinced that Mormon women could be easily seduced, the lieutenant wrote frankly of his amorous adventures with a married woman. ''Everybody has got one,'' he wrote with obvious pride, ''except the Colonel and Major. The Doctor has got three—mother and two daughters. The mother cooks for him and the daughters sleep with him.'' But though he described Utah as "a great country,'' the lieutenant waxed indignant over polygamy, which he condemned as self-righteously as any anti-Mormon minister: "To see one man openly parading half a dozen or more women to church . . . is the devil according to my ideas of morality virtue and decency.''

If the consciences of many Americans were troubled by the growth of red light districts in major cities, they could divert their attention to the "legalized brothels'' called nunneries, for which no one was responsible but lecherous Catholic priests. If others were disturbed by the moral implications of divorce, they could point in horror at the Mormon elder who took his quota of wives all at once. The literature of counter-subversion could thus serve the double purpose of vicariously fulfilling repressed desires, and of releasing the tension and guilt arising from rapid social change and conflicting values.

Though the enemy's sexual freedom might at first seem enticing, it was always made repugnant in the end by associations with perversion or brutal cruelty. Both Catholics and Mormons were accused of practicing nearly every form of incest. The persistent emphasis on this theme might indicate deep-rooted feelings of fear and guilt, but it also helped demonstrate, on a more objective level, the loathsome consequences of unrestrained lust. Sheer brutality and a delight in human suffering were supposed to be the even more horrible results of sexual depravity. Masons disemboweled or slit the throats of their victims; Catholics cut unborn infants from their mothers' wombs and threw them to the dogs before their parents' eyes; Mormons raped and lashed recalcitrant women, or seared their mouths with red-hot irons. This obsession with details of sadism, which reached pathological proportions in much of the literature, showed a furious determination to purge the enemy of every admirable quality. The imagined enemy might serve at first as an outlet for forbidden desires, but nativist authors escaped from guilt by finally making him an agent of unmitigated aggression. In such a role the subversive seemed to deserve both righteous anger and the most terrible punishments.

The nativist escape from guilt was more clearly revealed in the themes of confession and conversion. For most American Protestants the crucial step in anyone's life was a profession of true faith resulting from a genuine religious experience. Only when a man became conscious of his inner guilt, when he struggled against the temptations of Satan, could he prepare his soul for the infusion of the regenerative spirit. Those most deeply involved in sin often made the most dramatic conversions. It is not surprising that conversion to nativism followed the same pattern, since nativists sought unity and moral certainty in the regenerative spirit of nationalism. Men who had been associated in some way with un-American conspiracies were not only capable of spectacular confessions of guilt, but were best equipped to expose the insidious work of supposedly harmless organizations. Even those who lacked such an exciting history of corruption usually made some confession of guilt, though it might involve only a previous indifference to subversive groups. Like ardent Christians, nativists searched in their own experiences for the meanings of sin, delusion, awakening to truth, and liberation from spiritual bondage. These personal confessions proved that one had recognized and conquered evil, and also served as ritual cleansings preparatory to full acceptance in a group of dedicated patriots. . . .

As the nativist searched for participation in a noble cause, for unity in a group sanctioned by tradition and authority, he professed a belief in democracy and equal rights. Yet in his very zeal for freedom he curiously assumed many of the characteristics of the imagined enemy. By condemning the subversive's fanatical allegiance to an ideology, he affirmed a similarly uncritical acceptance of a different ideology; by attacking the subversive's intolerance of dissent, he worked to eliminate dissent and diversity of opinion; by censuring the subversive for alleged licentiousness, he engaged in sensual fantasies; by criticizing the subversive's loyalty to an organization, he sought to prove his unconditional loyalty to the established order. The nativist moved even farther in the direction of his enemies when he formed tightly-knit societies and parties which were often secret and which subordinated the individual to the single purpose of the group. Though the nativists generally agreed that the worst evil of subversives was their subordinaion of means to ends, they themselves recommended the most radical means to purge the nation of troublesome groups and to enforce unquestioned loyalty to the state.

In his image of an evil group conspiring against the nation's welfare, and in his vision of a glorious millennium that was to dawn after the enemy's defeat, the nativist found satisfaction for many desires. His own interests became legitimate and dignified by fusion with the national interest, and various opponents became loosely associated with the un-American conspiracy. Thus Freemasonry in New York State was linked in the nativist mind with economic and political interests that were thought to discriminate against certain groups and regions; southerners imagined a union of abolitionists and Catholics to promote unrest and rebellion among slaves; gentile businessmen in Utah merged anti-Mormonism with plans for exploiting mines and lands.

Then too the nativist could style himself as a restorer of the past, as a defender of a stable order against disturbing changes, and at the same time proclaim his faith in future progress. By focusing his attention on the imaginary threat of a secret conspiracy, he found an outlet for many irrational impulses, yet professed his loyalty to the ideals of equal rights and government by law. He paid lip service to the doctrine of laissez-faire individualism, but preached selfless dedication to a transcendent cause. The imposing threat of subversion justified a group loyalty and subordination of the individual that would otherwise have been unacceptable. In a rootless environment shaken by bewildering social change the nativist found unity and meaning by conspiring against imaginary conspiracies.

chapter nine

Cognitive Dissonance

It should be obvious by now that one of the major tasks historians have is the problem of understanding historical figures—either as individuals or in groups—whose behavior cannot be comprehended either by the historian or historical participants who have conventional expectations of behavior. There is also the problem of understanding actions that are plainly inappropriate, in view of the information that individuals are known to have had. For example, why did Leon Trotsky violate Communist Party rules—rules that he had fought to impose—thereby giving his opposition the effective weapon needed to block his attempt to gain control of the party, a succession that most people assumed would be his anyway? Why did the United States government during Reconstruction fail to secure the rights of former slaves by moving vigorously against obvious Southern terrorism? Or to pose the question contained in the following article, why, after the defeats of 1806 and 1807, did Prussian opposition to France, which was channeled into conspiracy to initiate guerrilla war against Napoleon in order to secure a treaty of peace, not cease when Napoleon indicated he was willing to agree to terms much like the Prussians wanted? Why did the plotters, led by King Frederick William's highest advisors, not put aside plans that were no longer necessary—plans that, after the betrayal of the plot, were unsuitable, dangerous, and irrational as well? To put the incongruity between perceived knowledge and actual behavior on a more everyday level, why do so many people continue the habit of smoking in the face of rather heavy evidence that cigarettes are associated with cancer and heart disease?

Sometimes there is a ready explanation for apparently inappropriate behavior, but frequently that explanation is either insufficient or absent. In the latter instance, the actions may be manifestations of the psychological phenomenon known as cognitive dissonance, which may be defined briefly as the perception of contradictory information leading to psychological discomfort in decision making. According to theory, we tend to filter perceptions so that information tends to justify our condition, plans, or activity. In the words of psychologist Leon Festinger, whose formulation is most known, the theory of cognitive dissonance "centers around the idea that if a person knows various things that are not psychologically consistent with one another, he will, in a variety of ways, try to make them more consistent."[1]

Cognition is defined as "any knowledge, opinion, or belief about the environment, about oneself, or about one's behavior." Inconsistency between what one knows (cognition) of one's behavior and what one knows (cognition) of reality as one perceives it creates psychological discomfort (dissonance) that the individual attempts to reduce. As long as the dissonance exists a person will try to evade circumstances that could create additional dissonance, even though the information (cognition) that would have been obtained might be valuable and highly accurate. Cognitive dissonance thus motivates "dissonance reduction just as hunger leads to activity oriented toward hunger reduction."[2]

Cognitive dissonance may occur for a number of reasons. First of all, people are unable to control all the information that comes to them; invariably some of it does not fit (the smoker hears about the results of cancer research, for example). Furthermore, there are few instances in which all information points to the same conclusion. The world of choices most people confront is not black and white but shades of gray. Whenever individuals must make an important decision or adopt an opinion they may experience dissonance created by the knowledge that alternative decisions and opinions also have positive and desirable features.[3] Dissonance becomes a significant motivator to the extent that a person has an emotional investment in a particular position. The mere awareness of alternate courses of action or conclusions is not sufficient to create a dissonance problem. But if an individual sees a particular decision as one that could affect his life significantly, the possibility of severe dissonance becomes important.

There are several ways in which dissonance can be reduced. First, when it is created by an inconsistency between knowledge and behavior either one can be changed so as to bring them into alignment. The simplest way is to change behavior, since few people are in such control of the world around them that they are able to change their environment—although it may be possible if one is able to surround oneself with people who share one's attitudes, such as, in this case, fellow conspirators who are equally dedicated to a plot that has little chance of success. A second possibility is to decrease total dissonance by adding new knowledge to offset dissonant elements. A third procedure reduces dissonance by distorting perceptions in order to reconcile apparently contradictory perceptions—thereby preventing the individual from comprehending the basic conflict of dissonant elements. Thus a smoker may stop smoking, examine the research reports to find their inadequacies, or simply disbelieve the reports. If none of these methods succeed in reducing dissonance it will continue, but so

[1]Leon Festinger, "Cognitive Dissonance," *Scientific American* 207 (October 1962):93. This article is a partial and popular summary of the theory that is presented at full length in Festinger, *A Theory of Cognitive Dissonance* (Evanston: Row, Peterson and Co., 1957).

[2]Festinger, *Theory of Cognitive Dissonance*, p. 3.

[3]Ibid., p. 5.

too will efforts at reduction.[4] It is important to be aware that cognition, or reality as the individual perceives it, may be highly inaccurate—what counts is not what *is,* but what the individual *thinks* is, however distorted that may be. This means that efforts to dissipate dissonance may be misdirected, much as passengers may get on the wrong train, and with the same result. They may think they are on the right train, and may therefore experience a temporary reduction in dissonance, but when they get to the wrong destination their problems (dissonance) will probably be increased rather than relieved.

Efforts to reduce dissonance may therefore fail. Sometimes the cognitive element that creates the inconsistency (dissonance) is resistant to change. This could be due to any one of several causes. Change may be painful, as Raack suggests about the leaders of the conspiracy of 1808 in Prussia, due to loss of face. Change might even be out of the question because of outside circumstances—such as the impossibility of altering past decisions. But the discomfort of dissonance may also be escaped by avoiding it; information may simply be ignored, as when the conspirators apparently thought of their plans as ends in themselves and continued their plot even though its initial goals (the peace terms) had been achieved by other means and the plot itself had inadvertently been revealed to the enemy. Furthermore, in group situations, where a number of people suffer the same dissonance, relief for each person may easily be obtained from the social support of the others since the dissonance is identical for each member of the group. More than that, members will attempt to persuade others of the correctness of their beliefs. The most essential point, in the context of Raack's study, is that if the group is firmly committed to its plans, dissonance reduction will not be aimed at changing the plans but at changing the cognition; information that undermines the belief or decision will be replaced by information that is more supportive, and conspirators will justify their schemes by permitting them to become ends in themselves.[5]

If this theory is correct, it is not surprising that the conspiracy was held together by a combination of bravado and recruiting when it was already too late. There is, as Festinger says, "an apparent paradox, namely, that after being exposed to evidence of one's own senses which unequivocally demonstrates a belief system to be wrong, people proceed to proselyte more vigorously for the belief system." Having made a decision, a person is faced with the discomfort created by the dissonance between the decision itself and the positive aspects of the rejected alternative. This postdecision dissonance is reduced by exaggerating the good points and minimizing the bad points of the accepted alternative. Individuals may also do the opposite; they may support their decision by downgrading the positive aspects and magnifying the negative attributes of the rejected alternative. Postdecision dissonance reduction thus leads "to an increase in the desirability of the chosen alternative and a decrease in the desirability of

---

[4]Ibid., pp. 19–24.
[5]Ibid., pp. 25–30, 195, 244–47, 265.

the rejected alternative.'' Baron Stein and his friends, for example, eliminated dissonance by downgrading the advantages of avoiding conspiracy while exaggerating the outcome of a success that seemed inevitable to them. Having initiated the conspiracy because acceptable terms of peace could not be obtained, Stein froze the decision and did not abandon the plot when the previously acceptable terms were offered to Prussia. ''Involuntarily exposed to information that will increase dissonance,'' says Festinger, an individual sets up ''quick defensive processes which prevent the new cognition from ever becoming firmly established.''[6]

In short, cognitive dissonance occurs when some of the things individuals ''know'' may not logically fit together. This dissonance creates a tension that causes individuals to take measures to bring dissonant elements into harmony. They may do this by changing their behavior, exposing themselves to new information, or changing their perceptions (as with Baron Stein), even to the point of tragic self-deception.[7] Emotional investment is an important factor in the tenacity with which inappropriate knowledge is believed, as people ''try to justify a commitment to the extent that there is information discrepant with that commitment''—a statement of the theory that fits the conspirators exactly.[8]

Festinger did not attempt to relate the theory of cognitive dissonance to other theories of personality or to individual differences in personality type, but the implications are there. Some individuals may be far more receptive to dissonance-reducing information than others. Postdecision dissonance may be created by cognitive elements introduced by the superego, to put it in Freudian terms (i.e., people's consciences may bother them). Or dissonance reduction may be thought of as the harmonizing of the id's desires with the reality principle of the ego. Erikson's identity crisis, when a young person ''half-realizes that he is fatally overcommitted to what he is not,'' could well be the result of an extreme case of cognitive dissonance, the youth suffering from discomfort created by knowing that he is able to take his place in society, and ought to—but has not yet done so. At any given time, says Erikson, speaking of youthful attachment to ideology, there is a tendency ''to make facts amenable to ideas, and ideas to facts, in order to create a world image convincing enough to support the collective and the individual sense of identity.''[9] On the other hand, the degree of success that an individual has in dissonance reduction may depend on the ''significant other'' from whom a person accepts new cognitive elements (information). Even the

---

[6]Ibid., pp. 32–34, 137, 247; and ''Cognitive Dissonance,'' p. 95.

[7]Festinger, *Theory of Cognitive Dissonance*, p. 31. See also Festinger, *Conflict, Decision, and Dissonance* (Stanford: Stanford University Press, 1964), and Jack W. Brehm and Arthur R. Cohen, *Explorations in Cognitive Dissonance* (New York: Wiley, 1962), which discuss both the theory and the experimental findings that support it.

[8]Brehm and Cohen, *Explorations in Cognitive Dissonance*, p. 300.

[9]Erik H. Erikson, *Young Man Luther: A Study of Psychoanalysis and History* (New York: W. W. Norton and Co., 1958), pp. 22, 43.

defense mechanism of projection may be involved. For in projecting desires on someone else, individuals reduce dissonance, attempting to eliminate the inconsistency between their cognition of their own desires and their cognition that having these desires is improper.

The discussion of the theory and of the following article may seem inconsistent at one point. Cognitive dissonance is usually discussed in terms of individuals, while Raack applies it to a group. Is the theory really susceptible to group application? The formulation seems to indicate that it is. Festinger himself employed it to analyze mass phenomena in which numbers of individuals experienced dissonance, such as victims of a 1934 earthquake in India, Japanese repatriates at the end of World War II, and the Millerites, a millennial religious movement active in upstate New York in the 1840s. Remember the oft-repeated warning, however. If our subject is a group we should be hesitant to conclude that all members remain committed to group goals simply because of successful efforts to reduce dissonance created by conflicting perception. We should also avoid the temptation inherent in many far-reaching theories to apply the concept everywhere. Once convinced of the theory, a researcher will find it easy to see its application in any historical situation—but many groups and individuals do not suffer from cognitive dissonance because the decision at hand is not particularly important to them or their awareness does not extend far enough to permit them to receive contradictory information. Sometimes people are wrong simply because they do not know any better.

Like other selections in this collection, Raack's article is an excellent demonstration of interdisciplinary approaches to historical problems, and it could be used to illustrate more than one methodological technique, including analogy (between historical events and artificial events created in social psychological experiments) and the dynamics of small-group behavior.[10] Most striking, however, is the use of the theory of cognitive dissonance (which is never explicitly mentioned in the body of the article). Perhaps it explains why the conspiracy's "supporters actually increased their dedication to it [the conspiracy] after its original *raison d'etre* . . . had disappeared," and after it had been betrayed. Perhaps the theory helps to explain their unrealistic failure to "believe that their military plans had led to the end of the reform government," and their foolhardy attempt to save "the state by making a success of the failure that seemed imminent" (pp. 145, 150).

---

[10] Although this aspect has not been emphasized, as a study of small-group behavior this article is a major milestone in historical methodology. Richard L. Schoenwald, "Using Psychology in History: A Review Essay," *Historical Methods Newsletter* 7 (December 1973):17, observes that "Raack appears to stand by himself in having solved a historical problem by using recent studies of the behavior of small groups."

When Plans Fail: Small Group Behavior and Decision-Making in the Conspiracy of 1808 in Germany
R. C. Raack

. . . My purpose here is to present the history of this anti-French conspiracy of 1808, and to analyze the historical evidence using available analogies and recent behavioral theory. Where gaps in the sources exist, I have reconstructed the record from historical examples of similar behavior and from the research results of other disciplines, especially recent systematic observations and laboratory studies in social psychology. I have tried to put together a study that might serve as a scholarly reference for those interested in unusual small group undertakings in the hope that my work will prompt additional research in which my general conclusions can be further tested and refined. . . .

History of the Conspiracy
In June 1808, Baron Karl vom Stein, famous in history as the chief architect of the Prussian reform movement, had just returned to the temporary capital, Königsberg, from Berlin. There he had made a fruitless effort to wrest final terms of peace from Napoleon's agents. Prussia, since its complete defeat in the war with France of 1806 and 1807, stood occupied by the French to the Vistula, with only East Prussia evacuated since the peace settlement at Tilsit, a year before. The purpose of Stein's quest in Berlin had been to find indemnity terms which would suit Napoleon and bring the French to leave the rest of the country, ending their costly occupation.

During the summer of 1808 the Prussian state appeared to be at the edge of bankruptcy. Stein and his friends in the reform government found their legislative work enormously complicated by the continuing occupation. Dealing with its effects and the rest of the legacy of defeat took up most of their energies. In addition, more recent actions of the ever restless Bonaparte appeared to pose new threats to the remaining crowned heads of Europe, and particularly to Prussia's fainthearted Frederick William III. He was helpless in defeat. He had relied wholly on Tsar Alexander's intercession with the French emperor to save his throne after the Prussian collapse in the summer of 1807. Then, in April 1808, Napoleon had brashly retired the King of Spain, invaded the Papal States, and imprisoned the Pope. Seeming to face a similar prospect as soon as a new opportunity was opened to Bonaparte, Frederick William and his advisers had come to despair of the future of their state and monarchy while the Corsican reigned supreme in Europe.

This excerpt from "When Plans Fail: Small Group Behavior and Decision-Making in the Conspiracy of 1808 in Germany," by R. C. Raack is reprinted from the *Journal of Conflict Resolution* Vol. XIV, No. 1 (March 1970) pp. 3–17 by permission of the Publisher, Sage Publications, Inc.

Suddenly in the summer of 1808 the dismally repetitious news of French triumphs was replaced by astonishing reports of the successful uprising of the Spanish people against the French thrall. Led by priests and other popular figures, they had risen in wrath against their newly imposed French king and his foreign armies. The surprising successes of the Spanish guerrilla legions, operating in familiar countryside against French lines of supply and communication, suggested the idea of a similar uprising to the Königsberg leaders. This response was duplicated in Vienna, where the Austrian emperor and his advisers had, for like reasons, come to a similar fear about their own future. Germany was filled with rumors of forthcoming conflict between France and Austria, the latter soon rapidly rearming. On the morrow of Stein's return from his futile journey to Berlin, his military advisers, Col. August Wilhelm Gneisenau and General Gerhard Johann von Scharnhorst, outlined for him the prospects for a similar undertaking in Prussia. Their idea was to join the Austrians in a coordinated uprising against France.

To Stein, the risky plot was worth considering, given the wretched state of the kingdom. Yet surely he appreciated that even the planning of insurrection would draw his and the state's energies from the course of domestic reform to which he was pledged. But as he must have seen the issue, even the most far-reaching changes would have no purpose if Prussia defaulted on the enormous reparation payments Napoleon had demanded and the lands to be redeemed thereby fell to the French. On the other hand, a successful military campaign might speedily free the country of both reparations and the French, thus restoring in a trice Prussia's glorious name and German national pride.

It is important to note that the military schemes put forward by Gneisenau and Scharnhorst, and approvingly passed along to the king by Stein, had sharp implications for social reform, some of them no doubt unsettling to the king and downright frightening to Stein's many powerful political opponents among the Prussian nobility. Gneisenau, for example, proposed a sort of mass *levée*, its peasant participants to elect their own officers and to be rewarded with liberation from their compulsory labor services. Nobles, on the other hand, were to forfeit their patents, and princelings to lose their thrones should they not show sufficient ardor by joining what Gneisenau described as the German cause.

Scharnhorst, while offering as his purpose "the liberation of Germans by Germans," prescribed fewer social reform goals, yet he too called for a mass uprising of the German people in emulation of the Spaniards. Both he and Gneisenau fancied using the clergy to stir up patriotic feeling and loyalty to the monarch; "these," he wrote, "are the things that speak to the common man."

Stein put these plans before the king, explaining the proposals in the context of an analysis of the general foreign policy situation which, with the Spanish affair and Austria's formidable rearmament, appeared so threatening to Napoleon's empire. He and his military advisers had good reason to expect that they could quickly gain the necessary recruits for their undertaking. The level of popular discontent with the severe

French occupation was high. Prussia and its former territories were full of discharged soldiers and officers and enlisted men on half-pay, veterans of a once proud army, ingloriously vanquished in the campaigns of 1806 and subsequently returned to civilian status with the forced reduction of the Prussian forces. Here was a large and restive group which, as the observations of scholars who have systematically considered the behavior of other corps of discharged veterans suggest, would happily seize an opportunity to return to military society with its promise of traditional social and psychological rewards.

With Stein's approval or not, Gneisenau and Scharnhorst had already got in touch with groups of ex-soldiers and civilian patriotic sympathizers all over Germany. We may imagine how quickly the secret news they sent was thereafter spread from leader to trusted follower, to friend and acquaintance: the initiated veteran, seeking to break away from his isolation in the relative chaos of civilian life, was, I submit, subtly prompted to find new personal status by joining the plot and then by self-importantly sharing the word about the dangerous game with a potential recruit. Thus the cells quickly grew and the secrets of the plot, with its promise of early success, were soon spread. The first steps toward successful recruiting appear to have been taken with remarkable ease. By mid-August, at the very time the Königsberg staff was designing arguments which Stein could put to the king, they were already in touch with a far-flung net of conspiracy lying across northern and central Germany. What they probably did not understand was that the very urge that had led to the quick expansion of the circle—the recruit recruiting by sharing his secret—inevitably would lead to a quicker betrayal to the enemy.

By mid-August, when the proposal for a conspiracy and mass uprising was brought before the king, who typically could not be brought to say a definite "yes" or "no" to its adoption as a contingent program, the planning was already advanced, major parts of the organization were long in being, and decisions on all aspects of military and foreign policy henceforth had to take into account the plan and its prospects as well as the very existence of the secret military groups. By refusing at this time to deny his advisers any further moves, the king was not reserving his decision for the future, as he must have thought. He had, in effect, ratified the contingency planning. In this way the plot was set in motion with results that none of its originators probably had imagined.

The separate outposts of the conspiracy were in touch with one another and with the leaders in Königsberg, though a great deal of the evidence that would complete a picture of the net of their communications has been lost. Since it was necessary in fact to operate largely under French eyes, except in unoccupied East Prussia, the work was perilous, connections were not easily made, and chosen leaders, who could not always be closely checked, were sometimes insufficiently ardent or unreliable. A dangerous overlapping of commands and the duplication and garbling of messages tended to blur the lines of central control. In time all of this might have been changed for the better. But given the slow communications of the day, even under the best of conditions the uprising was too ambitious a secret undertaking to be carried out with satisfactory timing. Neither the necessary interval for careful preparation nor the circumstances proper for haste existed. And in August, at the very time the leaders were trying to build a military chain of command, recruit, collect arms, and improve communications in a countryside occupied by a hostile army, events outside the control of the Prussians lurched forward precipitately, seeming to demand the setting of an immediate time of action. There came striking reports of French defeats in Spain and consequently necessary withdrawals of some French troops from Germany; rumors of Austria's stepped-up pace of rearmament, and of the widespread discontent in the German countryside suffering under the heavy-handed French military administration. This news only increased the zeal and determination of the chief plotters and their followers.

But withal, King Frederick William remained significantly unmoved in the midst of this agitation. And in his hands lay the power of command. Frederick William's confidence in himself and his state had been smashed at Jena. Just as he had put himself wholly under the protection of the tsar at Tilsit, he now wanted the backing of his guarantor before participating in any action, just in case his armies should come to grief once more. Hence he wrote to Alexander, inquiring hopefully of his attitude toward the prospective Austrian campaign against the tsar's new ally, Napoleon. Alexander replied prophesying disaster: he would stand by his French friend.

Given the king's dependence on the tsar, it was virtually certain that he would make no move to upset his protector. Moreover, the Russian emperor could at this moment point out that Napoleon had at last given his assurance that he was ready to seal up the treaty of peace with the Prussian delegation long biding its time in Paris. The Spanish debacle was surely the strongest reason for Bonaparte's sudden willingness to come to terms with the beaten Prussians. But whatever his other motives, his concession now brought to the Prussians the prospect of achieving almost everything that Stein had vainly sought in Berlin in the spring. And with this, the original arguments advanced to support the insurrection plan lost their force.

But the plans were not put aside. The king gave no order to take back what he had, in any case, only tacitly accepted. Probably it appeared to him that the murky future might yet bring a time when this would prove the best form of action. Who knew how far Napoleon's fortunes might fall in Spain or how successful the Austrians might someday be? Could Prussia stand aside unprepared at some future date while Austria alone led a victorious campaign for the liberation of Germany? There were good reasons of state for keeping the range of possible actions wide—and thus for keeping the insurrectionary groups and secret recruiting alive too.

But I want to contend that there were other reasons, less apparent to the participants, why the plot did not fade away in the new circumstances. In fact, its supporters actually increased their dedication to it after its original *raison d'être*—Napoleon's continued bleeding of a shattered Prussia to which he refused to grant any terms of peace—had disappeared. How may this paradox be explained? First of all, by this time not only the Austrians, but other displaced German princes as well were beginning to collect their own legions to join the Austrians. For them the ranks of unemployed

Prussian and other German veterans provided a pool of potential volunteers. Alien blandishments presumably meant little to the Prussian regulars. But the outside recruiters posed a threat to the very existence of groups composed in large part of unpaid professional soldiers. In consequence of these temptations, responsible Prussian commanders striving to hold their commands intact for some future day of deliverance found themselves under great pressure to act quickly. Thus conditions outside Prussia made it impossible to set a course in response to domestic needs alone lest they lose the forces which political common sense seemed to dictate they might soon need.

Yet the more subtle prompting to rash deeds came out of what we may argue was a psychological conditioning that developed from the members' involvement in the plot. For as these committed patriots met in their local cells it may be suspected that their zeal increased rather than decreased. Because of the newness of these groups and the original inequalities among the mixed membership of military and civilian volunteers (which the comradeship strengthened by the special intimacy of secret sharing could only superficially obscure), they and their leaders would have handled more outlandish opinions far less successfully than long-established groups whose members' opinions and roles within the small society were already known or predictable. Indeed, we may argue, in keeping with behavioral research analogy, that those most outraged—the glib and skillful, the most inflammatory orators—would have been those who spoke their pieces in group meetings. Uncritical arguments for wild schemes larded with strident references to the old manly virtues would have had the largest appeal as unequals outbid in bravura those within military society whom they subconsciously regarded as rivals, while at the same time proving to civilian counterparts their military worth. In such a situation, researchers have contended, the very hearing of others' willingness to take risks makes one's like inclinations appear less dangerous. For these reasons, as well as because of the very strength of patriotic feeling among these self-selected patriots, the combative spirits would have found it easy to reprobate the cautious. Appeals to moderation would, in any case, have been at odds with the intended quick, direct achievement of the tradition-sanctioned goals; and any urge to caution would have denied the very nature of the group that had been formed for the expression of hostile feelings. Indeed, in small societies like these, where, I submit, great prestige is attached to belonging and carrying out the task of the group, where the personal power of natural and self-selected leaders was strong, and solidarity among the followers tended to grow with their acceptance of a common fate, indirect pressure to cooperate by consenting to the group's behavior as normative was likely to have become especially strong. For these reasons as well, those who spoke out for riskier courses of action would have prevailed. The moderate would have inclined to prudent silence, their occasional hesitant interpositions presumably beaten down by the zealots who were made yet more rash by the very moods that they had helped arouse. For their part, the responsible planners of the conspiracy would have had to match these violent humors with promises of action sufficiently satisfying to meet members' demands, or face the withering of their commands through the flight of their recruits.

All of this suggests that within the local cells there developed a disposition to act faster than the leaders wished. There was emerging from within the movement itself a stimulus to get on with the undertaking. This was to become a potent influence on the Prussian commanders, an omnipresent blackmail which had been scarcely, if at all, anticipated, and whose causes could have been but poorly understood by the participants. This inner force, perceptible, if not definable, acted to tear control of the plot out of the hands of those who, in calmer days, had ordained the plot's existence. The tail, if it had not yet come to wag the dog, could at least set it atremble.

Stein, Gneisenau, and Scharnhorst were thus confronted by late summer with a state of mind among the plotters whose effects they perceived, but which they had not anticipated when they set their plans in motion. It seems reasonable to suppose that they had, by this time, taken the group's patriotic spirit as a true reflection of the state of mind of the country languishing under foreign rule. They were likely unaware of the further development of their own feelings which, as I shall now contend, had moved along event by event once they had joined their first energies to the adventure. By late summer the investment of their own spiritual and physical means was already great. Yet the prospect of a disgraceful peace, now apparently at hand with the proffering of the new French terms, would compel them to undo all their work without granting them an opportunity to attain any gratification—though other Germans might soon march on to success and glory. Their own conspiratorial bands would fade away as the enthusiasms of the ardent frittered away in discouragement, and the hope for action that was the sustenance of the less ardent dissolved. Hence they must have come to grasp very differently the political situations they had believed hopeless but a short time before. As their plans had so easily matured, so had their expectations of complete redemption. The once acceptable conditions of peace Bonaparte was now offering in his distress they could no longer reconcile with the seemingly reduced means he had of enforcing any peace terms. French debacles, the revival of German spirits, and the readily communicable enthusiasm of the groups had brought Stein and his friends to view their formerly contingent program as the only program. It appeared as the single tolerable alternative to the noisome peace treaty in spite of the fact that Stein, before his return from Berlin only a few months before, would have been desperately happy to sign terms hardly worse. Rejecting these conditions now, Stein and his allies seem to have become eager to pour ever-greater energies into a scheme fraught with risk in order to make their dreams come true. Judgments and actions taken so far they could justify to themselves only if allowed the opportunity to make their plan work. In effect, to thwart its undoing, which the acceptance of the peace terms could mean, they were subtly prompted to commit yet greater energies to make the original investment pay off. In this additional undertaking they quite likely took pleasure in viewing theirs as the sole path of honor and patriotism, on which they could best serve their state and their nation. But it appears in retrospect that they had merely surrendered themselves gradually, quite unknowingly all the while, to the inner momentum of the plot. Meanwhile, the king, that most timid of leaders, was willing for the nonce to shelve the conspiracy and take the mixed blessings Napoleon was offering.

Thus, whatever the inclinations of the conspirators, Bonaparte's concession of terms and the king's willingness to accept them meant that the forward movement of the plot had to be arrested at least temporarily while the situation was reconsidered. A stance that would keep open all the policy options had to be found. As for the plot this was at best a time to hold the groups together with promises of future action; to recruit, collect arms, and bind more tightly the separate units by improving the net of communications; and to gather information on the French and their movements. Tsar Alexander was expected to pass through Königsberg soon on his way to meet Napoleon at the congress of French-allied sovereigns at Erfurt. Frederick William and Stein would at last have a chance to hear his opinions directly on the still developing conflict between Austria and France. Stein evidently hoped that the tsar could be won over to support of the Austrian cause, which he wanted to make Prussia's, and that, with Alexander's blessing, his own king would then agree to carry on with the uprising plans. At the very least Stein expected to secure Alexander's promise of a strong representation to Napoleon of Prussia's case for better peace terms.

Yet when Alexander did arrive (18 September 1808), he refused to be budged from his alliance with Napoleon. His decision meant the conspiracy was dead as far as Frederick William was concerned. This attitude of the tsar the conspirators had at least anticipated. Hence the bad news was overshadowed completely by the disaster that befell Stein, who, at the very moment of the conference with the tsar, was being publicly ridiculed in the French-controlled European press for his involvement in the plot. He had been caught flagrantly spinning out the web of conspiracy. Circumstances suggest that he unintentionally showed himself as an implacable foe of France while eagerly yielding to the fatal temptation to spread the secret and widen the circle of intimacy.

Stein's incredible indiscretion had been revealed as follows. Acting on a tip, French officials had seized an official Prussian courier just outside Berlin. He bore several important letters from Stein to Baron Wilhelm Ludwig zu Sayn-Wittgenstein, a Prussian financial agent in Hamburg. One of them Stein had written at the height of his initial enthusiasm for the conspiracy, when he had had news of France's most recent misfortunes in Spain. All too candidly he had sought to convey to Wittgenstein, to whom he had no good reason to open up the secrets of the plot, his growing hopes for action and his optimistic assessment of the strength of anti-French feeling in the country. With this letter in their hands, the French knew even the chief of the Prussian government was caballing against them. The letter, along with other secret information on Prussia's recently more favorable financial status, Napoleon's agents had then suddenly pushed before the eyes of the long beleaguered Prussian representatives in Paris. Stein's own words, giving the lie to his ancient arguments for a reduction in the size of reparations and pointing directly to the threat that the Prussian military forces still posed to France's empire, were thus used to compel the Prussians to accept terms of settlement somewhat less advantageous than Stein had agreed upon in March. Stein's own errant letter appeared to contemporaries to have brought the state he served to the edge of disaster. Only his agitated state of mind and an urge to blurt out the secrets of the conspiracy can account for his blunder.

At this point we see Stein compromised because of his involvement in the plot before Napoleon and his marshals. They would hold effective power in occupied Prussia until the evacuation. He had been likewise made to appear foolish in the eyes of his own king. Frederick William saw the need to remove Stein forthwith from his *de facto* position as director of foreign affairs and send another agent off to Erfurt as Prussia's representative. Prussia could scarcely expect the leniency Alexander was to argue for after Stein's pleading if the appearance of the anti-French plotter himself should provoke Bonaparte's fabulous temper. Henceforth Stein's effectiveness as minister and reformer inevitably declined. Some influential Prussians, chiefly those conservatives who viewed Stein as the main force behind the reform measures they opposed, were quite ready to seize the occasion to persuade the king that his usefulness to Prussia had ended. Stein no doubt quickly sensed a change in his political weight, not only in his relations with the king and the court, and in his inability to represent Prussia diplomatically at Erfurt, but also in the gradual and subtle shift in attitudes he met in daily encounters with his rivals and enemies, open and secret, among his ministerial colleagues and in the civil service. From this time on, he was to watch helplessly as his power slipped away, not only in the forfeited area of foreign affairs. No longer could the weight of his opinions alone sustain his arguments as they once had. Yet, fateful for his political aims, the reform work was barely begun. For only with the end of the French occupation could his measures be brought to cover the vast majority of the state's territories. Major proposals had yet to be drafted and brought through the tedious wrangles of committees. With war between Austria and France looming, and a German insurrection being planned, Prussia's foreign policy role had to be carefully delineated. But Stein now saw himself shoved away from the foreign affairs that he had previously conducted, and meeting more and more resistance to his opinions and deeds in those areas of government yet remaining to him. Indeed, he was soon being challenged by his foes privately and publicly, as they sought to use his embarrassment and the animosity of the French to turn him out of office and thereby junk his radical domestic and military programs; recall that even the latter had social change as one goal. He must have now suddenly seen the consequences of his involvement in the conspiratorial movement. He faced the loss of all that he had fought to achieve: the reform of the state and the liberation of Germany from the French yoke.

Following the arguments already developed we ought to be able to hypothesize at this point the course of action that Stein and his friends would take in these new and dangerous circumstances which the revelation of their plot had brought on: they would grow yet more zealous in pursuit of the aims on whose achievement they had gambled so much. They would push forward their conspiratorial plans more singlemindedly than ever, asserting among other things that the onerous terms forced on the Prussian negotiators by Bonaparte would cast the state into bankruptcy and make its recovery as a power impossible. They would tell the king that, with so much already invested in the plan, the termination of the plot and the dismissal of the patriotic bands would end in the disillusionment of the loyal recruits and their loss to Prussia. They would make these arguments to themselves and to others, becoming more strident with each repetition. For they had come by this time to see the situation as even more critical than it had seemed at midsummer. They—Stein, of course, in particular—could not believe that their military plans had led to the end of the reform government; rather they counted upon redeeming their authority, and thus saving the state by making a success of the failure that seemed imminent. They were ready to do their utmost to avert the compromising of their own judgments. This they could do only by making their plot work, however much effort it would require.

Frederick William, in turmoil, resolved to ratify the odious terms, but failed (surprisingly) to inform any of his responsible counselors in Königsberg, including Stein, of his decision. He quietly sent his word off to his agent in Erfurt, to be delivered to the French. While it is easy to understand why the blundering Stein was not consulted, it is unaccountable that he, who still held important ministerial portfolios, and who as finance minister would have to arrange to raise the very reparations funds that the king was pledging, was not even informed. The military chiefs of the conspiracy were likewise not told of the decision, which of course created yet another new diplomatic situation that must force a rethinking of their plans.

Hence when Stein thereafter actually did go on plotting his campaign against the French with more zeal than ever, he had no official notice that new developments demanded a reconsideration of his work so far. He ought, in common sense, to have asked the king to take up the matter again, as soon as possible, considering all that had passed since the plot was first proposed. But he was obviously fearful that the king would then simply put an end to the affair; the more to be expected if he and his friends could not be on hand to deliver their powerful arguments in favor of it. As one of his first acts after the revelation of his plotting he therefore wrote the king a memorandum, probably unsolicited, calling for a rejection of the treaty terms—to repeat, virtually the same terms he had begged for a few months before. Meanwhile he had written to his trusted military agent in Silesia just as if nothing out of the ordinary had happened, in spite of the revelation of the plot and his own involvement in it. He urged him to go on with his activities and continue working up anti-French feeling. For Stein, publicly reprobated and reduced in political stature by the French, it appears that the campaign against Bonaparte was becoming a personal crusade for vindication. His own fate and that of the fatherland must have seemed to him to be merging. The conspiracy, whose success would reestablish his name and reputation, was to him more in order than ever before. Thus, while the king was secretively conducting Prussia's foreign affairs, perhaps out of fear of the arguments that Stein and his military advisers might mount against his decisions, Stein carried on determinedly the very policy that had been in part discredited, fearful that the king might order its abandonment. . . .

Discussion

Given the fact that conspirators normally obscure their traces, the large number of sources I uncovered on one conspiratorial undertaking offered a singular opportunity for a special type of historical study. I shortened some sections of the story line and expanded others with detail to elucidate those parts of the plot offering insights into evident attitudinal changes of the participants in these undercover groups. The attempted explanations in these extended sections on behavior in secret activity have been enhanced by using analogies gathered from laboratory studies and other systematic investigations. My hope is that this case study will contribute to a general theory of conspiratorial conduct that will center on the development of the attitudes of the individuals involved.

The pattern of events discussed here may prove to be that of other conspiracies. But it must be kept in mind that this one was first of all a military venture, though both Gneisenau and Stein (to name but two of the leaders) expected it to conduce toward social goals: freeing the serfs and breaking down class barriers. By contrast, most such plots whose outlines are recorded seem to have been hatched chiefly for the sole purpose of political and social revolution. Nonetheless, this conspiracy would appear to have enough in common with others having entirely different goals to be considered as a paradigm.

Interpreting my evidence in accordance with appropriate analogues drawn from history and social science, I have contended that the developments at issue followed organically, stage by stage, from the initial, hesitant conspiratorial planning decisions.

First, I tried to show that forces generated within the individual cells tended to heighten the influence of the risk-takers and stifle the voices of the more moderate. This radicalizing tendency appears to have become especially strong because of the particular composition of these groups. Their membership was largely drawn from a self-selected host of those who were extremely disoriented and disadvantaged by societal forces beyond their control. They came as unequals in status, unfamiliar with one another's points of view and behavior, holding a strong sense of the injustice they had supposedly been suffering. Once together, they found a traditionally approved outlet for their hostilities and a satisfying social attachment. Under these circumstances they vied with one another subconsciously for stature and leadership within the local organizations, which thereby became more bellicose than the central command. They were far readier than their general staff to accept risks they could not calculate.

Second, I argued that the plot itself developed an increasing internal momentum which imperceptibly gathered up leader and follower alike, pushing commanders to act more quickly than they thought wise and at variance with their original plans. This force, whose coming was unforeseen, and whose existence was not comprehended by the participants, even by those who nominally held the reins of power, abolished the likelihood of a reasoned direction of events.

A great part of this unanticipated momentum derived from the zeal developed within the cells. But another part came from the conspirators' coming to view their conspiratorial plans as ends in themselves, even after their original goals had been achieved by other means. One reason for this, I maintained, was that, once significant energies were invested in the scheme, the leaders felt the need to justify that investment by success—and the more so, the more they put into just keeping their scheme alive. The greater the threat to their brainchild, the greater their exertions to save it.

Third, I have singled out for particular attention the conditions originating in the need for secrecy. It contributed to group solidarity and, paradoxically, to recruiting new members. I have argued, in addition, that the subconscious impulse to spread the secret in order to expand the circle of intimacy meant that the plot was sure to be quickly revealed to the enemy—as it soon was by Stein, the leader, himself. Finally, I have stressed the importance of secrecy in creating the overwhelming problems in logistics and communications—most of them apparently unanticipated.

My contention throughout has been that those who were most deeply involved in the plot and whose fates hinged on its success and failure, Stein and his military advisers as well as many of their subalterns, were swayed at crucial moments of decision by the irrational forces generated within these particular group processes. To go beyond this imperfect generalization about behavioral motivation, common sense suggests to me that we must continue to investigate the shadowy tangle of influences on individual personalities. . . .

chapter ten

Informal Organization

There is always a difference between the real world and the world as it is supposed to be. In any organization there are lines of authority that are so formally established that they may be indicated on an organizational chart. But no organization is wholly formal. In day-to-day operation, we all depend on supplementary informal relationships, so that actual lines of authority may vary somewhat from those prescribed.

This readily noticeable condition of any organization has provided the basis for the social psychological theory of informal organization. It takes many forms. It has been observed, for example, that governmental agencies tend to develop informal lines of authority in addition to those legally established. Consultation may then take place, not vertically, with one's superior, but laterally, with one's equal, across the established lines of authority. Requesting advice from an equal does not involve the same possible admission of incompetence as asking advice of a superior; one tends to be wary of revealing ineptitude to the person who has control over one's career. Furthermore, the informal organization is likely to be composed of members who share the same or similar ideas.[1] More important, from a common-sense point of view, it is often far easier to consult with those who are not in the formal line of authority than it is to go to a supervisor. Social and occupational equals are more accessible and are usually seen more frequently. One analysis of a U. S. government agency found just such behavior as described above. The members of the agency not only held regular consultations across lines of authority, but also created an informal organization that established its own rules ("norms," even "taboos") to guide its conduct. One agency member who violated these extralegal rules (one of which, the taboo against reporting bribe at-

---

[1]See Edward A. Shils, "The Study of the Primary Group," in Daniel Lerner and Harold D. Lasswell, eds., *The Policy Sciences: Recent Developments in Scope and Method* (Stanford: Stanford University Press, 1951), p. 48.

tempts, was in flagrant violation of law) was isolated because he adhered to law and established authority, which alone were supposed to regulate the conduct of his job.[2]

Although an informal organization may merely supplement the formal organization, sometimes it becomes so extensive and fundamental to a group's existence that it spontaneously replaces the formal organization. In either event, all formal organizations have their informal parallels, and in some cases the former may not be able to function efficiently unless its decisions are approved by the latter.[3] Thus, in an instance quite familiar to veterans of army service, unofficial but very effective networks operate among enlisted men. These informal relationships manipulate everything from duty assignments to the well known ability of supply sergeants to borrow from each other to assure exact, correct inventories as each unit is inspected in turn.[4] Comparable behavior is often found in academic life. Important decisions are made by informal cliques composed of a few professors and administrators, some of whom may not hold any formal position of authority. Such was the situation during the U. S. Civil War, according to Thomas Lawrence Connelly and Archer Jones. These authors claim that a powerful informal organization in the Southern army was created by a combination of informal organizations, the "Abingdon-Columbia bloc," the "anti-Bragg bloc," the "Kentucky bloc," and the bloc clustered around the "personality and ideas of General P. G. T. Beauregard." This combined informal organization, the "western concentration bloc," eventually had a large voice in determining the military strategy adopted by the beleaguered Confederacy.

In view of what social psychologists have learned about informal organization, this development was hardly surprising. Indeed, it would have been more surprising if something similar to the western concentration bloc and its constituent informal organizations had not been formed. The Confederate Army was a new entity and the Confederate government created new lines of authority. This new formal organization

---

[2]See George Caspar Homans, *Social Behavior: Its Elementary Forms* (New York: Harcourt, Brace and World, 1961), Chapter XVII, especially pp. 360–63 and 373–75, which discusses the significance of some of the research findings of Peter M. Blau, *The Dynamics of Bureaucracy: A Study of Interpersonal Relations in Two Government Agencies* (Chicago: University of Chicago Press, 1955); (a revised second edition was published in 1963). For a good discussion of informal organization see Chester I. Barnard, *The Functions of the Executive,* anniversary ed. (Cambridge, Mass.: Harvard University Press, 1968), especially Chapter IX, and Herbert G. Hicks and C. Ray Gullett, *Organizations: Theory and Behavior* (New York: McGraw-Hill, 1975), Chapter VI.

[3]This has been shown to be true in factories and even in the World War II War Relocation Centers when U. S. Government communications with camp inhabitants were effective only if the authorities empowered to receive the communications were those whom the camp inhabitants preferred. Especially significant, in view of the following selection, is the finding that this also tends to be true in military organizations (as Confederate General Braxton Bragg discovered to his great chagrin). See Shils, "The Study of the Primary Group," pp. 48, 64–65.

[4]For a brief examination of informal organization as it operates in a military context, see Anonymous, "Informal Social Organization in the Army," *American Journal of Sociology* 51 (March 1946): 365–70.

was an overlay on preexisting networks of relationships that could not be erased immediately by the temporary authority of a newly created army. Kinship networks, as Connelly and Jones show, were extensive. They predated the Confederate Army's birth and they survived far longer. Equally important were the ties created by other organizations, such as the U. S. Army and the federal and state governments, in which many Confederate leaders had served. The events of the Civil War could hardly be expected to erase such prior relationships as superior-subordinate, fellow officer or legislator, or uncle-nephew. It is only natural to expect that when these informal organizations developed—as was inevitable—they would follow preexisiting lines of relationship.

Frequently the reason for the appearance of such informal organization is the inadequacy of the formal pattern. There may be flaws in the structural design or a deficiency in individual performance. In these cases there is a vacuum that must be filled if the goals of the organization are to be achieved—or sometimes if it is even to remain in existence. The members then develop their own informal organization to fill the vacuum by prescribing practices hitherto unprescribed, including such minutiae as how morning greetings are to be made or such vital procedures as the channels and occasions for command and consultation. Even in rather rigid and extensive organizational patterns, informal organization will inadvertently be created by the day-to-day relationships of group members.[5]

Another characteristic of the sort of organizational behavior that may lead to the creation of informal organizations is the development of ideological points of view (broadly defined); this too is illustrated by the western concentration bloc. Not all members of the formal organization are likely to have the same ideas. If some members feel strongly about their dissenting doctrines, they may attempt to establish alliances with other group members in order to make their ideas felt in the bureaucracy. A brilliant idea supported by one person alone remains just an idea. But if the sponsor gets allies the idea may become action. This being so, we may suppose that generals in an army (such as the Confederate Army), who favor a certain proposed strategy, will make the necessary alliances, thereby creating "small clusters of individuals who seek to act together both in 'putting across' decisions proposed by them and in attending to their respective interests in the institutional context."[6] Quite naturally we would expect that generals in other parts of the Army, politicians of like mind, and influential relatives would be brought into these clusters.

In addition, the western concentration bloc exemplifies the role of a key individual in providing the basis for an informal organization. Consultation across lines of author-

[5]See Herbert A. Simon, Donald W. Smithburg, and Victor A. Thompson, *Public Administration* (New York: Alfred A. Knopf, 1961), pp. 87–88.
[6]Fritz Morstein Marx, *The Administrative State: An Introduction to Bureaucracy* (Chicago: University of Chicago Press, 1957), p. 96.

ity may create the clusters necessary to support certain ideas, but it may also be that the ideas are inseparable from the man who conceived them. The cluster may then be held together by the force of this leading personality, who maintains the allegiance, in a wide sense, of the members of an informal organization. The pattern of relationship may become exceedingly complex, as "uncrowned leaders compete with crowned ones [and] informal and often unaccountable groupings brought to life for various purposes press against one another."[7] In any army this will be so; in the Confederate Army natural tendencies became absolute certainties, as shown by the disruptive behavior of General Bragg, the occasional obstinacy of Jefferson Davis, and the excessive individualism fostered by armchair generalship and state rights philosophy that encouraged many "uncrowned leaders" to seek authority.

Such key individuals are important to the working of an informal organization, but they are also a source of weakness in the application of the concept. Everywhere one can find uncrowned leaders, and it would be easy for the historian to examine their correspondence and discover informal organizations that did not exist, at least not in the way the historian may think they did. This is all the more true because all formal organizations will have informal parallels, and since there is no premeditation in their establishment and usually no conscious system in their interaction, it is difficult to determine their composition and leadership. Indeed, the leadership is likely to change, depending on the problems the group faces and the willingness of followers to continue following.[8] The problem becomes even greater when one understands that leaders may not be aware they are leaders and the members of the group are not even likely to realize that they have created an informal organization. Under such conditions one prominent member may appear to be as good a candidate for leadership as any other, and if proof of leadership roles is difficult to come by so is disproof. Like conspiratorial groups, informal organizations are unlikely to leave records for the historian to examine; it is no wonder that historians have been slow to link the shadow organizations they frequently encounter (e. g., Andrew Jackson's "Kitchen Cabinet") with the social psychological concept that helps to explain their existence.

To Connelly and Jones, General P. G. T. Beauregard was the uncrowned leader of the western concentration bloc, an informal organization that came into conflict with the formal organization it overlapped. The implications of such overlay and the conflict it created may be great. The consequences may include misunderstanding or even outright mutiny or revolution, as in an army or government. In this particular case, the four groups coalesced to form the western concentration bloc because their interests coincided as far as a western offensive was concerned. They could readily rally behind Beauregard, who could show that the offensive all desired was dictated by the

---

[7]Harvey C. Mansfield and Fritz Morstein Marx, "Informal Organization," Chapter XIII in Fritz Morstein Marx, ed., *Elements of Public Administration,* 2nd ed. (Englewood Cliffs, N. J.: Prentice-Hall, 1959); quote is from pp. 286–87.

[8]Hicks and Gullett, *Organizations,* pp. 107, 114.

Napoleonic principles of war. His articulateness and his tireless lobbying made the popular, magnetic general the natural focal point and leader in advocating a western strategy even though he was persona non grata to Jefferson Davis. The conflict was not resolved until the informal western concentration bloc was finally successful in winning over the *formal* organization; over Lee's opposition Jefferson Davis belatedly adopted the strategic ideas of the *informal* organization. The Confederate victory at Chickamauga was the result.

Note that the existence and nature of the informal organization is established with the aid of collective biography, without which it would have been difficult if not impossible to determine the extent of this inevitable shadow group. As a future essay demonstrates, however, these are not the same methods, nor are they even similar. In this case the nature of the evidence necessitated that the one device be employed as a complement to the other. The point here is not the tangled web of interrelationships, per se, but that the individuals involved interacted in conformity to the social psychological model of the informal organization.

The Western Concentration Bloc
Thomas Lawrence Connelly and Archer Jones

General R. E. Lee was Confederate President Jefferson Davis' official as well as unofficial military advisor. As Commander of the Army of Northern Virginia, Lee's advice stressed the importance of the Virginia front and the peril to his army and to Richmond, the Confederate capital, presented by unremitting Union pressure in Virginia. But many Confederate leaders, both military and civilian, strongly disagreed with Lee's advice to concentrate troops in Virginia. Lee's opponents, without his ready access to the Confederate President, worked through informal channels of communication. These channels included political leaders such as Senator L. T. Wigfall of Texas. As a member of the Military Affairs Committee of the Confederate Senate he had ready access to Secretary of War Seddon, who had been a fellow law student at the Universty of Virginia. In addition Wigfall had served in the United States Senate with Jefferson Davis. He was representative of many political leaders who had the opportunity to influence strategy and who also had wide contacts with dissident Confederate generals.

The formulation of an opposition strategy to Lee's and the exploitation of the many informal channels of communication to press it on Davis was the work of a formidable composite informal organization, the western concentration bloc. Although individual plans often varied, the group which appeared in 1862 was dominated by two ideas. First, its members rejected what appeared to be a governmental policy of a cordon

An adaptation of Chapter 3 from *The Politics of Command* by Thomas Connelly and Archer Jones, copyright © 1973, reprinted by permission of Louisiana State University Press.

defense of the West, and they advocated risking the loss of territory in order to secure an offensive concentration of western manpower. This type of concentration was not the same as the type often practiced by Richmond—responding to an enemy buildup on one line of advance by a Rebel concentration on that same front—instead, the western bloc embraced a Napoleonic concept. Concentration was to be effected upon one of the weakest of the multiple lines of advance used by the western Federals, followed by a rapid concentration for an offensive.

Second, the western concentration bloc was also motivated by a strong concern for the fate of the central South. Its members were preoccupied with the central corridor via Nashville, Chattanooga, and Atlanta into the lower South. Gradually, many of the group's strategic proposals centered on the need to thwart a Federal advance on the Chattanooga-Atlanta route into the lower South's munitions complex of Macon, Augusta, Selma, and Columbus.

The extensive influence of the western concentration bloc in Confederate history was probably the result of its relationship to other factions within the Confederate military system. Historians not only have underrated the western concentration bloc's contributions to strategic thought and action, but also have failed to examine the informal organizations which constituted it. These interrelated organizations, for the sake of identification, might be termed (1) the Abingdon-Columbia bloc (2) the anti-Bragg bloc (3) the Kentucky bloc, and (4) the Beauregard bloc. They not only combined to form the western concentration bloc, but they independently wielded substantial influence in Confederate affairs.

The keystone of the Abingdon-Columbia bloc was an intricate set of family relationships embracing many well-known Confederate names, such as Johnston, Floyd, Preston, Breckinridge, and Hampton. Many of these families, such as the parents of General Joseph E. Johnston, had dominated the society of the lower Appalachian Valley of Virginia. They had been the prominent families of southwestern Virginia, and had centered their living at the town of Abingdon.

Johnston was kin to many powerful families which at one time had flourished in the Abingdon vicinity and then had gradually migrated either to South Carolina or to Kentucky. Johnston's grandmother was a sister of Patrick Henry. Another Henry sister had married General William Campbell, a hero of King's Mountain. From this relationship Johnston was kin to the powerful Preston family. General William Campbell's daughter married Francis Preston of Abingdon. One son, John Smith Preston, practiced law in Abingdon before becoming prominent in prewar South Carolina politics. Preston, a South Carolina commissioner to Virginia in 1861, also had ties with Beauregard. In 1861 he had served with Beauregard as an aide, at both Charleston and Manassas; eventually the Creole (as Beauregard was sometimes called) recommended Preston for a brigadier generalship. Later Preston headed the Bureau of Conscription.

These Preston kinships were even more embracing. General William Preston, an avowed member of the anti-Bragg faction in the Army of Tennessee, was a son of

William Campbell Preston. Another relative, William Ballard Preston, was an influential Virginia lawyer, congressman, and cabinet member prior to the war. This Preston's grandparents also hailed from Abingdon, and during the war, William Ballard Preston was both a Confederate senator from Virginia and a strong supporter of Joseph E. Johnston.

Gradually the ties became more intermingled. General Wade Hampton, a wartime supporter of Johnston, was a distant relative of the general's. Hampton had married Margaret Preston. Margaret Preston was the sister of Johnston's relative and Beauregard's aide, the future head of the Conscription Bureau, John S. Preston.

The Floyd family of Kentucky and Virginia also was interconnected to this group. General John B. Floyd was tied by geography, sentiment, and kinship to the Abingdon-Columbia bloc. He also had been raised in the Abingdon vicinity, and had attended South Carolina College. Floyd's mother was the daughter of William Preston of Abingdon. This William Preston was also the grandfather of the Confederate General William Preston. Later, Floyd married his cousin, Sally Buchanan Preston, a granddaughter of General William Campbell. By these ties, Floyd was kin to Joseph E. Johnston, Wade Hampton, William Preston of Bragg's army, and the pro-Johnston Senator William Ballard Preston of Virginia.

Other Rebel families were tied to this network of in-laws. General John C. Breckinridge of Kentucky, former United States Senator and Vice-President, was a powerful member of the anti-Bragg faction in the Army of Tennessee. Breckinridge was related, at least by marriage, to Joseph E. Johnston, John B. Floyd, Wade Hampton, and William Preston. The interrelationship of the Breckinridge family with other bloc members was best expressed by the name given to General John C. Breckinridge's first cousin, who was a nephew of John Smith Preston of the Conscription Bureau. This Breckinridge, a colonel in General John Morgan's cavalry, was named William Campbell Preston Breckinridge. John C. Breckinridge had been Vice-President when Floyd served as Secretary of War.

The interweaving of this group embraced far more than family ties. Friendships, common strategic views, or even particular antagonisms toward the Richmond government connected a loose network of individuals, many associated with South Carolina. One such was General P. G. T. Beauregard, a leader of the Abingdon-Columbia faction. Beauregard had no kinship to others in this group, but he possessed their affection. Two thirds of Beauregard's Civil War career was spent in South Carolina: first as commander of the original Charleston defenses, and later as commander of the Department of South Carolina, Georgia, and Florida.

Another member of the faction, who also supported Beauregard heartily, was Senator Louis T. Wigfall of Texas. Wigfall had two ties with the Abingdon-Columbia bloc. He was a South Carolinian, born in the Edgefield District, and an alumnus of South Carolina College. His army service had been in Virginia under Johnston and Beauregard. Johnston and Wigfall were good friends and their wives also corresponded regularly. Johnston had recuperated in Wigfall's Richmond home from the wound suffered at Seven Pines. Later, after his removal from command in the Atlanta campaign, Johnston took up residence in Columbia, the home of Mrs. Johnston's sister. There Wigfall's two daughters lived with the Johnstons. They had been left with the general since June, 1864, when their parents had departed on a trip to Texas.

The Abingdon-Columbia faction maintained close ties with the members of other Confederate pressure blocs who also were generally antagonistic to administration policy. One such was the anti-Bragg faction—a powerful bloc within the Army of Tennessee, which was commanded by General Braxton Bragg. Not all members of the Abingdon group were, however, hostile to Bragg. Both Johnston and Beauregard maintained fairly good relationships with Bragg until 1864.

Yet Bragg seemed the vulnerable spot in Richmond's war policy. To Davis' opponents in Congress, this unfortunate general was a useful tool with which to criticize the government. By the summer of 1863 Bragg had a long record of defeats—Perryville, Murfreesboro, and the Duck River line. To demand a reinstatement of Johnston or Beauregard in Virginia, or to attack General Lee at all seemed foolish. Lee had turned back McClellan at the Seven Days' campaign, had destroyed General John Pope's reputation at Second Manassas, and had slaughtered General Ambrose E. Burnside's men at Fredericksburg. But Bragg was a loser, and by 1863 was extremely vulnerable.

The sentiment against Bragg within the Abingdon bloc went deeper than merely being a political device to attack Davis. Johnston and Beauregard exemplified a certain frustration. Both men had commanded the South's two main field armies. Yet in 1862, both had apparently been shuffled by Richmond to less important positions. Beauregard had been removed from the command of the Army of Tennessee in June. Johnston had been replaced by Lee after his severe wound at Seven Pines, and, after recuperating, was simply not reassigned to his old command. Instead, Johnston was given command of the vaguely defined Western Department.

From their base within the Abingdon-Columbia group both Johnston and Beauregard felt, for a large part of the war, a sense of exile. They had left the two chief field commands in June, 1862, when Confederate strength seemed to be rising. By the autumn of 1862, Confederate power, at least in the West, already seemed to be declining. The obvious conclusion drawn by these generals and their supporters was that had they commanded instead of Bragg, matters would have been different. Clearly Davis was playing favorites, and the Confederacy was suffering while Johnston and Beauregard languished in storage. This resentment against Bragg bound the Abingdon bloc to a second faction, the anti-Bragg bloc.

The anti-Bragg bloc was one of the most militant of the informal groups in the Confederacy. Centered within the Army of Tennessee, it also exemplified the overlapping of partisan groups. Several key members, such as Generals James Longstreet and Leonidas Polk were also in the western concentration bloc. Others, such as Generals John C. Breckinridge and William Preston, were among the interconnecting family groups of the Abingdon bloc.

The anti-Bragg bloc must be defined with caution. Not all who disliked Bragg were members. The term does not apply to general resentment throughout the Confederacy against Bragg's generalship. Instead, the true anti-Bragg faction was a combination of dissident generals within the Army of Tennessee who in late 1862 began to form a coalition to oust Bragg. By September of 1863 the coalition was so strong—embracing all four army corps leaders—that the group rose to challenge Bragg in an exhibition of near mutiny.

The power of the faction within the Army of Tennessee was obvious. Beyond the army, it was linked to the Abingdon bloc by family ties and a common resentment of Bragg. The uproar created by Bragg's opponents in itself focused attention on western matters. The correspondence of its members with Davis, Seddon, Wigfall, and others stressed the need for more attention to the West. Such correspondence also often urged the strategic policies of the western bloc.

The anti-Bragg faction was also influential because of its ties with another Confederate informal organization—the Kentucky bloc. This geographic faction was composed of a number of prominent Kentucky generals and politicians who maintained a close relationship throughout the war. Its military adherents included Generals John Morgan, William Preston, Joseph Lewis, Humphrey Marshall, Simon Buckner, and John C. Breckinridge. Its political members included the Confederate governor of Kentucky, Richard C. Hawes, and Senator H. C. Burnett.

The group was bound by a single ideal—to pressure the Confederates to attempt to regain Kentucky. This desire led to rapport with other factions. The Kentuckians' goals made them natural members of the western concentration bloc with its stress on the need for a concentrated offensive in the West. They were far less interested than other members of the western concentration bloc were in the fine points of Napoleonic strategy or in the threat to the Chattanooga-Atlanta front. An offensive meant a promise of redeeming their native state. Like the Abingdon-Columbia and the anti-Bragg factions, the Kentucky bloc generally was strongly opposed to Bragg because of that general's failure to recapture the state.

Bragg had problems with Kentucky generals because he did not comprehend their great pride and their widespread support. To the Kentucky bloc the war was a personal matter. Breckinridge and Humphrey Marshall, another of the powerful political figures in the state, had fled as fugitives to the Confederacy. Buckner had been a prominent military figure and Morgan a wealthy Lexington merchant. All of their prestige had been swept away, and these men had been cast as refugees. Thus the group was also bound together psychologically.

These three factions, the Abingdon-Columbia, anti-Bragg, and Kentucky blocs, formed a broad network of informal associations which largely composed the western concentration bloc. Yet the ties between all of these groups were based on family connections, friendships, state loyalty, or mutual hatreds. The final thread which connected these men was another informal but more embracing association, one that revolved around the personality and ideas of General P. G. T. Beauregard.

Beauregard's importance as a nucleus of several such factions goes beyond his membership in them. True, he shared the views of the western concentration bloc and, by virtue of his Carolina service, became a leader in the Abingdon-Columbia faction.

Furthermore, Beauregard, like Bragg and others, benefited from an informal association composed of admirers.

There was a mystique surrounding this general which in many respects seems unjustified. His vain, showy personality tended to alienate people. Yet he was influential in spite of, or perhaps because of, the fact that he was something of a fraud—a cocky, bombastic, foppish officer who was more powerful with pen than with sword, and who delighted in signing orders "within hearing of the enemy's guns" or in appealing for plantation bells to cast artillery. He was also a frantic correspondent with generals, governors, authors, and congressmen.

His ensuing correspondence is amazing for its breadth. He conferred in detail on western strategy with Senator Wigfall and generals Johnston, Bragg, Longstreet, and Breckinridge. He discussed diplomatic problems and blockade running with John Slidell. He outlined plans for a northwestern Confederacy with governors Joseph Brown of Georgia and F. W. Pickens of South Carolina. He discussed the defense of the Gulf with General Dabney Maury. Beauregard talked of the loss of New Orleans with General Mansfield Lovell. He advised General Chase Whiting on the defense of the North Carolina coast and Governor Isham Harris on the defense of the Mississippi River fortifications in Tennessee. To Congressman William Porcher Miles he sent advice on grand strategy and on the matter of a northwestern Confederacy.

Beauregard resembled a candidate for public office. He took pains to lecture on the Napoleonic principles of concentration—to Bragg and Johnston, to novelist Augusta Jane Evans, to Congressman Charles Villeré, and to Governor Joseph Brown of Georgia. He had a sympathetic word for the dissidents—for General Lovell after his loss of New Orleans, for the troubled Whiting on the North Carolina coast, and for a miserable Johnston on the Tennessee front in the spring of 1863. He never let the South forget him.

Because of his strategic views, he fit well into the western concentration bloc. His belief that concentration was needed in the West not only complemented the ideas of such officers as Bragg and Johnston, but also gained the appreciation of Senator Gustavus Henry of Tennessee, Governor Isham Harris of Tennessee, Vice-President Alexander Stephens, Governor Joseph Brown, and others. Beauregard also moved within the antiadministration bloc in Congress. Three of his former aides were in the Congress. Two of them, William Porcher Miles and Roger Pryor, were anti-Davis men, as was his brother-in-law by his first marriage, Charles Villeré of Louisiana. These, together with his supporter Wigfall, gave the Creole a base in Richmond.

Beauregard could identify with the anti-Bragg faction. The Kentucky bloc supported him warmly, for it was Beauregard who, in 1862, had drawn up two grand designs for the eventual reoccupation of their state. He maintained a correspondence with the bloc's leader, Breckinridge. When one considers Beauregard as a symbol of many varied Confederate frustrations, along with his relationship to the Abingdon-Columbia, the anti-Bragg, and the Kentucky blocs, a powerful undercurrent appears. These informal groups composed the western concentration bloc when they coalesced to advocate an opposition strategy. Together they had a broad power base and influence sufficient to counteract Robert E. Lee's Virginia-oriented strategic recommendations. The strategy of western concentration was therefore adopted; a brief period of Confederate victory in Tennessee was the direct outcome of the successful promotion of the ideas of an informal organization.

chapter eleven

Status and Reference Group

The notions and concerns of modern sociology are largely reactions to profound alterations in European society in the nineteenth and early twentieth centuries. Twin revolutions of industry and democracy destroyed older institutions and ways of life, thereby having a necessarily far-reaching effect in shaping our times; if Western society had remained static, feudal, and agrarian, surely the discipline would have evolved differently. The basic problems of sociology are thus the product of relatively recent history, as western society suffered the crises of "community, authority, status, the sacred, and alienation" that are still major subjects of sociological study. Robert A. Nisbet, a prominent American sociologist, calls these crises the "unit-ideas" which "constitute a reorientation of European thought."[1] The term unit-ideas is appropriate, for they are exactly that, and the usage provides a nice reminder of the relationship of sociology to intellectual history and the history of ideas.

The following selection deals with the unit-idea of status, which Nisbet defines as "the individual's position in the hierarchy of prestige and influence that characterizes every community or association," and which the pioneering German sociologist, Max Weber, defined as "a specific, positive or negative, social estimation of *honor*."[2] This concept is by no means new however, and certainly predates modern sociology. One thinks, for instance, of the great chain of being in Elizabethan thought, its hierarchy forming a society in which each individual's position was theoretically predetermined and constant. What is new in the modern age is that an individual's status might change, perhaps ought to change, in his or her own lifetime. And if status could change, those who held high status, whether due to their own merits (achieved status) or those of their ancestors (ascribed status), could possibly lose it; if it could be lost,

---

[1] Robert A. Nisbet, *The Sociological Tradition* (New York: Basic Books, 1966), pp. 4, 6, 8–10, 21 (emphasis omitted).

[2] Ibid., p. 6; H. H. Gerth and C. Wright Mills, ed. and trans., *From Max Weber: Essays in Sociology* (New York: Oxford University Press, 1946), p. 187, emphasis in original.

such individuals might well suffer from status anxiety and, motivated by this anxiety, might take measures to prevent loss of status or to regain it if it had already been lost.

Historical motivation has sometimes been explained in precisely such terms. To Richard Hofstadter, the early twentieth-century Progressive movement in the United States did not particularly appeal to those who were victims of economic misfortune but to those who suffered from "an upheaval in status that took place in the United States during the closing decades of the nineteenth and the early years of the twentieth-century. Progressivism . . . was . . . led by men who suffered from the events of their time not through a shrinkage in their means but through the changed pattern in the distribution of deference and power." Small businessmen, professionals, and gentry, once the leaders of their communities, were being overtaken by "the newly rich, the grandiosely or corruptly rich, [and] the masters of great corporations." "They were less important," says Hofstadter, "and they knew it."[3]

Hofstadter has not been the only scholar to examine historical phenomena in these terms. Sociologist Joseph R. Gusfield's study of the American temperance movement approvingly cites Hofstadter's theory of status anxiety and his hypothesis that Mugwump politicians in the latter part of the nineteenth century were trying to restore their old dominance and their rights to deference. Gusfield attempts to apply this model to the temperance movement. He sees America as a land of differing communities, where "drinking (and abstinence) has been one of the significant consumption habits distinguishing one subculture from another." "In its earliest development," says Gusfield, "Temperance was one way in which a declining [New England Federalist] social elite tried to retain some of its social power and leadership" in a country where "the socially dominant position of the Temperance adherent" was threatened "by those whose style of life" was different. Furthermore, the early movement "reflected the fears of an older, established social group at the sight of rising industrialism." Gusfield cites a third prominent historical use of the status anxiety model in the following essay by David Donald on the American antislavery movement. Like temperance reformers, abolitionists were supposedly individuals who launched into reform in an attempt "to regain their lost positions of leadership . . . and recoup their dwindled status."[4]

The mechanism that might trigger the activities of status-anxious individuals or groups is uncertain. The "tension-reduction theory of radicals" suggests that frustration caused by status dislocation may direct an individual toward agitation in an effort to vent aggressive tendencies.[5] Other research minimizes this theory and appears to

---

[3] Richard Hofstadter, *The Age of Reform from Bryan to F.D.R.* (New York: Alfred A. Knopf, 1956). See Chapter IV, especially pp. 131–47; the quotes are from pp. 135 and 137.

[4] Joseph R. Gusfield, *Symbolic Crusade: Status Politics and the American Temperance Movement* (Urbana: University of Illinois Press, 1963, pp. 3–6, 22–23, 40–41 (quotes from pp. 3–6, 41).

[5] Gerald Sorin, *The New York Abolitionists: A Case Study of Political Radicalism* (Westport, Conn.: Greenwood Publishing Corporation, 1971), pp. 4n2, 120–21, referring to Seymour Martin Lipset, "The Sources of the 'Radical Right,' " in Daniel Bell, ed., *The Radical Right* (Garden City, N. Y.: Doubleday and Co., 1963). However, Lipset believes this mechanism operates only during periods of economic prosperity (pp. 260, 280).

support the view that leaders of militant or extremist movements are not likely to be frustrated "political activists who find fulfillment in political action as such;" instead, they tend to be convinced idealists.[6] Thus Gerald Sorin, refuting David Donald's interpretation of the abolitionists, underlines the normality of one group of abolitionists and contends that the tension reduction theory is on its way out.[7]

If Sorin is right and abolitionists (or any other reform or agitation groups) were not merely venting aggression, then some other sort of trigger becomes necessary. Perhaps this may be found in status anxiety itself, for the very concept begs a question. Since status is a relative thing, it is important to know in each instance, relative to whom? The "whom" is what sociologists call a reference group. People feel status anxiety when they compare themselves to a reference group and see the reference group either as better off than themselves or as better off than they think it should be relative to themselves. As Gusfield puts it, "In status politics the conflict arises from status aspirations and discontents"; these "status discontents are likely to appear when the prestige accorded to persons and groups by prestige-givers is perceived as less than that which the person or group expects."[8]

Muzafer and Carolyn Sherif define reference group "as the group with which the individual identifies or aspires to belong." The implication is that an individual is motivated by his "sense of identity, the stability of this identity, his need for human company and mutual support, [and] his felt need to act in concert . . . for the effective attainment of his cherished goals" to choose "membership in informally organized groups."[9] Even this definition is too simple, for there are several kinds of reference groups. One is "the 'normative type' which sets and maintains standards for the individual and the second is the 'comparison type' which provides a frame of comparison relative to which the individual evaluates himself and others." The former is a "source of values" while the latter is "a context for evaluating the relative position [including status] of oneself and others."[10] The first informs a person how to think and act and the second tells one how well off one is. Further than that, the normative

[6]Sorin, *New York Abolitionists,* pp. 6–7, relying on Rudolph Heberle, *Social Movements: An Introduction to Political Sociology* (New York: Appleton-Century-Crofts, 1951), pp. 104–117. Heberle, a sociologist, makes an important distinction between enthusiasts, who are "primarily inspired by the ideals of the movement," and fanatics, who are "primarily concerned with action." The latter, the activists, "can pass from one militant movement to another, without pangs of conscience" (pp. 114–15).

[7]Sorin, *New York Abolitionists,* pp. 133, 123.

[8]Gusfield, *Symbolic Crusade,* p. 17.

[9]Muzafer and Carolyn W. Sherif, *Reference Groups: Exploration into Conformity and Deviation of Adolescents* (New York: Harper & Row, 1964), p. 55 (italics omitted). While the authors are concerned with the application of the theory to adolescents, the definition applies equally to other age groups (p. 55).

[10]Robert K. Merton, "Continuities in the Theory of Reference Groups and Social Structure," Chapter XI in Merton, *Social Theory and Social Structure,* enlarged ed. (New York: The Free Press, 1968), pp. 337–38. Merton and Alice S. Rossi are most responsible for formulating the concept and theory of the reference group. See their joint paper, "Contribution to the Theory of Reference Group Behavior," Chapter X in *Social Theory and Social Structure.*

reference group should be subdivided, for an individual's behavior may not be the result of conscious adoption of one group's norms but the consequence of absolute rejection of another group's norms; thus, not all reference groups are positive ones to which individuals aspire to belong or to imitate—there are also negative reference groups, whose norms are emphatically disapproved. The positive reference group is used to adopt norms for evaluating one's own position while the negative reference group marks rejection and formation of opposing standards.[11]

Although historians often appear unaware of the connection between concepts of status and reference group, Hofstadter did mention it in a footnote when he remarked of one alienated professional that "he was unhappy not because he had actually lost out but because the 'reference group' by which he measured his position was a different one" than formerly.[12] Gusfield is more oblique, discussing the abstainer's "point of reference," the operation of a "status group . . . with an image of correct behavior which it prizes," and negative reference groups that serve as "models of what *not* to do."[13]

The theoretical framework of the reference group opens new doors to historical interpretation, as Donald's essay indicates. But it is more complicated than it sounds. Since everyone is a member of more than one potential reference group (defined by age, region, occupation, interests, ethnic background, and the like), one of the central problems is to determine which is the operative reference group at any given time. An individual may not always have the same reference group and he may or may not be a member of the group that provides his frame of reference. It is not necessary that the reference group be perceived accurately, or even that it exist, as long as the individual aspires—however irrationally—to be like its members. Just as important may be the possible effect when a person is equally attracted to conflicting reference groups.[14] Even deviant behavior is explained by the theory; the criminal may be as conformist as anyone else—it is only that he has a different reference group, and follows different norms accordingly.

Put at the simplest level, the basic questions involved in reference group theory are, "Who do I want to be like?" and "Who do I not want to be like?" To Hofstadter, Gusfield, and Donald, the status-anxious subjects of their studies would unconsciously reply, "like my ancestors before me, because they dominated their society and re-

[11]Ibid., pp. 354–55.
[12]Hofstadter, *Age of Reform*, p. 153n8.
[13]Gusfield, *Symbolic Crusade*, pp. 10, 27–28.
[14]Merton, *Social Theory and Social Structure*, pp. 287, 298. For a wide range of readings on reference group theory, see Herbert H. Hyman and Eleanor Singer, eds., *Readings in Reference Group Theory and Research* (New York: The Free Press, 1968). See also W. G. Runciman, "Relative Deprivation and the Concept of Reference Groups," Chapter II in *Relative Deprivation and Social Justice: A Study of Attitudes to Social Inequality in Twentieth-Century England* (Berkeley and Los Angeles: University of California Press, 1966).

ceived proper deference, but not like the present leaders of society, who are vulgar parvenues and *nouveaux riches,* and representative, not of the old world of agriculture and trade, but of the new world of banking and manufacturing.''

The findings of historians using reference group theory have not gone without challenge. The usefulness of Hofstadter's characterization of the Progressive reformers has not been questioned because of inaccuracy, but on the ground that it does not take the opposition into consideration. Using Toledo, Ohio, from 1905 to 1913 as an example, Jack Tager shows that supporters of the conservative machine and the corporations came from the same middle class background as the Progressives themselves. And it is a truism that an attribute equally common to all cases cannot by itself explain the distinctive behavior of any one set of cases. Thus, says Tager, ''the status-revolution theory based on collective middle class action . . . did not exist in Toledo and might not have existed elsewhere.''[15] In regard to abolitionists, Gerald Sorin even denies the basic premise. He claims that abolitionist leaders had higher status than their fathers, thus appearing to contradict the whole status-anxiety thesis. Examining the Liberty Party in New York, 1838–1845, Sorin concludes that ''abolitionist leaders pursued the most influential occupations in their communities and were actively engaged in public service. They generally seem to have had higher status in their respective communities than their fathers had had in theirs.''[16]

Donald's application of status anxiety and (by implication) reference group theory has been disputed on similar grounds as Hofstadter's. Robert A. Skotheim's critique gets to the heart of the problem when he asks whether it would ''not be desirable or perhaps necessary to present . . . evidence showing by comparison that other individuals did *not* have the same social background as the abolitionists?''[17] In reply, Donald remarked that he made ''no claim that my group of abolitionist leaders was unique'' and suggested parallel studies of other reform groups.[18] Donald's disclaimer was perhaps deceptively simple (if the attribute is not unique, at least in degree, its explanatory power is open to question).

That the status revolution did not motivate other middle class citizens to react as the reformers did, however, does not necessarily invalidate the concept or its specific usage here. Although Donald has not undertaken research on parallel reform movements, his examination of a select group of Southern proslavery apologists seems to indicate that the influences of status revolution and reference group do not necessarily

[15]Jack Tager, ''Progressives, Conservatives and the Theory of the Status Revolution,'' *Mid-America* 48 (July 1966):162–75 (quote is from p. 175). Other studies have come to conclusions similar to those of Tager. See, for example, E. Daniel Potts, ''The Progressive Profile in Iowa,'' *Mid-America* 47 (October 1965):257–68.

[16]Sorin, *New York Abolitionists,* p. 119.

[17]Robert Allen Skotheim, ''A Note on Historical Method: David Donald's 'Toward a Reconsideration of Abolitionists,' '' *Journal of Southern History* 25 (August 1959):356–65 (quote is from p. 363).

[18]David Donald, ''Communications,'' *Journal of Southern History* 26 (February 1960):156–57.

motivate all their victims to react the same way. What is most important, perhaps, is that such people may be moved to act in *some* way. Stand patters might have been so shaken by their loss of status that they would hold on to the status quo with unusual tenacity. Among Donald's proslavery advocates, the clear pattern is that of "unhappy men who had severe personal problems relating to their place in southern society. . . . Most looked back with longing to an earlier day of the Republic when men like themselves—their own ancestors—had been leaders in the South." These apologists were repelled by the changing South in which they lived and by the forces that were transforming it, such as urbanization and democratization. Nostalgically, they "looked longingly to a bygone pastoral Arcadia," and "hoped, as did so many New England abolitionists, for a restoration of social order and hierarchy."[19]

Even more surprising are the findings of Leonard L. Richards, who examined mob action directed against northern abolitionists. "The typical anti-abolition mob consisted largely of 'gentlemen of property and standing' . . . whose careers were identified not only with the mercantile economy of preindustrial America, but also with the local political establishment." The rioters, who felt "their leadership and their traditional values" were being threatened, were merely attempting to hang on to their old values and status.[20] In brief, Richards would have us believe that the anti-abolitionists were the sort of people David Donald thought the abolitionists were.

How is this to be explained? Perhaps, as Donald's study of the proslavery apologists seems to indicate, it does not matter which side of a question the advocate takes. If it is true that abolitionists, apologists, and antiabolition mobs had the same status anxiety, the question may become not one of pro or con but rather action or inaction. Possibly the vocal activists of society, whether radical, conservative, or neither, are motivated to act by the anxiety resulting from comparison of their status with that of their reference group.[21] Or more likely there is some as yet unexplained psychological factor that moves some victims of status anxiety to action and impels others to act not at all.

Whatever the final outcome of the historiographical debate about abolitionists or Progressives, it is beyond the scope of this discussion. But some important cautions must be kept in mind. The determination of individuals' and groups' status or the reference groups which provide their standards is a formidable task. It is difficult to judge the status of any member of society unless one uses such objective criteria as wealth or occupation—information that might not be available and might not be an

---

[19]David Donald, "The Proslavery Argument Reconsidered," *Journal of Southern History* 37 (February 1971):3–18 (quotes from pp. 12, 16–17).

[20]Leonard L. Richards, *"Gentlemen of Property and Standing": Anti-Abolition Mobs in Jacksonian America* (New York: Oxford University Press, 1970), pp. 149–50.

[21]Richards also concluded that some of the abolitionists were exactly the opposite from what Donald thought they were, being less rather than more likely to be native born or engaged in the professions. See ibid., Chapter V.

adequate measure of status at all. So too the question of the particular reference group operative in any given situation may be more a matter of informed conjecture than established proof. But if one is sufficiently resolved to structure a historical event by the concepts of status and reference group, no doubt a plausible way will be found to do it. Men and women always seek status, even to the point of bragging about who is the most humble. With this in mind, one may find status anxiety to be a major motivating force in any given situation. And since everyone has reference groups, even if they be imaginary, a suitable one can be dredged up for any occasion. The danger with these tools is that the researcher may be tempted to use them to pervert the past in order to structure his arguments to suit a sociological theory. As with a shoe, so with a methodology—make sure it fits before you put it on. More important, the discovery of behavioral abnormalities in a reformer or anyone else should not prejudice the investigator's conclusions. Whatever they are, the abnormalities may be quite irrelevant to the reform, or perhaps a somewhat warped mind may be required to understand the problem in the first place. Neurotic individuals often channel their drives into socially productive ends; perhaps society owes a debt of gratitude to some of its deviates. In any case the personal character or anxieties of the reformer should not be allowed to discredit the reform.

In this selection Donald acts on the observation that abolitionists sometimes behaved in extraordinary ways, responding ''with excessive vehemence to a mild stimulus.'' He assumes that under such conditions violent reaction may be ''the symptom of some profound social or psychological dislocation.'' He assumes further that since slavery had existed long before the creation of abolitionism, there must be something unusual and remarkable about the 1830s. The article, then, attempts to explain why a drive for immediate abolition developed when it did.[22]

Note again the use of collective biography to provide a conceptual stage for the application of sociological theory. Note too the distinction between reference group theory and informal organization. Reference groups will operate for the members of any organization, formal or informal, and may determine the form or function the group may take. But abolitionists were no shadow. This discussion does not concern the form of the organization in which abolitionist forces combined; instead, it concerns the motivations that caused people of like attitude to join a formal movement involving active, even frenetic recruitment of new members for formal antislavery organizations. As is often the case when sociological or psychological theories are applied to history, the thread of proof from cause to effect may sometimes seem tenuous. Nevertheless the essay serves as a highly stimulating suggestion about the nature of antebellum American society.

[22]The comments in this paragraph are based on the omitted first section of Donald's essay, ''Toward a Reconsideration of Abolitionists,'' in *Lincoln Reconsidered: Essays on the Civil War Era* (New York: Alfred A. Knopf, 1956); the quote is from p. 20.

Toward a Reconsideration of Abolitionists
David Donald

. . . I believe that the best way to answer this difficult question [of the source of abolitionism] is to analyze the leadership of the abolitionist movement. There is, unfortunately, no complete list of American abolitionists, and I have had to use a good deal of subjective judgment in drawing up a roster of leading reformers. From the classified indexes of the *Dictionary of American Biography* and the old Appleton's *Cyclopaedia of American Biography* and from important primary and secondary works on the reform generation, I made a list of about two hundred and fifty persons who seemed to be identified with the antislavery cause. This obviously is not a definitive enumeration of all the important abolitionists; had someone else compiled it, other names doubtless would have been included. Nevertheless, even if one or two major spokesmen have accidentally been omitted, this is a good deal more than a representative sampling of antislavery leadership.

After preliminary work I eliminated nearly one hundred of these names. Some proved not to be genuine abolitionists but advocates of colonizing the freed Negroes in Africa; others had only incidental interest or sympathy for emancipation. I ruthlessly excluded those who joined the abolitionists after 1840, because the political antislavery movement clearly poses a different set of causal problems. After this weeding out, I had reluctantly to drop other names because I was unable to secure more than random bits of information about them. Some of Weld's band of seventy agitators, for instance, were so obscure that even Barnes and Dumond were unable to identify them. There remained the names of one hundred and six abolitionists, the hard core of active antislavery leadership in the 1830's.

Most of these abolitionists were born between 1790 and 1810, and when the first number of the *Liberator* was published in 1831, their median age was twenty-nine. Abolitionism was thus a revolt of the young.

My analysis confirms the traditional identification of radical antislavery with New England. Although I made every effort to include Southern and Western leaders, eighty-five per cent of these abolitionists came from Northeastern states, sixty per cent from New England, thirty per cent from Massachusetts alone. Many of the others were descended from New England families. Only four of the leaders were born abroad or were second-generation immigrants.

The ancestors of these abolitionists are in some ways as interesting as the antislavery leaders themselves. In the biographies of their more famous descendants certain standard phrases recur: "of the best New England stock," "of Pilgrim descent," "of a serious, pious household." The parents of the leaders generally belonged to a clearly defined stratum of society. Many were preachers, doctors, or teachers; some were farmers and a few were merchants; but only three were manufacturers (and two of these on a very small scale), none was a banker, and only one was an ordinary day laborer. Virtually all the parents were stanch Federalists.

These families were neither rich nor poor, and it is worth remembering that among neither extreme did abolitionism flourish. The abolitionist could best appeal to "the substantial men" of the community, thought Weld, and not to "the *aristocracy* and fashionable worldliness" that remained aloof from reform. In *The Burned-Over District,* an important analysis of reform drives in western New York, Whitney R. Cross has confirmed Weld's social analysis. In New York, antislavery was strongest in those counties which had once been economically dominant but which by the 1830's, though still prosperous, had relatively fallen behind their more advantageously situated neighbors. As young men the fathers of abolitionists had been leaders of their communities and states; in their old age they were elbowed aside by the merchant prince, the manufacturing tycoon, the corporation lawyer. The bustling democracy of the 1830's passed them by; as the Reverend Ludovicus Weld lamented to his famous son Theodore: "I have . . . felt like a stranger in a strange land."

If the abolitionists were descendants of old and distinguished New England families, it is scarcely surprising to find among them an enthusiasm for higher education. The women in the movement could not, of course, have much formal education, nor could the three Negroes here included, but of the eighty-nine white male leaders, at least fifty-three attended college, university, or theological seminary. In the East, Harvard and Yale were the favored schools; in the West, Oberlin; but in any case the training was usually of the traditional liberal-arts variety.

For an age of chivalry and repression there was an extraordinary proportion of women in the abolitionist movement. Fourteen of these leaders were women who defied the convention that the female's place was at the fireside, not in the forum, and appeared publicly as antislavery apostles. The Grimké sisters of South Carolina were the most famous of these, but most of the antislavery heroines came from New England.

It is difficult to tabulate the religious affiliations of antislavery leaders. Most were troubled by spiritual discontent, and they wandered from one sect to another seeking salvation. It is quite clear, however, that there was a heavy Congregational-Presbyterian and Quaker preponderance. There were many Methodists, some Baptists, but very few Unitarians, Episcopalians, or Catholics. . . .

Only one of these abolitionist leaders seems to have had much connection with the rising industrialism of the 1830's, and only thirteen of the entire group were born in any of the principal cities of the United States. Abolition was distinctly a rural movement, and throughout the crusade many of the antislavery leaders seemed to feel an instinctive antipathy toward the city. Weld urged his following: "Let the great cities *alone;* they must be burned down by *back fires.* The springs to touch in order to move them *lie in the country.*"

In general the abolitionists had little sympathy or understanding for the problems of an urban society. Reformers though they were, they were men of conservative economic views. Living in an age of growing industrialization, of tenement congestion, of sweatshop oppression, not one of them can properly be identified with the labor movement of the 1830's. Most would agree with Garrison, who denounced labor leaders for trying "to enflame the minds of our working classes against the more opulent, and to persuade men that they are condemned and oppressed by a wealthy aristocracy." After all, Wendell Phillips assured the laborers, the American factory operative could be "neither wronged nor oppressed" so long as he had the ballot. William Ellery Channing, gentle high priest of the Boston area, told dissatisfied miners that moral self-improvement was a more potent weapon than strikes, and he urged that they take advantage of the leisure afforded by unemployment for mental and spiritual self-cultivation. A Massachusetts attempt to limit the hours of factory operatives to ten a day was denounced by Samuel Gridley Howe, veteran of a score of humanitarian wars, as "emasculating the people" because it took from them their free right to choose their conditions of employment.

The suffering of laborers during periodic depressions aroused little sympathy among abolitionists. As Emerson remarked tartly, "Do not tell me . . . of my obligation to put all poor men in good situations. Are they *my* poor? I tell thee, thou foolish philanthropist, that I grudge the dollar, the dime, the cent I give to such men. . . ."

Actually it is clear that abolitionists were not so much hostile to labor as indifferent to it. The factory worker represented an alien and unfamiliar system toward which the antislavery leaders felt no kinship or responsibility. Sons of the old New England of Federalism, farming, and foreign commerce, the reformers did not fit into a society that was beginning to be dominated by a bourgeoisie based on manufacturing and trade. Thoreau's bitter comment, "We do not ride on the railroads; they ride on us," was more than the acid aside of a man whose privacy at Walden had been invaded; it was the reaction of a class whose leadership had been discarded. The bitterest attacks in the journals of Ralph Waldo Emerson, the most pointed denunciations in the sermons of Theodore Parker, the harshest philippics in the orations of Charles Sumner were directed against the "Lords of the Loom," not so much for exploiting their labor as for changing the character and undermining the morality of old New England.

As Lewis Tappan pointed out in a pamphlet suggestively titled *Is It Right to Be Rich?*, reformers did not object to ordinary acquisition of money. It was instead that "eagerness to amass property" which made a man "selfish, unsocial, mean, tyrannical, and but a nominal Christian" that seemed so wrong. It is worth noting that Tappan, in his numerous examples of the vice of excessive accumulation, found this evil stemming from manufacturing and banking, and never from farming or foreign trade—in which last occupation Tappan himself flourished.

Tappan, like Emerson, was trying to uphold the old standards and to protest against the easy morality of the new age. "This invasion of Nature by Trade with its Money, its Credit, its Steam, its Railroads," complained Emerson, "threatens to upset the balance of man, and establish a new universal monarchy more tyrannical than Babylon or Rome." Calmly Emerson welcomed the panic of 1837 as a wholesome lesson to the new monarchs of manufacturing: "I see good in such emphatic and universal calamity. . . ."

Jacksonian democracy, whether considered a labor movement or a triumph of laissez-faire capitalism, obviously had little appeal for the abolitionist conservative. As far as can be determined, only one of these abolitionist leaders was a Jacksonian; nearly all were strong Whigs. William Lloyd Garrison made his first public appearance in Boston to endorse the arch-Whig Harrison Gray Otis; James G. Birney campaigned throughout Alabama to defeat Jackson; Henry B. Stanton wrote editorials for anti-Jackson newspapers. Not merely the leaders but their followers as well seem to have been hostile to Jacksonian democracy, for it is estimated that fifty-nine out of sixty Massachusetts abolitionists belonged to the Whig party.

Jacksonian Democrats recognized the opposition of the abolitionists and accused the leaders of using slavery to distract public attention from more immediate economic problems at home. "The abolitionists of the North have mistaken the color of the American slaves," Theophilus Fisk wrote tartly; "all the real Slaves in the United States have pale faces. . . . I will venture to affirm that there are more slaves in Lowell and Nashua alone than can be found South of the Potomac."

Here, then, is a composite portrait of abolitionist leadership. Descended from old and socially dominant Northeastern families, reared in a faith of aggressive piety and moral endeavor, educated for conservative leadership, these young men and women who reached maturity in the 1830's faced a strange and hostile world. Social and economic leadership was being transferred from the country to the city, from the farmer to the manufacturer, from the preacher to the corporation attorney. Too distinguished a family, too gentle an education, too nice a morality were handicaps in a bustling world of business. Expecting to lead, these young people found no followers. They were an elite without function, a displaced class in American society.

Some—like Daniel Webster—made their terms with the new order and lent their talents and their family names to the greater glorification of the god of trade. But many of the young men were unable to overcome their traditional disdain for the new money-grubbing class that was beginning to rule. In these plebeian days they could not be successful in politics; family tradition and education prohibited idleness; and agitation allowed the only chance for personal and social self-fulfillment.

If the young men were aliens in the new industrial society, the young women felt equally lost. Their mothers had married preachers, doctors, teachers, and had become dominant moral forces in their communities. But in rural New England of the 1830's the westward exodus had thinned the ranks of eligible suitors, and because girls of distinguished family hesitated to work in the cotton mills, more and more turned to schoolteaching and nursing and other socially useful but unrewarding spinster tasks. The women, like the men, were ripe for reform.

They did not support radical economic reforms because fundamentally these young men and women had no serious quarrel with the capitalistic system of private ownership and control of property. What they did question, and what they did rue, was the transfer of leadership to the wrong groups in society, and their appeal for reform was a strident call for their own class to re-exert its former social dominance. Some fought for prison reform; some for women's rights; some for world peace; but ultimately most came to make that natural identification between moneyed aristocracy, textile-manufacturing, and Southern slave-grown cotton. An attack on slavery was their best, if quite unconscious, attack upon the new industrial system. As Richard Henry Dana, Jr., avowed: "I am a Free Soiler, because I am . . . of the stock of the old Northern gentry, and have a particular dislike to any subserviency on the part of our people to the slave-holding oligarchy"—and, he might have added, to their Northern manufacturing allies.

With all its dangers and all its sacrifices, membership in a movement like abolitionism offered these young people a chance for a reassertion of their traditional values, an opportunity for association with others of their kind, and a possibility of achieving that self-fulfillment which should traditionally have been theirs as social leaders. Reform gave meaning to the lives of this displaced social elite. "My life, what has it been?" queried one young seeker; "the panting of a soul after eternity—the feeling that there was nothing here to fill the aching void, to provide enjoyment and occupation such as my spirit panted for. The world, what has it been? a howling wilderness. I seem to be just now awakened . . . to a true perception of the end of my being, my duties, my responsiblities, the rich and perpetual pleasures which God has provided for us in the fulfillment of duty to Him and to our fellow creatures. Thanks to the A[nti]. S[lavery]. cause, it first gave an impetus to my palsied intellect. . . ."

Viewed against the backgrounds and common ideas of its leaders, abolitionism appears to have been a double crusade. Seeking freedom for the Negro in the South, these reformers were also attempting a restoration of the traditional values of their class at home. Leadership of humanitarian reform may have been influenced by revivalism or by British precedent, but its true origin lay in the drastic dislocation of Northern society. Basically, abolitionism should be considered the anguished protest of an aggrieved class against a world they never made. . . .

chapter twelve
Class and Mobility

Class, the subject of this chapter, and status, the subject of the previous chapter, are quite distinct ideas. Yet they are similar enough to invite comparison, if only to avoid confusion by pointing out some differences between them.

In the middle of the twentieth century the concept of class is tied closely to the ideas of Karl Marx, who thought that class played a central role in historical change. Looking at nineteenth-century European society, he thought he detected social divisions determined by the existence of three major classes. These were characterized by their relations to "the capitalist mode of production" and were totally irreconcilable and always in conflict. They included "wage laborers, capitalists and landlords," "whose respective sources of income are wages, profit and ground-rent."[1] People's places in society were thus determined by the economic function of the class to which they belonged.

Although Marx did not specifically examine the distinction between class and status, his writings imply that he knew the difference. He once maintained that growth of capital brought an equal growth of wealth and diversion. But the contentment this growth provided workers would fall when compared to the increased gratifications available to capitalists. Satisfaction was therefore relative. A man with a small house might be content until someone built a larger house beside his; then he might become dissatisfied even though the small house were perfectly adequate.[2] On another occasion Marx pointed out that when prices and wages both dropped, but profits rose, the laborer's purchasing power would be unchanged and his standard of living would also remain the same. However, "his *relative* wages, and therewith his *relative social position*, as compared with that of the capitalist, would have been lowered."[3] In both

[1]Karl Marx, *Capital: A Critique of Political Economy,* 3 vols. (Chicago: Charles H. Kerr and Company, 1909), 3:1031–32.

[2]Karl Marx, "Wage-Labour and Capital," in V. Adoratsky, ed., *Karl Marx: Selected Works,* 2 vols. (Moscow and Leningrad: Cooperative Publishing Society of Foreign Workers in the U.S.S.R., 1935), 1:268, 269.

[3]Karl Marx, *Value, Price and Profit,* Eleanor Marx Aveling, ed. (New York: International Publishers, 1935), p. 51.

of these instances Marx was really discussing reference group theory and its relation to status.

Early twentieth-century German sociologist Max Weber was more explicit in his exploration of the relationship of class and status. Although both were related to the distribution of power, a "status situation" was "determined by a specific, positive or negative, social estimate of *honor*." It was descriptive of the social order, grouping together people with a common style of life and forming a community, though "often of an amorphous kind." At its extreme, status could evolve into caste, which was usually based on ethnic distinctions.[4]

In contrast, Weber thought a "class situation" was determined by "life chances," and that the class was not necessarily composed of people with similar life-styles but individuals with common "life chances." "Always," wrote Weber, "this is the generic connotation of the concept of class: that the kind of chance in the *market* is the decisive moment which presents a common condition for the individual's fate. 'Class situation' is, in this sense, ultimately 'market situation.'" If status were of the social order, class was of the economic order. A class was not even an amorphous community, though it could be a basis for joint activity. Although class and status distinctions could be linked by means of property, status honor would not necessarily be connected to class situations. Indeed, thought Weber, status was usually opposed to the claims of property alone. Both status groups and classes were stratified, but while the former was "stratified according to the principles of their *consumption* of goods as represented by special 'styles of life,'" the members of the latter were "stratified according to their relations to the production and acquisition of goods."[5] The essence of status was life-style and honor, while production and chance in the market were the keys to class.

Class, then, was neither social nor communal. It was economic, and it was not necessary that there be a conscious feeling of cohesion among its members (unlike status). Certainly there might be points of similarity between a certain class and a given status, but one could not be defined in terms of the other. It was economic position, rather than honorific attributes, which was the basic factor in determining class membership. Perhaps if Weber's useful and clear-cut differentiation had been maintained, confusions of definition would not have occurred. Thus Robert A. Nisbet's definition of status quoted earlier ("the individual's position in the hierarchy of prestige and influence that characterizes every community or association"[6]) was rather lucid. But class, which would appear on the surface to be a more concrete notion than status, is actually less so. Although people seem to be able to define their status, their fumbling attempts to define their class betray confusion. Query a large cross section of respondents as to their class, and the majority will insist they are middle class.

[4]H. H. Gerth and C. Wright Mills, ed. and trans., *From Max Weber: Essays in Sociology* (New York: Oxford University Press, 1946), pp. 181, 186–89.

[5]Gerth and Mills, *From Max Weber*, pp. 181–84, 187, 193.

[6]Robert A. Nisbet, *The Sociological Tradition* (New York: Basic Books, 1966), p. 6.

This muddle can only be reinforced by studies that reveal that, as groups, the members of different classes do not necessarily agree in their characterizations of the status of other classes. In some instances researchers have ranged classes in a six-level continuum from "upper-upper" and "lower-upper" through "upper-middle" and "lower-middle," to "upper-lower" and "lower-lower." This impossible six-class theory, found in the works of W. Lloyd Warner and his students, is really a theory of status, as the subtitle to Warner's procedural manual clearly indicates. Studies that attempt to circumvent this confusion by using the categories upper class, middle class, working class, and lower class, introduce a new difficulty: three classes are defined by vertical concepts of stratification and one, in a loose way, by occupation.[7] Class and status are therefore hopelessly entangled; although they may be similar, they are not the same. Blue-collar workers may report they are working class, yet any objective inquiry must take into account the fact that while some of them appear to be considered lower class, many others are clearly middle class, possessed of better opportunities in the marketplace and thus better "life chances" (to use Weber's term) than many poorly paid teachers, librarians, bookkeepers, and shop clerks, who, by virtue of education, occupation, family, or other attributes, might have higher status. That class is often explained in terms of status—or vice versa—indicates a lingering scholarly chaos that makes comprehension of both theories rather difficult.

Robert L. Heilbroner, for example, recognizes the difficulty of distinguishing the "working class" from either the poor or the well-paid skilled middle-class workers. Without bothering to define class—although he appears to agree with Weber that "class situation" is "market situation"—Heilbroner nevertheless goes on to divide classes into poor, working, middle, upper, and rich, thereby maintaining the confusing combination of occupational and income categories. But working class, to Heilbroner, is simply *every* family, regardless of occupation, earning between $6500 and $15,000—since many teachers, nurses, clergymen, and even lawyers fall into this income range, we are faced with a rather mind-boggling sort of working class; no less strange is Heilbroner's "middle" class, the 35 percent of the families who are not really middle income at all, since fully 60 percent of the nation's families fall into lower income categories. Using this contrived scheme, Heilbroner points to the great possibility that the working class and middle class are likely to come into confrontation and conflict when economic growth slows due to diminishing resources and dangers of

---

[7]W. Lloyd Warner, Marchia Meeker, and Kenneth Eells, *Social Class in America: A Manual of Procedure for the Measurement of Social Status* (Gloucester, Mass.: Peter Smith, 1957 [originally published 1949]). Berton H. Kaplan, *Blue Ridge: An Appalachian Community in Transition* (Morgantown, West Virginia: Applachian Center, West Virginia University, 1971), attempts to overcome the tendency of all respondents to label themselves middle class by using a model based on three classes, labeled "better," "get by," and "sorry." The novel labels may avoid some methodological problems, but the classes are clearly treated as status groups, and are described as "Upper Group," "Middle Group," and "Lowest Group," respectively. See Kaplan, *Blue Ridge,* pp. 17–18, 36, for example. Such imprecise terminology, unfortunately common, indicates continuing confusion between class and status.

pollution. As growth winds down, its benefits cannot be expanded to cover everyone; competition for goods thus becomes inevitable and "the working class must come into conflict with the middle class." The author's thesis is interesting, provocative, and highly important, but because of Heilbroner's blurred and arbitrary distinctions we may miss the full significance of the thesis if we pay particularly close attention to the method by which the conclusion is reached.[8]

Sociologists and others who use the concept of class have thus had to face the sticky problem of definition. Although Marx and Weber met the difficulty by relating class directly to economics, more recent students are dubious about a system which leaves no place for ethnic, kinship, or cultural distinctions. British scholar G. D. H. Cole believes "that no . . . single criterion [for definition] exists and that the very notion of class, as distinguished from that of caste [status] or legally recognized estate, is imprecise." The matter is made more difficult, thinks Cole, because one person may be a member of more than one class while another may not belong to any at all. He further disputes the possiblity of arranging classes in a hierarchy and points out that any objective method of class assignments would have to take income, occupation, and education into account; but even these have their limitations (and how is the relative importance of each to be determined?). Cole suggests that if an objective approach is to be used, it is probably best to use occupation as the class criterion.[9]

Another scholar thinks of status as one of the attributes of people who occupy certain social strata, but he is careful to distinguish between strata and classes. The class, to social psychologist Richard Centers, is based on class consciousness (and here he agrees with Marx and contradicts Weber); more than that, however, it is a psychological attribute, to be defined in psychological terms as "a part of . . . [a man's] ego, *a feeling on his part of belongingness to something;* an *identification* with something larger than himself." Noting that people of quite differing status may be members of the same class, Centers agrees that "the concept of class has often been confused or wholly identified with that of status or social position," and that class designations can not be made "wholly on the basis of social inferiority and superiority and without any consideration of their own feelings of belongingness."[10]

Although Marx and Weber determine class by economics, Centers sees it as a psychological feeling of identification, and Cole sees no single test, the issue is complicated further by Ralf Dahrendorf. Dahrendorf, Director of the London School of Economics and Political Science, agrees with Centers that classes are not layers of social strata or status groups. But he also agrees with Cole that class cannot imply

---

[8]Robert L. Heilbroner, "Middle-Class Myths, Middle-Class Realities," *Atlantic* 238 (October 1976):37–42. Quote is from p. 41.
[9]G. D. H. Cole, *Studies in Class Structure* (London: Routledge and Kegan Paul, 1955), pp. 1–8 (quote from p. 1).
[10]Richard Centers, *The Psychology of Social Class: A Study of Class Consciousness* (Princeton: Princeton University Press, 1949), pp. 27, 226–28.

some sort of hierarchy; if it does, then it may be a status group but it is not a class. Instead, classes are "conflict groups," based not on economic considerations but on "differential distribution of authority."[11] There is no way around it—the notion of class is complicated and difficult to define.[12]

Regardless of its definition, too often class is discussed in political and polemical terms, rather than in descriptive and clinical terms. It tends, in this way, to become synonymous with class conflict. To Dahrendorf, for example, "*class* is always a category for purposes of the analysis of the dynamics of social conflict and its structural roots."[13] Whatever the inevitability of class conflict may be, however, any study of class must consider the fact that frequently classes are not in any but theoretical conflict. One of the reasons for this lack of clash in the United States, suggested by the early twentieth-century German scholar, Werner Sombart, is that members of suppressed classes had significant opportunity for social and geographic change.[14] Thus the study of class leads inevitably to the study of mobility, since mobility is the movement between classes. To recast the statement along lines that Max Weber would have approved, class mobility means changing one's market situation and hence one's "life chances." This usually implies changes in one of, or some combination of, four critical characteristics: occupation, wealth, education, and intelligence, with emphasis on the first. (Note that the first three of these variables are those suggested by Cole for determining class.) The change is generally thought of as an improvement or a deterioration, and hence is often referred to as upward or downward mobility, though upward and downward simply mean better or worse "life chances" and should not necessarily be construed to imply the existence of some hierarchy.

In America the degree of mobility has often been exaggerated. The key is appearance versus reality. How much mobility did people *think* there was? It is evident from examination of literature and politics in nineteenth-century United States that a high degree of mobility was thought possible. This is demonstrated, for example, by the Horatio Alger stories about the hardworking young men who started poor but worked their way to the top. The supposedly archetypal self-made businessman of the Gilded

---

[11]Ralf Dahrendorf, *Class and Class Conflict in Industrial Society* (Stanford: Stanford University Press, 1959), pp. 76, 204.

[12]Cole, *Studies in Class Structure*, p. 147. According to Dahrendorf, *Class and Class Conflict*, p. 74, one scholar, writing as far back as 1928, counted over thirty different modifications of the idea of class. "The history of the concept of class in sociology," writes Dahrendorf (pp. 74–75), "is surely one of the most extreme illustrations of the inability of sociologists to achieve a minimum of consensus even in the modest business of terminological decisions. . . . Whoever reads these definitions may well be tempted to regard sociology as rather a frivolous discipline."

[13]Dahrendorf, *Class and Class Conflict,* p. 76.

[14]Ralf Dahrendorf, *Conflict after Class: New Perspectives on the Theory of Social and Political Conflict* (London: Longmans, Green and Co., 1967), p. 9. This hypothesis is still viable. See Stephan Thernstrom, *The Other Bostonians: Poverty and Progress in the American Metropolis, 1880–1970* (Cambridge: Harvard University Press, 1973), pp. 258–59.

Age, who is partly responsible for the American success myth, is frequently found in American fiction. In *The Rise of Silas Lapham,* William Dean Howells portrayed a young man who found a mineral on the family farm that could be employed in the manufacture of paint, went into business with great success—and so on, *up.* In *A Hazard of New Fortunes,* Howells' protagonist, after an unsuccessful career in the insurance business, becomes editor of a new magazine. It is a success, and his career propels him *up.* Impressionistic evidence from the real world leads to a similar conclusion. John D. Rockefeller started working for a commission merchant, earning the meager sum of $3.50 per week. He formed his own partnership after a few years' experience, was promptly successful, and so on, *up.* Andrew Carnegie worked for $1.20 a week as a bobbin boy in a textile factory. After learning telegraphy he became secretary to the superintendent of the Pittsburgh Division of the Pennsylvania Railroad, then superintendent himself, and so on, *up.* More recent studies have indicated that such individuals were not as representative as was once thought, yet the idea remains; with class one must also study mobility. Where class lines are rigid, there may be little mobility, while high mobility may tend to indicate a fluid class structure.[15]

The historian who wishes to study class and mobility is faced with a number of problems. Since class means different things to different people it should be defined at the outset. And since mobility implies some sort of movement, usually from one category of something (such as occupation or wealth) to another, it may be necessary to establish carefully defined classifications in order to ascertain what movement took place.[16] Unfortunately, class analysis of history frequently employs a scheme that has only three or four classes. The implication may be that these classes were monolithic. Instead of a restless mass of millions of individuals, one sees instead only three or four united "interests" poised in opposition to each other. The distinction is vital and makes the difference between seeing history as people or merely as vague, nebulous forces. Failure to make the differentiation may result in ponderous, sweeping, almost mechanical assertions about one interest or class in its relations to a second or a third. But such oversimplification of history will leave knowledgeable readers unimpressed and will cause others to miss much of the rich, exceedingly intricate pattern in the

---

[15]In addition to this vertical mobility, there is also horizontal mobility. The son may be of the same class as the father, but may be following a different occupation. Both of these must be distinguished from geographic mobility, which is the easy opportunity to move from place to place. Both vertical and horizontal mobility are sometimes associated with geographic mobility.

[16]See, for example, Jonathan M. Wiener, "Planter Persistence and Social Change: Alabama, 1850–1870," *Journal of Interdisciplinary History* 7 (Autumn 1976):235–60; and Donald J. Treiman, "A Standard Occupational Prestige Scale for Use with Historical Data," ibid., 283–304. This entire issue is devoted to problems of social mobility. See also Theodore Hershberg and Robert Dockhorn, "Occupational Classification," *Historical Methods Newsletter* 9 (March-June 1976):59–98.

historical fabric. It is far more satisfying to follow Pessen's example and examine those people who shared chances in the market to see who they were, what values they had in common, and how they interacted with each other and with individuals who had different chances in the market.

The subjects of Edward Pessen's study were obviously people who usually held high status, and Pessen frequently uses the term status to describe them (although the usage appears to pertain to nothing more than condition or state of being). However, the most distinctive thing about these individuals—indeed, it was their common denominator—was not the honorific attribute, but their class—the "life chances" that created, and were created by, their wealth. In the following excerpt Pessen relies primarily on wealth to establish class and measure social mobility, asking whether (as he indicates in the title to this chapter) rich Americans were self-made men in the so-called "Era of the Common Man"—although the remainder of the book also relies heavily on personal associations and intimate circles, marriages, residences, neighborhoods, and life-styles. Impressionistic evidence had long indicated that mobility was high and class lines relatively fluid in the Age of Jackson. Pessen tests this belief by studying the backgrounds of the richest citizens of New York, Brooklyn, Boston, and Philadelphia in the 1820s, 1830s, and 1840s. For family background, his sources include genealogical information, private papers, local histories, and diaries; for wealth, the major reliance is on tax records. The results vigorously contest the older notions of a highly mobile society.

But older ideas cannot be laid to rest so simply. Each reader must decide whether a hypothesis based on study of four northeastern cities may be applied to the entire, predominantly rural nation of the pre-Civil War era. Perhaps in the newer cities of the West, Chicago and Cincinnati, for example, or in the rural South, one might find that men of riches tended to have more humble backgrounds. And the real test of mobility in the Age of Jackson might be the extent to which older men of middling wealth in the 1850s were in more modest circumstances in the 1820s and 1830s;[17] such a test should be applied throughout the country, sampling not only big cities, but also, as Pessen suggests, smaller cities, small towns and villages, rural areas close to centers of high population density, and isolated rural areas. And it should be applied to individuals and not their families.

Pessen's painstaking work throws generally accepted views of class structure and social mobility during the Age of Jackson into serious doubt, and drastically erodes the

---

[17]Pessen does discuss his four cities along these lines in Chapter VII of the book from which this essay is taken. He finds no great mobility among the very rich, who, while generally increasing their wealth, were nevertheless at the top to begin with. But national wealth was also increasing during this period; the rich were not necessarily getting larger slices of the pie. Instead, the pie was getting larger.

underpinnings of the success myth.[18] As he indicates, it would be an interesting study in intellectual history to determine the reasons for the persistence of that myth. Perhaps the success of the few were symbols of the egalitarian "life chances" the American people wished had existed; perhaps American egalitarianism is a fit subject for the history of ideas; and it could be that the myth has been accepted for so long because of the successful reduction of cognitive dissonance, as an unpleasant reality was offset by the creation of a new and mythical cognitive element.

Were Rich Americans in the "Era of the Common Man" Self-Made Men?
Edward Pessen

> *In America most of the rich men were formerly poor. . . .*
> *They have felt the sting of want; they were long a prey to*
> *adverse fortunes.*
> Tocqueville, *Democracy in America,* I:54; II:138

In a speech to the United States Senate on February 2, 1832, Henry Clay advised his colleagues and the nation that almost all of the successful factory owners of his acquaintance were "enterprising self-made men, who have whatever wealth they possess by patient and diligent labor." Made in the context of a pro-tariff argument, Clay's remarks were hardly original, nor did they purport to be. The Kentuckian was merely proclaiming a social belief he had reason to think was held by most of his countrymen.

The notion that not only factory owners but almost all wealthy Americans were self-made men came close to being a secular article of faith during the "era of the common man," so widely did it appear to be subscribed to. There is, of course, no way of determining either the extent of its acceptance or the depth of conviction of those who did adhere to it. Certainly the idea was persistently propagated by orators and publicists. In this instance, at least, the Tocquevillean conclusion that rich Americans had been born poor only confirmed what his American audience evidently believed it already knew.

---

[18] The subject is still open to debate. Using more refined methodology, for example, Stephan Thernstrom discovers more upward mobility in post-Civil War Boston than Pessen's study of the prewar period would seem to suggest. "If Horatio Alger's novels were designed to illustrate the possibility not of rags-to-riches but of rags-to-respectability, as I take them to have been, they do not offer wildly misleading estimates of the prospects for mobility open to Americans." Thernstrom, *The Other Bostonians,* especially pp. 256–61. Quote is from p. 257.

Reprinted by permission of the publisher, from Edward Pessen: Riches, Class and Power Before The Civil War, (Lexington, Mass.: D. C. Heath and Company, 1973).

Moses Beach and the other compilers of the lists of wealthy citizens reminded their readers that the great fortunes they immortalized through publication were characteristically self-made. Boston's "first men" ostensibly "were once poor themselves, or their fathers were;" their wealth "came to them through toil and labor. . . . " Many of New York City's Midases too had "by honest and laborious industry . . . raised themselves from the obscure and humble walks of life, to great wealth and consideration." The anonymous editor of the Philadelphia rating reported that most of the city's "wealthy citizens are plain men . . . [who] pride themselves for having made their own money." Such contemporary historians of successful merchants as Freeman.Hunt and Stephen N. Winslow glorified their subjects above all for having risen to the top through heroic struggle. "Philadelphia," wrote Winslow, "is remarkable for the number of self-made merchants and manufacturers in it; men who feared not 'those twin-jailors of the aspiring soul low birth and misfortune.' " To the question, what is a self-made man? he responded: "the reply is easy. A man who, without any extraordinary family or pecuniary advantages at the commencement of life, has . . . by indomitable industry and unwavering integrity achieved both character and fortune." The nation was told that such men abounded here. Not long after Clay's tariff speech, the respected Calvin Colton affirmed that "this is a country of self-made men," whose wealthiest citizens had started "from an humble origin and small beginnings," and whose success was "the reward of merit and industry." These roseate judgments were confidently uttered by men who gave the impression of harboring no doubts concerning their accuracy.

The great merchant William E. Dodge even offered a detailed estimate as to the proportion of his wealthy mercantile contemporaries who were self-made. "If the history of our citizens of wealth were written," he advised a lecture audience, "we should find that full three fourths had risen from comparatively small beginnings [with little or nothing] to their present position." Neither Dodge nor the other contemporary purveyors of the rags-to-riches myth reached their conclusions on the basis of detailed factual investigation into the origins of wealthy men. Drawing on a few examples, which they evidently had no difficulty in convincing themselves represented a universal American tendency, they said, above all, what they wanted the American people to believe. As ideologists of a sort, they were less concerned with the accuracy of their sunny social judgments than with their popularity. This is not to impugn their sincerity; for few men are more sincere than those who seek to convince others of what they themselves know intuitively. What is in question is not the motives of these contemporary yeasayers but their accuracy.

It is well known that Tocqueville, one of the influential architects of the rags-to-riches belief, was at times prone to spin his marvelous social theorems by recourse more to logic than to pedestrian data. What is fascinating is the extent to which scholars ordinarily skeptical of unverified observation have relied on it in discussing the origins of the rich in the "age of the common man." If few modern historians would commit themselves to a precise ratio, as did William Dodge, many have nevertheless agreed that a remarkable movement up the social and economic ladder, did take place during the second quarter of the nineteenth century. The author of an influential modern interpretation of voting behavior in antebellum New York State, in explaining why economic class allegedly influences voting less than does ethnic and religious identity, states that "since the United States is highly heterogeneous, and has high social mobility, I assume that men tend to retain and be more influenced by their ethnic and religious group membership than by their membership in economic classes or groups." One marvels that so significant a theory would be based on a premise of high social mobility that is merely asserted rather than demonstrated.

Modern factual studies have been undertaken to test the validity of the rags-to-riches thesis for most periods in American history. The twentieth century, the post-Civil War decades, the colonial and the Revolutionary eras have all been subjected to detailed investigations of varying intensity. The "age of egalitarianism," however, has heretofore escaped inquiries of similar scope. One surmises that a major reason for this neglect is that constant repetition of the theme of fluidity has convinced scholars that for the Jacksonian period the facts are in: intergenerational economic and occupational mobility were the rule. Actually, it is not the facts that are in, but rather a continuing series of firmly stated generalizations that essentially do nothing more than assume that the facts bear them out. I have, therefore, gathered evidence on the wealth and status of the parents and families of the several hundred wealthiest persons in each of the major cities of the northeast during the era in order to subject the belief that typically they were born poor to the kind of empirical test it has previously been spared. . . .

Some of the best known among the wealthy citizens did, in fact, have the kind of background ascribed to them by the egalitarian thesis. Although John Jacob Astor's story is perhaps improperly described as "rags to riches," there is some question as to the precise wealth or status of his father. Whether the latter was a "very worthy" minor office-holder, as some described him, or a poor man devoted more to tippling than to industry, as others saw him (and it is not clear that the two judgments are mutually exclusive) it seems fairly certain that the great merchant was indeed a self-made man of humble origin. The same can be said with even more certainty of his sometime partner, Cornelius Heeney, who migrated from Ireland apparently with less than a dollar in his pockets and went on to become one of the wealthiest residents of Brooklyn. Lewis A. Godey, publisher of the popular *Ladies Book,* John Grigg, and Joseph Sill were wealthy Philadelphians of humble beginnings. In Boston, Daniel P. Parker, Ebenezer Chadwick, John R. Adan, and the three Henshaw brothers also appear to have been of poor or humble birth. Anson G. Phelps, Marshall O. Roberts, Gideon Lee, Saul Alley, and possibly the Lorillard brothers were New York City eminences whose backgrounds appear to have been plebeian, as was John Dikeman's in Brooklyn. Stephen Girard's claim that he too had been a destitute youth was evidently accepted by most contemporaries, although there is some doubt as to whether it was well founded. No matter how Girard's family is finally appraised, evidence is not lacking that some rich men had in fact been born poor. The most interesting feature of such evidence however is its uncommonness.

During the age of alleged social fluidity, the great majority of wealthy persons appear to have been descended of parents and families that combined affluence with high social status. The small number of these families that had been less than rich had typically been, not poor, but well-to-do. . . . In terms of occupation, the well-to-do or the middling category was composed of less-than-rich ministers, professionals other than very successful lawyers and doctors, petty officials, shopkeepers, skilled artisans who doubled as small tradesmen, and independent or moderately prosperous farmers. Included in the middle are the families of Peter Cooper, William E. Dodge, Gerard Hallock, Joseph Sampson, Cornelius Vanderbilt, Moses Yale Beach, Peter Chardon Brooks, Amos and Abbott Lawrence, Thomas Handasyd Perkins, George C. Shattuck, George Hall, Thomas Everitt, Jr., Samuel R. Johnson, Cyrus P. Smith, and Samuel Smith, all of whom appeared to have been both better off and of higher-status occupations than the mechanics, cartmen, milkmen, and laborers who predominated in the cities. The evidence for these generalizations, inevitably imperfect, requires elaboration.

Table 1   The Wealth and Status of Parents and Families of the Richest Persons in Antebellum Northeastern Cities (by percentage)

Cities	Rich and/or Eminent	Middling	Poor or Humble
New York City	95	3	2
Brooklyn	81	16	3
Philadelphia	92	6	2
Boston	94	4	2

It was, of course, impossible to obtain reliable information on the family status of all rich persons. Fortunately, abundant evidence exists on the backgrounds of most of the very wealthiest persons in the great cities. Data were secured on 90 per cent of the more than 100 New Yorkers who in 1828 were assessed for $100,000 and upward and in 1845 at $250,000 or more; on 85 per cent of the more than 100 Bostonians worth $100,000 or better in 1833 and $200,000 or more in 1848; and on about 90 per cent of the 75 Brooklynites who in 1841 were evaluated at $60,000 or more. For Philadelphia, as indicated earlier, the nature of the tax records does not permit them to be used to disclose the total assessed wealth of individuals. One can differentiate the "super rich" of that city from other wealthy persons only by accepting at face value the sums attributed in the anonymous *Memoirs and Auto-Biography of Some of the Wealthiest Citizens of Philadelphia.* Varied evidence does point to the credibility of that document. Information was obtained on 75 per cent of the 365 persons each claimed by the *Memoirs* to be worth $100,000 or more. As Table 1 indicates, the pattern of the social backgrounds of the urban rich was strikingly similar for the four leading cities. If the families of Brooklyn's smaller number of rich persons were more often than elsewhere of middling or well-to-do rather than wealthy status, an explanation may lie in Brooklyn's more recent origins as an independent city, its much smaller population, its lesser wealth, and its more limited economic development. It appeared to be easier for newcomers to the city proper (or to its most envied ranks) to find a niche in Brooklyn's elite than in larger cities richer in both wealth and tradition.

Evidence was not as freely available for the lesser rich of the great cities. Data were obtained on about 70 per cent of the more than 450 New Yorkers assessed at between $25,000 and $100,000 in 1828, and for 63 per cent of the 950 New Yorkers who in 1845 were worth between $45,000 and $250,000; on about 60 per cent of the 260 Bostonians evaluated at between $50,000 and $200,000 in 1833, and on the same percentage of the 400 Bostonians similarly appraised in 1848; and on 63 per cent of the 100 Brooklynites assessed in 1841 at between $30,000 and $60,000. These are not unsubstantial proportions, yet it is possible that the backgrounds of the missing persons were unlike those of the much larger numbers of individuals for whom information was obtained. It can be fairly argued that the omissions concern less-eminent persons whose families probably were neither as wealthy nor of as high status as the families whose careers and records are better publicized. Yet a significant feature of the evidence is its disclosure that there appeared to be no difference in the social origin patterns of the lesser wealthy as against the "super rich"; nor did the patterns of family background of the relatively little-known rich for whom information was obtained differ from those of the eminent rich. Vastly rich or fairly rich, celebrated or obscure, it mattered not: the upper 1 per cent of wealthholders of the great cities—the rich of their time—almost universally were born to families of substance and standing.

These are amazing findings. Startled at the great disparity between previous beliefs and actuality, I went over the evidence for each wealthy person a number of times, assessing it as conservatively as possible in order to make certain that the delights neither of revisionism nor iconoclasm would affect the evaluations made of family rank. Determining relative wealth and standing involves judgment, in contrast, say, to determining religion or date of birth. Among the chief factors that went into the appraisal of a family were wealth (actual and alleged), occupation, reputed standing in the community and the period of time during which they had status, religious denomination, kinship ties, and the kind of material life and opportunities provided the eminences of the 1820s, the 1830s, and the 1840s in their youth. That, for example, a young person attended so prestigious an institution as Harvard, Columbia, or the University of Pennsylvania in an era when only one-tenth of 1 per cent of the population attended any college at all was a significant fact. For all their unevenness and inevitable deficiencies, the data are so abundant that even concise descriptive summaries alone would require a substantial volume. More than a thousand case histories are involved in all. . . . Such material conveys more forcefully than the statistical analysis derived from it the characteristic social routes taken by the rich. Impervious to the mood of the interpreter, the evidence stands, sharply refuting prevalent views about the backgrounds of the wealthy in the "era of the common man."

What accounts for the popularity of this false notion? How could so many intelligent and informed persons have been so wrong? A number of explanations come to mind. Men of conservative persuasion such as Moses Beach, Calvin Colton, and Edward Everett evidently hoped that popular acceptance of the "sound doctrine" of rags to riches would have happy social consequences: unfortunates would be deflected from radical thought and action. The Malthusian teaching so popular with social conservatives here and abroad—that "the poor are the authors of their own misery"—was thus complemented by its corollary—that "the rich are the authors of their own success or happiness." Successful men, eager to convince their less fortunate countrymen that their successes were due to innate ability, virtue and honest labor—rather than to mere luck or unfair advantages, such as inheritance—had little trouble in convincing themselves in the process. Nor was it entirely a matter of the wish being father to the thought.

Contemporary writers, particularly the small army of European visitors who toured the United States during the era, were for the most part convinced that in the society of the fabled young republic the social ladder was easily climbed. That most of the visitors actually found little evidence of upward social movement hardly detracted either from their own conviction that such mobility was a reality or from their American audience's acceptance of a conclusion both logical and comforting. These same visitors also agreed, in the words of one of them, that "the most striking circumstance in the American character was the constant habit of praising themselves." Not the least of the features of their civilization that Americans boasted of was the alleged opportunity it afforded ordinary men to rise to the top.

The rags-to-riches ideology had so penetrated American thought during the era that men whose own publications contradicted the thesis, nevertheless insisted it was true, often reaching conclusions at odds with their evidence. . . . One Boston publicist described as a "poor boy" Robert G. Shaw, whose family was a prosperous one; another, overlooking the connections and the wealth accumulated by the eminent Huguenot family, the Sigourneys, wrote that Henry Sigourney amassed his wealth by his "own industry" alone. The eulogists of Philadelphia's merchants were also prone to this form of self-delusion. Overlooking the "respectability and wealth" of the Beck family in Germany, old Ritter wrote that Paul Beck, Jr., "was the architect of his own fortune." Winslow, after noting that the parents of Isaac R. Davis were in "moderate circumstances" and that a prosperous friend to the family took interest in the lad, wrote that Davis began "without a single dollar." John Hare Powel, an ornament of the Philadelphia elite, could assert that "influence and standing should be won and maintained by individual merit," as though his own life illustrated this wholesome principle. This comment came from a man whose father, Robert Hare, was an eminent Englishman and speaker of the Pennsylvania Senate; whose mother was Margaret Willing of the fabulously wealthy family; who before he was 21 years old managed to earn $20,000 in one commercial voyage alone—undertaken while he was with the counting house of his relatives the Willings—; who on attaining his majority took the Grand Tour "for improvement and pleasure," his tastes catered to in the most opulent manner by his paternal relatives in England; who had his surname changed in order to gratify—and become the heir to the fortune of—his aunt Elizabeth (herself the wife of Major Samuel Powel, and the daughter of Charles Willing and Anna Shippen of the great Philadelphia family); and who as an adult lived a refined and elegant life made possible by his inheritance!

Perhaps the most Pollyannaish contemporary [mis]interpreter of biographical evidence was Freeman Hunt, devoted and enthusiastic admirer of America's merchants, whom he extolled in his charming *Merchants' Magazine*. According to Hunt, Stephen Girard had left his "native country . . . in the capacity of a cabin boy, without education, excepting a limited knowledge of the elements of reading and writing." From this description one would hardly guess that the great merchant's father was a shipping merchant who "piled up a good-sized fortune," and left a substantial inheritance to young Girard, or that "there had never been the slightest thought that Stephen Girard would remain a junior officer." Mathew Carey, we are told, landed "at the wharf at Philadelphia . . . with scarce a dozen guineas in his pocket," information that does not quite convey either the wealth that had been accumulated by this great publisher's father in Ireland as an "extensive contractor" or the kind of education the latter had provided for the younger Carey and his fortunate brothers. Hunt could also somehow describe Walter Restored Jones of the old, eminent, and wealthy family of Cold Spring, Long Island—truly one of fortune's favorites—as a "self-taught and self-made man."

Of course, evidence that one form of social mobility was absent in antebellum cities by no means rules out the possibility that other forms flourished. That, in technical terms, an "in-flow" study of a social and economic elite reveals little upward movement is no assurance that there was equally small "out-flow" movement from society's low and middle levels upward. . . . In the absence of the requisite data, we know very little at this time about the later fate of the poor and the middling. A recent statistical investigation of upward and downward mobility among different socioeconomic strata in antebellum Philadelphia does disclose relatively slight movement; and that the changes that occurred were confined to contiguous rather than to widely separated categories. As it relies chiefly on the criteria of occupation and residence, that study is admittedly not definitive for Philadelphia, let alone for other cities. But if the need for continued exploration of early-nineteenth century mobility patterns—particularly among the poor—reduces the universality of generalizations drawn from the careers of the rich, it in no sense detracts from their importance.

Why so many historians accepted the rags-to-riches version of antebellum success is a fascinating question, a problem in psychology and intellectual history which is beyond the scope of this essay. One suspects that unwitting yeasaying, nationalism, a belief in American exceptionalism, and unwillingness to tamper with a historical belief that was both comforting and logical, among other reasons, played a part. Whatever the ultimate explanation, it seems clear that historians' belief in this most dramatic form of social mobility—the alleged leap from the bottom to the top in one generation—is untenable. The detailed evidence . . . indicates that the ''self-made man''—recently shown to have been more fantasy than fact in the post-Civil War decades—was similarly a creature of the imagination a generation earlier, at the very time when the great Henry Clay was asserting the phantom's corporeality and ubiquitousness.

4 Quantitative History

"That Bitch-goddess, QUANTIFICATION"! cried social and intellectual historian Carl Bridenbaugh in his 1962 presidential address to the American Historical Association.[1] His exclamation has been echoing throughout the profession ever since. With equal frustration Jacques Barzun declared more recently that although "the contemporary search for a persuasive myth . . . has been found in numbers, it does not follow that their promiscuous use with other forms of magic, namely words, is permissible." He contended that when the reader's "eye ranges across a chart in all directions . . . he is not *reading history*."[2] Another historian claims that "the high degree of isolation of feelings permitted by the use of statistics gives them an attractiveness to social scientists who wish to avoid their own painful emotions. . . . [Quantitative] methods are ego syntonic for personalities who need emotional defenses against experience."[3]

What is it about quantification that provokes such intense reaction? Perhaps the answer is to be found in psychology rather than history. Cushing Strout keenly noted that historians on the methodological defensive may only be expressing their "ignorance and fear of the unfamiliar, [with] an unearned and inflated professional pride that masks an anxious fear for a threatened status in an academic world in which other subjects currently have more prestige."[4] C. Vann Woodward, one of the leading American intellectual historians, similarly observed that "traditional historians have reacted defensively and belligerently" when "confronted with equations they cannot read, with techniques they cannot understand, [and] with copious data beyond their comprehension. . . . They see their authority challenged, their humanistic values threatened, their canons of criticism ridiculed, and their cherished classics derided as

[1] Carl Bridenbaugh, "The Great Mutation," *American Historical Review* 68 (January 1963):326.

[2] Jacques Barzun, *Clio and the Doctors: Psycho-History, Quanto-History, & History* (Chicago: University of Chicago Press, 1974), pp. 24, 26.

[3] Peter Loewenberg, "The Psychohistorical Origins of the Nazi Youth Cohort," *American Historical Review* 76 (December 1971):1475n52.

[4] Cushing Strout, "Ego Psychology and the Historian," *History and Theory* 7 (1968):281.

'soft,' impressionistic, and unscientific. It is not surprising that some of them have overreacted."[5] It is appropriate to remember David Donald's remark a propos the abolitionists, noted just a few pages back, that "when a patient reacts with excessive vehemence to a mild stimulus, a doctor at once becomes suspicious of some deep-seated malaise."[6]

History is in a state of malaise. Student interest declines and ignorance increases correspondingly, but for reasons having nothing to do with methodology. Pulitzer Prize-winning historian Oscar Handlin talks with disillusionment of "intellectual pressures emanating from within that have fragmented the discipline, loosened its cohesive elements, and worn away the consciousness of common purpose." It becomes obvious from his discussion that to him one of these pressures, one of the roots of the crisis, is quantitative methodology. "At worst," he wrote, "we find elaborate ways of telling time by algebra," and he ominously but properly warns that "we have long known the danger of depending on translators; we must now learn the danger of depending on programmers."[7] The muse's doctors are searching frantically for any change in the patient that may have accompanied and supposedly caused her malaise. History has turned to quantification and its handmaiden, the computer, more in recent years than in the past. Is this a reason for the decline? The analysis of Bridenbaugh, Barzun, and Handlin would seem to lead to that conclusion, although it is more likely that quantification—the use of measurement—is no more the cause of history's current difficulties than it is the remedy. To be sure, even its detractors guardedly admit that quantification has a place. Barzun allows that "tables are digestible and welcome if their size and contents help support or illustrate the text and not the other way around,"[8] and Bridenbaugh concedes that once a historian has achieved "a thorough, imaginatively molded knowledge of the life of a former epoch" (which, we might add, is likely to take a lifetime) he could go on to study another kind of history if he wishes, "yes, even quantification, for we need to know about such matters."[9]

In general, there are four apprehensions at the bottom of the naysayers' objections to historical quantification and the New History with which it is associated. One of these is the tendency that all of us have to pooh pooh what we do not understand. Many critics oppose quantification and computer techniques because they have not had sufficient opportunity to learn something about them. This intellectual anti-intellectualism may prove, paradoxically, to be the threat to history that the antiquantifiers are so busily rooting out. A second criticism is found in the mistaken

[5]C. Vann Woodward, "The Jolly Institution," *New York Review of Books* 21 (May 2, 1974):3.
[6]David Donald, "Toward a Reconsideration of Abolitionists," in *Lincoln Reconsidered: Essays on the Civil War Era* (New York: Alfred A. Knopf, 1956), p. 20.
[7]Oscar Handlin, "History: A Discipline in Crisis?" *American Scholar* 40 (Summer 1971):450, 455.
[8]Barzun, *Clio and the Doctors,* pp. 24–25.
[9]Bridenbaugh, "The Great Mutation," p. 327.

notion that quantitative methods are mere mechanical procedures that imply no unique theoretical assumptions. Actually, the idea of measurement, on which all quantitative methods are based by definition, is a good deal more complex than it appears to be on the surface; this will become apparent in the pages below.

The other objections must be taken more seriously. Perhaps the best-put warning has come from historian Arthur Schlesinger, Jr. Speaking to the 1962 meeting of the American Sociological Association, Schlesinger confessed his awareness of how vague, impressionistic, and imprecise historians could be, and agreed that quantification could often be useful. But he maintained that "most of the variables in an historical equation are not susceptible to commensurable quantification." Quantification was imprecise because it could only be used with evidence that has the capacity to be measured. It was Schlesinger's contention "that almost all important questions are important precisely because they are *not* susceptible to quantitative answers."[10] Immediately and instinctively most historians, advocates of Schlesinger's humanist views, see the truth in his position. But one must also be wary of his conclusions. It is true that many vital issues cannot be solved quantitatively, but one fears that many of Schlesinger's questions cannot be answered at all. Perhaps one value of quantification is that it has a good chance of coming up with some answers, however limited, to some of the questions that hitherto were unanswerable.

A fourth exception to quantification is on literary grounds. This aversion must be taken very seriously, because it involves an important problem for which no satisfactory solution is in sight. Whatever else it is, history is a literary art. But the art is being lost; the decline of literary grace in historical writing is an underlying theme in the complaints of those who would deny the claims of quantification and the New History. Overwhelmed by tedious percentages and detailed footnotes, for example, one book reviewer complained that humanity had been squeezed out of a book, leaving nothing but "the fibrous rind. Quantification once more has gagged the muse."[11] Upset by much the same thing, another reviewer remarked that quantitative details were "very scholarly, very scientific, and very impressive. They are also quite boring and for all except a few specialists quite meaningless. The average person, even the average professional historian, will not understand them, he will not even want to understand them, and he will either pass them by or throw the books down in annoyed frustration!"[12]

It is easy to point to this communication problem, but quite another thing to point to a solution other than to say that historians must attempt to maintain technical precision and overall clarity at the same time. Meaningless verbal thickets must always be

---

[10]Arthur Schlesinger, Jr., "The Humanist Looks at Empirical Social Research," *American Sociological Review* 27 (December 1962):768–71.

[11]Review by Robert J. Taylor, in *William and Mary Quarterly,* 3d ser. 30 (January 1973):163.

[12]Review by Albert Castel, in *Civil War Times Illustrated* 11 (January 1973):49.

avoided; however, strange words cannot be abandoned just because some people do not understand them. In every discipline there is a necessary technical language that must be used, with precision, if the message is to be perceived accurately by other members of the discipline. Daniel Boorstin, a historian of such wide-ranging accomplishments that one hardly knows how to describe him except to say that he is not a quantifier, puts it more bluntly: if the historian finds the vocabulary to be unfamiliar he ought to try to learn it.[13]

More important than the communcations gap between professional historians (this can be bridged) is that between the quantifier and the general reading public, including students. If some historians will not tolerate a chart or a correlation coefficient, what of the ordinary intelligent reader who simply likes to read history? Of course, the popularizers play a very important role in solving the problem, but the quantitative historians must involve themselves by improving their communication. If they do not, their audience will be confined to a small band of the initiated.

On a practical level, however, if one's research involves technical findings and charts and tables, how is one to write about it without mentioning the technology, the charts, and the tables? One way to avoid that dilemma is to eliminate the technical apparatus altogether, using it merely as a research guide for an ordinary prose discussion. This is surely what many historians would prefer, and it is sometimes done. Peter Laslett's fine study, *The World We Have Lost,* is an example of such a work; the chapter on "Births, Marriages and Deaths," which is a key part of his discussion, and which required the use of a demographic technique called family reconstitution, contains two quotations from Shakespeare, one from another contemporary playwright, one from a contemporary account book—and only three simple tables. Laslett's work is exceedingly well written, quite readable, and very scholarly; but, as the introduction indicates, it is a report preliminary to a work that will be more academic.[14] In short, it is an early and somewhat popularized account.

Many scholars, including the quantifiers, welcome the disappearance of the technical apparatus. As historians become more familiar with various quantitative techniques and the computers that manipulate them, their use is taken for granted and passed over in silence. To most readers a correlation coefficient means little; but are we to ignore the reader who does find the coefficient meaningful? The question answers itself. The disappearance of scholarly apparatus, whether it consists of tables, coefficients, technical terms, or even footnotes, is not necessarily a welcome event. Indeed, the necessity of these details should be made clear in the ensuing pages.

One of the most important virtues of quantification is that it supposedly produces replicable results, that is, findings that can be repeated by another researcher using the

---

[13]Daniel Boorstin, "Enlarging the Historian's Vocabulary," Introduction to Robert William Fogel and Stanley L. Engerman, eds., *The Reinterpretation of American Economic History* (New York: Harper & Row, 1971), p. xi.

[14]Peter Laslett, *The World We Have Lost* (New York: Charles Scribner's Sons, 1965), p. x.

same data. We are rightly suspicious of results that cannot be repeated. It is to permit replication that a traditional historical study uses footnotes; for the same reason a quantified study must use whatever charts, tables, and coefficients are necessary. It may aid the literary qualities of the work to put the apparatus in footnotes or, as is increasingly being done, in appendices—but they must be there. As Jacques Barzun points out (and he would be surprised to see his reasoning used to support quantification), "the inner check in any historian, plain or 'scientific,' is intellectual honesty, but the one *external* discipline for the subjectivity that all share is evidence accessible to others."[15] If correlation coefficients, tables, and the like are not reproduced it will be difficult to check results—and entirely too easy to accept conclusions uncritically.

Another significant strength of quantitative history, made so because large quantitative projects require the use of the computer, is a sharpening of the investigator's thinking. Karl Kroeber, whose field is English literature, writes of his naiveté when he went to a university computer center to inquire about the use of the machine to analyze prose style. The response was immediate and positive—with the proviso that he would first have to explain what he meant by style. Kroeber confessed that months later he was still trying to figure out the answer to that query.[16] In order to use quantitative data, and in order to manipulate that data with a computer, one must think very carefully about each operation, define all variables precisely, devise tests, establish thresholds, and make assumptions which he can justify to others. Data must be coded before the computer can process it; but to be coded that data must first be defined, which requires making conscious choices that must be compatible with the logic one builds into one's program. At this very point, quantification is revealed to be no more objective than any other methodological technique, for the act of making choices automatically incorporates subjectivity.[17] The assumptions and simplifications inevitably involved here are not unique to quantitative history. The difference is that quantitative historians are more likely than other historians to be aware of their assumptions—and hence their weaknesses—and their oversimplifications should be obvious to their readers at every step of the way. With traditional techniques, the operating mechanisms of assumption and simplification are often obscured from the reader—and occasionally from the investigator as well.

Sometimes quantification is condemned because it lumps people together into groups, submerging their individuality in a series of code categories. Carl Bridenbaugh objected to it on just such grounds. History, he thought, "concerns itself with the 'mutable, rank-scented many,' " creating "a sense of individual men living and having their daily being, men acting in time and place, or there will be no

[15]Barzun, *Clio and the Doctors,* p. 59.

[16]Karl Kroeber, "Computers and Research in Literary Analysis," in Edmund A. Bowles, ed., *Computers in Humanistic Research* (Englewood Cliffs, N.J.: Prentice-Hall, 1967), pp. 135–36.

[17]François Furet, "Quantitative History," *Daedalus* 100 (Winter 1971):160.

comprehension.''[18] Far from defeating such a goal, however, quantification promotes it. The documents and letters from which traditional history is written can seldom reflect the thoughts of the silent multitude of the past. Archival collections bulge with letters from and to senators, representatives, governors, generals, and businessmen. Printed documents, whether newspapers, government publications, memoirs, and the like, are also primarily the accounts of an articulate elite. Indeed, in the days before widespread literacy, letters and newspapers could seldom reflect anyone except the elite and their friends. But turn forward to the demographic chapter, and note how the veil of obscurity is torn away from the humble inhabitants of Nueces County, Texas, in 1850. Although few names are mentioned, more is known about the life of this small, obscure population than would ever have been known had not the authors tried to measure some of its demographic characteristics. In the same way, in legislative analysis minor politicians, whose vote is all that remains to posterity, may be understood in their role as part of the dynamic machinery of political decision-making, thanks to quantitative techniques.

Not everything can be quantified, and much that can be should not be. Sometimes material is extremely susceptible to measurement but is not of sufficient quality to make the effort worthwhile. Data based on faulty assumptions, with too many missing figures, or gathered in a suspect manner may be quantified as easily as any other. The computer or calculator will make no distinction between what can be done and what ought to be done. That job is left to the investigator, who ought never to forget the cliché of the computer users: GIGO—meaning Garbage In, Garbage Out. The report of an official of the British government, apparently in the early twentieth century, should give us pause:

> The Government are very keen on amassing statistics. They collect them, add them, raise them to the Nth power, take the cube root and prepare wonderful diagrams. But you must never forget that every one of these figures comes in the first instance from the village watchman, who just puts down what he damn pleases.[19]

If we were fortunate enough to possess two or three of George Washington's laundry lists they would be precious *qualitative* documents; and no one would attempt to quantify the numbers in a telephone directory—although marvelous charts and diagrams could doubtless be generated from them. Or if we possessed only 1 percent of the listings from the 1860 census, the information therein could be measured as easily as any other census data. But, unless limited geographical areas were virtually complete in coverage, it would be foolish to do so. And sometimes the meaning of the result would make measurement of dubious value. If a county has only one baker in 1850,

---

[18]Bridenbaugh, ''The Great Mutation,'' pp. 326–27.
[19]I regret that the source of this quotation has been lost.

and only two in 1860, there is little point in reporting that the number of bakers increased 100 percent during the intervening decade. One must always consider whether the data can or should be measured, and this often requires what some historians would call qualitative or traditional historical knowledge.

The determinism of the method is another serious shortcoming of quantification. Schlesinger pointed out that many important historical questions are not susceptible to measurement. Some of these questions may not even be susceptible to answers, but the historian who is overcommitted to measurement may not even bother to conjecture about other questions, or may not even recognize them when they are encountered. Quantifiers run the risk of overlooking important aspects of human experience simply because their methods are applicable only to certain types of data. This problem will be amplified in the pages below. For now it is sufficient to warn that numbers do not guarantee objectivity, comprehensiveness, or understanding, and may actually limit the researcher's insight by blinding him or her to other important kinds of evidence.

Perhaps the greatest difficulty in quantitative history comes when computers or calculators have stopped humming and one has graphed or charted the output. Then the researcher is faced with the ultimate question that every investigator must ask sooner or later: there it is, but what does it mean? It is easy to claim too much and easier still to claim nothing and expect neatly typed tables to say it for you. But the tables are silent unless the writer interprets them. "And often in the end," as Oscar Handlin points out, "after the calculations are in, we still revert to a literary issue—the choice of adjectives." For the number means little without the author's brief description. Should one say "only" 15 percent or "fully" 15 percent? The figure remains the same but its meaning changes with addition of a single qualitative modifier.[20] Certainly historians are as subjective when they use quantification as when they use literary analysis or social or psychological theory, and they require an extensive, basic knowledge of their field in order to understand their findings no matter what their methodology.

Quantification attempts to compensate for this inevitable subjectivity by making it explicit and by introducing greater precision into history. It is based on the assumption that it makes more sense to say "15 percent" rather than "a few," or "97 percent" rather than "virtually everyone." One is precise, then, in direct proportion to the extent that one can establish that there is relatively more evidence pointing to one conclusion and relatively less evidence pointing to another. Few historians would go so far as Lord Kelvin, who asserted that "when you can measure what you are speaking about and express it in numbers you know something about it; but when you cannot measure it, when you cannot express it in numbers, your knowledge is of a meager and unsatisfactory kind."[21] But many would agree that measurement is essential to basic

---

[20]Handlin, "History: A Discipline in Crisis?" p. 456.
[21]William Thomson, *Popular Lectures and Addresses*, 2nd ed., vol. 1, *Constitution of Matter* (London: Macmillan and Co., 1891), p. 80.

knowledge and that there are many more historical phenomena susceptible to intelligent measurement than most scholars suspected a few years ago.

If any history may be called "scientific," quantitative history probably is (although no particular superiority should be claimed for it on that account). As such it is often placed at the polar opposite from other historical methods, which are sometimes called subjective, other times called humanist, and occasionally labeled qualitative. The subjective-humanist-qualitative historian is skeptical of the idea that behavior can be reduced to numbers, and is supposed to be suspicious of numbers based on faulty evidence. But so too is the quantifier. In short there is an implied dichotomy which does not exist. No responsible quantifier, observes William O. Aydelotte, "would assert that all historical information can be quantified . . . , that quantitative procedures can achieve finality and eliminate subjective judgment, or that the adoption of these methods precludes the use of speculation, imagination, intuition, [and] logic." He goes on to contend that the notion of such a polarity is based on nothing more than "an intellectual time-lag."[22]

Today's New History is reminiscent of another time of professional soul searching early in the twentieth century, when a group of young historians wished to upset the prevailing notions of scientific history. While some critics complained that history was becoming unreadable (this was over half a century ago!), others, social scientists among them, questioned the failure of orthodox historians to seek and discover the laws that governed history. The young historians agreed, wishing to put away the distant past. They concentrated instead on the useful, recent past, emphasizing the everyday life of the masses. They wanted to be relevant, and they crossed disciplinary lines to embrace the social sciences.[23] Their thought was epitomized by James Harvey Robinson. "The 'New History,'" claimed Robinson, "is escaping from the limitations formerly imposed upon the study of the past. It will come in time consciously to meet our daily needs; it will avail itself of all those discoveries that are being made about mankind by anthropologists, economists, psychologists, and sociologists."[24] Like that of sixty years ago, today's New History is interdisciplinary, for it attempts to use theory developed in economics, psychology, sociology, anthropology, and political science. And like the older "New History" it emerged as a protest against the methods of traditional historians and a desire to substitute more systematic inquiry.[25]

[22] William O. Aydelotte, *Quantification in History* (Reading, Mass.: Addison-Wesley Publishing Co., 1971), pp. 4, 36.
[23] John Higham with Leonard Krieger and Felix Gilbert, *History* (Englewood Cliffs, N.J.: Prentice-Hall, 1965), pp. 104–116.
[24] James Harvey Robinson, "The New History," in Robinson, *The New History: Essays Illustrating the Modern Historical Outlook* (New York: Macmillan Co., 1912), p. 24.
[25] Aydelotte, *Quantification in History*, pp. 17–18.

The term "systematic" implies quantification, but that is only part of the New History. Sometimes quantitative historians are called behaviorists, "understanding behavioural to connote, in this instance, a strong interest in the methods, results, and implications of measurement, combined with some desire to produce research that is respectable by social-science criteria."[26] What today's New History requires is merely that useful data be subject to measurement where measurement is potentially valuable, that the assumptions and hypotheses adopted to aid the analysis of data be explicitly stated, and that social science theory be utilized when appropriate. In this way the last two selections in the psychosociological section relate to this discussion of quantitative history, as they make tentative probes in the direction of quantitative collective biography for the purpose of ordering data around sociological theory.

Each of the following essays illustrates some aspect of the New History. The first four, dealing with southern elites, development of colonial perceptions of nationalism, and demographic studies of the American cattle frontier and the medieval peasantry, may be categorized under the heading of the New Social History. The next two selections concern voter behavior in the post-Civil War Midwest and legislative behavior of the United States Congress just prior to the War of 1812. They are clearly products of the New Political History; the first essay under social history could also be placed in this category. The New Economic History is represented by the last selection, which considers the relation of the Populist movement to railroad rates. Generally speaking, the articles are arranged in order of difficulty, according to the complexity of the quantitative procedures employed. Taken together, these selections illustrate the interrelationship of the three points of the New History: quantification, explicit assumptions and hypotheses, and social science theory. Their presence here also indicates that the methodological wars fought since quantification began to be accepted by the historical profession seem to be coming to an end. The victory is not going to the shrill naysayer, nor to the zealous, presumptuous quantifier who thinks numbers can explain all—there are no longer many of either anyway. Rather quantification is being generally accepted as an additional and highly useful tool. One should emphasize both sides of this issue equally. If there can be no real question of the validity of quantification when properly used, there can also be no question as to the appropriateness of traditional methods when properly used. Neither quantifiers nor nonquantifiers need to apologize for their procedures. All that is required, on both sides, is an open mind and a willingness to learn.

---

[26]Allan G. Bogue, "United States: The 'New' Political History," *Journal of Contemporary History* 3 (January 1968):6.

chapter thirteen

Quantitative Collective Biography

The last selections in the psychosociological section illustrate inevitable methodological overlapping by introducing a new conceptual element. Attempting to determine whether rich Americans in the Jacksonian era were self-made men, Edward Pessen examined local histories and tax, census, and genealogical records in order to draw profiles of wealthy citizens he wished to study. Not only did he ascertain their wealth, but also their family background, occupation, education, religion, and ties of kinship. Although the results, for the most part, are not tabulated, Pessen was using collective biography for the purpose of applying the sociological concepts of class and mobility to the resident elite of four eastern cities. By the same token, when David Donald applied the theories of status and reference group to abolitionists he was also using collective biography, although in a somewhat more obvious form than Pessen, for he reports the number of individuals on his list of abolitionists and makes some calculations intended to underline the nature of the abolitionist movement.

Collective biography is the simple English term for this method. It can be made to sound far more technical if obscured by the jargon of career-line analysis and will be totally unrecognized when referred to as prosopography (literally, the collection of biographical information, originally used to describe an individual). But students should not be discouraged by fancy labels. Collective biography is a simple and frequently used historical method. While employed more often now than formerly, it is not new. Charles A. Beard used collective biography in *An Economic Interpretation of the Constitution of the United States,* which first appeared in 1913, and Sir Lewis B. Namier employed it in *The Structure of Politics at the Accession of George III* and *England in the Age of the American Revolution,* the first editions of which came out in 1929 and 1930, respectively.[1]

---

[1]Charles A. Beard, *An Economic Interpretation of the Constitution of the United States* (New York: The Macmillan Co., 1913); Lewis B. Namier, *The Structure of Politics at the Accession of George III,* 2 vols. (London: Macmillan and Co., 1929); and Namier, *England in the Age of the American Revolution* (London: Macmillan and Co., 1930).

A renewal of interest in collective biography and a geometric increase in the research that utilizes the method is the result of three developments. The first is the increasingly interdisciplinary orientation of history. Today's students and their instructors are likely to have some sort of sociological knowledge, even if informally acquired via newspapers, radio, and television. The thoughts of such historians are likely to be quite concerned with the mode of conduct of formal and informal groups. Under this influence, it is to be expected that some of the more interesting groups (a legislative body, the civil service, the wealthy establishment of a particular city, abolition or other reform movements) would become the subject of intense investigation. At first this work was necessarily done by hand; machine techniques were not readily available to academicians until the early 1960s, and in the absence of machines, or at least of true computers (as opposed to keypunches, sorters, tabulators, and the like), research tended to be concentrated on elites. This was not because they were especially important, although a case could be made that they were, or because of a desire to reduce elites to a common stature by showing the common motivations which determined their behavior. Instead, it was because elite groups are small and the smaller the group the easier it is to process data. The second and third developments occurred simultaneously. One of these was the growing desire to examine larger groups, such as the population of an entire community or a sample of the rank and file membership of a large organization. Granted that small elites are important, so too are large elites and mass aggregates. But if a large group is to be examined, electronic data processing becomes necessary. The third development was therefore the rapid proliferation of the computer, which removed the size limitations imposed by hand tabulation on collective biography projects.

The basic questions collective biography is able to answer are those that involve the "who were . . . ?" query. That is, we can partially understand the nature of a group by discovering something about its members. As Richard Jensen put it, the method will "free the historian from dependence on the haphazard generalizations of journalists, novelists, and the biographers of famous men."[2] In the following selection, for example, we learn that Confederate Congressmen were more likely to be wealthy secessionist Democratic slaveholders, engaged in law and/or agriculture, than anything else; although there was a substantial minority who may have been unionists and/or Whigs, there were very few who were poor, nonslaveholding, or had other occupational interests. Collective biography is thus a prime tool for historical reinterpretation. Were Loyalists mostly clergy and political placeholders? Was the Whig party leadership composed of a mercantile and professional elite? Were local governments in the

---

[2]Richard Jensen, "Quantitative Collective Biography: An Application to Metropolitan Elites," in Robert P. Swierenga, ed., *Quantification in American History: Theory and Research* (New York: Atheneum, 1970), p. 405. Jensen's essay is an excellent example of the application of refined statistical procedures to collective biography.

immediate antebellum South controlled by local oligarchies? Questions like these are good opportunities for the employment of this extremely useful technique.

Collective biography has a wide range of applications. As one of its practitioners explains, it can be used "to make sense of political action, to help explain ideological or cultural change, to identify social reality, and to describe and analyze with precision the structure of society and the degree and the nature of the movements within it."[3] Thus the key issue that the researcher in collective biography wishes to resolve is usually not what proportion of a group behaved in a certain fashion but what is unique or different about those who behaved in that manner.

The findings of collective biography illustrate the usefulness of the method. For example, Ruth B. Bordin examined Richard Hofstadter's contention that the influence of propertied and educated "gentlemen" in American politics declined during the first fifty years of the nineteenth century. One of the places Hofstadter found evidence of this was in Congress, so Bordin compared congressmen in the Sixth Congress (1799–1801) with those in the Thirty-first Congress (1849–1851) with regard to educational level and occupation, which are certainly key tests in the determination of whether or not an individual in the early years of the nation had acquired the stature of a gentleman. The differences are so minor as to deny the contention that the gentleman was becoming a rare breed in Congress[4]—if one accepts Bordin's criteria as reliable indicators of what determines a gentleman. Some historians might wish to add tests for wealth (which Hofstadter considered to be an essential characteristic of those early gentlemen) and family background or to add additional congresses so as to avoid overreliance on only two data points, either of which could be atypical. However that may be, the testing method here is collective biography.

In a similar vein, the middle-class revolt interpretation of early twentieth-century Progressivism published by George Mowry and Alfred D. Chandler, and accepted by Hofstadter,[5] was challenged (at least for Iowa) by the use of collective biography. E. Daniel Potts examined 137 county histories and other biographical sources, and concluded that Roosevelt Progressives in Iowa differed little from other Republican factions between 1900 and 1912 except in age and previous politics. They were equally middle class and their national origins, education, religion, and occupation did not vary appreciably from the members of the other factions. Far from a middle-class

[3]Lawrence Stone, "Prosopography," *Daedalus* 100 (Winter 1971):47.

[4]Ruth B. Bordin, "Hofstadter and the Decline of the Gentleman—Fact or Fancy," *Mid-America* 48 (April 1966):119–25, analyzing Richard Hofstadter, *Anti-Intellectualism in American Life* (New York: Alfred A. Knopf, 1963), Chapter VI.

[5]George E. Mowry, *The California Progressives* (Berkeley and Los Angeles: University of California Press, 1951), especially pp. 86–89; Alfred D. Chandler, Jr., "The Origins of Progressive Leadership," in Elting E. Morison et al., *The Letters of Theodore Roosevelt*, 8 vols. (Cambridge, Mass.: Harvard University Press, 1951–1954), 8:1462–65; and Richard Hofstadter, *The Age of Reform: From Bryan to F.D.R.* (New York: Alfred A. Knopf, 1956).

revolt, therefore, the Progressivism of the Bull Moose party was a rebellion of the young.[6]

The analytic procedure in collective biography need not be difficult. A population is first selected for study—a congress, an elite of some sort, the inhabitants of a specified area, the members of a church or union—and the names of the individuals composing that population are ascertained by referring to government documents, local histories and biographical directories, newspapers, organizational records, or other appropriate sources. A series of questions is then asked of each group member to determine his or her key biographical characteristics. The questions must be well thought out so the responses will satisfy the queries posed by the project; if one seeks to determine whether Populists were led by farmers or small-town businessmen, for example, one had better secure data on occupation and residence.

These questions are called variables, since the answers vary from case to case. Variables are usually divided into categories, and the task in data collection is to place each individual case in the proper category for each variable: for example, age (0–20 years, 21–40 years, 41–65 years, 65 years or more), occupation (farmer, professional, small business, white collar, skilled labor, unskilled labor), marital status (single, married, divorced, separated, widowed). The researcher then determines frequencies: farmers, 156, or 58 percent; lawyers, 206, or 77 percent, and so on. If desired, these counts can then be divided further by other variables. One might find that 40 percent of the 206 lawyers were Whigs and 60 percent were Democrats. This procedure "controls" for occupation, that is, occupation (or any other variable one might choose to control) will be the same (held constant) for all members of the subgroup being examined. Although these tabulations will usually be easy to compile, comprehending their significance is likely to be a problem of much greater magnitude. For the most meaningful results in collective biography, a particular group (Progressives, for example), should be compared with other groups, if they exist, which are oriented around the same subject but from a different point of view (i.e., conservatives); it may be equally useful to compare the same group, or groups of a similar nature, at different points in time as Ruth

[6] E. Daniel Potts, "The Progressive Profile in Iowa," *Mid-America* 47 (October 1965):257–68. It is interesting to note that Richard Hofstadter, who was greatly interested in the application of social science theory to history, bears the brunt of criticism in a number of quantitative studies that seem to undermine conclusions based on his use of that theory. The student ought to consider whether this is a sign of the insufficiency of social science concepts or is instead the usual heavy criticism directed toward the pioneer in any field, the censure being due to the new concepts the pioneer introduces as well as to his inevitable mistakes as he fumbles about adapting techniques from another discipline which the next generation will use without a second thought. In this instance, as another historian remarks, "collective biography *per se* will never tell us whether the . . . Progressives [or anyone else] perceived a decline in their status. Before the argument can be settled, it will be necessary to add a psychological dimension." Burton W. Folsom II, "The Collective Biography as a Research Tool," *Mid-America* 54 (April 1972):108–122 (quote on p. 121).

Bordin did in her comparison of the membership of the Sixth Congress and the Thirty-first Congress.[7]

One of the sociological concepts used to amplify the significance of collective biography is Max Weber's "ideal typical means of orientation," or ideal type, which Weber intended not as an exact delineation of reality but only as a potentially adequate portrayal. It is created by combining a multitude of varied instances until it is possible to draw up both a generalization about a given phenomenon and a standard by which to compare its real-life parallels.[8] The typical congressman sketched toward the end of this selection (p. 220) is an ideal type. He did not exist in the real world, for none of the congressmen fit all of the characteristics mentioned; all vary in greater or less degree from the ideal type. This device is not often developed clearly, although a summation of statistical findings such as this one may unconsciously employ Weber's idea. However, it is not necessary to employ a statistical technique in order to take advantage of the concept of the ideal type. In a chapter added to the second edition of his Pulitzer Prize-winning study of immigration, Oscar Handlin wrote that he had used the ideal-type method to sum the experiences of the immigrant European peasant, but only one reviewer understood what he was doing.[9] That reviewer was Richard Hofstadter, whose social science orientation has already been remarked and whose main criticism was that Handlin gave no indicator of how representative his ideal type was. This was a question, wrote Hofstadter, which "could have been answered with a figure or two."[10] Back to statistics!

In presentation, collective biography may take varying forms. It may be confined largely to quantitative discussion, including frequency counts and tabulation tables, as in the accompanying article. It may also consist of a comprehensive narrative description, perhaps accompanied by biographical sketches, of the dovetailed interests and interrelationships of the group members. In the latter instance there may be little tabulation, if any, as illustrated by Beard's *Economic Interpretation of the Constitution,* Namier's two works on the British Parliament, or the Jones and Connelly essay in

[7]For an excellent recent use of comparative collective biography, see Richard D. Brown, "The Founding Fathers of 1776 and 1787: A Collective View," *William and Mary Quarterly,* 3d ser. 33 (July 1976):465–80, which compares the signers of the Declaration of Independence with the members of the Constitutional Convention and contrasts this combined elite to the general population in such characteristics as age, occupation, ethnic origin, family size, and the like.

[8]H. H. Gerth and C. Wright Mills, trans. and eds., *From Max Weber: Essays in Sociology* (New York: Oxford University Press, 1946), pp. 294, 323–24; and Edward A. Shils and Henry A. Finch, trans. and eds., *Max Weber on the Methodology of the Social Sciences* (Glencoe, Illinois: The Free Press, 1949), pp. 90–93, 101–102.

[9]Oscar Handlin, *The Uprooted,* 2nd ed., enl. (Boston: Little, Brown and Co., 1973), p. 304.

[10]Richard Hofstadter, "West of Ellis Island," *Partisan Review* 19 (March-April 1952): 252–56. Hofstadter called the ideal type "a valid but usually bloodless sociological method" (p. 255).

the previous section on informal organization in the Confederate Army. But these are not really *quantitative* collective biographies. On the other hand, the presentation may consist of some combination of the two. In either event, the best use of quantitative collective biography utilizes the results as a starting point for further analysis. For this reason, collective biography, which seems so mechanical, is often employed in connection with theories of status, reference group, legislative behavior, and the like—if not explicitly, at least implicitly. This article, in a revised form, thus provided one point of departure for a study of the Confederate Congress in which the important variables marked out in the collective biography were examined for their relationship to the way congressmen voted on major issues.[11]

Collective biography rests upon several concepts, some of which are equally applicable to other quantitative methods. One is found in the rather rigid behaviorism that the method implies. It suggests the possibility that a few usually obvious characteristics have perhaps indirect but nonetheless major roles in determining or at least ascertaining how people behave. It is the antithesis of the popular conception of developmental psychology (for example) that might predict that on the basis of an individual's childhood experiences he or she would behave in a certain manner. Collective biography, at least as applied to politics, usually assumes that the roots of behavior lie in such variables as age, occupation, residence, political affiliation, economic situation, ethnic background, religion, place of birth, and education, some of which an individual cannot control.[12] The assumption is often made unconsciously, being built into a study by the ready availability of such information. This iron-bound determinism is not without basis. Many studies do show that a variation in some crude biographical attribute is highly correlated with certain types of behavior—thus Richard Jensen's article, reprinted toward the end of this quantitative section, demonstrates a strong association between voter behavior and membership in a liturgical or nonliturgical church.

This behavioral concept can easily lead the researcher into difficulty. It is too easy to take for granted that any significant variations between subgroups in the frequencies of a given characteristic indicate causation. Often they will, but just as often the historian does not know whether there is a causal connection or not. One advantage of collective

---

[11]Thomas B. Alexander and Richard E. Beringer, *The Anatomy of the Confederate Congress: A Study of the Influences of Member Characteristics on Legislative Voting Behavior, 1861–1865* (Nashville: Vanderbilt University Press, 1972).

[12]Whether some variables might in turn be determined by childhood experience is a pertinent but as yet unexplored question. Would persons born in one part of the country have a sufficiently different cultural upbringing that they would be more likely to repress their feelings than those born in another part? Would farm youth be more or less likely to suffer from an identity crisis than city youth? Would these developmental differences, if they exist, be sufficiently strong to affect educational goals, occupations, or consumption habits which might then cause distinctive political behavior? The questions are worth asking, but, so far as I am aware, no one has yet attempted to do so with collective biography.

biography is that it points to areas of potentially useful speculation along lines of causation, but one danger is that causal connections will be made where they actually do not exist. More often than not, one has no direct causal linkage between characteristic A and behavior B; rather, both have been the consequence of some unknown cause, C. In this situation the most that one can say about the relation of A and B is that they are associated, meaning they tend to occur together. Presented with problems like this, the quantifier inevitably becomes a pluralist as he or she realizes the impossibility of ascribing a single cause to any significant event.

Another important warning is that whatever the findings of collective biography they are obviously not going to fit each individual. One must not confuse collective biography with biography per se. If Southern Democrats in 1861 tended to be secessionists and Whigs tended to be unionists, there are, nevertheless, Whig secessionists and Democratic unionists whose behavior runs counter to the direction in which the variables seem to point. (Even then one can sometimes point to some variable among these exceptions which is associated with their behavior.) The lesson: beware of exceptions, draw conclusions with appropriate modesty, and remember that the essence of quantitative collective biography is the study of *groups* (not individuals) by means of a statistical profile—as indicated by the title of the following article. Since most applications of collective biography are to elites, one must also avoid the temptation to extend the findings to an anonymous rank and file. Whatever the reality behind the status anxiety thesis as applied to Progressive leaders, for example, the case could be quite different for the followers. Remember that elite groups, legislatures, executive committees, and the like, are not a cross section of the entire population.

One last warning concerns the nature of the data, which necessarily determines and restricts the conclusions that can be drawn. If the only variables are economic and political, one can be sure that any causal suggestions will point to economic or political motivations; on the other hand, if variables are confined to more personal attributes, such as family background, age, and sex, causation will point in entirely different directions. To a large extent, as with all other methods, the nature of the data sets up the parameters within which explanations are likely to be discovered. To compensate for this bias, one should have a reasonably wide range of variables and a ready willingness to confess the possibility that characteristics one is unable to assess may be fully as important as any others. This is especially true because sufficient records of thoughts, emotions, and beliefs are rarely available—even for elites—to allow them to be used as variables, thereby creating an inevitable, anti-intellectual bias in one's conclusions.

Quantitative collective biography is clearly one of the most promising historical techniques. It is simple enough to be used by anyone who has forgotten high school mathematics, for all that is absolutely necessary is the ability to count. Even when done poorly it may be of value. If the analysis is insufficient or inadequate, the accompanying tables nevertheless will be useful to future researchers provided only that the figures have been added correctly. Even before reading the following article alert students should therefore be able to examine the tabulations and reach some tentative conclusions of their own about the interrelationships of party affiliation, secession stand, wealth, and other variables among the Confederate political elite.

This discussion presents a composite quantitative picture of the economic, political, and personal background of the 267 men who served in the Confederate Congress. The emphasis is on measurement so that an accurate profile may be developed. Collective biography in this instance is not used to illustrate a sociological model; it is, instead, an end in itself. The sources that provided the necessary information include biographical directories, county histories, and the manuscript enumerations from the 1860 census. Full information was not available for all members, but there was sufficient data to make the results reliable. However, readers should consider whether the full significance of these findings might not be obscured by the lack of references to parallel studies of other legislative elites.

A Profile of the Members of the Confederate Congress
Richard E. Beringer

. . . The first Confederate Congress was actually the Provisional Congress. This body emerged by default when delegates chosen to create a provisional government and draft a permanent constitution realized that the exigencies of the times required they exceed their limited authority. Legislative power was more or less usurped as the delegates transformed themselves into congressmen. But necessity overcame nicety; and most Southerners acquiesced in an action which seems rather incongruous for a people revolting to defend proper constitutional order. The Congress of this provisional government held five sessions, lasting from February 4, 1861, to February 17, 1862, when it was superseded by the Congress of the permanent government. This First Congress met in four sessions between February 18, 1862, and February 17, 1864, while the Second Congress held two sessions between May 2, 1864, and March 18, 1865. The total of 267 members of the Confederate Congress includes 36 senators and 231 congressmen who served as representatives in either the provisional or permanent Congress or in both. . . .

Richard E. Beringer, "A Profile of the Members of the Confederate Congress." *Journal of Southern History*, XXXIII (November 1967), 519–27, 530–41, abridged, footnotes deleted. Copyright 1967 by the Southern Historical Association. Reprinted by permission of the Managing Editor.

. . . Of the 146 legislators who sat at one time or another in the First Congress, only 46, about a third, had been in the Provisional Congress. Literally overnight the legislative body of the Confederacy was transformed from a fairly close balance between lifetime Democrats and former Whigs to a three-to-two ratio, due mainly to the overwhelmingly Democratic allegiance of the freshman legislators. An influx of farmers (owning less than twenty slaves) replaced many small planters (designated as those owning from twenty to forty-nine slaves), and there were more men who had been secessionists in the 1861 crisis. In other essential characteristics, such as wealth and political experience, however, the two Congresses were much the same; but the drastic change in membership must have had its effect upon the legislative function.

Turnover between the First and Second Congresses was also considerable, though not nearly so great as earlier; only 39 per cent of the 137 members of the Second Congress were newcomers (this includes 3 men who had sat in the Provisional Congress). Some states, however, furnished more than their share of replacements. Nine of the 12 Georgians and 8 of the 12 North Carolinians in the Second Congress, for example, were new. There were fewer secessionists, as the new senators and representatives in the Second Congress had been overwhelmingly pro-Union in 1861. A similar shift occurred in party affiliation, with the ex-Whigs appearing in strength. The effect of this rotation of membership can be understood better by realizing that newcomers made up only about 20 per cent of the Eighty-sixth United States Congress and about 15 per cent of the Eighty-seventh Congress. They constituted two-thirds of the first Confederate Congress and one-third of the Second.

The party background of these legislators . . . is especially significant. At least five of those who sat in the Confederate Congress were early Jacksonians, being born before the Treaty of Ghent and the Battle of New Orleans. Two, former President John Tyler and William Cabell Rives, had even been Jeffersonian Democratic-Republicans. But it is membership in the leading parties of the prewar years that is especially important (Table 1), for it is this allegiance that helped to determine behavior in the crisis of 1860–1861. Ninety-one former Whigs (with only a few nostalgic exceptions, no one called himself a Whig in 1861) served at one time or another in the Congress of the Confederacy. Of those whose views are known, only 31 per cent were secessionists, while 68 per cent were Unionists. Only one, Walker Brooke of Vicksburg, Mississippi, was a co-operationist; and the secession views of six others are unknown. The former Americans or Know-Nothings were divided in the same proportion, Union over secession. Of the forty-seven Constitutional Unionists an overwhelming 80 per cent were Unionists; what is more remarkable is that 20 per cent (nine men) became secessionists after the 1860 presidential election. Of course, most of the Know-Nothings and Constitutional Unionists had been Whigs earlier in their careers.

Foremost, however, were the 154 Democrats in the Congress. Seventy-two per cent of those whose views are known were secessionists and only 23 per cent were Unionists. Predictably, the 118 lifetime Democrats were even more heavily secessionist, favoring disunion over Union by 78 per cent to 17 per cent in the case of the 108 of

Table 1 Former Political Affiliations of Confederate Congressmen Arranged by Views on Secession

	Secession		Co-operation		Union		Sub-total		Un-known	Total
	No.	%	No.	%	No.	%	No.	%		
Whig	26	31	1	1	58	68	85	100	6	91
American	8	31			18	69	26	100		26
Const'l Union	9	20			36	80	45	100	2	47
Lifetime Democrat	84	78	6	6	18	17	108	100	10	118
Converted Democrat	18	53	1	3	15	44	34	100	2	36
Total Democrat	102	72	7	5	33	23	142	100	12	154
Party Unknown	18	67	2	7	7	26	27	100	21	48
All Members	134	58	9	4	87	38	230	100	37	267

Vertical totals would be meaningless since many congressmen had belonged to more than one party, and are therefore included in more than one category. Virtually all "converted Democrats" had once been Whigs, as had 85 per cent of the Americans and 81 per cent of the Constitutional Unionists. Due to rounding off, percentages may not always total exactly 100 per cent.

known opinions. The Democracy was indeed the party of disunion in the South. There were 48 congressmen (18 per cent of the membership) whose party affiliations are unknown. All but one of the 15 South Carolinians were lifetime Democrats, and the other's affiliation is unknown. Missouri and Texas were also heavily Democrat, while Georgia and North Carolina gave an edge to former Whigs, about two-thirds of both delegations having been in that party at one time. In view of party feelings on secession, it is not surprising that North Carolina was strongly Unionist while South Carolina and Confederate Missouri were not. The Louisiana congressmen, on the other hand, contradict this relationship. Heavily Whig, they were also heavily secessionist; this, however, may be related to their wealth, for the richer an ex-Whig in the Confederate Congress was, the more likely he was to have been a secessionist in 1861. The economic upper half of the Whigs was split in a close five-to-four ratio for Union, but the lower half gave a decisive seven-to-two ratio for the Union. None of these men was really poor, however, only eight having estates worth less than $10,000, with the lowest being valued at over $3,000. Democrats were split evenly on secession in both halves of the economic scale.

Knowledge of secession views is more complete. Based on information for 230 members, 58 per cent of the lawmakers were secessionists, while only 38 per cent were Unionists. Co-operationists ran a poor third with 4 per cent. Although most of the 134 secessionists were lifetime Democrats, there were also quite a few former Whigs, demonstrating that both major parties of the early 1850's contributed strongly to the secession movement. The Florida, Kentucky, Louisiana, Mississippi, Missouri, South Carolina, and Texas delegations were heavily secessionist. Arkansas, North Carolina, and Tennessee congressmen had generally been pro-Union in 1860, while the Alabama, Georgia, and Virginia delegations were rather evenly split on this point.

These secession views suggest how the politicians felt about the 1860 election. The general assumption that the majority favored the Southern Democratic nominee John C. Breckinridge seems to be true. Complete data are unfortunately lacking, as the views of over half the men are unknown. But 54 of the other 115 favored Breckinridge, 45 approved of John Bell, and only 16 supported Stephen A. Douglas. Such meager information can be supplemented by county election results, which show that 49 per cent of the congressmen came from counties which gave a majority to Breckinridge in 1860, while another 34 per cent resided in neighborhoods favoring Bell. Only 7.5 per cent of the congressmen's counties were carried by Douglas. Others were split or unknown; and two Missouri congressmen were from St. Louis County, which gave Lincoln a majority in 1860. Of those congressmen for whom information is available, however, only half voted the same way as their counties, with more voting contrary to local sentiment in the upper South than was true in the lower South.

Only a little less important is the political experience of these lawmakers (Table 2). Far from being newcomers thrown into the political arena by the revolutionary events of 1860-1861, these were to a large extent experienced public men. Only 10 per cent had no political experience whatever. Even this figure is undoubtedly too large, since it

Table 2 **Prior Political Experience of Confederate Congressmen**

	Number	Percentage
State Legislature	172	64
Federal Congress	85	32
State Secession Convention or Equivalent	86	32
State Supreme Court	13	5
State Circuit, Superior, and Other Courts	25	9
Governor or Lieutenant Governor	14	5
Other State Offices	25	9
City Offices	10	4
Federal Cabinet or Diplomatic	8	3
Other Political Experience	140	52
No Political Experience	28	10

Percentages are based on total membership and do not equal 100 since most legislators had several types of experience.

may be assumed that pertinent information for some individuals was lacking. Furthermore, every political body finds itself with some members who have had no prior experience. Only 7 of the inexperienced lawmakers sat in the Provisional Congress, 10 more in the First Congress, and another 11 in the Second Congress. This experience level is remarkable considering that many Southern leaders preferred military to civil service. No less than 172, or 64 per cent, had served in state legislatures, where many had held the speakership, and 85, or 32 per cent, had served in the United States Congress (62 men had served in both). Many had been judges, in positions ranging from a lowly justice of the peace to the chief justice of a state; 14 were former governors or lieutenant governors; some held other state or city offices. In addition, 86 Confederate congressmen had been delegates to their state secession conventions (or the equivalent legislature in Kentucky). . . .

The occupational breakdown of the senators and representatives on the eve of civil war shows a wide variety of careers (Table 3). Eleven were journalists, 10 were promoters and financiers, and another 10 were merchants; others were clergymen, physicians, manufacturers, or teachers. Still others had followed these callings, especially journalism and teaching, earlier in life, generally before turning to law or agriculture. The latter were the two most important occupations, but lawyers were far more prevalent than agriculturalists. Seventy-seven per cent of the congressmen were practicing law, and another 9 per cent had once prepared to do so. Occupational breakdown shows no relation to previous political affiliation. The tendency toward dual occupations can be illustrated by the fact that 40 per cent (107) of the congressmen were engaged in both law and agriculture. Farmers and planters were thus the second largest occupational group, claiming 156, or 58 per cent, of the legislators.

Table 3   Occupations Held by Confederate Congressmen, c. 1860

	Number	Percentage
Agriculture		
Farmers (0–19 slaves)	39	15
Small Planters (20–49 slaves)	45	17
Large Planters (over 50 slaves)	62	23
Unknown slaveholdings	10	4
Total agriculture	156	58
Lawyers	206	77
Physicians	6	
Merchants	10	
Manufacturers	5	
Clergymen	4	
Journalists	11	20
Promoters and Financiers	10	
Teachers	5	
Others	3	

Percentages are based on total membership. Vertical totals would be meaningless since most congressmen had two or more occupations; the total percentage for agriculture is fractionally less than the sum of the percentages for the separate categories.

If this seems to be a rather large number, it is because all those with substantial slaveholdings who lived in rural areas are considered agricultural, unless there is good information to the contrary. A rural lawyer with thirty or forty slaves, for example, was usually engaged in agriculture, although he may not have participated actively in the overseeing of his estate. . . .

The most important part of the analysis of Confederate congressmen, however, is the breakdown by size of estate and slaveholding. It is here that the manuscript census returns become so valuable. Most information on estates and slaveownership comes from that convenient source, though in a few instances it was obtained elsewhere. Of course, the census is not completely reliable. Some people thought census takers were tax men and therefore gave little account of their fortunes. Others like to brag, making themselves a little more prosperous than perhaps they were. Still others were apparently omitted altogether.

Even though the census may give an erroneous picture of any given individual, the composite picture it produces should still be relatively reliable. One is thus permitted to study the entire economic range of the congressmen and not just the wealthy, who are so often the only ones about whom one can discover anything. Edward Sparrow of Louisiana was easily the richest man in Congress and was one of the wealthiest in the

Confederacy. Worth over a million dollars in 1860 and the seventh largest producer of cotton in Louisiana in 1859, he towered economically over his colleagues, including poor Robert B. Hilton of Florida, who confessed an estate of only fifty dollars when the census taker came to his door in 1860, and Thomas C. Fuller of North Carolina, who admitted having no estate whatever. But if Sparrow was the richest, others also had estates which would seem large even today, while Hilton and Fuller at the other extreme were not the only poor men at Richmond. Some of the 31 delegates classed as unknown may simply have had nothing to say when the assistant United States marshal came to call. The rest of the 236 men do cover the full spectrum, however, with the median estate being $48,000.

The richest congressmen were not well distributed geographically. The top twenty-five estates, ranging from $180,000 to Sparrow's $1,248,000 in value, include five from Louisiana (which only sent eleven delegates to the three Congresses), six from Virginia, and three from Mississippi, with the other eleven scattered among six other states. The richest South Carolinian, Memminger, was twenty-eighth, the leading Missourian was thirty-seventh, and the wealthiest of the Kentucky congressmen ranked sixty-fifth. This "poor" man, Willis Benson Machen, was still worth about $94,000. Predictably, of the eight from Louisiana and Mississippi in the top twenty-five, five were from the river and delta regions.

The distribution of the poorer lawmakers shows less pattern, for the twenty-five smallest known estates were well distributed and ranged up to $8,800 in value. Every state had at least one, except for Louisiana, whose poorest congressman (Thomas Jenkins Semmes of New Orleans) ranked ninety-second from the bottom. Kentucky had three of the twenty-five, while Arkansas, Georgia, South Carolina, Texas, and Virginia each had two. But Missouri easily won dubious honors, having no less than six of these poorer legislators. Over half of the twenty-five, however, were worth $5,000 or more, a figure which denoted a rather respectable estate by the standards of the 1860's.

But raw figures do not carry the entire meaning. Also important was the relative economic standing of a congressman, not in the entire Confederacy, but in his own local area. The advantage of such a consideration may be seen by comparing Wiley Pope Harris of Jackson, Mississippi, with Hiram P. Bell of Cumming in northern Georgia. Harris' $36,000 estate was only 130 per cent of the local average, while Bell's $5,360 estate was 350 per cent of his county's average.

To measure this relative status, the average estate valuation for each congressman's home county was determined by dividing the aggregate estate valuation of that county by the number of families (including single adults) residing there. Leaving aside the 31 individuals for whom figures are not available (Table 4), we find over half (130 or 55 per cent) of the congressmen had much-above-average estates (that is, 600 per cent or more of average) in their home counties, and another 63 were above average. Only 43 were average or below. Although Missouri and Arkansas had the largest proportion of the state delegations in the two bottom groupings, in every state the majority of

Table 4 **Views of Confederate Congressmen on Secession Compared to Relative Value of Estate**

	Secession		Coopera-tion		Union		Un-known		Total
	No.	%	No.	%	No.	%	No.	%	
Below Average (1-50%)	7	5					3	8	10
Average (51-200%)	14	10	2	22	14	16	3	8	33
Above Average (201-600%)	34	25	2	22	21	24	6	16	63
Much Above Average (600%+)	62	46	4	44	47	54	17	46	130
Unknown Estate Category	17	13	1	11	5	6	8	22	31
Total	134	100	9	100	87	100	37	100	267

Percentages are based on the number whose secession views are known. Due to rounding off, percentages may not always total exactly 100 per cent.
Relative estate categories are based upon computed average values for each congressman's county of residence.

congressmen possessed above- or much-above-average estates. North Carolina, Tennessee, and Virginia all had at least ten members in the highest categories for every one in the lowest, and all known Louisiana congressmen were in the top category (ex-Whigs were a majority in each of these four delegations). This confirms the long held but never really demonstrated opinion that the Confederate Congress was primarily composed of members of an economic class that was far richer than the mass of the Southern population. If these men acted like rich men, it is because most of them were rich men, not only in the South as a whole, but in their own neighborhoods as well. As the table indicates, however, these relative estate evaluations had little correlation with the congressmen's views on secession. While Unionists may have tended to be somewhat richer than secessionists on a relative basis, the small difference may well have been due to the rather large number of unknowns.

On an absolute basis ... it is the secessionists who appear to be wealthier as a group. The difference is so negligible however, that it may be said that economic standing cannot explain opposing views on secession. On the problem of former party affiliations, however, the story is slightly different. A tendency for former Whig congressmen to be richer than lifetime Democrats can be illustrated by comparing the one hundred poorest lawmakers with the one hundred richest. Twenty-nine per cent of the bottom hundred were ex-Whig, while 42 per cent of the top hundred belonged at one time to the party of Clay and Webster. But for lifetime Democrats the division was almost equal. Former Know-Nothings and Constitutional Unionists, however, belie their Whig origins, as they both had more in the bottom hundred than the top. Or, to demonstrate the point another way, the median estate for all congressmen was $48,000, which was also the approximate median estate for both secessionists and Unionists. While lifetime Democrats were also close to this over-all figure, the median estate for Whigs was $60,000.

Equally as important as the estates of these congressmen are their slaveholdings. Again the major source of information is the manuscript census. . . .

Just as these legislators cover the scale from rich to poor, so too they cover the full range from those who owned many slaves to those who owned none at all. The largest holding belonged to Duncan F. Kenner of Louisiana, who late in the war led the ill-fated Confederate mission to Europe which attempted to trade abolition for recognition. He was the eighth largest owner in Louisiana in 1860 and was the fourth largest sugar producer the year before. With 473 slaves, he had one of the greatest holdings in the country, for only eighty-eight men in the nation owned as many as 300 slaves in 1860. Of these eighty-eight, three became Confederate congressmen, for Kenner was followed by Edward Sparrow, also from Louisiana, who owned 460 slaves. They were far ahead of John Perkins, Jr., Louisiana, who owned 340 and ranked third. (The fourth man, who owned 275 slaves, was also from Louisiana.) These planters were in sharp contrast to their colleagues at the other end of the scale. Twenty-two congressmen owned no slaves at all, and another eight had only one each. Only a few of these nonslaveholders could be considered poor by 1860 criteria, however; Wiley Pope

Harris of Mississippi, for example, owned no slaves, but his estate in 1860 was worth about $36,000. Again, some of the twenty-five unknowns undoubtedly belong in the category with the nonslaveholders.

The largest slaveholders are poorly distributed geographically, as the twenty-five biggest holdings (115 slaves or more) include five of the eleven Louisiana congressmen. Another five are from Georgia, followed by three each from Alabama and Virginia. Four states had no congressmen in this select group: the largest North Carolina holding was in twenty-sixth place, the most important Texas holding was thirty-eighth, that among Kentuckians was sixty-second, and the largest Missouri ownership was ninety-third—but John B. Clark, Sr., of Missouri, still counted twenty-seven human beings as his property.

The other end of the spectrum shows a somewhat better geographic distribution. Leaving aside the unknowns, among the thirty congressmen who owned no more than one slave, five each came from Missouri and Kentucky, four from Virginia, three each from Arkansas and Tennessee, and the rest were scattered. In the Alabama and North Carolina delegations, however, the smallest holding was two slaves. That Missouri and Kentucky would lead is rather to be expected; that Virginia would rank with them is due to the large size of her delegation and her location, for all four came from the mountains, including three from what is now West Virginia.

But again raw figures do not tell the whole story. Figuring the average holding in each county and comparing congressional holdings with this average, congressmen can be categorized by the same method used to determine relative estates. Omitting those for whom we have insufficient data, 113 congressmen had slaveholdings significantly larger than average (this was most noticeable in the long-established states of Georgia, Louisiana, and South Carolina), while another 128 had average or below-average holdings (especially the border and frontier states of Arkansas, Kentucky, Missouri, and Texas). This relative ranking shows only insignificant correlations between slaveholding and secession views, but there does seem to be an indication that Whigs were more likely to be relatively large slaveowners in their home counties than lifetime Democrats. . . .

Other things are important besides a man's political and economic background. The congressmen ranked rather high, for example, in education. Of the 208 whose educational level is known, at least 80 per cent went to a college or university and at least 62 per cent were graduates. They attended no less than sixty-one institutions scattered throughout the country, some of which are no longer in existence. The most popular was the University of Georgia (or rather its predecessor) followed by the University of North Carolina. Four went to West Point, and one, George B. Hodge of Kentucky, went to Annapolis. Most received at least part of their education in some small college, which was attended by only one, or at most two, other congressmen.

As to age, most were in the prime of political life, though they were younger than congressmen of the present. Thirty-nine per cent were in their forties in 1860, and another 34 per cent were in their thirties. Nine of the youngest congressmen were born in 1830, and another seven were born later that decade. The youngest were Robert J. Breckinridge, Jr., of Kentucky and Elias C. Boudinot, Cherokee Nation, both of whom were born in 1835. Only 25 per cent of the legislators, on the other hand, were fifty or more years old. . . . Politically, the younger they were, the more likely these senators and representatives were to have been lifetime Democrats, even though most of them came to maturity when the Whig party was still active. Men in their fifties and sixties were former Whigs, Americans, or Constitutional Unionists by a three-to-two ratio; but of those in their thirties at least 65 per cent had been Democrats all their lives. Younger men were also more likely to be secessionists. While those in their fifties and sixties, for example, were divided evenly between secession and the Union, those who were between thirty and fifty years old in 1860 were about two to one in favor of secession. . . .

From the small amount of research that has been done on the Confederate Congress, one might conclude that it was an unimportant body, composed largely of men who were unknown even in their own time. But this picture is quite misleading. The average congressman was by no means obscure, though he was not necessarily a leading statesman. Rather he was a man of some political experience, having served in his state legislature and perhaps in the United States Congress, the state courts, or the state secession convention. He came to Congress knowing, and knowing of, many of his colleagues, and was in turn known by many of them. He was probably a Breckinridge Democrat and secessionist; and he sat in two of the three Congresses, most likely in the House of Representatives. He lived in a rural area away from the mountains, and, while he practiced law, he also had agricultural interests. He was born in one of the established seaboard states of the South, and the chances are a little better than even he was sent to Congress by the state of his nativity. He had a substantial estate which was probably worth between $40,000 and $50,000 in 1860. He was better off than most of his neighbors; in fact, his estate valuation was much above the average for his county. He owned about sixteen slaves, which was usually somewhat above the average holding in his community. He was between the ages of thirty and sixty, a Protestant, and had at least some college education. He probably never served in the army. . . .

It is very apparent that the members of the Confederate Congress were far from being a cross section of their communities. But they were chosen by their constituents to serve, and they did so as well as the circumstances of the time would allow. Unlike their counterparts in the United States Congress, they did not see their efforts crowned by victory. But this was not due to lack of effort, for these men were probably on a par with Northern congressmen in education, ability, wealth, age, experience, and the intangible item of dedication. Future research into the background of United States congressmen of the period may make a detailed comparison possible.

chapter fourteen

Content Analysis

Since historians must always analyze the content of their sources, we could say that all historical research employs content analysis. In this sense, however, the term is so broad that it is meaningless. Here we will employ the restricted definition of Ole R. Holsti, who believes that "content analysis is any technique for making inferences by objectively and systematically identifying specified characteristics of messages."[1] As Alexander George puts it, "quantitative content analysis . . . substitutes controlled observation and systematic counting for impressionistic ways of observing frequencies of occurrence."[2]

All content analysis involves some of the same principles. After a working hypothesis has been chosen, the sources to be studied are also selected, if there is a choice. (Some research may involve a hypothesis so closely connected to a specific source that no choice is possible.) If the body of material to be studied is large, there may be the additional problem of selecting a sample. Procedures are specified, including the implications, words, or (in more complex procedures) contexts to be identified. A measurement device is then adopted and applied to the text in order to establish the frequency of occurrence for certain communications—words, situations, attitudes, issues, and the like. The investigator then infers the appropriate conclusions from the resulting measurement.

Although we may not be aware of it, content analysis is in everyday use. It is used in a number of academic disciplines, including law, art, music, literature, marketing, history, journalism, and psychology. It even has implications for national policy. During World War II important work was done analyzing German propaganda, and today some of the basic texts in the field are aimed at the study of national or international crisis. Policy involvements are also demonstrated by newspaper reports. James

[1] Ole R. Holsti, *Content Analysis for the Social Sciences and Humanities* (Reading, Mass.: Addison-Wesley Publishing Co., 1969), p. 14.
[2] Alexander L. George, "Quantitative and Qualitative Approaches to Content Analysis," in Ithiel de Sola Pool, ed., *Trends in Content Analysis* (Urbana: University of Illinois Press, 1959), p. 8.

J. Kilpatrick's syndicated column of October 13, 1974, reported that two members of the U.S. Senate attempted to study the use of emergency powers by feeding the U.S. Code into a computer, programming "the machine to respond to such words as 'emergency' and 'crisis.' " The result was the startling discovery that Congress had authorized use of emergency executive power "in some 470 areas." Jack Anderson's syndicated column of June 3, 1975, reported a study of television programming for children which even designated the proportion of total TV violence for which each network was supposedly responsible.[3]

One of the easiest quantitative procedures in content analysis is a simple frequency count of overall impressions or contexts. Melvin Small used this approach with an evaluation panel and a simple sampling procedure in order to measure the usefulness of content analysis of magazine articles as a substitute for opinion polls. Using the Truman Doctrine as a case study, he tried to determine when Americans felt "they had passed the point of no return with the Russians." He assumed that because of the need for high circulation, magazines publish articles people want to read; hence they reflect readers' opinions to some degree. Twenty-three magazines were therefore surveyed for general political outlook and assigned a liberal, moderate, or conservative political position. A sample of 1300 articles was then evaluated by a panel, which indicated whether the contents "presented a favorable, unfavorable, or neutral impression of the Soviet Union." Results indicate that the content of the articles generally turned strongly unfavorable to Russia in 1945, although liberal magazines always gave a better press to the Soviet Union than conservative magazines. The more numerous moderate magazines were much like the liberals from Pearl Harbor through 1944; they held a middle position in 1945 and took a conservative position in 1946 and 1947. Small finds a strong correspondence between opinion polls and magazine articles for 1945 and 1946. Although polls were always more favorable to Russia than articles, the rate and direction of change was similar. Ruminating over his results, Small contends that if polls and articles generally indicate change in the same direction, as they do in his research, then magazine articles are potentially reliable indicators of opinion for periods when no polls are available. Hence the utility of content analysis.[4]

[3] Anderson's report illustrates that content analysis need not be confined to written sources. For example, Morton Cronin inspected 205 of the almost 7000 prints published by Currier and Ives between 1835 and 1907 and determined, by a simple tally of the frequencies with which certain subjects appear, the attitudes they revealed toward agriculture, industry, and racial minorities. Morton Cronin, "Currier and Ives: A Content Analysis," *American Quarterly* 4 (Winter 1952): 317–30.

[4] Melvin Small, "When Did the Cold War Begin?: A Test of an Alternate Indicator of Public Opinion," *Historical Methods Newsletter* 8 (March 1975): 61–73, quotes on pp. 61, 67. Members of the panel agreed in their evaluations of 90 percent of the articles; the panel agreed with the author on 85 percent of the evaluations. One warning should be added. The parallel attitudes indicated by public opinion polls and magazine articles may apply only to a highly literate society, in which the literate adult population approximates the total adult population. Before widespread literacy it may be that an educated elite would hold opinions quite different from the mass of the population—as Martyn J. Bowden's research seems to indicate.

A somewhat more complex technique of content analysis goes beyond general impressions and employs instead frequency counts of key words and phrases. For example, Martyn J. Bowden tested the commonly accepted thesis that between 1825 and 1870 Americans thought of the western interior as a great desert. Among his techniques was the examination of over 200 nineteenth-century geography textbooks having more than 120 words depicting the western interior, seeking references to desert and synonymous phrases; the frequency distribution of these terms seems to indicate the desert image was significant from the 1820s to the 1850s. In contrast to geography books, however, newpapers for the 1840s and 1850s rarely labeled the western interior a desert, which suggests that an average, newspaper-reading citizen knew more about the area than the educated elite, which read geography. For the most part, concludes Bowden, the Great American Desert was a myth confined to the northeastern elite.[5]

A more intricate procedure adds to this simple frequency count of words and phrases the contexts in which the subject appears. An early example of this technique, under the label of personal structure analysis, is psychologist Alfred L. Baldwin's study of the letters of Jenny Masterson, an elderly and rather lonely and abrasive lady. Baldwin tallied the frequency with which certain concepts occurred, and measured their context by checking the contiguity of some concepts to others. He assumed that frequency is a measure of importance and that repeated conjunction of two thoughts indicates a significant relation in the mind of the writer. After a preliminary survey of the letters, a list of fifteen topical categories was drawn up, each broken down by contextual attitudinal categories: the topic of Jenny's son was subdivided by such attitudes as favorable, unfavorable, protected, attacked, and the like. The number of incidents and contexts were tabulated and each pair of concepts and attitudes intercorrelated. Taking the highest correlations, Baldwin then drew a diagram indicating idea clusters in his subject's life. For example, Jenny frequently made references to nature and art, usually in close contiguity to favorable references to her son; she made unfavorable comments about other women, often in the context of her own social superiority. One cluster indicated Jenny's ambivalence by including both favorable and unfavorable attitudes toward her son.[6] There is no reason why this technique could not be applied to other collections of the letters of a single individual.

Since the rapid growth of computer technology in the 1950s, more complex systems of content analysis have been developed to permit more categories of ideas to be analyzed and larger sets of data to be used. However, it is usually necessary to reduce

[5]Martyn J. Bowden, "The Great American Desert and the American Frontier, 1800–1882: Popular Images of the Plains," in Tamara K. Hareven, ed., *Anonymous Americans: Explorations in Nineteenth-Century Social History* (Englewood Cliffs, N. J.: Prentice-Hall, 1971), pp. 48–79.

[6]Alfred L. Baldwin, "Personal Structure Analysis: A Statistical Method for Investigating the Single Personality," *Journal of Abnormal and Social Psychology* 37 (April 1942):163–83. The letters are reproduced in Gordon W. Allport, ed., *Letters from Jenny* (New York: Harcourt, Brace and World, 1965), which also discusses the various interpretive techniques applied to the letters, including Baldwin's content analysis.

similar ideas, expressed in various words, to some sort of common denominator. The word self, for example, may be considered a common denominator for such words as I, me, mine; in the same way, alike, same, and consist may be subsumed under equal. This approach is employed in a package of programs, known as General Inquirer, which was developed at Harvard University. The system uses a "dictionary" of about 3000 to 4000 "entry" words. This dictionary and the source text are fed into the computer, which reads the text and assigns a "tag" to each text word listed in the dictionary. A number of dictionaries have been developed to be used with this program package, for each project may have somewhat different needs; research areas using General Inquirer include psychology, anthropology, marketing, political science, and literary analysis.[7]

One of the most widely used of these dictionaries is the Harvard III Dictionary, which was designed primarily for uses in psychological and sociological research, but which has also had historical application. Each of almost 4000 entry words is placed in that one of 55 first-order tags "which represents the 'primary explicit denotative' meaning of that word," and, additionally, in as many of the 28 second-order tags as may be required for proper definition. This second-order tag "represents the connotative meaning of dictionary entries." If desired, each entry word may be further identified according to its use, whether subject, verb, object, or other. When entry words have been tagged, frequency counts or percentages may be used to determine which tags have been used the most, and for what purpose. For example, *affection* (first-order tag, denotative meaning) directed toward the *family* (second-order tag, connotative meaning) can be compared in its various uses as subject or object of a sentence, or with other tags, such as *anger* directed toward *community*. All sentences containing emotional tags can also be counted, or retrieved in a special printout that lists only sentences containing the desired tags.[8]

This system has been used by Jeffery M. Paige to analyze the *Letters from Jenny* that Baldwin studied (p. 223). The results indicated that Jenny directed aggression primarily against her son and other women and secondarily against her own work and travel. At the same time it was apparent that she needed and at times enjoyed her son; this confirms the ambivalence that Baldwin discovered, but is more precise than Baldwin as to the situations that shaped this dualism.[9] The same program package and dictionary have been adopted for the examination of literary texts in historical problems. In one instance they were applied to a comparative study of sixteenth- and

[7]Philip J. Stone et al., *The General Inquirer: A Computer Approach to Content Analysis* (Cambridge, Mass.: M.I.T. Press, 1966), and Holsti, *Content Analysis for the Social Sciences and Humanities,* Chapter VII. Entry word dictionaries frequently cover as much as 90 percent of a text.

[8]Charles M. Dollar and Richard J. Jensen, *Historian's Guide to Statistics: Quantitative Analysis and Historical Research* (New York: Holt, Rinehart and Winston, 1971), pp. 207–210.

[9]See Allport, *Letters from Jenny,* pp. 199–205, and Jeffery M. Paige, "Letters from Jenny: An Approach to the Clinical Analysis of Personality Structure by Computer," in Stone et al., *General Inquirer,* pp. 431–51.

twentieth-century catechisms in order to supply some reasonably precise notion of the differences in religious values between the two eras;[10] in another, they were used to investigate social and psychological stress in three documents from the American Revolution, including John Dickinson's *Letters from a Pennsylvania Farmer,* the *Declaration of Independence,* and Thomas Paine's *Common Sense.*[11] Such complex textual analysis may point out hitherto unsuspected dimensions and confirm intuitive methods of inquiry, but it is also likely to indicate the relative importance of one attitude over another in a more precise way than an impressionistic method would permit.

The possible applications of this technique in conjunction with other methods are almost limitless. Would Henry Nash Smith have found it helpful to use content analysis in his examination of the log cabin symbol or the germ theory metaphor? Perhaps Cushing Strout would have found it a useful aid in his application of Eriksonian developmental theory to William James. In 1954 intellectual historian John Higham expressed the belief that "any advance toward mathematical precision should clearly seem desirable to those who value exact knowledge," and surmised that examiniation of literature for loaded words or phrases might be extremely helpful in charting changing attitudes. By 1970 he admitted he was less hopeful about this interdisciplinary approach, believing that the necessity to establish categories and allocate evidence to them would constrict the data that could be studied.[12] Students should consider the merits of Higham's fear that the inflexibility thus introduced into history would more than balance the advantages of increased precision, but the potential of the method is both great and relatively untapped.

It must be clear by now that content analysis is not simply a mechanical procedure. It is more than just counting, involving a sophisticated and subtle knowledge of the word symbols being studied. The basic concept, which appears logical, and which seems to be sustained by research results, is that words and phrases contain hidden messages and that these may be ascertained by close examination of both consciously and unconsciously revealed clues found in historical literature. To put it more simply, there is more to what people say than is apparent on the surface and a simple thing like frequency counts may actually reveal an author's unspoken point of view.[13] Content analysis may be a nonpsychological method of exploring the unconscious.

As in the case of other historical methods, the assumptions underlying content analysis may have the unintended effect of structuring the investigator's conclusions. The technique demands that we understand word symbols as they were used in the

---

[10]Ralph Dengler, "A General Inquirer Analysis of Sixteenth Century and Contemporary Catechisms," *Computers and the Humanities* 8 (January 1974):5–19.

[11]Dollar and Jensen, *Historian's Guide,* pp. 210–13.

[12]John Higham, "Intellectual History and Its Neighbors," in Higham, *Writing American History: Essays on Modern Scholarship* (Bloomington: Indiana University Press, 1970), pp. 36, 38–39.

[13]T. F. Carney, "Content Analysis: Construing Literature as History," *Mosaic* 1 (October 1967):25.

past, capturing significant nuances and understanding the favorable and unfavorable contexts in which an otherwise neutral word may have been placed. If our knowledge is inadequate in this respect our findings will leave something to be desired. But in the study of the past content analysis is only applicable to the written word, since we have very little record—often none at all—of the spoken word for societies prior to the invention of electronic recording. When dealing with societies in which a significant minority of the population was illiterate, content analysis may be of little assistance in revealing the emotions, aspirations, and attitudes of any but the literate elite. The method may lead its user to forget the great mass of humanity.

Despite the great potential of content analysis, therefore, the method can only be used with great care. Like most quantitative techniques, it is a helpful tool but is unlikely to be of much use if other methods are not used to supplement it. Neither is it a substitute for a thorough knowledge of the sources and of the general historical context of the era that produced them. Failure to understand that point can lead to serious difficulty, especially because there are limits to the meanings that codes and categories can convey. The study of the Jenny letters, for example, turned up a clear instance of incorrect tagging due to the inability of the programs to instruct the computer how to detect sarcasm. "I have a truly noble son," meant as a deprecation of Jenny's son and his morals, was tagged GOOD.[14] A computer is not able to read between the lines. Furthermore, the viability of content analysis rests upon the questions one asks of the data. If a study does not ask the right questions it is all a waste of time. An equally dangerous snare is the tendency of words to change their meanings over time. One should be wary of employing the method on sixteenth century documents without ascertaining whether key words had the same meaning then as they do now. One might wonder, for example, at Richard L. Merritt's use of the term "America." Today it is frequently used by citizens of the United States to denote only their own country; can we always be sure how it was used 200 years ago? On the eve of the Revolution, "Britain's American colonies" referred to more than those which later became part of the United States, and included Newfoundland, the Maritimes, and the island colonies of the West Indies. Merritt's commentary indicates he is aware of this problem, but it is possible that he has not always interpreted the term correctly. Over 200 years later, we cannot always be sure what contemporary newspapers meant when they printed "America."

Merritt's work is a good example of the word frequency count method of content analysis. The author sought to discover when English colonists began to consider themselves Americans. To do this he tabulated the frequency with which self-referent word symbols, such as "Americans," "the colonies," "England," or pronouns and other substitutes referring to them, occurred in colonial newspapers during the period 1735 to 1775; he based this procedure on the assumption that a person's words uncon-

---

[14] Allport, *Letters from Jenny,* p. 203.

sciously symbolize his attitudes. To what degree, Merritt sought to discover, do these self-referent symbols "associate the land or its population with the British political community or with a distinctly American community" (p. 230)? Since it was impossible to examine and code all colonial newspapers, or even all issues of a few papers, Merritt was forced by the size of his task to sample his sources. Accordingly, he used a randomly selected sample of four issues a year for papers from five centers of population—a total of over 800 issues.[15] With such a large body of source material, Merritt certainly had no choice but to use some form of sampling. But are urban newspapers a reliable source of national opinion when very few citizens live in urban areas? And to what extent do newspapers reflect mass opinion in an age when a large proportion of the population was illiterate? Does the author claim too much? Perhaps his discussion would be just as interesting and useful if his claims were more circumscribed.[16]

The Emergence of American Nationalism:
A Quantitative Approach
Richard L. Merritt

The symbolism of names plays a significant role, not only in the magic of the primitives and the games of children, but in the process of group development and emerging nationalism as well. The designation of a group by a name—a specific name that serves as a symbol under which all would-be members of the group can unite, no less than as a means to differentiate the group from other such groups—is indicative that a group has come of age. In a situation where people are beginning to shift their primary group loyalties, the symbolism of names is particularly important.

Such was the case in the emerging American political community of the eighteenth century. The point at which the colonists stopped considering themselves Englishmen and began more often to think of themselves as Americans was of signal importance in the rise of American nationalism. . . .

. . . When *did* the transition to Americanism take place? When did the colonists stop referring to themselves as "His Majesty's subjects" or as "British colonists"—perceptions compatible with membership in a British (or possibly

[15]In a footnote deleted for this presentation, Merritt indicates that he compared samples of four issues a year for ten years with independent samples of twelve issues a year for ten years, with the result that in nine of the ten yearly comparisons the larger sample produced no significant difference in findings.

[16]Students who wish to examine this problem more extensively should read Merritt's book, *Symbols of American Community, 1735–1775* (New Haven: Yale University Press, 1966).

Richard L. Merritt, "The Emergence of American Nationalism: A Quantitative Approach," *American Quarterly*, vol. XVII (Summer 1965 supplement), 319, 321, 323–26, 330–35. Published by the University of Pennsylvania. Copyright, 1965, Trustees of the University of Pennsylvania. Reprinted with deletion of notes and abridgment by permission of the author and *American Quarterly*.

Anglo-American) political community—and start more often calling themselves
"Americans"? Did this shift occur in all the colonies at approximately the same time?
. . . Above all, what was the timing of the transition? Did American nationalism
blossom in the space of a few weeks or months, in response, perhaps, to some
spectacular event or British pronouncement of policy? Or did the colonists "learn" to
become Americans over a much longer period of time?

A useful approach to such questions is the method of communication research
known as "content analysis." Now, at first blush, the term seems to imply nothing
new. Is that not what we do daily when we "analyze" the "content" of a book, letter,
speech or other communication? In the modern social sciences the term "content
analysis" has come to mean something much more specific. Quantitative content
analysis, in the words of Alexander George, "substitutes controlled observation and
systematic counting for impressionistic ways of observing frequencies of occurrence"
of content variables. Examples of such content variables include words (or symbols),
concepts, images, words in context, sentence lengths or structures, and so forth. Thus
content analysis is the systematic tabulation of the frequency with which certain predetermined symbols or other variables appear in a given body of data—newspapers,
letters, books, speeches or any other form of recorded communication—covering a
specific period of time.

This essay uses the type of content analysis that concentrates on words or symbols to
explore a key aspect of the emergence of American nationalism: the terms used by the
colonists to refer to themselves and to the land they inhabited. .*. .

. . . Taking an example from colonial history, if a Tory newspaper, such as the
Massachusetts Gazette, devoted an increasing share of its space to American symbols
and events as the colonial years passed, or if it increasingly more often identified its
readers as "Americans" rather than as "His Majesty's subjects" or even "colonists,"
we might say that, despite its pro-British point of view, the latent content of its symbol
usage encouraged its readers to think of themselves as members of a distinctly American community and to turn their thoughts inward toward that American community. . . .

Once he has decided that a symbol analysis would be feasible and useful, the analyst
must frame his questions (or form his hypotheses) so that quantitative data can answer
them clearly, directly and simply. Symbol analysis is not merely a counting process,
nor is it what might be termed "brute empiricism"—the amassing of statistics in the
hope of finding interesting relationships. Effective symbol analysis is designed to test
specific hypotheses by establishing a limited universe of relevant items as well as their
alternatives, and by establishing their distribution or changes in the frequency of their
appearance. On the basis of the evidence the hypotheses can then be accepted or
rejected. An example of such an hypothesis might be: "The colonists' sense of group
identification shifted from the British political community to a strictly American political community gradually but steadily from 1735 to 1775." This proposition asserts that
the colonists turned away from their British ties in favor of an intercolonial allegiance;

and, further, that a trend line showing the growth of an American sense of community would be generally linear, that is, not characteristically marked by sharp shifts in the colonists' community ties. . . .

How could we test the hypothesis suggested above—that "The colonists' sense of group identification shifted from the British political community to a strictly American political community gradually but steadily from 1735 to 1775"—using symbol analysis? Since one crucial aspect of group identification is the recognition, both by members of the group and outsiders, of the group's existence apart from other such groups, we can examine the use of self-referent symbols in colonial newspapers. To return to some questions suggested above, when did the colonists (or at least their newspapers) stop referring to themselves as "colonists" or as "His Majesty's subjects," and begin more often viewing themselves as "Americans"? When did they begin identifying the land that they occupied as "America" rather than as "British-America" or the "colonies"? Another aspect of group identification is the amount of attention paid by the members of the group to one another, in contrast to the attention paid to outsiders. When did the colonists begin devoting more space in their newspapers to local events and occurrences in America than they did to European wars and English court gossip? A simple count of symbols in the colonial press referring to place names throughout the world would give us substantial information about the colonists' focus of attention, and about the changes in this focus as they reached the end of the colonial era. . . .

Finally, the analyst must interpret the results of the symbol count in terms of his theoretical framework. That the colonists' use of self-referent symbols changed considerably from 1735 to 1775 is in itself an interesting fact. But where does that fact fit into the development of an American sense of community, the growth of sentiments of separateness from the mother country, the emergence of a desire for independence? It is this relationship—conclusions "formed by means of an inference from observed data to nonobserved continua" [in the words of Harold D. Lasswell]—that is the crux of research in the social sciences. . . .

A systematic analysis of self-referent symbols in the colonial press would tell us much about patterns of nationalism in eighteenth-century America. With this view in mind I examined the news columns of four randomly selected issues per year of newspapers from each of five colonial population centers—Boston, New York, Philadelphia, Williamsburg and Charleston in South Carolina—tabulating each appearance of place-name symbols (such as "Boston," "England," "the colonies," "Americans" or other names of actual places or their inhabitants) during the 41 years from 1735 to 1775. The place-name symbols of particular importance here are self-referent symbols referring collectively to either the colonists or the colonies as a single unit. The tabulation includes both direct symbols (that is, those symbols actually specifying the group or the area, such as "the colonists" or "the colonies") and indirect symbols (those that replace the specific name of the group or area with such terms as "they," "that place" and so forth).

The collective self-referent symbols are categorized in two different ways. One means is by their primary identification content: Do they denote the geographic area that later became the United States, or its population? A second means of categorization is according to the specific label, a so-called secondary symbol, that the self-referent symbols attach when identifying the primary content: Do they associate the land or its population with the British political community or with a distinctly American community? In this respect we can differentiate five groups of such symbols: (1) Symbols of explicit British common identity: "British North America," "the English colonies," "British-America," or "British colonists," "British-Americans," "English provincials"; (2) Symbols of identification with the British Crown: "His Majesty's colonies," "royal colonies," or "crown colonies," "His Majesty's subjects in America," "Royal Americans"; (3) Symbols of implicit British common identity: the "colonies" or "provinces," "our colonies in America" (only when used in articles with British datelines), "colonists" or "provincials"; (4) Symbols of implicit American common identity: the "continent" or "country," the "American colonies" or the "colonies in America," the "United Colonies," the "continentals," "American colonists"; and (5) Symbols of explicit American common identity: "America" or "North America," "Americans" or "North Americans." In this paper I shall collapse the first three categories into a single one comprising symbols identifying the colonies and colonists as essentially British, and the last two categories into one of symbols identifying the colonial lands and population as American. Elsewhere I have considered the difference it makes if we categorize self-referent symbols according to whether they appeared in articles with American, British or other foreign datelines; here I shall consider the distribution of symbols only in respect to the total image of the American community presented to the newspapers' readers.

The first point to be noted about the distribution of collective self-referent symbols in the press is that their salience increased dramatically in the years from 1735 to 1775. In the late 1730s, the newspapers as a whole paid little attention indeed to the colonies or colonists as a collective unit. The average issue contained .66 such symbols, that is, in every three issues of a newspaper approximately two self-referent symbols appeared. This figure represented somewhat over 4 per cent of the total number of symbols in the press referring to American place names. The average issue from 1771 to 1775 contained almost 22 collective self-referent symbols, an increase of over 3200 per cent over the 1735–39 period. During the last five colonial years the press devoted about one-quarter of its news space to collective symbols, another quarter to symbols of place names in the colonies publishing the individual journals and about one-half of its space to symbols of place names in other colonies. In sum, a concept that was extremely marginal in the late 1730s was quite salient by the early 1770s.

The process by which the salience of the collective concept for the colonial press increased was cyclical. As may be seen in Table 1, the number of collective self-referent symbols per issue fluctuated considerably during the 41 years from 1735 to 1775. The low points of the cycles occurred in 1736 (or possibly earlier), 1745, 1761 and 1772; the peaks were in 1740, 1756, 1769 and 1775 (or later). Two points are of interest here. First, the peaks of the cycles no less than the troughs were on increasingly higher planes as time passed. Second, in general the cycles were of increasingly shorter duration. Thus, despite fluctuations in the curve, the secular trend in the use of collective self-referent symbols was clearly climbing upward at an ever greater rate.

That the salience of the collective concept in the newspapers rose is of course no indication that the colonists were becoming ever more "nationalistic." It is possible that they could merely have been stressing their allegiance to the British political community more often. As it turns out, however, such was not the case. For the period as a whole about six in ten collective self-referent symbols (58 per cent) identified the colonies or colonists either implicitly or explicitly as American. Again the propensity to use American self-referent symbols rose: from roughly 43 per cent in 1735–39 to about 63 per cent in 1771–75. In no year after 1755 did less than 50 per cent of these symbols identify the land and people as American rather than British.

Collective self-referent symbols referring to the people appeared in the newspapers far less frequently than did those referring to the land. In fact the latter outnumbered the former by more than five to one. In only one year (1760) before 1765 did the average issue refer collectively to the colonists at least once; the ensuing decade found each newspaper printing an average of 3.7 such symbols, reaching a high point of 10.9 in 1775, the year in which fighting broke out between the Americans and the Redcoats.

It was not until the years after 1764 that the distinction between "His Majesty's subjects" or "British colonists" and "Americans" became a real one in the colonial press. Before then the newspapers were all but unanimous (97.1 per cent) in identifying the colonists with the British political community. By far the most popular terms during these 29 years were those identifying the colonists as subjects of the British Crown —"His Majesty's subjects," "His Majesty's colonists," and, after 1756, the regimental name "Royal Americans"—which together comprised 108 (or 79.4 per cent) of the total of 136 symbols. From 1764 to 1775 almost six in ten (57.0 per cent) of the collective self-referent symbols identified the colonial people as American rather than as British. But even during this period the relative paucity of symbols resulted in wide fluctuations in the distribution of symbols from year to year. If the data for these 12 years are fitted to a linear trend line, however, a clear picture of changing perceptions emerges. The average increase in the use of symbols identifying the colonists as American was 2.3 percentage points per year. The threshold of self-conscious or explicit "Americanism," an imaginary 50 per cent line, was crossed in 1770, although it is true that there were two years before that date when the curve was above the 50 per cent level, and at least two years after 1770 when it was below the halfway mark. (By way of comparison, the linear trend line for symbols identifying the land as American rose 0.8 percentage points per year from 1735 to 1775 and crossed the 50 per cent threshold in 1762, thus suggesting that the perception of the land as being a part of an American rather than a British community clearly preceded a similar perception of the inhabitants of that land.)

Table 1 **THE FREQUENCY OF COLLECTIVE SELF-REFERENT SYMBOLS IN THE COLONIAL PRESS, 1735-1775**

Note: For easier visualization the data are on a semi-logarithmic graph.

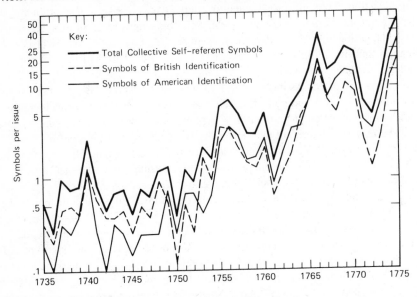

As far as newspapers from the individual colonies are concerned, there were some marked differences in their presentation of an image of the American community. The New England prints—the Tory *Massachusetts Gazette* from 1735 to 1764 and, after its level of "Americanism" slipped somewhat, the patriot *Boston Gazette* from 1765 to 1775—led in this respect; the journals of the middle colonies (the *New-York Weekly Journal*, the *New-York Mercury* and the *Pennsylvania Gazette*) lagged until the 1760s; and the southern newspapers (the *Virginia Gazette* and the *South-Carolina Gazette*), after an initial period of rather high awareness of an American political community, seemed to draw closer in their symbol usage to the British political community in the two decades between 1745 and 1764. With the passage of time the individual newspapers not only became more aware of the collective concept, as indicated by the inclusion of an ever larger number of collective self-referent symbols in their columns, but their choice of symbols tended to become quite steady and congruent. Not until the early 1760s, however, did the newspapers of the middle colonies join with the New England prints in a symbol revolution that preceded the outbreak of fighting by more than a decade.

These findings are suggestive of the value of symbol analysis for putting events or specific statements of individuals into a larger time perspective. It becomes clear, for instance, that the "Americanism" that appeared during the War of Jenkins' Ear was not without precedent. Nor did a spirit of American nationalism strike the colonists like a bolt from the blue during the French and Indian War. That spirit was already there. Similarly, the newspapers, which at once reflected and helped to shape the images of the politically relevant strata of colonial society, revealed an upsurge in sentiments of American community during the 1760s. The point, however, is not that such a trend emerged for the first time during the conflicts of that decade. The trend already existed. The crises of the 1760s merely accelerated the pace of that trend toward symbolic separation from the British political community. In short, the changing processes of symbolic identification in the American colonies seem to have been neither revolutionary nor evolutionary in the strictest sense of these terms. Rather, like other learning situations, they were both gradual and fitful, with a few periods of extremely rapid advances (or breakthroughs) interspersed with other periods of more or less mild relapses. Symbol analysis gives us a useful means to examine this process by which the colonists learned to be Americans.

chapter fifteen

Historical Demography

One of the most fascinating developments accompanying the growth of quantification in history is its application to demography—the study of fertility, mortality, and migration, and their effect on the size, structure, and composition of population. The relation of demography to the likelihood that Romeo and Juliet were married at the normal age for brides and grooms has already been mentioned. Edward Pessen's study of mobility involved some demographic analysis, and in the next chapter Emily R. Coleman's use of regression and correlation was intended as a preliminary to a demographic study. For the last decade this has been one of the truly mushrooming fields in the historical profession, stimulating studies of social and geographic mobility, urban history, economic history, and the history of the family. Computer techniques have contributed to its continued development by facilitating linkage of data from such varied sources as census returns, tax assessments, deeds, county histories, parish registers, city directories, and similar documents.

There are two methods of analysis, family reconstitution and aggregation. The first, sometimes called the nominal method, consists of "bringing together . . . scattered information about the members of a family to enable its chief demographic characteristics to be described as fully as possible."[1] Using a variety of sources, all original record entries for each individual in a given community are compiled from birth through marriage, baptism of children, and death, and then transferred in chronological order to previously prepared forms, one form for each type of event: marriage, baptism, and burial. The forms are then sorted alphabetically, which groups them by

---

[1] E. A. Wrigley, "Family Reconstitution," in Wrigley, ed., *An Introduction to English Historical Demography from the Sixteenth to the Nineteenth Century* (New York: Basic Books, 1966), p. 96. This book is the prime source for the methodology of historical demography, although it was written with pre-modern English documents in mind. Many of the techniques were adapted from an earlier French publication by Michel Fleury and Louis Henry, *Des registres paroissiaux à l'histoire de la population: manuel de dépouillement et d'exploitation de l'état civil ancien* (Paris: Éditions de l'Institut national d'études démographiques, 1956). Students wishing to pursue this topic further should turn first to Wrigley.

surnames, thus clustering family names and placing family events in chronological order. The investigator then transfers this information to other forms, called Family Reconstitution Forms, recording all events for all families of one surname before proceeding to the next surname. This step requires a number of clerical operations, the most important of which is the linkage of baptisms to the subsequent marriages of the persons involved. After the Family Reconstitution Forms have been filled out the investigator uses them to determine, for as many individuals as possible, such information as age at marriage or death, birth intervals, and number of children, always relying upon the forms to supply necessary dates. Since the process of reconstitution reveals both the size of the population at risk and the total events in a given category, key demographic rates (mortality and age-specific fertility, for example) may be derived.[2]

The painstaking, detailed reconstitution process is too time consuming and expensive except for lightly populated geographical units (when the task involves large areas, however, it could be lightened by sampling if the research involves comprehensive, modern records). Furthermore, the technique depends on positive identification, which requires records that indicate not only births, marriages, and deaths, but give full names of individuals, their parents or spouses ("son of . . ." or "wife of . . ."), and accurate dates. Since the historian is attempting to follow a cohort through time, it is also essential that the records be well kept for an extended period, for age at marriage or death obviously cannot be determined from the original record until many years after birth; family reconstitution for a period of less than 100 years, therefore, is probably not feasible. Additional problems are created when the geographic area covered by the documentation is too small. Many people migrated to or took spouses from other counties or parishes, which necessarily creates a gap in the record of the area under study. Naturally this tendency increases as the geographical area grows smaller. Indeed, migration is the major reason why usually only a small fraction of families can be reconstituted.[3]

The alternative to family reconstitution is aggregation, in which the total of a given kind of event is determined periodically for the purpose of ascertaining trends. Individual families are not involved, although the method may lay the basis for reconstitution by indicating places and periods that are worthy of more detailed examination if the quality of the data permits.[4] Aggregation is less complicated than family reconstitution. Each baptism, marriage, or burial is noted from the records as it appears and added up whether there is reference to parentage or not, along with such incidental

---

[2]Wrigley, "Family Reconstitution," pp. 111–53. An age-specific rate is the annual number of occurrences per 1000 people (death rate, for example) or women (birth rate) of a specific age in a given area. The population at risk is that subject to the event being considered. Thus the population at risk when calculating birth rates consists of women of childbearing age.

[3]Ibid., pp. 102–104. A cohort is a group of individuals who have experienced a common statistical event, such as birth in the same year or period of years.

[4]D. E. C. Eversley, "Exploitation of Anglican Parish Registers by Aggregative Analysis," in Wrigley, ed., *Introduction to English Historical Demography*, pp. 44–45.

information as the record may supply, including occupation, legitimate or illegitimate birth, residence of bride, groom, or deceased, and so forth. Events are transcribed by month and totaled yearly, or perhaps decennially if one is examining an extended period. From this data one can measure past population structure, including growth, fertility, marriage rates, infant mortality, and sex ratios of the community. This is often facilitated by using moving averages to smooth out fluctuations over time.[5] The final step in the analysis is to check findings against each other and against other evidence. When presented visually, as in line graphs for example, peaks or troughs vividly indicate population configuration, often providing clues about crop failures, epidemics, or high or low wages; data such as birth rates may also be checked against female mortality, prices, or other relevant information.[6]

Aggregation has three important advantages. First, historians often work with documents that modern demographers would consider incomplete—such defective records may be worked to advantage by aggregation when reconstitution is impossible. Second, it is quicker than reconstitution and thus less expensive, regardless of the quality of the record. Last of all, it uses all information, not just that which pertains to the small proportion of families that can be reconstituted. Applied to early data, such as the parish registers kept in sixteenth- or seventeenth-century England and France, or colonial America, aggregation tends to be limited to determination of gross trends. However, the most important difference between the two methods, when applied to historic and usually incomplete data, lies in the questions they answer, and from this point of view reconstitution has the advantage. Reconstitution permits determination of birth intervals and the approximate ages at which marriage, giving birth, or death occurred, information that, until governments kept detailed vital statistics and took elaborate censuses, is otherwise unobtainable for significantly large segments of the population. Reconstitution thus permits the investigator to trace historical changes in important demographic trends, including age-specific fertility and mortality. On the other hand, modern data, having been gathered for demographic purposes, has fewer limitations than that gleaned from centuries-old civil or church records, and hence permits the calculation of age-specific information without resort to the cumbersome reconstitution technique.[7]

Perhaps a sample of the findings of historical demography may be illustrated by the work of Peter Laslett, whose proof that Elizabethan brides were not as young as Shakespeare's Juliet has already been alluded to. In this instance the information was

---

[5]A five-year moving average records as the frequency for any given year the average of that year plus the two prior and two successive years. By the same token, a nine-year moving average of deaths is the arithmetic mean of the number of deaths from 1846 through 1854, for example, which would be recorded for 1850; the 1851 figure would be the arithmetic mean for 1847 through 1855 and so on. In this way peaks and troughs due to unusual events are less likely to distort general trends.

[6]Eversley, "Aggregative Analysis," pp. 61–90.

[7]Wrigley, "Family Reconstitution," pp. 71, 97–100.

found easily, simply by glancing at old marriage licenses. Laslett also contends that for preindustrial England "the starving peasant" is merely a cliché. Although there surely were occasional crises of subsistence, in only one parish has the pattern of documentation been found that is characteristic of a starving time: a sharp drop in conceptions, an abrupt rise in mortality, and starvation or the like listed frequently as the cause of death.[8]

Another generalization, which illustrates the close tie-up of demographic history and the newly emerging field of the history of the family, concerns the supposedly omnipresent extended family of the preindustrial past, including three generations and consisting of husband and wife, an unmarried brother or sister, perhaps one or two of their parents, and some of their married siblings and their spouses. This patriarchal, welfare-oriented family supposedly shouldered responsibility for the care of sick or unemployed family members. But the facts, reports Laslett, are that in seventeenth-century England average family size was small; children started their own homes when they married (they did not marry unless they could); and resident in-laws were infrequent, one reason being shorter life expectancy. Few parents could expect to live long enough to reside with a married child for a prolonged period of time. In short, the conjugal family was normal; the extended family was not.[9]

Laslett points out that the consequences of the extended family "delusion" are important, "for the view we take of ourselves, and the plans we make for our society and its welfare" are often based on this myth,[10] which thus has important implications for the setting of public policy. One of the solutions proposed for the plight of older people today is a return to the traditional extended family, that provided a comforting, loving home to aged parents. It would be nice if this had been so; nicer yet if it could be so again. But the proposed solution rests on an unsound premise. In many areas of the world, there is no traditional extended family to return to: Laslett's findings in this regard are duplicated by John Demos for colonial Bristol, Rhode Island, and early colonial Plymouth; by Lynn H. Lees for Irish slum dwellers in London; and by Richard Sennett for middle-class Chicago.[11] In an international sampling reported by

---

[8]Peter Laslett, *The World We Have Lost* (New York: Charles Scribner's Sons, 1965), pp. 81–83, 113.

[9]Ibid., pp. 89–92, 236.

[10]Ibid., p. 89.

[11]John Demos, "Families in Colonial Bristol, Rhode Island: An Exercise in Historical Demography," *William and Mary Quarterly,* 3d ser. 25 (January 1968):40, 44–45; Demos, *A Little Commonwealth: Family Life in Plymouth Colony* (New York: Oxford University Press, 1970), pp. 62–64, 78–79; Lynn H. Lees, "Patterns of Lower-Class Life: Irish Slum Communities in Nineteenth-Century London," in Stephan Thernstrom and Richard Sennett, eds., *Nineteenth-Century Cities: Essays in the New Urban History* (New Haven: Yale University Press, 1969), pp. 375–80; and Richard Sennett, "Middle-Class Families and Urban Violence: The Experience of a Chicago Community in the Nineteenth Century," in Thernstrom and Sennett, eds., *Nineteenth-Century Cities,* pp. 401–405.

Laslett, only Japanese communities appear to have had a significant number of extended families or multiple households prior to the coming of industrialization.[12]

Another important intersection between historical demography and public policy concerns the birth rate. At a time when population limitation is becoming a problem of worldwide concern, it is important to note surprisingly early declines in birth rates in some parts of the globe. Demographic research indicates that, as early as the eighteenth century, birth control of some sort was practiced in France, and was probably common throughout the country by 1789; in England family limitation began to occur perhaps as much as a century earlier.[13] This appears to indicate that under certain conditions even a poorly educated population may voluntarily and gradually limit births over an extended period of time without modern techniques of contraception.

Like other techniques, demographic methods must not be used without full awareness of their limitations. Family reconstitution, for example, is so painstaking that it is seldom employed except for areas of small population, such as colonial New England towns. Whether such findings can be generalized to include large urban areas or small towns in other locations is uncertain. Furthermore, reconstitution does not reveal the history of all families. Because of defects in the record, ranging from gaps to lack of uniformity in the spelling of names, between 10 and 50 percent of the population are all that can be included in reconstituted families.[14] One obvious factor eliminating some individuals is migration. Those who left the town, county, or parish to take up residence elsewhere are lost; the result is that the demographic picture is composed largely of stay-at-homes, who are not necessarily a reliable sample of the entire community.

There are also problems using the aggregative method on relatively modern data, for example, that provided by the nineteenth-century United States census. By its very nature the U. S. census is chronologically incomplete. Taken just once every ten years, it provides only limited basis for determining events in the other nine years. Furthermore, it always overlooks a significant floating population. These people are usually members of the lower economic segments of society, which means that the census is automatically biased—and so too are findings based on it, although the bias may not

---

[12]Peter Laslett, "Introduction: The History of the Family," in Laslett, ed., *Household and Family in Past Time* (Cambridge: Cambridge University Press, 1972), pp. x, 61. Of course the predominance of nuclear families does not by itself refute the use of extended families, insofar as they did exist, for "social security" purposes. Given a small number of old people, the most frequent household form could not possibly include dependent parents.

[13]Louis Henry, "Historical Demography," *Daedalus* 97 (Spring 1968):392; Pierre Goubert, "Historical Demography and the Reinterpretation of Early Modern French History: A Research Review," *Journal of Interdisciplinary History* 1 (Autumn 1970): 44–46; E. A. Wrigley, "Family Limitation in Pre-Industrial England," *Economic History Review,* 2d ser. 19 (April 1966):100–105.

[14]Maris A. Vinovskis, "The Field of Early American Family History: A Methodological Critique," *The Family in Historical Perspective,* No. 7 (Winter 1974):2, 3.

always be significant. Totals are thus approximations only. It is unlikely that the U. S. enumerations contain the names of very many nonexistent persons (even though census takers were paid by the head), but it is certain that underenumeration is a serious problem. There is always that floating population; in frontier areas, census takers might not even be aware of some settlements; and sometimes householders would fail to report absent members of the family. The reliability of figures on wealth are questionable (does the citizen exaggerate his economic position so he can cut a finer figure in the community or does he minimize it, fearing the tax assessor is peeping over the census taker's shoulder?). Ages are frequently inaccurate, often being reported in round numbers (ages ending in 5 and 0 are far more prevalent than probability permits) or inflated by elderly persons, some of whom had no certainty as to when they were born. Occupations may be those which an individual usually followed, or hoped to follow, rather than the one being pursued at the time of enumeration. Place of birth may also mislead, for it gives no indicator of places of residence since birth. A person born in Massachusetts may not be from Massachusetts when the census taker comes to his Iowa door in 1870; to some extent this problem can be overcome for married adults by noting the place of birth of their children. Even names may be a source of confusion, being spelled differently from one census to the next. Many names simply changed. A single woman marries between enumerations, takes her husband's name, and disappears (unless the historian has access to marriage records). German immigrants named Schmidt may change their names to Smith, Norwegians add "son" to the father's name or, like many of their countrymen in the United States, change their names to that of their place of origin in the old country—and they too vanish without a trace. Not the least of the problems of working with the U. S. census is that some enumerators had abominable handwriting.[15]

Demography will supply insights into the historical process that other methods will not, but this advantage is not provided simply because of the mechanical procedures involved in aggregation or family reconstitution. Far more important than mechanics is the assumption that the world we have lost may be recaptured to some extent by detailed examination, sometimes down to the level of the single individual, of the population that composed it. This requires analysis of population structure, such as sex ratios and geographic distribution; it also necessitates examination of the most basic events of all lives—birth, marriage, migration, death—as experienced by the population of another era. In this way we may gain insight into social and cultural history that

---

[15]For further information about the problems involved in use of the United States manuscript census see Melvin Zelnik, "Age Heaping in the United States Census: 1880–1950," *Milbank Memorial Fund Quarterly* 39 (July 1961):540–73; Peter R. Knights, *The Plain People of Boston, 1830–1860: A Study in City Growth* (New York: Oxford University Press, 1971), appendices; Susan E. Bloomberg et al., "A Caution to the Unwary from the Burned: A Note on Sources and Methodology," *Journal of Social History* 5 (Fall 1971):44–45; and Henry C. Binford, "Never Trust the Census Taker, Even When He's Dead," in *Urban History Yearbook, 1975* (Leicester: Leicester University Press, 1975).

traditional methods would leave undetected. What layman would have guessed that the parish registers of France and England would provide insight into popular attitudes toward and methods of birth control two centuries ago?

At the same time, however, demographic methods may focus the investigators' attention so narrowly to population trends that they quite forget that other things are important too. In some areas and at some periods, for example, a crisis of subsistence may be verified by weather observations if any are available, or even by tree rings (the width of which vary according to a year's moisture) thereby pointing out droughts. More to the point, demographic techniques are primarily descriptive—that is, they demonstrate that certain types of events (such as a drop in birth rate or an increased marriage rate) occurred, but they are limited in their ability to tell us why. If primitive methods of birth control were used in Europe as early as the seventeenth or eighteenth century, why was this so? Twenty-first century demographers looking at birth rates in the United States in the 1960s and 1970s will be hard put to explain their figures if they are not well acquainted with the social and intellectual history of our time.

One old saying has it that a case study is a generalization based on a single instance.[16] Robert Higgs and H. Louis Stettler attempted to overcome the tendency of other investigators to generalize from insufficient and perhaps unrepresentative instances. They applied family reconstitution to a sample of twenty colonial New England towns, selected on the basis of location and quality of records. Findings indicate that marriages were not early (although not so late as in Elizabethan England), fewer than 17 percent of the women died from causes relating to childbirth,[17] and the birth rate was high—forty per thousand women, perhaps somewhat more, but less than the national birth rate in 1800. These results partly confirm the discoveries of other scholars, but they also indicate significant variations in the demographic experience of individual communities.[18] The authors' sampling technique provides a better basis for generalization than the individual case study. Even so, the historian is left out on a limb, for the sample includes only New England towns. Perhaps there were some

---

[16] As Stephen Thernstrom put it, "The easiest tactic is to describe one's microscopic examination of an obscure group or neighborhood or community as a 'case study,' a useful phrase which lends an attractive aura of generality to one's painstaking study." Thernstrom, "The Historian and the Computer," in Edmund A. Bowles, ed., *Computers in Humanistic Research* (Englewood Cliffs, N. J.: Prentice-Hall, 1967), pp. 77–78.

[17] This necessarily recalls Oscar Handlin's warning (above, p. 199) that, in the end, quantification still finds historians groping for appropriate adjectives. Higgs and Stettler seem to be saying that "only" 17 percent of the women died in childbirth; but some readers might think it more appropriate to say that "as many as" 17 percent died. Handlin's point is well taken.

[18] Robert Higgs and H. Louis Stettler III, "Colonial New England Demography: A Sampling Approach," *William and Mary Quarterly,* 3d ser. 27 (April 1970):282–93.

significant differences between these and their middle-state or southern counterparts.

One way to overcome obstacles created by narrowly based investigations is by parallel studies, such as those of George M. Blackburn and Sherman L. Ricards, Jr. In a series of articles these authors have applied aggregative analysis to counties on the cattle, mining, and timber frontiers, in an effort to determine the characteristics of these counties and compare them with attributes uncovered in parallel work by other researchers.[19] For example, the authors point here to the woefully unbalanced sex ratio (although it was not nearly so skewed as that of Butte County, California) that was characteristic of frontier populations, and to the unusual and deceptive age distribution of the inhabitants of Nueces County and other frontier counties; although these communities appear to have an older population than that of the nation as a whole or an average agricultural county, this is due to the relative absence of children. Note also the use of regression in this article. In order to determine the values in Table 6, the authors evidently took known data for five years between 1848 and 1856 and computed a regression line using the data as the dependent variable and time as the independent variable. This permitted them to estimate values for missing years. To be consistent, however, all values entered in the table are the regression line values for the indicated years; they do not supply an accurate picture for any one data point, but presumably they do provide a reliable indicator of trends.

The article raises some interesting questions illustrating the problems encountered in using census returns. For example, the authors appear to accept the records' indication that Nueces County, where cattle raising was the most important agricultural undertaking, had no butchers. Figures for real wealth, on the other hand, may well be correct, but when analyzing the distribution it might have been more practical to exclude the individual who held 75 percent of the recorded wealth of the county. Despite these questions, the article illustrates that United States census data permits the application of aggregative analysis to the calculation of an age-sex and socioeconomic status description of the population. The results support the conclusion that despite the rhetoric of Manifest Destiny, in Nueces County Americans "were creating a bifurcated society" in which the Mexican inhabitants were relegated to a secondary position.

This sort of county-level comparative history has obvious limitations in an article such as this, for usually the findings were matched with only three other counties. Presumably Blackburn and Ricards will continue their work in other counties, and be

---

[19]See the accompanying article, plus Sherman L. Ricards, Jr., "A Demographic History of the West: Butte County, California, 1850," *Papers of the Michigan Academy of Science, Arts, and Letters* 46 (1961): 469–91; George Blackburn and Ricards, "A Demographic History of the West: Manistee County, Michigan, 1860," *Journal of American History* 57 (December 1970):600–618; Ricards and Blackburn, "The Sydney Ducks: A Demographic Analysis," *Pacific Historical Review* 42 (February 1973):20–31.

joined by other investigators until a sufficient sample of varying types of communities has been examined to make comparative results more meaningful. Although this article covers only a single census year and hence is more like a snapshot than a motion picture, the element of change could easily be added by doing the same sort of analysis for other census years and comparing results.

A Demographic History of the West: Nueces County, Texas, 1850
George M. Blackburn
Sherman L. Ricards

To many mid-nineteenth-century Americans, the acquisition of Texas, New Mexico, California, and Oregon marked the fulfillment of the nation's manifest destiny. To others, like Senator Daniel S. Dickinson of New York, much remained to be done. With expansion came obligations, he explained to the Senate in 1848. "New territory is spread out for us to subdue and fertilize; new races are presented for us to civilize, educate, and absorb; new triumphs for us to achieve for the cause of freedom." Even as Dickinson was speaking, in places like Nueces County, Texas, the process of Americanization had already begun. What manner of Americans were these disciples of destiny? What new races did they subdue and civilize? Two years after the senator's speech, census enumerators recorded for the seventh decennial census of the United States such demographic data as the name, age, sex, occupation, property, and nativity of each resident, thereby furnishing later generations of Americans with insights into the characteristics and composition of frontier society.

Nueces County is an appropriate microcosm for the 1850 period because of its strategic, commercial, and agricultural location. Situated on the Gulf Coast west of the Nueces River, the county was part of the disputed territory after the Texas Revolution that provided the ostensible cause for the Mexican War. Although the issue had been settled by 1850, the area retained military importance because of the warlike Comanche and Apache Indians and the threat of Mexican invasion. At the same time Nueces County was part of the frontier and experiencing rapid growth. . . .

For a time following the war with Mexico, the economic development of Nueces County remained in jeopardy because of the sharp increase in Indian depredations. The Treaty of Guadalupe Hidalgo transferred responsibility for controlling the border tribes to the United States, enabling the Indians to roam at will through the region until the federal government was able to establish a military defense system over the vast new

George M. Blackburn and Sherman L. Ricards, "A Demographic History of the West: Nueces County, Texas, 1850," *Prologue* IV (Spring 1972), 3–4, 7–9, 11–20. Reprinted from *Prologue: The Journal of the National Archives,* with deletion of notes and abridgment.

territory. In August 1849 when Indians raided within three or four miles of Corpus Christi, citizens petitioned for federal protection. The government responded the following February by establishing Fort Merrill on the Nueces River, some sixty miles from Corpus Christi. Two companies of mounted troops were garrisoned at the fort and two companies were stationed at Corpus Christi.

Besides posing problems for army authorities, the Indian troubles created special circumstances for taking the 1850 census in Nueces County. Yet A. W. Hicks, the only individual who signed the census schedules, reported that he completed the assignment over a four-day period, in three days of actual counting. . . . The short period of enumeration, primitive transportation, and widespread disorders are consistent with the concentration of population in a few defensible locations—Corpus Christi and its vicinity and occasional settlements on the Nueces and San Antonio rivers.

Race

Of the 698 persons in Nueces County in 1850, only 47 were slaves . . . no doubt because there was no lucrative opportunity to utilize slaves. The region did not grow a staple crop, such as cotton, which required extensive unskilled labor, while commerce was not suited to slave labor. The use of slaves for cattle herding would have been particularly risky. ''The frequent escape of slaves from the American side of the Rio Grande into Mexico,'' according to one observer, ''and the folly of any attempt to recapture them although you often meet your own property in Matamoras'' discouraged owners from bringing valuable slaves near the Mexican border.

Only three male slaves were between fifteen and forty, the prime working age . . .; the median male age was a low 9.50 years. On the other hand, fifteen of twenty-eight females were between fifteen and thirty, and the median female age was 21.67. There were approximately twice as many females as males. The diffusion of ownership, comparatively large number of females, and higher median age of females indicate that slaves served primarily as domestic servants.

In 1850 the slaves of Nueces County were owned by thirteen men and one woman. Seven of the owners had but one slave; one owned ten, while another owned eight. The institution of slavery seems to have been as popular with those of northern or foreign birth as with those of southern birth. Six of the slaveholders were born in the South, five in the North, and three were foreign-born. No Mexicans owned slaves. Most of the owners were married with young children in the family. All the slaveholders except three farmers said they possessed real estate; the total declared wealth of slaveholders was $389,300, which constituted 95 percent of the wealth of Nueces County. Not surprisingly, slaveholders were markedly older (early forties) than the average inhabitant of the county.

One free Negro was enumerated in 1850, a woman of forty living by herself. Only two slaves were listed as mulattoes, suggesting that little miscegenation had occurred. Indians, a major racial group in Nueces County, were not enumerated in the 1850 census.

Sex

The sex ratio for the United States in 1850 was approximately 106 (106 males for every 100 females). Such a ratio, however, was seldom found on the frontier, as Table 1 shows. Trempeleau County, Wisconsin, showed a sex ratio of 120 in 1860. Jack E. Eblen's model frontier territory for the years 1840 to 1860 had a sex ratio of 140, while his average agricultural county had a sex ratio of 125. Sherman L. Ricards's study of Butte County, California, a gold rush area, showed an exceptionally high ratio of 3,329 because of the distance of migration, the uncertainty of the life, and the physical hardships of mining. The timber frontier of Manistee County, Michigan, produced a fairly high sex ratio of 168.51 which can be explained by the slight need for women in the occupation of timber cutting.

Table 2 shows that the sex ratio of the civilian component of Nueces County was 144.24. Fairly high even for a frontier, that figure would have been even higher except for the presence of the Mexican-born. If the Mexican-born herdsmen and their families had been subtracted from the civilian component of the population, the sex ratio would have risen to 270.63. As might be expected, the military component of the population had a very high sex ratio of 1,883.33. On the other hand, the slaves had a very low

Table 1   Selected Sex Ratios: 1840-60

Area	Sex Ratio
United States, 1850[a]	105.20
United States, 1860[b]	104.84
Average Agricultural County, 1840-60[c]	125.00
Average Territory, 1840-60[c]	139.50
Butte County, California, 1850[d]	3,329.81
Trempeleau County, Wisconsin, 1860[e]	120.22
Manistee County, Michigan, 1860[f]	168.51
Nueces County, 1850[f]	177.29

[a]Derived from *Historial Statistics of the United States: Colonial Times to 1957* (Washington, 1960), p. 10.
[b]Derived from J. D. B. DeBow, *Statistical View of the United States . . . Seventh Census* (Washington, 1854), p. 55.
[c]Jack E. Eblen, "An Analysis of Nineteenth-Century Frontier Populations," *Demography* 2 (1965): 405, 406
[d]Sherman L. Ricards, "A Demographic History of the West: Butte County, California, 1850," *Papers of the Michigan Academy of Science, Arts, and Letters* 46 (1961): 481.
[e]Derived from Jack E. Eblen, "Age and Sex Characteristics on the Northwestern Agricultural Frontier, 1840–1860" (M.A. thesis, University of Wisconsin, 1961), pp. 71–73, Table 9.
[f]Derived from original census returns.

Table 2   **Population of Nueces County by Sex and Socioeconomic Status: 1850**

Status	Males	Females	Sex Ratio
Civilian	313	217	144.24
Military*	113	6	1,883.33
Slave	19	28	67.85
Total	445	251	177.29

*This category includes the enlisted men, five officers, and seven civilian members of their families at Fort Merrill, and two soldiers residing in Corpus Christi. Two of the persons enumerated with army personnel and listed as male gave their names as Jane Flinn and Janett Shaffer.

ratio of 67.85. The high sex ratio of 177.29 for the entire Nueces population is not surprising in view of the living conditions and the area's unsettled character.

Age

The population of the United States in 1850 had a median age of approximately 19. According to Table 3, males on the frontier tended to be older. In Nueces County the median male age of 25.00 was markedly higher than the national figure, while the females of the county were only slightly older (20.31 years) than their counterparts in the nation. Only 3 percent of the population in Nueces County, however, were over 45 years of age, while almost 11 percent of Trempeleau and 8 percent of Eblen's average territory were over 45. Seven percent was the comparable figure for the gold-seeking male population of Butte County. Nueces and Butte counties did, however, have a common pattern of few elderly females.

Fertility

The measurement of fertility, that is, the rate of reproduction, has long occupied the attention of demographers. They have been concerned with overcoming the poor quantity and quality of extant data in seeking to make comparisons between modern and historical fertility rates. P. K. Whelpton devised a ratio based on the number of children under five years of age per one thousand women twenty to forty-four years of age standardized to 1930 national norms. A figure of more than one thousand means higher fertility than in 1930. Various ratios for 1850 and 1860 are shown in Table 4.

According to Whelpton, the fertility of the United States was declining throughout most of the nineteenth century, from 1,342 in 1800 to 892 in 1850. The decline was most pronounced in New England and the Middle Atlantic States. The ratio for the west south central states, which included Texas, was 1,061 in 1850, however, and coincided with a social structure which emphasized the family as the basic social unit. Life was organized along *gemeinschaft* lines: face-to-face contacts were common,

Table 3 Median Ages of Selected Frontier Areas by Sex: 1840-60

Area	Male	Female
United States[a]	19.51	18.81
Average Territory, 1840-60[b]	22.73	17.21
Average Agricultural County, 1840-60[b]	20.27	16.63
Trempeleau County, Wisconsin, 1860[c]	20.19	17.35
Butte County, California, 1850[d]	27.84	22.60
Manistee County, Michigan, 1860[e]	23.85	18.78
Nueces County, 1850[e]	25.00	20.31

[a]DeBow, *Seventh Census,* p. 55.

[b]Eblen, "An Analysis of Nineteenth-Century Frontier Populations," p. 404.

[c]Derived from Eblen, "Age and Sex Characteristics on the Northwestern Agricultural Frontier," pp. 71-73, Table 9.

[d]Ricards, "Butte County," p. 481.

[e]Derived from original census returns.

Table 4 Children under 5 per 1,000 Women 20 to 44 for Selected Areas

New England[a]	636
Middle Atlantic	776
East North Central	1,037
West North Central	1,122
South Atlantic	957
East South Central	1,115
West South Central	1,061
Mountain	875
Pacific	896
United States	892
Manistee County, Michigan, 1860[b]	989
Trempeleau County, Wisconsin, 1860[c]	1,101
Average Agricultural County, 1840-60[d]	1,202
Average Territory, 1840-60[d]	1,156
Butte County, California, 1850[e]	454
Nueces County, Texas, 1850[b]	818
Matagorda County, Texas, 1850[b]	985

[a]This and the following 9 ratios for 1850 appear in Donald J. Bogue, The Population of the United States (Glencoe, Ill., 1959), p. 295, and are from P. K. Whelpton, Forecasts of the Population of the United States, 1945-1975 (Washington, 1947), p. 16.

[b]Derived from original census returns.

[c]Derived from Eblen, "Age and Sex Characteristics on the Northwestern Agricultural Frontier," pp. 71-73, Table 9.

[d]Derived from Eblen, "An Analysis of Nineteenth-Century Frontier Populations," p. 405.

[e]Derived from Ricards, "Butte County," p. 481.

religion was highly emphasized, traditional modes of behavior were demanded, emotional rather than rational judgments were normal, and the authority of the father was predominant. These cultural factors tend to be associated with high fertility.

The Nueces County fertility ratio of 818 was thus considerably below the ratio of its section of the country and the nation as a whole. Several reasons help explain this. Unlike the rest of the South, Nueces County was not predominantly agricultural and commercial activity was significant. . . . Another explanation for low fertility lies in the sex ratio in the fertile years for females, fifteen to forty-four. In this age grouping, the United States has a sex ratio of 106.33 and a fertility ratio of 892. The high sex ratio of 154.17 in the fertile ages for Nueces County is consistent with a low fertility ratio of 818. . . .

Labor Force

The census enumerator recorded the occupations of all males fifteen and older. The listed occupations may be divided into three major categories: protection, agriculture, and various town activities. The protective function involved army personnel, who accounted for 35.67 percent of male occupations, as shown in Table 5. Fortunately for Nueces County, the army was supported by the national government, because a single frontier community could scarcely afford to support such a high proportion of its population in a solely protective role. Since the army garrison was located some sixty miles from Corpus Christi and the census schedules for the county do not list a sheriff, constable, or any other law enforcement official, presumably day-to-day protection was performed on an informal or militia basis under the direction of leading merchants. Such a procedure would have been typical of a Spanish or Mexican community.

The census data indicate that 38.85 percent of the labor force was devoted to agriculture, in which cattle raising predominated. In almost every instance where a male described himself as a farmer the enumerator listed one, two, or more Mexican-born herdsmen and their families before listing the next farmer. Thirty males described themselves as farmers and ninety-two were listed as herdsmen. The census manuscripts indicate that none of the farmers, but all of the herdsmen, were Mexican-born. These data leave no doubt that Americans secured occupations of importance and value and the Mexican-born were relegated to positions only slightly above that of laborer.

The third component in the Nueces County population was the townsfolk of Corpus Christi. A lawyer, a physician, and a surveyor constituted the entire professional personnel of the community. Nine merchants, one hotelkeeper, one manufacturer, and two ship captains constituted the managerial category. The development of commerce is suggested by the presence of seven clerks, a watchmaker, and a printer who doubtless did job printing as well as publishing the newspaper. Other skilled persons were a saddler and a shoemaker, both essential on the frontier.

The dependence of Nueces County on the outside world can be inferred from the absence of certain skilled occupations necessary for frontier settlement. The town had no gunsmith, tinsmith, tailor, painter, butcher, sawyer, cigar maker, wheelwright, or

Table 5   Occupations of Free, Civilian Males in Nueces County: 1850

Occupations	Number	Percent
Professional and Semiprofessional	3	.96
Managers and Officials	13	4.14
Clerks	7	2.24
Protective Service	112	35.67
Agriculture	122	38.85
Skilled	11	3.50
Semiskilled	5	1.59
Unskilled	37	11.78
Unknown	4	1.27
Total	314	100.00

weaver. Although Corpus Christi was a seaport and transfer point for goods, no one declared an occupation related to unloading ships and preparing goods for further shipment. Even more striking was the absence of any stage drivers, wagoners, or draymen. Perhaps some of these unlisted occupations were filled by the surprisingly small portion of the Nueces County male labor force (11.78 percent) who were listed in the unskilled labor category. Presumably these males, most of whom lived in Corpus Christi, worked at "town" jobs and the Mexican-born herdsmen did the agricultural labor.

Notably absent from the census schedules were government officials. No judge, jailer, postmaster, schoolteacher, notary public, county clerk, tax assessor or collector was listed. Probably the leading citizens of Nueces County performed legislative, judicial, and administrative functions in a rough-and-ready fashion. It is entirely possible that some of the clerks carried out routine functions of government under the direction of leading merchants. Clearly the census is not a suitable instrument for analyzing the structure of a government in which the major roles are performed by those who regard another occupation as primary. For example, William Aubrey, a partner of Henry Kinney, was made postmaster in 1846; in the census of 1850, however, he listed his occupation as merchant. Similarly, no one was identified in the census as a teacher, although there is evidence of three schools in Corpus Christi by 1850 and the census records indicate some children attended within the previous year.

That no woman was listed as a schoolteacher may seem surprising; in fact, no woman was listed as gainfully employed in Nueces County in the census records. Whether the females performed functions other than that of mother, wife, and daughter remains to be determined. Two hundred and twenty-three women appear on the Nueces County census records. Eight, most of whom were over forty, were either widows or heads of families, and unaccompanied by a male who could be assumed to have been a husband. Ninety-two were evidently married, since they are listed immediately after a male, bear the same last name, are of the same generation, and have children listed immediately after of a different and generally younger generation. Ninety-three females under seventeen apparently lived with their families; nineteen over seventeen were clearly living with either their own or other families. Two females living with merchants were probably employees, while one female living alone was over fifty. These constituted about 96 percent of the feminine population. The only conclusion to be derived from the Nueces County census manuscripts is that there were few prostitutes on this frontier. Some of the women might be improperly categorized. More likely, the prostitutes avoided the census enumerator or he avoided them; the schedules also list no saloonkeeper and only one hotelkeeper.

Nativity

. . . Approximately two-thirds of the free, civilian population of Nueces County in 1850 were foreign-born, largely Mexican-born. Significant numbers were born in Germany and, to a lesser extent, in Ireland. Persons born in southern Europe were as absent in this particular migration stream as they were from the total migration stream to the United States. Approximately one-third of the free, civilian population of the county in 1850 had been born in the United States. . . . Approximately equal proportions of the males were born in the northeastern and southern states, 9.43 and 10.37 percent respectively. Of the females only 4.48 percent had been born in the Northeast while 13.00 percent had been born in the South. The contrast is particularly evident in Texas which produced 7.23 percent of the males and 13.45 of the females. . . .

The nativity data also can be utilized to show migration routes within the United States. There were twelve familes with native-born parents in Nueces County in 1850. Two families appear to have gone directly from New York to Nueces County. One family originated in Maine and tried Michigan before going to Texas. In one family the father from Connecticut and the mother from Pennsylvania came to Texas from Illinois. Two families went to Texas from Kentucky, one from Arkansas, and one from Missouri. Four families appear to have come from the deep South to Texas. The data show two basic migration streams: one from the South through Louisiana and the other directly south, possibly by ocean or the Mississippi River. Except that they were largely native-born, the soldiers of the army detachment did not differ very much in nativity from other migrants to Nueces County. Only 8 of the 106 enlisted men were foreign-born, approximately one-third were from the Northeast (mainly New York) and one-third from the South (mainly Louisiana, Kentucky, and Mississippi). The remaining one-third originated about equally in either the north central or western states.

Wealth

Persons with wealth—that is, persons who were listed in the census manuscripts as possessing real property—in Nueces County in 1850 were few, male, old, town-based, non-Mexican, and to a slight extent foreign-born. There were only twenty-nine persons who cited any wealth and twenty-five of these were males. The median age of these males was 37.68 which suggests they had acquired their wealth before migrating to Corpus Christi. The entire wealth of the county was $408,125 most of which ($300,000) was in the hands of Henry Kinney, then twenty-seven, who listed his occupations as "various." Merchants possessed 92 percent of the wealth. Most farmers and herdsmen residing in the county professed to have no property; of the farmers who claimed wealth, the median figure was $796. Only one Mexican, a herdsman, had any wealth, and he was worth $4,500.

Compared to other frontier areas for which data are available, the wealth of Nueces County was highly concentrated. Merle E. Curti analyzed the distribution of wealth from those with the least to those with the greatest amount. Curti divided his property holders into deciles and calculated the percentages of wealth of each decile. In both Curti's study and the study of the timber frontier in Manistee County, Michigan, the highest decile possessed about 37 percent of the wealth. Nueces County, in contrast, had 85 percent of the wealth concentrated in the highest decile. Conclusions about the validity of Turner's thesis that the frontier was a land of opportunity must await further studies of individual frontiers over a number of years. Available data suggest, however, that at least initially the frontier was the land of opportunity for middle-aged property holders rather than for poor, young, landless pioneers.

The assessment of the wealth of an area utilizing the self-declared net wealth of its citizens is but one method of determining its relative prosperity. Another is to establish the number and value of the material goods or implements which produce wealth. Since Nueces County and Corpus Christi were centers for both agriculture and transhipment in 1850, it is appropriate to consider items utilized in these endeavors: cattle, horses, mules, and land. Fortunately, the comptroller of the state of Texas computed extremely helpful figures. The calculation of linear regressions from these data may be found in Table 6. Such calculations suggest that in 1850 there were 359 horses and mules with a total value of $4,442 or $12.37 per animal and 6,220 head of cattle with a total value of $16,482 or $2.65 per animal. Thus, there were about 10 longhorns in the county for every person and about 1 horse or mule. By similar calculations, land in Nueces County in 1850 was worth about $0.23 per acre. According to Table 6, cattle must have been an excellent investment, because $100 invested in cattle in 1850 would have produced $202.64 six years later. Investments in land, horses, and mules produced no such dividends.

Miscellaneous Social Data

From the census materials certain clues to the social structure of Nueces County can be derived. Since every male over fifteen listed an occupation, the present delay of youths entering the labor force and adulthood did not exist. In short, there was no period of adolescence. The census records show but one marriage between a person of Mexican descent and a person of non-Mexican descent. Only one Mexican was considered literate; none of the non-Mexicans were listed as illiterate. None of the Mexicans had

Table 6   Number and Value of Horses and Mules, Cattle, and Land in Nueces County: 1848-56*

Year	Horses and Mules			Cattle			Land Per Acre†
	Number	Total Value†	Per Animal†	Number	Total Value†	Per Animal†	
1848	58	288	3.93	4,021	947	.24	.20
1849	209	2,365	11.31	5,120	7,768	1.52	.22
1850	359	4,442	12.37	6,220	16,482	2.65	.23
1851	510	6,519	12.78	7,319	25,198	3.44	.24
1852	661	8,596	13.00	8,418	33,913	4.03	.25
1853	812	10,673	13.14	9,518	42,628	4.48	.27
1854	962	12,750	13.25	10,617	51,343	4.84	.28
1855	1,113	14,827	13.32	11,717	60,058	5.13	.29
1856	1,264	16,904	13.37	12,816	68,773	5.37	.30

*Calculated using linear regressions from data from the comptroller of Texas as cited in Paul S. Taylor, *An American-Mexican Frontier: Nueces County, Texas* (Chapel Hill, 1934), p. 71. The records of the comptroller of Texas indicate the number of horses and mules and the number of cattle for 1848, 1849, 1853, and 1856. The records also indicate the average value of land per acre. Taylor, *Nueces*, p. 181. The 1850 figures have been determined by linear regression; the reader should be cautioned about the possibility of nonlinear growth. The authors are indebted to Tim Shaffer for his suggestions and aid in the construction of this table.

†In dollars.

attended school within the year previous to the census enumeration; sixteen non-Mexican children had attended school. The students' fathers had ''town'' occupations, and all but one were property holders.

Senator Dickinson had proclaimed the American mission to civilize, educate, and absorb new races. If Nueces County is representative of the territory wrested from Mexico in the war, Americans paid scant heed to the rhetoric of manifest destiny. In Nueces County presumably the new race included those of Mexican descent, while Americans included those born in the United States and Europe. The census records indicate that Americans in Nueces County in 1850, rather than civilizing, educating, and absorbing the Mexicans, were creating a bifurcated society. Only Americans owned slaves; no Mexicans owned slaves. Americans could read and write English; no Mexican could. The land was predominantly owned by Americans; only one Mexican owned land. The employers were Americans; Mexicans were herdsmen and employees. American families were large; Mexican families were small. In a remarkably short time, the Americans in Nueces County had emerged as the dominant economic force, establishing social patterns that survived well into the twentieth century.

Federal census records contain a wealth of social data about all nineteeth-century communities. Since the records are readily available on microfilm, historians through similar studies can construct a thorough demographic history of the entire American frontier.

chapter sixteen

Simple Correlation and Regression

Correlation suggests that one circumstance is related to another. We say that things are correlated when the presence of one indicates the presence, in more or less degree, of the other. During the summer ponds of stagnant water are correlated with the mosquito population; in winter snowfall depth is correlated with the use of snowplows. In a more technical sense, correlation implies not only that one circumstance is related to another but also that it is related in a measurable way. For example, there is a direct and measurable correlation between the total depth of a winter's snow and the amount of gasoline the local highway department uses for plowing. And there is an ascertainable degree of relationship between student grades and hours spent in study. The key question is not whether there is a relationship, but, instead, "how much"?

Statisticians have developed a variety of measurements to answer this question. Which to use depends on the task at hand. Thus, sometimes figures indicate only that one case has more of something than another but cannot indicate how much more, as in the rankings given the participants in a gymnastics contest or diving competition. In other instances figures supply a more precise idea of measure, as in population figures, railroad mileage, prices, or acreage. Historians, political scientists, and sociologists frequently encounter data of this type.

Given the latter sort of information, how do we measure the strength of correlation between two variables? The particular measurement illustrated by the accompanying article is called the Pearson product moment coefficient of correlation, which is usually designated r.[1] It has the prime advantage of being applicable to the raw data historians

---

[1] "Pearson product moment coefficient of correlation" may best be understood by reversing the terms. CORRELATION means "*co-relation*," the relationship between two variables. A COEFFICIENT is an index number, here measuring the co-relation, or association, between two statistical variables. MOMENT is a term from the physical sciences referring to a distance from a particular point or axis. Here correlation is determined by the PRODUCT of two moments away from their respective reference points. The mathematics of this coefficient were developed by Karl PEARSON. It is probably more useful to define the term as related to the slope of the straight line of best fit by the least squares method.

frequently encounter (e.g., percent voting Democratic correlated with percent blue collar). It is also a standarized measure, used so frequently in history and the social sciences that if a study makes no mention of which correlation coefficient has been employed, one assumes it is Pearson's r. Equally important, the coefficient conveniently ranges from -1 (meaning perfect negative correlation) through 0 (no correlation) to $+1$ (perfect positive correlation).

Data used to calculate a measure of "co-relation" could be fed into a calculator or computer without a second thought. However, it is highly preferable to proceed as the author of the following article has done, plotting the two variables being examined to provide a visual indicator of the degree to which they are correlated (see Appendices II and III to Emily R. Coleman's article). Using the figures listed in Appendix I the author drew a scatterplot, or scattergram. In this diagram each dot represents the relation of two variables in one particular case, also called a data point or observation (e.g., 10 people per farm and sex ratio of 138.1). The first feature to be noted is that the data points are not scattered all over the chart, in a haphazard manner; if they were, the coefficient of correlation, r, would be close to 0. One also notices that although the data points do not follow one another in a straight line across the page, they do seem to have some direction. This indicates that the two variables being compared are correlated to some degree.

The strength of this correlation is determined by a series of formulas that are too complicated to be reproduced here. These determine the line of best fit, called a regression line, which can be drawn through the cluster and which generalizes the direction it indicates (see Appendices II and III for examples). By definition, if the vertical distance between each data point and the regression line is calculated, and the differences squared, the total of the squared differences will be the smallest sum possible using the given data points. A regression line sloping up to the right, with data points tightly clustered in cigar shape about it, would indicate high positive correlation. A line sloping down to the right, with data points similarly clustered, would be a sign of high negative correlation. The same line with data points only loosely clustered along it is characteristic of moderate to low negative correlation, as illustrated by the article.[2]

[2] The average history student, who has usually forgotten most of his or her high school mathematics and statistics but who wishes to pursue the details of this technique, should examine some basic text for necessary formulas and instruction. V. O. Key, Jr., *A Primer of Statistics for Political Scientists* (New York: Thomas Y. Crowell Co., 1966) is easy to follow and more logically presented than most instructional manuals. Roderick Floud, *An Introduction to Quantitative Methods for Historians* (Princeton: Princeton University Press, 1973), and Edward Shorter, *The Historian and the Computer: A Practical Guide* (Englewood Cliffs, N. J.: Prentice-Hall, 1971) are extremely lucid and probably as easy for non-statistically oriented students to follow as any; the latter is especially helpful on theory since it is relatively unencumbered by the mathematical details that become necessary when one attempts to transform theory into practice. Charles M. Dollar and Richard J. Jensen, *Historian's Guide to Statistics: Quantitative Analysis and Historical Research* (New York: Holt, Rinehart and Winston, 1971) is more complex than Key, Floud, or Shorter, but has the advantage of being more comprehensive. The computing formulas for r and the regression line are presented with great clarity in Key, *Primer of Statistics*.

Correlation and regression are important tools for the analysis of historical statistics. The scattergram may point to hitherto unsuspected phenomena which "often make relevant to the relation—or to specific deviations—random pieces of information apparently meaningless when they stand alone," and a case study becomes much more useful if it may be understood in terms of its association with similar instances.[3] The devices are equally important for their predictive capability. If the correlation is reasonably high, and the scatter diagram shows a linear function, then the regression line may be considered a trend line and extended either into the future or into the past. Such prediction has obvious hazards. It is altogether too easy to extend a regression line infinitely into the future in the expectation that data points as yet nonexistent will eventually lie along it. Stock speculators may do this and win a million or lose their shirts; boards of education may do it and be surprised when enrollments drop. It is best to use regression for short-term predictions only. Using much the same reasoning, one may use a regression line to supply missing data. If the percent Democratic vote for a given set of counties is known for every presidential election except one from 1872 through 1916, the vote for the missing year may be approximated from the information provided by the regression line. This device for filling in unknowns has already been encountered in the demographic chapter, where it was used to estimate the number and value of farm animals in Nueces County, Texas. Obviously the technique is of doubtful utility when there are too many unknowns or a correlation coefficient is low.

Correlation and regression are not mere mechanical procedures, any more than any other quantitative method is. As the use of regression both here and in the Nueces County article demonstrates, the method assumes a certain mathematical order in the universe. It operates under the premise that one can obtain valuable numerical information indirectly by analysis of other numerical information, and that the procedure is so precise that other investigators using the same technique on the same figures would get the same results—although they might well interpret them differently. Furthermore, the theoretical justification for correlation is that one can reduce measures of association between measurable attributes to a single index figure, or coefficient, and that this figure will be a useful indicator of a complex interrelationship. Moreover, and all quantitative methods once again may be included here, those who employ correlation techniques accept the assumption that statistical relationships may permit the investigator to make conclusions about cause and effect.

As in the case of any historical method, simple correlation and regression should not be used without due regard for limitations. One problem is that the technique assumes a linear function, that is, it assumes that the regression line should be a straight line. But sometimes data points are clustered in such a way that the line of best fit is a curve (e.g., studies of population, subsistence, epidemic disease, and income distribution). Data must not be fed into a machine without visual inspection of the scattergrams first. The resulting "eyeball correlations" will not be precise; but since a straight line can be drawn through any cluster, this is the only way to determine true linearity.

---

[3]Key, *Primer of Statistics*, p. 125.

A second problem is that correlation is most helpful when there are a large number of cases, or data points. Any correlation based on but a few cases will be quite volatile and could be swayed unduly by the addition or deletion of a single data point. If there are only a half-dozen observations the correlation coefficient must be rather high before it is worth looking at. Conversely, if the computation is based on several hundred observations, the measurement will be extremely stable. In that event, a correlation of .4 or .5 may be important. Here Coleman used over 2000 cases, aggregating them so that each scatterplot has over twenty data points and represents the average of a number of observations. Her otherwise low correlations are therefore worth further study.

An additional pitfall to be noted is that of the "outlier," an isolated data point sufficiently far from the cluster of other points that it inordinately influences the value of the correlation coefficient. In Appendix II there are two outliers. The first is not indicated because it would have to be plotted about a foot off the top of the page, and the second is the circled data point. Obviously, a ready explanation for these deviations is that an error has been made; but if a data check indicates the contrary, correlation and regression computations should be performed a second time without outliers, as Coleman has done, to indicate how strongly they have influenced results. In this instance, $r = -.52$ when the deviant cases are removed. Furthermore, identification of outliers may provide an opportunity. They beg special consideration and in the end their distinctiveness may prove to be of greater interest than more normal cases. In one voting study of a predominantly rural state, for example, outliers proved to be urban areas. By definition, of course, many outliers will be a sign of nothing more than low correlation. Percentages add a problem of their own. If one correlates percentage units one risks perverting results if the raw totals on which those percentages are based vary widely, and if outliers are present. In the analysis of county level data, if an outlier represents a county with a population of less than a hundred souls, for example, the use of percentages will cause all counties to weigh equally—thus wildly inflating the influence of the small county outlier and distorting the correlation even more than any other outlier would do.

Another snare in the use of Pearson's r for linear functions paradoxically lies in one of its prime attributes. One can determine how much variance the correlation "explains" simply by squaring the coefficient. If $r = .9$, then $r^2 = .81$, meaning that change in the independent variable (cause, if there is one) accounts for 81 percent of the concomitant change in the dependent variable (effect).[4] But beware the plunge in the explanation of variance as the coefficient drops. Cut r in half, from .9 to .45, and it accounts for only 20 percent of the variance. Note that Coleman got $r = -.40$ in both scattergrams, which is enough to explain 16 percent of the variance. Given enough observations, $-.40$ is sufficient to assure us that more than chance is involved in the association of sex ratios and units of arable land or people per farm. But obviously the

---

[4] This is a comfortably large proportion. Significant real-life data seldom produces correlations much above .95. If it does, the two variables are probably the same characteristic under different labels.

researcher must be on the alert for other explanatory variables—a point that was made at greater length in the discussion of collective biography.

It is clear that any variable omitted from the investigation will automatically be excluded from any causal considerations. If one attempts to ascertain the degree of association between political success and social success, one had better include a variable that measures social success. But mere association will not indicate a causal relationship no matter how high the correlation. Remember the difference between causation and association. Percent voting Democrat in one election will be highly correlated with percent voting Democrat in the next election, but there is no direct causal relation between the two—the 1972 election results did not cause the 1976 election results, except in a roundabout way. By the same token, Coleman would not maintain that people per farm cause the sex ratios (Appendix III). But they are significantly associated. The current controversy over cigarettes and cancer is an example of the confusion of causation and association. In the opinion of some persons, whether or not smoking is a cause of cancer is still an open question. That the two phenomena are associated, however, no longer seems open to doubt. Even if the doubters are correct in asserting that lung cancer is not caused by smoking but rather by some undetected third variable, the association nevertheless provides a strong indicator of possible corrective action; even if smoking does not *cause* cancer, the fact of their correlation would seem to indicate that manipulation of the smoking variable may possibly cause change in the cancer variable. Even when causation is not established, therefore, association is often significant enough to provide important insights into the problem at hand. This causation-association question must be handled with common sense. While purists may contend that correlation never proves causation, often the connection is so logical that it ought not to be denied. There is a strong correlation between rainfall and the amount of water in your rain gauge, and only a pedant would demand that we call the relationship a mere association.[5]

Obviously correlation and regression should be employed only when the historian's questions may be answered by manipulation of measurable attributes. However, in any given historical situation there are important variables that cannot be measured at all, or cannot be measured any longer because the participants are dead. Suppose a researcher wishes to investigate the co-relation of farm production and immigrant population in nineteenth-century United States to test the conjecture that in one way or another crop yields for native born would differ from those for the foreign born. It would be easy enough to select sample crops and run correlations between yields and immigrant population in a number of counties. If the subjects of the investigation still

---

[5] For good brief discussion of the improper use of correlation, see Shorter, *Historian and the Computer*, pp. 110–11; Floud, *Introduction to Quantitative Methods*, pp. 151–52; and Dollar and Jensen, *Historian's Guide*, pp. 90–100. For a more advanced critique of correlation techniques see J. Morgan Kousser, "The 'New Political History': A Methodological Critique," *Reviews in American History* 4 (March 1976):1–14, which discusses correlation in voting studies.

lived, one could use interviews to measure their education and perhaps their skill and experience. But further explanation would also require some knowledge of the sense of values and commitment to a work ethic of the people involved; this could necessitate examination of the *Zeitgeist,* the intellectual and social climate, which influenced farmers with different backgrounds.

It must be apparent by now that the users of any historical technique are frequently so captivated by it that they tend to use it despite its drawbacks. Simple correlation and regression are useful and vital tools, but they can be sadly deficient when the investigator attempts to deal with very complex phenomena. It frequently becomes obvious that change in the independent variable is an insufficient explanation for change in the dependent variable, and that both have been affected by a third, perhaps a fourth variable. A few years ago Walter Dean Burnham, a political scientist, appealed to historians to use more powerful statistical tools for multivariate analysis that would permit the employment of control mechanisms. Burnham observed that failure to use such techniques predetermines results, as "quantitative analysis becomes excessively subject to the 'law of the instrument.' " He accordingly called on historians to use multiple and partial correlation.[6] Such multivariate analysis reveals the relative importance of each of a number of variables, points to previously unknown influences, or may demonstrate that two supposedly independent variables are actually the same. Multiple and partial correlations are too complex to be discussed here; suffice to say that they can provide a picture of the relative contribution of each of several independent variables to change in the dependent variable. The reader should note that Coleman is aware of such problems, for in her second-to-last paragraph she indicates her intention to use more complex techniques in the future.

Coleman's use of simple correlation is especially interesting. Pointing out that few sources are available for study of the lives of medieval peasants, she examined an ecclesiastical survey for Saint Germain-des-Prés in an effort to uncover demographic information. Although potentially useful, the document is suspect because of the unusually high sex ratios that it reveals. The value of Coleman's analysis is that it validates an otherwise dubious document and thereby permits her to use the data it contains. The correlation coefficients are not high, but they are high enough to indicate the relationship is significant, considering the large number of cases involved. Specifically, the abnormal sex ratios are explained sufficiently so that there need be no further reluctance to use the source, at least for the author's purposes. But the discussion raises a few questions. What is the nature of the outliers in Appendix II? The one

---

[6]Walter Dean Burnham, "Quantitative History: Beyond the Correlation Coefficient. A Review Essay," *Historical Methods Newsletter* 4 (March 1971):62–66, quote from p. 65. This appeal is repeated in Kousser, "The 'New Political History.' "

for less than one bunuarium (a unit of land) refers mostly to lands newly cleared and settled by unmarried men. But what is the explanation for the other outlier? Since this document includes over 2000 families, most of the aggregated observations must include about 80 families (Coleman does not say how she aggregated her data). This outlier is more than an anomaly—too many people were anomalous to make that supposition believable. Surely this is an excellent example of the outlier that demands further investigation. And what of the thrust of the entire article: that the larger the agricultural unit the more likely it could afford the relative luxury of a number of female inhabitants? Perhaps there is another important variable, one not likely to be susceptible to correlation techniques. Recent research in the history of childhood has underlined the prevalence of infanticide, especially of girls. The result, says Lloyd deMause, the historian of childhood, "was a large imbalance of males over females which was typical of the West until well into the Middle Ages."[7] If we assume a birth rate for both sexes comparable to that of today, and if we note the high sex ratios on all units of land, regardless of size (with only one exception in Coleman's data), we are forced to wonder what happened to so many females. Elsewhere Coleman herself has suggested female infanticide and death in childbirth as possible explanations for the imbalance.[8]

A Note on Medieval Peasant Demography
Emily R. Coleman

The demography of the early medieval peasantry—like that of many peasant or servile populations—is particularly difficult to study because the peasants themselves left virtually no records; in fact, there are few enough documents that have anything to do with them at all. Those rare sources which do deal with this class are almost entirely polyptychs or ecclesiastical surveys. These are tax records and contain only information which was financially remunerative to the lords; they have no information whatever on any of the more personal aspects of peasant life. Recently I have been working with the ninth century polyptych of Saint Germain-des-Prés, one of the oldest and most complete medieval tax surveys. What follows is based on my analysis of this document.

[7] Lloyd deMause, "The Evolution of Childhood," in deMause, ed., *The History of Childhood* (New York: Harper and Row, 1974), pp. 25–30, quote from p. 26.
[8] Emily R. Coleman, "Medieval Marriage Characteristics: A Neglected Factor in the History of Medieval Serfdom," *Journal of Interdisciplinary History* 2 (Autumn 1971):209. See also Coleman, "L'infanticide dans le Haut Moyen Age," *Annales: économies, sociétés, civilisations* 29 (1974):315–35 which is a more fully developed discussion and explanation of the data discussed here.

Emily R. Coleman, "A Note on Medieval Peasant Demography." Copyright © 1971 Department of History, University of Pittsburgh. This essay is a revision of an article originally published in the *Historical Methods Newsletter,* Vol. 5, No. 2 (March, 1972), 53–58, reprinted by permission of the author and the publisher.

The basic taxing unit in the polyptychs was the manse, the farming unit. It is around this feature that the demographic, as well as fiscal, information was arranged. The tax collectors recorded the household head and his status, his wife and her status, and their children, usually by sex; if there was more than one family living on the farm, the information about them was recorded according to the same formula. This was followed by the size of the farm and the types of land it encompassed. Finally, there was a listing of the taxes and dues for which that farm and its inhabitants were responsible.

This data is available for some 2600 households on some 1700 farms. Though it is quite incomplete by modern standards, simple counts of the populations thus described produce important results. The average household and family size may be roughly posited and the size of the average peasant farm and the number of people each farm supports may be quickly gauged. Moreover, sex ratios (the number of men per 100 women in a population) can be determined.

Yet the sex ratios found in such manner lead to questions concerning the reliability of the source and thus the worth of any of the demographic information derived from it. For the sex ratios which are found in the polyptych of Saint Germain-des-Prés and other tax registers from this period are extraordinarily high. The normal modern ratio is about 105; but the areas within the jurisdiction of Saint Germain, in the Paris Basin, range from 110.3 to as high as 177.10, taking the population as a whole. These figures have disturbed historians for generations. They have usually been ascribed to the imperfection of the source—if the source were correct, the ratios would be more normal. In true tautological fashion, then, it follows that a faulty source has given us faulty sex ratios. And if the sex ratios are incorrect because the source is not reliable and not fully recording the women on the land, then there is no way to accurately estimate household size, population density, etc. All the population data is called into doubt.

I do not believe the original premise to be correct. Through the use of simple correlation and regression I have found that the population of Saint Germain-des-Prés is a complex one albeit with discernable trends hidden within the rough form of a tax roll. I used the sex ratios as dependent variables to consider factors which might conceivably influence them, such as household size, the economic potential of the land (in terms of amount of arable), and the population size of the individual family farms.

Certain patterns began to emerge from the population as a whole. The farming units with the most land were supporting the most people. But while sheer size accounts reasonably well for the number of people per farm, it does not summarize all there is to know. It only partially accounts for the demographic breakdown by sex ratio. When the population was broken down according to tenurial units differing by size, the sex ratios ran from a high 421.05 for the people on lands of less than one *bunuarium* (unit of arable land) to a low 97.33 for the people on lands with between 17 and 18 *bunuaria*. These sex ratios are based on data aggregated for each villa or estate. The correlation was r = −.40 (see Scattergram I, Appendix I, and Appendix II) showing an inverse relationship between the arable land and the sex ratios; the larger the arable land area, the fewer men per woman on it or—relatively, the more women on it.

There is also a negative relationship between the size of the population on the land and the sex ratios, regardless of the amount of arable. Controlling for population per farm, the sex ratios go from 78.6—on farms with 25 people—to 156.6 on those with 3 inhabitants; here the correlation is r = −0.40 (see Scattergram II, Appendix I, and Appendix III): the larger the number of tenants on a farm, the larger the relative number of women among them.

On the other hand, the relationship of sex ratios to the number of people in individual households (discounting for the moment the number of households per farm) is quite different. There is correlation of r = +0.52 between the number of people per household and the sex ratios in them.

These correlations might possibly be considered relatively low; but in dealing with an early medieval tax census, we have a document of practice, not a model. The correlations above suggest a definite, if subtle, pattern within the overall population on the lands of Saint Germain-des-Prés. On a significant number of farms and in an important proportion of families the presence of women had an economic basis. Where women were most useful and supportable, they were most obviously in attendance. A larger, richer farm could simply afford more women than a smaller, poorer one. The greater population on these lands could cooperate more efficiently and be more productive than small individual nuclei. The land could perhaps be forced to produce enough food for an extra mouth or an extra dowry or so. At the same time, women would be more useful because of proportional increase in their work. In these cases, females would have been more useful and feasible, both economically and socially. On the other hand, where economic subsistence was most precarious and their special skills and talents expendable, they were fewer. The means by which these patterns developed are not within the province of this essay, but it was only by using correlation and regression that they became clear. That these patterns emerge clearly and definitely is, at the very least, a strong indication that the documents are not necessarily erroneous or inadequate. Instead, it is possible that the sex ratios hide subtle trends which, if found, might reveal a great deal about the peasant society of the time—beyond the premise that the census-takers were less than systematic and comprehensive in their work.

Obviously correlation and regression are not new techniques of analysis. What I have found particularly useful, however, is their application to relatively intransigent documentation. The problem of limited data is endemic in early medieval history; and what information exists is difficult to get at. Just because of these complexities, this approach to the polyptych has been helpful; it has enabled me to go behind and beyond the formulas left by ninth-century assessors. Just as clearly, it does not solve all the problems of early medieval demography. The product-moment coefficient, for example, is very sensitive to an individual idiosyncracy within a large set of data, and the correlation can consequently be thrown off. Also, multiple regression will be of even greater utility with its ability to interrelate a greater variety of data than can simple correlation. Of course, the problem of interpreting the correlations will always remain with the historian.

No doubt there are many applications of this technique and many other techniques of which I am unaware and of which I would like to hear. But what I think to be important here is not the specific method of statistical analysis (the relative abstract merits of which statisticians continue to debate) but that documents of great difficulty, tax documents whose cryptic reporting have made them unresponsive to the usual demographic questioning such as by fertility and death rates, may successfully be probed by the relatively simple statistical methods of correlation.

Appendix I   Scattergram Data

Scattergram I		Scattergram II	
Units of Arable	Sex Ratios	People/Farm	Sex Ratios
less than 1	421.05		
1	145.28		
2	143.46	2	129.9
3	138.89	3	156.6
4	125.82	4	127.0
5	128.10	5	119.5
6	119.92	6	119.2
7	127.41	7	129.4
8	131.73	8	109.0
9	141.67	9	125.0
10	141.62	10	138.1
11	110.71	11	115.1
12	119.85	12	120.7
13	129.25	13	101.0
14	131.62	14	94.9
15	117.54	15	105.9
16	128.16	16	150.9
17	97.33	17	131.8
18	130.49	18	114.3
19	100.00	19	90.0
20	123.08	20	81.8
21	103.33	21	110.0
22	170.59		
23 and over	135.00	23	155.6
		25	78.6

Appendix II: Bunuaria to Sex Ratios*

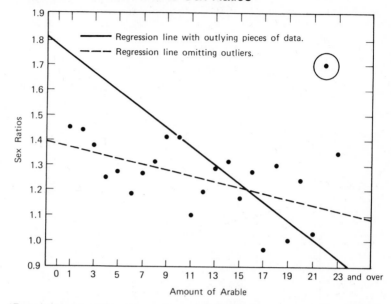

*For purposes of graphic presentation, the sex ratio is shown on a scale of one rather than 100. The regression line is distorted and less strong due to the reduction of scale. Also, this scattergram is based on aggregated data. The correlation remains strong with unaggregated data, but for purposes of visual demonstration it becomes unwieldy.

Source: *Polyptyque de l'Abbaye de Saint Germain-des-Prés rédigé au temps de l'abbé Irminon,* ed., A. Longnon, 2 vols., (Paris, 1886–1895).

Appendix III People per Farm to Sex Ratios*

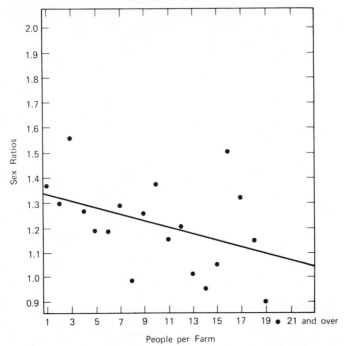

* For purposes of graphic presentation, the sex ratio is shown on a scale
of one rather than 100. This scattergram is also based on aggregated
data. The correlation remains strong with unaggregated data, but for
purposes of visual demonstration it becomes unwieldy.

Source: *Polyptyque de l'Abbaye de Saint Germain-des-Prés rédigé au temps de
l'abbé Irminon,* ed., A. Longnon, 2 vols., (Paris, 1886–1895).

chapter seventeen
Voter Behavior

At election time American voters are the most plentiful yet most prized of all big game. They are hunted out in every corner of the land. They are probed by pollsters, wooed by candidates, and dragged to the voting booth by eager precinct workers. Long pursued by political scientists, who attempt to determine those characteristics of their habitats supposedly responsible for their current behavior, within the last decade voters have also been stalked by historians. These scholars seek to determine which factions had most appeal, which issues proved most divisive (or cohesive), and which ideologies commanded allegiance. This is psephology, or the "scientific" study of the determinants of electoral behavior.

Interest in this topic goes back to the origins of representative democracy and the building of the first political machines. It is reputed, for example, that in 1800 Aaron Burr had a card file index of New York City voters, which recorded their attitudes and previous political preferences. Subsequent politicians often kept similar records, but not necessarily on a systematic basis. After the Civil War political organizations sometimes attempted to gauge their strength by the use of primitive polling techniques. Benjamin Harrison authorized a survey of Civil War veterans in Indiana for his 1880 senatorial campaign and in 1896 the G.O.P. interviewed every voter in Chicago three times to monitor the effectiveness of its campaign.[1]

Journalists also had an early interest in voter responses. Election results were not only to be reported, they were to be explained. Richard Jensen, author of the following article, has discovered newspaper analyses of the Massachusetts election of 1787 when an unpopular decision to suppress Shays' Rebellion led to the defeat of the incumbent governor. Journalistic interest was also reflected in numerous nineteenth-century publications of election statistics, notably the yearly *Tribune Almanac* published under the

---

[1]Richard Jensen, "American Election Analysis: A Case History of Methodological Innovation and Diffusion," in Seymour Martin Lipset, ed., *Politics and the Social Sciences* (New York: Oxford University Press, 1969), p. 229.

editorship of Horace Greeley. Most such publications printed raw figures only; percentage breakdowns were rare until well into the twentieth century.[2] Like politicians, journalists also used polls, although their reliability was always open to question. In 1936 the *Literary Digest* poll indicated a landslide victory for Alf Landon over Franklin Roosevelt, and in 1948 the pollsters predicted that Thomas E. Dewey would beat Harry Truman.

Scholarly interest in electoral behavior emerged in the latter decades of the nineteenth century through the combination of statistics and cartography. Displaying political, social, or economic variables for a given political unit along with party percentages, statistical maps could display a wide variety of information in readily comprehensible form. Frederick Jackson Turner, who taught the mapping technique to his students, was one of the early scholars to employ statistical cartography. However, Turner did not teach basic statistical methods, which are a necessary concomitant to such studies; ill-equipped historians therefore turned to simplistic explanations of behavior, including a rather unsubtle economic determinism.[3] Between World War I and the middle of the twentieth century the behavioral approach to electoral conduct was thus left to the social scientists, who were acquainted with statistical procedures, and who were willing to use complex methods with only the aid of simple calculators, paper, and pencil.

As was to be expected, the social scientists' election studies found strong relationships between voters' decisions and vital social, economic, and psychological variables. In a 1944 publication, for example, Paul F. Lazarsfeld, Bernard Berelson, and Hazel Gaudet used survey techniques in an intensive investigation of a single county. The purpose was to observe the presidential campaign and the influences which may have persuaded a voter to change preference during its course. The most important cause of change appeared to be personal contact with party workers, but other important variables included religion, location of residence (whether urban or rural), traditional family allegiance, opinion leadership, and cross pressure—the pressure on individuals who are members of several groups with conflicting political loyalties. The authors' social science orientation was underlined by their conclusion that "a person thinks, politically, as he is, socially. Social characteristics determine political influence." However, a 1954 study by Angus Campbell, Gerald Gurin, and Warren E. Miller downgraded "the simple classification of voters into sociological categories." They employed survey methods to probe party images in the popular mind and to determine the association of social characterisitics and voting for both the 1948 and 1952 elections. A new dimension was added as the investigators also examined "attitudes, expectations, and group loyalties, the *psychological variables* which intervene between the external events of the voter's world and his ultimate behavior"; both studies, the authors concluded, actually illustrated "the basic

[2]Ibid., pp. 226–28.
[3]Ibid., pp. 230–35.

psychological principle that when strong and opposing forces act on an individual the resultant behavior will demonstrate the characteristics of conflict."[4]

Among the earliest quantitative social science studies of voting behavior, however, was that by political scientist Harold F. Gosnell. His *Machine Politics* not only employed interviews but also standard deviations, scatterplots, regression lines, the Pearson product moment coefficient of correlation *(r)*, partial correlation, and even factor analysis, a full generation before historians began their tentative probes beyond simple percentages.[5] Gosnell's pioneering study was well received, but with reservations. One baffled reviewer flippantly asserted that "reducing everything to algebraical equations, looked to me like an interesting experiment, but when I found that . . . 'h' turned out to be a political clown like Big Bill Thompson, 'v' the median rental, and 'z' equaled the Roosevelt vote, I shook my head. . . . There are only eight pages of that to skip."[6] Gosnell himself complained about one reviewer of *Machine Politics* who thought its major value lay in the fact that Gosnell's approach produced the same results as traditional methods plus "grade school arithmetic."[7] These misgivings are carbon copies of those generated by the behaviorally and quantitatively oriented New Historians of the last decade or so.

Current interest in electoral behavior stems largely from the work of V. O. Key. His impressive publications provided basic instruction both in the political process and in the techniques of political analysis. In *A Primer of Statistics for Political Scientists* he opened new doors not only to members of his own discipline but also to the historians who followed; even today it is one of the best introductions to the statistical study of voting behavior. This is only appropriate, for Key was one of the few political scientists of his time who concerned himself with the historical implications of the problems he examined.[8]

Historians moved from their traditional approaches rather timidly. When Lee Benson published *The Concept of Jacksonian Democracy*,[9] which marked the emergence of the New Political History, it was generally well received, perhaps because of the

---

[4]Paul F. Lazarsfeld, Bernard Berelson, and Hazel Gaudet, *The People's Choice: How the Voter Makes Up His Mind in a Presidential Campaign,* 2nd ed. (New York: Columbia University Press, 1948), preface to the second edition, pp. ix-xxvi, 27; and Angus Campbell, Gerald Gurin, and Warren E. Miller, *The Voter Decides* (Evanston: Row, Peterson and Co., 1954), pp. 85–86, 183, emphasis mine. This conclusion is a strong reminder of Leon Festinger's theory of cognitive dissonance.

[5]Harold F. Gosnell, *Machine Politics, Chicago Model* (Chicago: The University of Chicago Press, 1937).

[6]Review by Joseph F. Dinneen, *Saturday Review of Literature* 16 (September 25, 1937):23.

[7]Harold F. Gosnell, *Grass Roots Politics: National Voting Behavior of Typical States* (Washington: American Council on Public Affairs, 1942), p. 139.

[8]V. O. Key, Jr., *A Primer of Statistics for Political Scientists* (New York: Thomas Y. Crowell Co., 1954, 1966.) Much of the foregoing discussion has been suggested by Jensen, "American Election Analysis." See also Jensen's essay, "History and the Political Scientist," which is also in Lipset, ed., *Politics and the Social Sciences.*

[9]Lee Benson, *The Concept of Jacksonian Democracy: New York as a Test Case* (Princeton: Princeton University Press, 1961).

simple statistical presentation. Arguing that American political history had long been placed within an overly simplistic framework, Benson rejected the idea of distinctive economic lines drawn between rich and poor, few and many, which is implied by the term "Jacksonian Democracy." He substituted for this view an ethnocultural voting model that has since become one of the hallmarks of the New Political History. Religious and ethnic variables were more important than economic differences in determining voting behavior, but voters were also influenced, thought Benson, by negative reference groups—as dislike for citizens of another heritage created hostile antagonisms that were carried into the political arena. Working along much the same lines, more recent historians have used a variety of techniques to relate voting behavior not only to religion and ethnic background but also to other common social and economic variables, including age, educational level, occupation, and rural or urban residence. Political beliefs and behavior, many students of voting analysis imply, are closely associated with the culture that imposed its patterns of conduct upon the voter.[10] These voters make their electoral selections on the basis of the cues offered by their cultural background and their reference groups, and the selections may seem strange to today's students. "Real" issues are not ignored; instead the perception of what issues are "real" varies. Thus prohibition, public support of parochial schools, and other "moral" issues were not false at all, but were rendered significant by many voters' reference groups and culture.[11]

Historical data and contemporary surveys seem to support the assumptions of this ethnocultural orientation, and modern politicians are unremitting in their efforts to attract and hold the alliance of various ethnic groups. Political aspirants usually run issue-oriented campaigns, but it is often discovered that certain ethnic groups are more aroused by some issues than others (e.g., support for Israel, school busing, affirmative action, and the like). That this is true both now and in the history of American politics is no sign that it will always be so in the United States or that it is necessarily so in other countries; the experience of the United States cannot be generalized to any open political system at any time. Change occurs, and a nation that is ethnoculturally homogeneous will have other bases for political division. Even current politics in the

---

[10]The ethnocultural view generally holds that religion and ethnicity are the most important predictors of behavior. For recent critiques of this approach, which avoid return to the opposite extreme of simple economic determinism, see Richard B. Latner and Peter Levine, "Perspectives on Antebellum Pietistic Politics," *Reviews in American History* 4 (March 1976):15–24; James E. Wright, "The Ethnocultural Model of Voting: A Behavioral and Historical Critique," in Allan G. Bogue, ed., *Emerging Theoretical Models in Social and Political History* (Beverly Hills, Cal.: Sage Publications, 1973), pp. 35–56; and Richard L. McCormick, "Ethno-Cultural Interpretations of Nineteenth-Century American Voting Behavior," *Political Science Quarterly* 89 (June 1974):351–77. Two prominent criticisms, for example, are that insufficient attention is paid to the often large proportion of the population that was unchurched or nonvoting. There is also some question about how the ethnocultural model translates voting power into formulation of major public policy.

[11]Wright, "Ethnocultural Model of Voting," p. 37. Note use of the term reference group.

United States is usually issue oriented, witness the slogan that when the economy is down voters turn to the Democrats. But since economic distress may not affect all ethnic groups to the same degree (as the higher than average unemployment rate among blacks testifies) it may sometimes be very difficult to distinguish between ethnocultural and issue-oriented voting behavior. Voters, then, are neither foolish nor automatons; their vote is not necessarily predetermined by ethnocultural attributes. But members of different ethnocultural groups do perceive policy issues differently, and they may react with a cohesive response when an issue encroaches on the attitudes or welfare of their group. In a very real sense such voters send their political leadership sometimes subtle, sometimes brutally blunt messages either ratifying or repudiating the past, and rejecting or confirming the candidates' visions of the future.[12]

One of the most important devices for studying voting behavior is correlation and regression. Percent Democrat, for example, may be plotted against percent Catholic or Italian for each city ward in order to determine how much these variables are associated with the voters' decisions. Another method of electoral analysis is simply to talk to the voters on an informal basis.[13] Far more objective, however, is the use of the systematic sample survey, or poll, a device developed as an adjunct to market research. The essence of the survey lies in the proper selection of a sample. In a random sample each individual has an equal chance to be selected; this is usually done after classifying the population by region, sex, occupation, age, or wealth. Survey techniques, as well as formal interviews with politicians, are frequently used by political scientists to study contempory political behavior. But the historian usually wishes to investigate periods for which no scientific surveys exist, and for which no survivors remain to be interviewed.[14] In such cases the sampling of opinion (if it is to be done at all) may have to be done through newspapers, which may strongly bias results because editors usually do not represent the full spectrum of opinion among all voters. Perhaps content analysis, discussed previously, may prove to be a way around that difficulty. But if one thinks of an election ballot as an instance of a standard questionnaire being presented to a large segment of the population, then, if interpreted correctly, that election becomes an excellent device for determining public opinion.

Drawing conclusions about electoral behavior is not easy. Electoral records, and the

---

[12]For further discussion along this line, see V. O. Key, Jr., *The Responsible Electorate* (Cambridge, Mass.: The Belknap Press of Harvard University Press, 1966).

[13]The best example is Samuel Lubell, *The Future of American Politics,* 3rd ed., revised (New York: Harper & Row, 1965). Among other things, Lubell identified key isolationist counties and attempted "to penetrate beyond the statistics" by visiting those areas and "talking first-hand to voters of every type, to see whether the Korean War had stirred the same emotional responses as had the last two wars." These interviews led him to "question whether isolationism, as generally pictured, ever really existed" (p. 133).

[14]Paul F. Lazarsfeld, "The Obligations of the 1950 Pollster to the 1984 Historian," *Public Opinion Quarterly* 14 (Winter 1950–51):617–38, urged pollsters to avoid overemphasis on the present and to ask those questions that will provide data historians will need in the future. "What," he asks, "will the future analyst, in retrospect, wish that we had ascertained today?" (p. 631).

materials often correlated with them, are aggregative in nature. They record the action of groups, often defined by artificial geographical boundaries. But usually the investigator is not particularly interested in the behavior of a political unit, unless it permits inference about the behavior of some other group: Roman Catholics, liturgical Protestants, farmers, blue-collar workers, immigrants, or the elderly, for example. It may be a difficult jump from observing that county X voted Republican to proving the hypothesis that one type of farmer voted Republican but another did not. An investigator who assumes that the behavior of individuals flows directly from the recorded opinions and values of the communities in which they live risks committing the ecological fallacy. When there is a high correlation between percent Democratic and percent Catholic for the counties of a given state, for instance, we cannot necessarily conclude that Catholics vote Democrat; we can reasonably assert that Democrat and Catholic are associated variables, and that Democrats are likely to do better in those counties that are more Catholic. But those counties might also be poorer, or more industrialized, so which factor determines the vote?[15] And we must always remember that the population of any given area may not match that portion of the population that actually goes to the polls.[16]

A major purpose of individual electoral studies is to generalize the findings, on the theoretical assumption that a particular case may provide useful clues to behavior in other instances. Voter investigations are repeatedly concerned with the same variables: age, occupation, economic status, sex, geographical area, race, religion, party preference, agricultural prices, unemployment, rate of inflation, crime, and even soil type or climate. Whatever variables we employ, the very fact of utilizing this sort of theoretical framework forces the investigator to assume that if attitudes, values, and roles govern "how people respond to a given situation, then a test population confronted with that situation ought to respond in a pattern that conforms to the presence or absence of the attitude,"[17] or, we might add, any other variable. In short, if percent liturgical seems to be a determining factor in one election presumably it will be so in others as well. Thus the new political historians of voting behavior may be less interested than their traditional counterparts in the unique, that is, the infighting, personalities, and singular results of a particular election. They will surely be more interested than historians used to be in the problem of generalization.

[15]Charles M. Dollar and Richard J. Jensen, *Historian's Guide to Statistics: Quantitative Analysis and Historical Research* (New York: Holt, Rinehart and Winston, 1971), pp. 97–99.

[16]One recent study underlines the subtle implications of this point. David A. Bohmer suggests that individual voting in Maryland during the first American party system (1796–1816) was strongly influenced by ethnocultural, environmental, and personal considerations, but that election results were not. Outcomes seemed to hinge on variations in voter turnout, for the key individuals were not committed party followers. Instead, the swing vote was cast by occasional voters who decided to vote at one election but not at another. See Bohmer, "Voter Behavior During the First American Party System: Maryland, 1796–1816" (Ph.D. dissertation, University of Michigan, 1974).

[17]Robert M. Zemsky, "Numbers and History: The Dilemma of Measurement," *Computers and the Humanities* 4 (September 1969):32.

We can examine, then, party loyalty and the characteristics associated with affiliation with one party or the other, but this loyalty and these characteristics do not necessarily pertain to individuals; instead, they pertain to voting units. Although a city, county, or ward may behave consistently over a long period of time, we must never forget one of the basic lessons of demographic analysis. At least in the United States, the population is in constant motion. That a county votes heavily Republican in 1880 and again in 1900 shows stability in the behavior of the county. Since many voters died, came of age, moved in, or moved out during that period, we may not be able to make the remotest inference about individual behavior unless we can show that people moving in resembled those moving out in religion, ethnicity, economic class, and the like. The greater the time difference between the two elections, the stronger this rule becomes. Supposedly the individuals of a voting unit who tend to vote a certain way share a mix of socioeconomic variables that creates a political subculture. Sharing ethnic background, race, religious views, and occupational outlook, the members of the subculture also share the world view that their shared characteristics create.[18] Many recent studies of voter behavior, including that of Richard Jensen reprinted here, necessarily rest on such concepts, which generally seem consistent with the findings.

In the following selection Jensen explores the association of religious affiliation and occupation with voter behavior. He does not present regression or correlation coefficients (though these were part of his preliminary research); instead, he uses the simple but effective percentage to indicate relationships. Utilizing county directories published in the 1870s that identified individual voters by name and indicated their occupation, religion, party preference, and sometimes age, place of birth, and farm values, Jensen is, in effect, using extensive interview data just like the Gallup polls of a century later. Although the voters themselves have long passed from the scene, these particular county directories had been compiled by editors who took pains to interview the individuals they reported about.

Jensen concludes that "one of the most accurate ways to determine a voter's choices in the late nineteenth century was to ascertain his religious preferences (except in the South, where one ascertained his race)." He finds that religion and occupation were the determinants of voting behavior in Illinois and Indiana. He calls these "the basic roots of party identification for the average citizen."[19] At least in the Midwest, any voter analysis that goes no further than countywide election returns, which show Republicans and Democrats to be equally strong, ignores the deep cleavages (obscured

---

[18]Ronald P. Formisano, "Analyzing American Voting, 1830–1860: Methods," *Historical Methods Newsletter* 2 (March 1969):2–25.

[19]Richard Jensen, "The Religious and Occupational Roots of Party Identification: Illinois and Indiana in the 1870's," *Civil War History* 16 (December 1970):325, 326.

by aggregate returns) that were so closely associated with religion and occupation. The interesting twist is that the religious influence is not determined by a simple Catholic-Protestant classification. Instead, distinctive voting behavior seems to have been associated with a dichotomy of liturgical versus pietist religion (i.e., "high" church —Catholic, Anglican, orthodox Calvinist, and German Lutheran—as opposed to revivalistic church—Congregational, Disciples of Christ, Methodist, some Presbyterians, and Scandinavian Lutheran), and a second dichotomy of white-collar versus blue-collar occupations. Note the effect of parallel pressures: pietist businessmen were far more likely to be Republicans than unskilled liturgicals, who tended to vote Democrat. Unskilled pietists and liturgical businessmen fell in between, because they were subject to the cross pressures of conflicting loyalties.

The Religious and Occupational Roots of Party Identification: Illinois and Indiana in the 1870's
Richard Jensen

. . . Religion was relevant to social and political behavior in three ways. First, different theological positions produced different interpretations of morality and of the behavior most appropriate for the Christian citizen. Second, organized religious bodies formed fundamental social groups of the highest importance to their adherents. The members of a particular congregation or denomination knew other members intimately—they worshipped together, intermarried, and probably discussed political issues with each other over long periods of time. Thus a strain toward political uniformity within a particular religious group would not be unexpected. If like the German Lutherans a particular religious group was sufficiently inwardly directed, they might be said to constitute a distinct subculture. This usually happened in the case of immigrant groups sharing a common religion. Thirdly, the denominations as formal groups sometimes took active parts in political controversies. Thus the Methodists before the Civil War came to adopt a semiofficial antislavery stance through the actions of respected elders, ministers, bishops, educators and editors. These positions were transmitted to the general membership through voluntary associations, special meetings, regular sermons, and an influential network of church periodicals. By working with denominations rather than specific congregations, the three modes of religious influence can all be incorporated into an interpretation of how religious differences generated political differences.

The importance of religion in nineteenth-century America cannot be overestimated.

Richard Jensen, "The Religious and Occupational Roots of Party Identification: Illinois and Indiana in the 1870's," *Civil War History,* XVI (December 1970), 328–332, 334–343. Copyright © 1970 by the Kent State University Press. Reprinted with deletion of notes, abridgment, and minor revision by permission of the author and publisher.

In 1789 the United States was a largely de-Christianized nation. Wave after wave of revivals, from the 1790's to World War I, converted the major part of the population to Protestantism. The depth and breadth of the revivals forced a revamping of the fundamentals of Protestant theology. The revivalists, led by a few powerful intellectuals at Yale and Oberlin and hundreds of preachers in the field, rejected the orthodox Calvinist theory of predestination, and the Catholic-Anglican-Lutheran established church styles of theology which emphasized patience, gradualism and incrementalism and which made no allowance for massive and sudden revivals. The antirevivalists fought back bitterly and often brilliantly, producing major theological and liturgical renaissances in the Episcopalian, Presbyterian, Reformed, Lutheran and Catholic denominations. The result was a century-long conflict between the revivalist or "pietistic" outlook, and the antirevivalist or "liturgical" outlook.

While this conflict was not the only divisive force in American religion, it was the most intense and long-standing. By the end of the century, when the revivalist circuit riders had dismounted and ministers searched for new methods to tend their flock, the pietistic-liturgical conflict rapidly faded in the major denominations. This in turn set off another wave of formation of new sects and denominations by men who felt the dimension was all-important.

The liturgical (or "ritualistic" or "high church") outlook stressed the institutionalized formalities and historic doctrines of the established churches of Europe—Calvinist, Catholic, Lutheran and Anglican. Salvation required faithful adherence to the creed, liturgy, sacraments and hierarchy of the church. The quintessence of liturgical style could be found in Catholicism's lavish use of ornamentation, vestments, esoteric languages, ritualized sacraments, devotion to the saints, and vigorous pursuit of heretics, all directed by an authoritarian (and after 1870 infallible) hierarchy. Comparable ritualism became firmly established among Episcopalians and Orthodox Jews. German Lutherans (of the Missouri Synod, especially) and orthodox Calvinists (the "Old School" Presbyterians and many Baptists) similarly fixed ritualistic practices, clung to old theologies, and rejected both revivals and the manifestations of pietism.

One key element in the liturgical outlook was particularism, the conviction that their denomination was the one true Church of God, and most outsiders were probably damned. This attitude was strong not only among Catholics, but also among orthodox Calvinists, who clung to predestination, high church Episcopalians, Missouri Synod Lutherans and Landmarkean Baptists. For the liturgicals, moralistic social action groups that were not an integral part of the church structure were illegal, unscriptural and unnecessary; the church could attend to all matters of morality without outside help. Thus the orthodox Calvinists ejected half the Presbyterian membership in 1837; the Baptists split over missionary societies in the 1830's; the Catholics underwent a great crisis in the 1890's regarding missions to Protestants; and the Episcopalians ordered their Church Temperance Society to disband in the 1920's.

Heresy, pride and innovation, rather than impure behavior, were the cardinal sins for the liturgicals. Consequently they responded to pietism by stressing orthodox theology and developing seminaries and parochial schools to preserve their faith unchanged. Catholics and German Lutherans relied on their parochial schools to the exclusion of public schools, thus opening a line of political battle that climaxed in 1890 in intensely bitter elections in Wisconsin and Illinois. The courageous pursuit of duty was the highest virtue for liturgicals, and the most outstanding exemplar of this trait was the son of a Calvinistic Presbyterian minister, Grover Cleveland.

The pietistic outlook rejected liturgicalism. It had little respect for elaborate ceremonies, vestments, saints, devotions, and frequently opposed organ music in church. Theologically the key to pietism was the conviction (called Arminianism) that all men can be saved by a direct confrontation with Christ (*not* with the Church) through the conversion experience. The revival was the basis of their strength—the preaching of hellfire, damnation and Christ's redeeming love, the anxious bench for despondent sinners, the moment of inner light wherein a man gained faith and was saved. While the liturgicals routinely baptized all the children in their community, and then went out to baptize heathens, the pietists insisted on the conversion experience before membership could be granted, and demanded continuous proof in the form of pure behavior. The Methodists, for example, did not hesitate to expel a member whose conduct was unbecoming to a true believer. Creeds and formal theology were of little importance, and heresy was not a major concern. Denominational lines were not vital either, and pietists frequently switched churches. The pietists fostered interdenominational voluntary societies to distribute Bibles, conduct missionary work, abolish slavery and promote total abstinence. . . .

The bridge linking theology and politics was the demand by pietists that the government actively support the cause of Christianity by abolishing the sinful institutions that stood in the way of revivals. Specifically, midwestern pietists demanded that the government halt the spread of slavery (or even abolish it), overthrow the saloon and the sale of liquor, and (among many pietists) restrict the "pernicious" and "corrupting" flood of Catholic immigration. (Nearly all the abolitionists were prohibitionists, and most were anti-Catholic.) Antiliquor, antislavery and nativism were the immediate causes of the realignment of parties in the mid-1850's that produced the third party system, pitting Republicans against Democrats.

Liturgicals, as a rule, opposed prohibition, denounced abolitionists (even if they disliked slavery), and avoided the nativist agitation. The intrusion of government into affairs of morality was, in their eyes, a threat to the primacy of the Church in the spiritual realm, and an unconstitutional abridgment of individual liberties. Although the liturgicals did not favor the pernicious evils of the saloon any more than did pietists, they did not demand total abstinence of their members, nor did they discipline their slave-holding adherents. While the major piestic denominations each suffered a north-south rupture *before* the Civil War, none of the liturgical churches was divided. The liturgicals feared that "fanatical" (their favorite epithet) pietists would use the government to further their moralistic crusades.

The liturgical fears were well grounded. Beginning with the Maine Law of 1851, a wave of prohibition legislation swept the country, instigated by the pietists, first through the Whig party, and then through the Know-Nothings and Republicans. After 1854 the slavery issue became paramount, and the pietists of the North mobilized into the moralistic, crusading Republican party. The Democrats, who had always claimed the support of most liturgical voters, sought to blunt the Republican attack by vigorously defending a wet, antinativist, antiabolitionist position. During the Civil War itself, the pietists were the mainstay of the Union war effort, while the liturgicals held back. Catholics, both Irish and German, rioted against the draft and emancipation; Old School Presbyterians refused to fly the American flag at their 1863 convention; and not a few Episcopalians were denounced as Copperheads. The Episcopalian church in Indianapolis was even ridiculed as the "Church of the Holy Rebellion." The only appeal that finally gained liturgical support for the war was Lincoln's emphasis on loyalty, patriotism, and nationalism.

It seems reasonable to hypothesize that when party lines reformed in the 1850's, the great majority of pietists in the Midwest became Republicans, and liturgicals Democrats, and that the phenomenon of political inheritance through families and long-term stability of individual partisan identification maintained this basic division for the remainder of the century. This hypothesis has to be modified slightly in view of the fact that after 1869 and the victory of Radical Reconstruction, the temperance issue reemerged as the most salient political issue on the state and local level throughout the Midwest. In the mid-1870's, with the formation of the Woman's Christian Temperance Union, the prohibition movement again attained the status of a continuous crusade. Thus the religious-political correlation established before the Civil War was reinforced afterwards. (The Republicans, furthermore, used the "bloody shirt" issue, and the anger of Methodists about southern religious developments, to maintain the Civil War cleavages.) . . .

The effect of the prohibition issue in differentiating liturgical and pietistic voters of similar background can be traced in aggregate election returns. Most Norwegians in Iowa were pietistic Lutherans and voted 90 per cent Republican year in and year out. In Winneshiek county, however, liturgical Norwegian Lutherans predominated. The three towns of Pleasant, Glenwood and Madison voted 93 per cent Republican in 1881, before the temperance issue became salient. In 1882, the same towns voted 55 per cent against a prohibition amendment to the state constitution and, as the temperance crusade continued, the Republican share of the vote slipped 33 points to 60 per cent in 1891. In 1893, after the prohibition issue had been temporarily resolved to the satisfaction of the liturgicals, the vote in the towns shot up to 76 per cent. In heavily liturgical-German Dubuque, where the Republicans had taken 50 per cent of the vote in 1881, the prohibition amendment received only 15 per cent of the vote, and the Republican vote plunged at the next election to 28 per cent. (Dubuque's ward five, a German center, which had been 63 per cent Republican, voted 94 per cent wet, and the Republican vote then plunged to 22 per cent.) The professionals in the Republican party finally learned that support for prohibition meant defeat at the polls and after 1891 generally refused to permit the pietists to dictate dry platforms.

Religious outlook seems also to have affected occupational status. The pietistic faith, by placing heavy emphasis upon individual initiative and responsibility for salvation, attracted entrepreneurs, while the passive liturgical faith was more amenable to less adventuresome men. . . .

Occupational status had a more direct connection with politics; the Republican party always offered a comfortable home to the businessman, while the Democrats throughout the century consistently attacked the wealthy and privileged. . . .

So far, men without religious affiliations have not been accounted for. The very fact that they did not belong to a church in an age of revivals suggests that most of these men would either be young voters who had not yet been converted, or else were reluctant to join in voluntary organizations. It can therefore be expected that their partisanship would be weak. And since they lacked religious affinities toward either party, they should be located midway between pietistic Republicans and liturgical Democrats. Furthermore, the two parties were very closely matched before 1894 and election campaigns very intensely fought. As every extra vote counted, both parties probably endeavored to enlist these men, thus dividing them 50-50. If they were in business or professional occupations, however, they might be drawn to the Republicanism of their colleagues and repelled by the antibusiness animus of the Democracy. If they were factory workers, the Republican high-tariff position would be especially appealing. If they were laborers or farmers, they might have been drawn to the Democracy as the party of the common man. All of these possibilities can be explored with interview data.

* * * *

The detailed analysis of one urban and seven rural townships in northern and central Illinois, and six rural townships in central Indiana reaffirm . . . the hypotheses. . . . Table 1 shows the partisan distributions by denomination for the Indiana townships,

Table 1   **Party, by Denomination, Hendricks County, 1874**

Denomination	% Rep.	% Dem.	% None or other	N
Friends (Quaker)	96.4	1.2	2.4	83
Christian (Disciples)	73.6	23.7	2.7	291
Methodist*	72.8	21.9	5.2	232
Presbyterian	64.3	31.4	4.3	70
Missionary Baptist	57.4	38.6	4.0	101
Misc. Prot. denoms.	52.1	39.1	8.7	23
No denomination given	47.0	48.3	4.6	699
Regular Baptist	17.0	78.7	4.3	94
Roman Catholic	4.2	83.3	12.5	24

*Methodist Episcopal plus African Methodist

where the coverage was unusually good (in part because the editors lived in one of the townships); all names were included except for twenty-four (1.5 per cent) who failed to return any information on party or religion, and who usually had no age data listed. Less than 25 per cent of the eligible men were missed by the canvassers here and, according to aggregate election returns, they voted the same way as the men who were included. Table 2 shows the party breakdown by denomination for the Illinois data. In this case, only Republicans and Democrats listed in the directories were included; otherwise coverage was comparable to that in Indiana.

Table 2   **Party, for Pietistic Denominations, 8 Illinois Twps., 1877-78 (Per cent Republican of two-party total)**

Denomination	% Rep.	N
Congregationalist	82.0	39
Methodist	75.2	289
Disciples, Christians & Cumberland Presbyterian	71.8	220
Lutheran (pietistic synods only)	60.5	38
Presbyterian	57.7	108
Baptist	55.7	61

The four most Republican denominations, Quakers, Congregationalists, Disciples and Methodists, were strongly pietistic in the Midwest. The Presbyterians were predominantly pietistic, but the traces of Old School liturgical Democracy were evident. The Baptists present an interesting special case. The Missionary Baptists were pietists, while most of the "Regular" Baptists in Hendricks county clung to orthodox Calvinist views and were especially hostile to missionary and temperance societies. Only 4.2 per cent of the Hendricks county men were independent—including several "Greeley Republicans," two Grangers, three Prohibitionists, and one "Old Whig." Occupationally, only half the independents were farmers, in contrast to over three-fourths of the partisans; the independents were also a bit younger, but the small N's prevent more exact conclusions. The "Civil War" generation (born 1832 to 1845) in Hendricks county was only slightly more Republican than other age cohorts, controlling for religion and occupation, although 189 of the 236 Union veterans in the county (80 per cent) in 1880 were reportedly Republicans, with Democrats outnumbering Greenbackers two to one among the remainder. Sectional origins were not significant in Hendricks—the great majority of all the voters had been born in the South or had fathers born in the South. Southern origins, less than a decade after the Civil War, did not affect the partisanship of these Hoosiers; the effect in Illinois was very small.

The interview records do not, of course, specify whether a man was pietistic or liturgical in orientation. Some oversimplification is necessary: all members of predominantly liturgical denominations must be classified as liturgicals, and all members of pietistic denominations as pietists. Obviously some men will be misclassified, but the effect of this error will be to weaken the true patterns. That is, if the hypothesis is true, most of the true liturgicals misclassified as pietists would be Democrats, and the misclassification therefore lowers the observed proportion of pietists who were Republicans. If the errors of misclassification could somehow be rectified, the estimated proportion of Republicans among pietists (already high) would be further increased and the estimated proportion of Republicans among liturgicals (already low) would be further lowered.

All members of Protestant denominations were classified as pietistic with the exception of Episcopalians, German Lutherans, Old School Presbyterians, Primitive Baptists, and Anti-Missionary Baptists. Everyone else, including the handful of Jews, was classified as liturgical. . . .

The Illinois returns for each religious and political group are shown by their occupational distributions in Tables 3 and 4. Bear in mind that low-status occupations probably were under-represented in the directories. Several striking patterns appear. An urban-rural split occurs on party identifications. The great majority (83 per cent) of independents were non-farmers, while Democrats were somewhat more likely to be farmers than Republicans (51 per cent versus 41 per cent). There was, however, no urban-rural difference between liturgicals and pietists, while non-members were slightly more likely to be non-farmers. Age probably accounted for this—young men, who had not yet been converted, were leaving the farms for the nearby towns.

Among the non-farmers (not all of whom lived in towns or cities), the Republicans were especially strong and liturgicals weak. This was the age of the Yankee mechanic, and the Republican protective tariff. To scotch one old myth, blacksmiths (in Indiana) were just as religious and partisan as anyone else, though it is true that the only "naturalist" and the "free and easy" independent in Hendricks county were both blacksmiths. The pietists were especially strong among professionals and weak among unskilled labor, with just the reverse for liturgicals. The religious literature of late-nineteenth century is full of warnings that the Protestant churches had abandoned the lower classes to the "Romanists."

By removing the political independents (and non-responders) the relative party strength among occupational groups, controlling for religion, can be discriminated. Table 5 shows the Republican share of the two-party vote for each occupational group by religious subgroups.

The basic pietistic-liturgical correlation with party holds true for every occupational group, with two exceptions. Among high-status businessmen, Republican liturgicals barely outnumbered [liturgical] Democrats. Among low-status farm renters and laborers pietistic Democrats outnumbered Republicans. The unchurched groups hovered around the 50–50 mark, except among businessmen, white collar workers and, inexplicably, among adult sons living on their fathers' farms. The unchurched fell midway politically between the pietists and liturgicals in every occupation except white collar workers (but the N is small), and among those farmer renters and laborers. (The reason here is that only 3 of 35 Republican farm laborers were pietists, in contrast to 14 of 28

Table 3   Non-Farm Occupation, by Party and Religion, 8 Illinois Twps., 1877-78 (Read Down)

	% All	Party			Religion		
		% Rep.	% Neither	% Dem.	% Piet.	% None	% Lit.
Professional	8.5	9.6	8.9	6.8	13.4	7.3	4.6
Business	21.1	24.0	25.5	13.3	23.3	21.6	15.3
White Collar	6.8	6.9	7.3	6.3	5.8	7.6	5.3
Skilled Blue Collar	32.7	36.0	30.4	30.9	33.8	35.2	21.4
Unskilled Blue Collar	8.2	5.8	7.1	12.0	3.1	8.2	16.5
Unskilled Common Labor	15.2	10.2	13.6	22.9	11.0	13.2	30.4
Unknown	7.5	7.5	13.2	7.8	9.6	6.9	6.5
Total	100.0	100.0	100.0	100.0	100.0	100.0	100.0
N	1717	669	506	542	447	1009	261

Table 4   Farm Occupation, by Party and Religion, 8 Illinois Twps., 1877-78 (Read Down)

	% All	Party			Religion		
		% Rep.	% Neither	% Dem.	% Piet.	% None	% Lit.
Farm Owners	75.2	76.0	73.3	74.9	78.9	70.5	81.5
Sons of Owners	9.7	10.5	8.6	9.3	9.6	12.3	3.0
Renters & Laborers	15.1	13.5	18.1	15.8	11.5	17.2	15.5
Total	100.0	100.0	100.0	100.0	100.0	100.0	100.0
N	1129	467	105	557	374	553	201
Farmers as % of All Voters	39.7	41.1	17.2	50.6	44.5	35.5	43.5

Table 5   Party Strength by Occupation and Religion, 8 Illinois Townships, 1877-78
(Per cent Republican of two-party total) (N in parentheses)

Occupation	Pietists	Not Affiliated	Liturgicals	All
Professional	75.9 (N = 58)	50.0 (34)	33.3 (9)	63.4 (101)
Business	81.4 (97)	62.8 (105)	51.5 (31)	69.1 (233)
White Collar	60.0 (25)	61.9 (42)	38.4 (13)	57.5 (80)
Skilled Blue Collar	73.1 (145)	55.6 (218)	30.4 (46)	58.9 (409)
Unskilled	65.0 (60)	48.0 (123)	8.0 (113)	36.1 (296)
Unknown	65.9 (38)	52.6 (38)	31.2 (16)	54.4 (92)
All Non-farm	72.9 (423)	55.1 (560)	22.8 (228)	55.3 (1211)
Farm Owner	59.1 (279)	49.1 (348)	13.1 (145)	46.1 (772)
Sons of Owner	70.6 (34)	41.0 (61)	0.0 (6)	48.5 (101)
Renters & Laborers	42.5 (40)	52.4 (84)	7.4 (27)	41.7 (151)
All Farm	58.4 (353)	48.7 (493)	11.8 (178)	45.6 (1024)
All	66.2 (776)	52.2 (1053)	18.0 (406)	50.9 (2235)

renters.) Note also that farmers were 10 points less Republican than non-farmers (14.5 points for pietists, 6.4 points for nonmembers, 11.0 points for liturgicals). As far as age is concerned, a random sample (N = 314) from Indiana gives a median age of 36 or 37 for the Republican farmers and non-farmers, and for the Democratic non-farmers, but a median age of 44 for Democratic farmers—indicating again the special affinity for Jacksonian Democracy among older farmers.

The four rows in Table 5 representing the largest nonfarm occupational groups, businessmen, professionals, skilled blue collar workers, and unskilled laborers, illustrate the complex relationship among party, religion and occupation. (White collar clerks, for whom the numbers are small, are somewhat exceptional.) The Republican strength in the four groups ranged from 65 to 81 per cent among pietists, from 48 to 63 per cent among unaffiliated, and from 8 per cent to 52 per cent among liturgicals. Three factors account for these patterns . . .: religion itself, occupation itself, and the joint effect (interaction) between religion and occupation.

For each occupational group taken separately, the Republican strength depended greatly on religious grouping. Pietists were 30 points more Republican than liturgicals among businessmen, and a remarkable 57 points more Republican among the unskilled. Secondly, among men in the same religious group, there was a wide range between the most and least Republican occupation, with businessmen highest and unskilled lowest for each group. Among pietists, businessmen were 16 points more Republican than [unskilled] laborers, while among liturgicals the businessmen were 43 points more Republican. Occupation was thus more influential among liturgicals than among pietists or the unaffiliated. Clearly religion and occupation were both "real" factors that cannot be explained away by statistical controls. The independent effects of religion and occupation added together so that pietistic businessmen had the extra Republicanism of pietists added to the extra Republicanism of businessmen, and were an amazing 73 points more Republican than unskilled liturgicals. This immense range between two polar groups living in the same community was far greater than the average differences in voting patterns between different communities. Considering the farmers too, the 2235 voters in the eight townships who expressed a political preference were almost exactly divided between the parties (50.9 per cent Republican versus 49.1 per cent Democratic). In aggregate terms, therefore, the townships hovered around 50–50, yet the constituent groups typically hovered around the 75–25 level (except for the nonaffiliated group which was 50–50). Any analysis of the social correlates of partisanship that depends upon aggregate election returns will miss the most important dimension of midwestern voting patterns, the deep internal conflicts, because the votes of the various religions and occupational groups were usually mixed together in aggregate data.

The factors of religion and occupation interacted so that the liturgicals concentrated in the heavily Democratic low-status occupations (see Table 3). Thus [in Table 5] the non-farmer pietists, taken all together, were 50 points more Republican than the liturgicals (72.9 versus 22.8), which is larger than the spread in any occupation group except unskilled. It is impossible to explain the reasons for this interaction, but the theological and social group functions of religion were factors, along with positive anti-liturgical job discrimination. If the interaction had not existed and the pietists, liturgicals and unaffiliated had been proportionately represented in each occupation, then the pietists would have been 71.5 per cent Republican instead of 72.9 per cent, the unaffiliated would have been 54.8 per cent instead of 55.1 per cent, and the liturgicals would have been 29.8 per cent instead of 22.8 per cent for a range of 71.5−29.8 = 42 points instead of 72.9−22.8 = 50 points. Thus, different occupational profiles increased the political difference between pietists and liturgicals from 42 to 50 points, an increase of 20 per cent.

[The first column of Table 3 shows the occupational profile of all 1717 non-farmers; the last three columns show the profile for each religious group. If the occupational profile for each religious group had been identical, 8.5 per cent of the pietists, non-members and liturgicals would be professionals, of whom 75.9 per cent, 50.0 per cent and 33.3 per cent, respectively, would be Republicans (according to the first row of Table 5). Arithmetically, the proportion of pietists who would then be Republicans is: 8.5% × 75.9% + 21.1% × 81.4%, + . . . + 7.5% × 65.9% + 71.5%. This procedure, called ''standardization,'' was repeated for each religious group, and a similar standardization by religion was computed for each occupational group.]

Conversely, if the religious profile of each occupational group had been identical, the businessmen would have been 67.1 per cent Republican instead of 69.1 per cent, and the unskilled would have been 46.4 per cent Republican instead of 36.1 per cent. Thus the different religious profiles of the occupations stretched the difference between businessmen and unskilled from 67.1–46.4 = 21 points to 69.1–36.1 = 33 points, an increase of over 50 per cent. Hence, the religious distribution produced relatively greater effects than the occupational distribution did or, in other words, religion exacerbated the political tension between high and low status occupations.

The 21 point spread between the Republicanism of businessmen and unskilled laborers which remains after correction for the lopsided religious distribution has been made stands in need of further explanation. Unfortunately, no profound insights can be squeezed out of the tables. A variety of hypotheses could explain the result. Perhaps the Republicans were simply the party of the classes and the Democrats the party of the masses. This may be true, but it merely restates the results and does not explain when, how, and why such a difference emerged. If the pattern first emerged after the Civil War, it could be best explained in terms of Reconstruction race and economic policies and, perhaps, the effects of the depression of 1873–1877. If the pattern first emerged during the war, emancipation policies, conscription, economic conditions and Republican appeals to patriotism would seem to offer the best leads. If the patterns first emerged before the war, a different set of explanations is required. Until the dating problem is solved the occupational differences cannot be explained.

New data is also needed to settle conclusively whether the relationships among religion, occupation and party can be generalized for the entire country. Clearly a different framework of analysis is necessary to explain the racially-oriented patterns of partisanship in the postwar South. The political history of the northern states was relatively uniform in the 1850's, 1860's and early 1870's, but the East differed sharply from the Midwest by its more industrialized occupational profile and the tendency in some denominations (Congregationalists, Quaker, Presbyterian) for liturgical elements to be stronger than they were in the Midwest. Congregationalists in New England in the 1850's, for example, were less committed to temperance and antislavery than their counterparts in the Midwest. The tentative conclusion is that the strong links among religion, occupation and politics that existed in Illinois and Indiana were typical of the Midwest, and perhaps the Northeast too, but not the South.

chapter eighteen

Legislative Behavior

The obvious sources for the study of legislative behavior are the proceedings and journals of deliberative bodies, which provide records of motions, referrals to committee, committee reports, and debates. However, the insight into legislative proceedings that these materials supply is not always satisfactory. What legislators say about an issue—if they say anything at all—does not necessarily agree with how they vote. In the first place, many speeches are pure buncombe. Second, even when legislators support a measure wholeheartedly, they may vote against it at several stages of the legislative process—even perhaps at final passage—because amendments have so changed its effect that they no longer find it acceptable. Third, many printed debates are inaccurate because they are not a literal representation of the events they describe; in order to insure accuracy, avoid embarrassment, and reduce the temptation of loquacious lawmakers to talk on and on, congressmen today are routinely granted permission to "revise and extend" their remarks in the *Congressional Record*.[1] Fortunately for students of legislative behavior, however, deliberative bodies frequently include the full roll-call record in their published reports.

Roll calls have always been useful for politicians, journalists, and voters, who find a more or less precise indicator of a lawmaker's point of view in the overall record of the votes cast on important pieces of legislation. Scholars also have found roll calls to be useful indicators of party or sectional alignment. As with election studies, however, statistical mapping was a prelude to systematic exploitation of the data. Thus, the earliest scholarly analysis of legislative voting was done by Orin G. Libby, who had

---

[1]This is not a new problem. The *Annals of Congress*, which include the debates of the House and Senate of the United States from 1789 to 1824, were not contemporaneously compiled and are incomplete; the *Register of Debates*, covering 1824 to 1837, is contemporary but not always literal; the *Congressional Globe*, 1833–1873, is also contemporary but, at least in the earlier years, is incomplete. Verbatim reports of congressional debates were not made officially until 1874. See U. S., Superintendent of Documents, *Checklist of United States Public Documents, 1789–1909*, 3rd ed., rev. and enl. (Washington: Government Printing Office, 1911), pp. 1463–75.

learned political mapping at the University of Wisconsin from the director of his doctoral dissertation, Frederick Jackson Turner. Libby sought to test the hypothesis that the supporters and opponents of the ratification of the U.S. Constitution could be determined by their proximity to the Atlantic coastline. In *The Geographical Distribution of the Vote of the Thirteen States on the Federal Constitution, 1787–8*, Libby "determine[d] systematically the areas of support for, and opposition to, the new instrument of government." On a reconstructed map of the United States for 1787 and 1788, he coded the degree of support given the constitution, as indicated by the *votes of the delegates* to state ratification conventions and the geographic location of the districts they represented. He concluded that cleavage on the ratification question was economic, between commercial interests on one hand and agricultural interests on the other. Even after the publication of this study in 1894, and his move to the University of North Dakota in 1902, Libby continued to use mapping techniques to examine legislative behavior.[2] Some of his maps—finely, carefully, almost painfully drawn —remain in dusty corners of the University of North Dakota to this day.

Libby fully realized the inadequacy of debates as a reflection of legislative sentiment, and, pointing out that most representatives never spoke on major issues, he asserted that "to base judgement of what these silent majorities thought and did upon what these insignificant minorities said is a grotesque application of the rule of the best which has no place in our history." He demanded that votes in the House of Representatives, whose members would reflect more closely than Senators the interests of their constituents, be related to geographic location and economic data for the counties composing a member's district.[3]

With varying techniques and a wider range of variables, this is precisely what many historians have been doing—but only in the last ten to fifteen years. Why the delay? For one thing, the proper analytical techniques had to be developed; as with election studies, mapping was a poor substitute for statistical methods. Generally speaking, even political scientists, whose work is often so closely allied to that of the historian, did not possess the necessary methodological tools for the full exploitation of roll-call records.[4] No doubt the most important factor, however, is the development of the computer, which permits the manipulation of large masses of data with a degree of accuracy and speed undreamed of a generation ago. For instance, clustering the members of a legislative body by checking the extent of voting agreement between partners in every possible pair of lawmakers requires nothing more than the ability to count; if there were only 5 or 10 members the task would be simple, for there would be only 10

[2]Robert P. Wilkins, "Introduction: Orin G. Libby: His Place in the Historiography of the Constitution," pp. 6–11 in the reprint edition of Orin G. Libby, *The Geographical Distribution of the Vote of the Thirteen States on the Federal Constitution, 1787–8* (Grand Forks: University of North Dakota Press, 1969).

[3]Orin Grant Libby, "A Plea for the Study of Votes in Congress," American Historical Association *Annual Report* 1 (1896):321–34, quote from p. 327.

[4]Richard Jensen, "History and the Political Scientist," in Seymour Martin Lipset, ed., *Politics and the Social Sciences* (New York: Oxford University Press, 1969), pp. 8–9.

or 45 possible pairs. But if the body contains 100 legislators there are 4950 pairs, and if there are 435 members (as in the current House of Representatives) there are 94,395 pairs! To compute agreements and print results in a form suitable for analysis for so many pairs, for a session of 500 or so roll calls, could tie up a small computer for the better part of an afternoon.

The easiest method of legislative analysis is a simple index or performance score. This requires selection, based on the investigator's judgment, of a group of roll calls that supposedly measure the degree to which a lawmaker supports a given issue, leader, or pressure group. The *Congressional Quarterly Almanac,* for instance, ranks congressmen according to their agreement with a "conservative coalition." Roll calls on which a majority of Republicans and a majority of southern Democrats vote the same way, and in opposition to a majority of other Democrats, are presumed to test conservatism. Each member's record is then compared to this supposedly ideal conservative record and scored accordingly. From time to time one reads of other congressional voting scores that attempt to measure a legislator's sympathy with labor, the environment, agriculture, or some other interest.

The difficulty with this approach is that it does not really establish the existence of the attitude it attempts to measure. In the case of the conservative coalition of the *Congressional Quarterly Almanac,* no real test of conservatism is involved. To determine conservatism by agreement of Republicans and southern Democrats presumes that they are, in fact, conservative; by definition, the *Almanac* therefore discovers that most conservatives are Republicans and southern Democrats. This is a circular argument; in the event there were no roll calls on issues that had a truly conservative dimension the *Almanac* would still list the members of a non-existent conservative coalition, provided only that parties and sections voted according to the requirements of the rigid model. By the same token, special interest groups may not always pick votes that reflect the attitude that the interest wishes to put into focus. The crude performance score therefore does not permit precise inference about legislators' attitudes. On the other hand, the device is relatively uncomplicated and allows the salvage of data that may not be susceptible to more refined techniques, such as cumulative scaling. In a study of the Confederate Congress, for example, legislative attitudes were so ill-defined that scaling was often impossible; the use of a performance score was absolutely essential and, on topical areas that could be scaled, sometimes produced similar results by ranking congressmen in much the same relative position regarding the topic being explored.[5]

An index or performance score often assumes the existence of measurable attitudes. A more precise technique for identifying those votes that measure the same attitude (or dimension, as it is sometimes called), is cumulative scaling. Also known as

---

[5]Thomas B. Alexander and Richard E. Beringer, *The Anatomy of the Confederate Congress: A Study of the Influences of Member Characteristics on Legislative Voting Behavior, 1861–1865* (Nashville: Vanderbilt University Press, 1972).

Guttman scaling, this procedure was originally developed by social psychologist Louis Guttman to ascertain whether all queries on interview questionnaires measured the same attitudes. Analyzing roll calls as if they were interview questions, the investigator uses one of several methods to determine which votes measured the same attitude. These votes are then ranked in order from easiest to accept to hardest to accept (according to the original vote totals). Each lawmaker who does not have an excessive number of absences or "error responses" is then assigned a scale score or scale position according to his own votes, in such manner that the score indicates the legislator's relative degree of support for a policy or attitude. A score of 4 will indicate that a congressman took a stronger stand than a colleague with a score of 2, but the numbers do not indicate how much more. If, on any particular vote, an excessive number of legislators had "error responses" ("excessive" may be measured by any of several statistical tests), the roll call does not measure the attitude being studied and accordingly is dropped out of the tentative scale.[6]

It might appear logical enough that six or eight votes on a specific measure—to amend, table, postpone, pass, reconsider, and the like—would fit into one attitude scale. What is more revealing is that votes that are not so obviously related may be a part of a single dimension. Historian William O. Aydelotte found a scale covering Chartism, corn laws, income tax, and livestock duties in the British House of Commons in the 1840s, for example,[7] and political scientist Duncan MacRae, Jr., discovered a scale in the United States' Eighty-first Congress that included such varied items as rent control, social security, and the Taft-Hartley Act.[8] Having detected the presence of a scale and discovered the roll calls that compose it, however, the investigator may have a great deal of difficulty determining exactly what attitude it measures. And it goes without saying that attitudes can be detected only if votes have been held on the germane issues; some positions inevitably remain undetected.

Scale analysis is an important technique in Ronald L. Hatzenbuehler's article, below. Just as prominent is Rice-Beyle cluster-bloc analysis. In this procedure, each legislator's voting record is compared with that of every other legislator and the level of agreement of every possible pair of lawmakers is inserted into a matrix. The numbers in the matrix represent the percentage of the total number of roll calls on which the paired legislators voted alike, although some investigators may insert the

---

[6]For detailed discussion of scaling techniques, see Lee F. Anderson, Meredith W. Watts, Jr., and Allen R. Wilcox, *Legislative Roll-Call Analysis* (Evanston: Northwestern University Press, 1966), Chapter VI, and Duncan MacRae, Jr., *Dimensions of Congressional Voting: A Statistical Study of the House of Representatives in the Eighty-first Congress* (Berkeley and Los Angeles: University of California Press, 1958). For comparison of index (performance) scores and cumulative (Guttman) scaling, see Allan G. Bogue, "The Radical Voting Dimension in the U.S. Senate During the Civil War," *Journal of Interdisciplinary History* 3 (Winter 1973):449–74.

[7]William O. Aydelotte, "Voting Patterns in the British House of Commons in the 1840s," *Comparative Studies in Society and History* 5 (January 1963):137.

[8]MacRae, *Dimensions of Congressional Voting*, p. 225.

number of agreements instead. Lawmakers who achieve a specified minimum level of agreement with every other member of a cluster may then be considered a bloc. Because of the overwhelming number of pairs in large legislative bodies, this method has not been used as often as scaling. Allan G. Bogue, however, used cluster bloc analysis to supplement scale analysis: percentages of agreements used to create clusters served also to indicate a reasonable division point between Republican scale scores that distinguished Radicals from Moderates in the second session of the Thirty-seventh Congress.[9] Similarly, a study of the Confederate Congress used cluster bloc analysis to verify the factional divisions uncovered by scaling,[10] while an investigation of the Senate of the Forty-fourth through Forty-sixth Congresses used this scheme to determine the composition of the Stalwart faction of the Republican Party.[11]

A third device in Hatzenbuehler's article is an index of cohesion, developed by sociologist Stuart A. Rice. This is nothing more than a simple measurement of the extent to which a selected subgroup (determined by party, section, age, or any other appropriate attribute) of a deliberative body votes together. Hatzenbuehler uses it to measure party unity by determining the difference between the percentage of a party voting yea on a given vote and the percentage voting nay. If the party is split, 50 percent voting yea and 50 percent voting nay, the index is 0; if the vote is 60 percent to 40 percent the index is 20.[12]

The theoretical foundation of roll-call analysis lies in the assumption that legislators' votes are more likely to be informative than their speeches and that, when compared to the record of other legislators, these votes will reveal some sort of identifiable and measurable pattern of association, if only that certain types of legislators tended to vote alike (a not insignificant finding). The method also implies that roll calls do measure something worth measuring (whatever it is) and that this something, be it basic attitudes or merely agreed-on behavior, can provide insight into the legislative process. Like representative government itself, roll-call analysis goes on to the further assumption that the vote of legislative representatives will somehow reflect the wishes of those who elect them.

---

[9]Allan G. Bogue, "Bloc and Party in the United States Senate: 1861–1863," *Civil War History* 13 (September 1967):231.

[10]Richard E. Beringer, "The Unconscious 'Spirit of Party' in the Confederate Congress," *Civil War History* 18 (December 1972):312–33.

[11]William G. Eidson, "Who Were the Stalwarts?" *Mid-America* 52 (October 1970):235–61. For variations of this technique, see Charles M. Dollar, "The South and the Fordney-McCumber Tariff of 1922: A Study in Regional Politics," *Journal of Southern History* 39 (February 1973):45–66, which employs a correlation coefficient, phi, instead of a percentage to indicate the extent of agreement between pairs of legislators; and Mary P. Ryan, "Party Formation in the United States Congress, 1789 to 1796: A Quantitative Analysis," *William and Mary Quarterly,* 3d ser. 28 (October 1971):523–42, which adjusts the index of agreement by eliminating "the probable number of chance agreements" (p. 526). For more detailed discussion of cluster-bloc analysis, see Anderson, Watts, and Wilcox, *Legislative Roll-Call Analysis,* Chapter IV.

[12]For further information on the use of this and similar indices, see Anderson, Watts, and Wilcox, *Legislative Roll-Call Analysis,* Chapter III.

One difficulty with these techniques is that we may become so taken with the craftsmanship of a method that we pyramid assumptions, apply overly elegant tools to rough data, or, in general, pursue the method rather than the result. For this reason a simple unweighted performance score may be more suited to some legislative data than more complex procedures. And it may not always be true that lawmakers accurately represent their constituents; the claims of party, sectional loyalty, or personal obligation sometimes overcome the tie that binds the legislator to those he represents. Moreover, any technique used for roll-call analysis may have the effect of circumscribing possible conclusions. It tells us nothing about important issues that may not have come to a vote and it tempts the researcher to overemphasize the political process at the expense of the total historical context. Since this may result in an overemphasis on political history, conclusions are likely to be stated in political terms when economic or social explanations may have been more appropriate.

It is also sobering to realize that despite the rigid determinism implied by the quantitative analysis of legislative behavior, the margin of individuality remains great and unpredictable. Not everyone fitting into a neat socioeconomic or political category behaves the way the category predicts. This warning is underlined by interviews that political scientist Wilder Crane, Jr., held with members of the 1957 Wisconsin Assembly. Much to his surprise, Crane discovered that roll calls that behavioral techniques indicated were party votes often were the result of nonparty pressures and frequently were not even perceived as party votes by the legislators who cast them. In fact, concluded Crane, "Party cohesion was most easily maintained on those issues about which legislators were least concerned and apparently regarded as least important." It thus appears that party loyalty and party interests are not necessarily measured by the voting record of the members of that party.[13]

In the following article, Ronald L. Hatzenbuehler uses three of the techniques discussed above to analyze the House of Representatives in 1812. In a deleted portion of the essay the author indicates that he did not study all roll calls but instead eliminated votes on which there were excessive absences, those with less than 10 percent dissent from majority opinion, and those on which there was less than 5 percent dissent within either party; inclusion of such roll calls would muffle divisions and present a false picture of inter- and intraparty harmony. Note the detail in Table I. Q refers to the statistical test used to eliminate roll calls with too many error responses. Given the information in this table, any student could duplicate Table II, thereby checking its accuracy; in addition to providing an indicator of the subjects that measured the war dimension, Table I also serves much like a footnote, allowing anyone to look up the source of the individual information in Table II.

[13]Wilder Crane, Jr., "A Caveat on Roll-Call Studies of Party Voting," *Midwest Journal of Political Science* 4 (August 1960):237–49, quote from p. 247.

Readers should decide for themselves whether the author succeeds in disentangling the intermingled strands of section and party. The two attributes created the attitudes Hatzenbuehler tries to measure, and it is often difficult to separate them. Nevertheless, the author concludes that Roger H. Brown was correct in contending that party was more important than section or attitude in determining representatives' support for the War of 1812.[14]

Party Unity and the Decision for War in the House of Representatives, 1812
Ronald L. Hatzenbuehler

. . . The present study utilizes an index of cohesion, scaling, and cluster-bloc analysis to study roll calls related to foreign policy in the House of Representatives during the first session of the Twelfth Congress, from November 4, 1811, to June 18, 1812, the date of the final votes on the bill declaring war. This presentation involves a wider range of roll-call behavior within a larger universe than has previously been attempted, but the special tactical problems arising from such a decision do not outweigh the potential benefits. For the purpose of a more nearly complete roll-call analysis, the House provides greater possibilities than the Senate for three reasons: (1) the larger number of roll calls dealing specifically with foreign affairs which the House recorded during the first session; (2) the larger sectional groupings; and (3) the larger number of Federalists potentially in opposition to the Republican majority.

Of the 166 roll calls in the House during this timespan, 113 non-unanimous votes were generally related to foreign affairs, with Federalists and Republicans in opposition to one another on 98 of the votes (87 percent). From a graph of the two parties' indexes of cohesion over time (Figures 1 and 2 in Appendix), one sees this divergence of party policies even more clearly. In particular, two trends are obvious. First, both parties were able to maintain a relatively high degree of unity throughout the session. Republicans fell below an index of fifty (a 75-25 percent split) forty-two times from November through June 18. The Federalists fell below it only twenty times. Secondly, a point arose in the session when the cohesion of both parties increased sharply . . . the Republican jump corresponding with the second reading of a bill to borrow $11 million on February 24, and the Federalist tightening with the first war tax resolution on

[14]Roger H. Brown, *The Republic in Peril: 1812* (New York: Columbia University Press, 1964), pp. 39–66, 73. For further examination of the War Hawk controversy using quantitative methods to analyze legislative behavior, see Ronald L. Hatzenbuehler, "The War Hawks and the Question of Congressional Leadership in 1812," *Pacific Historical Review* 45 (February 1976):1–22.

Ronald L. Hatzenbuehler, "Party Unity and the Decision for War in the House of Representatives, 1812," *William and Mary Quarterly*, 3rd ser., XXIX (July 1972), 371–390. Copyright © 1972, by the Institute of Early American History and Culture. Reprinted with deletion of notes and abridgment by permission of the author and the *William and Mary Quarterly*, in which it first appeared.

February 27. From February 24 through the final war votes, Republicans fell below the fifty mark only fifteen times (20 percent of the votes as compared to 68 percent prior to this point). Once again, the Federalists attained a higher degree of party unity as they fell below the mark only three times after February 27, a miniscule 4 percent.

The loan and the war taxes were direct responses by the Republican majority in the House to President James Madison's State of the Union Message presented to Congress on November 5, 1811. In his message, the President asked the lawmakers to "feel the duty of putting the United States into an armor and an attitude demanded by the crisis, and corresponding with the national spirit and expectations." Specifically, he recommended that the military establishment be strengthened and that new sources of revenue be tapped to provide for military preparedness. After nearly a four-month delay, on February 26 the Ways and Means Committee finally presented fourteen resolutions for raising taxes to support a war with a European nation.

The financing of the war marked an especially significant stage for the Federalists in cementing their party unity. As a whole, the Federalist congressmen generally took no part in the debates of the first session, believing that the Republicans used Federalist opposition only to consolidate their own party's position. As one Federalist explained, "The cry of British party, and British influence has been managed with great adroitness and success. This [silence] has stript them of this weapon, and now they have not to plead . . . Federal opposition as an apology for the continuance of the restrictive system.". . .

Another way to test the strength of party unity than a cohesion index is to compare party loyalty with other explanations for a legislator's vote, such as attitudinal or sectional reasons. In a scale reflecting a representative's position toward roll calls related to foreign policy (Tables I and II), the diversity one might expect within rankings from zero to fourteen does not occur. The construction of the scale purposely emphasizes the extreme positions (zero and fourteen), and yet one finds 46.5 percent of the total number of scaled legislators (58 of 125) in these most extreme categories (Table II).

When one adds to these two groups of legislators others whose scale positions may be viewed as similarly extreme, the division between aggressives and non-aggressives becomes even more striking, and the moderate position virtually disappears (Table III).

In our own day, issues of foreign policy often evoke a comparable polarization of attitudes. Are there other explanations for this extreme divergency? A breakdown of the legislators into sectional groupings (Table IV) revealed that the South and West section was most favorable to war and the Northeast was least favorable. The Middle States were the most diverse with six of the seven moderates in the scale belonging to this section.

A division of the legislators by party as well as section, however, proved to be more informative than the attitudinal or sectional groupings alone (Table V). Two patterns are evident from such a presentation. First, Republicans and Federalists opposed one

Table I   **Sample of Foreign Policy Roll Calls**
Q = .8 or Higher

Scale Number	Volume and Page (Annals)	Date	Subject	Positive Response	Cohesion Index		Number of Ties
					Rep.	Fed.	
1	1/545-6	Dec. 16	Raise additional troops for a period of three years.	Y	91	3	6
	1/800-1	Jan. 17	Raising a volunteer corps—final vote.	Y	88	20	
2	1/716-7	Jan. 9	Postpone consideration on bill to raise additional troops as amended by the Senate.	N	87	44	3
	1/1092	Feb. 25	Borrow $11 million—final reading.	Y	91	43	
3	1/617	Jan. 2	Raise additional troops—second reading.	Y	76	45	0
	1/691	Jan. 6	Raise additional troops—final reading.	Y	75	44	
4	2/1636-7	June 4	Motion to adjourn.	N	74	82	0
	2/1635-6	June 4	Postpone decision on bill to declare war until June 5.	N	67	89	
	2/1635	June 4	Postpone decision on bill to declare war until the first Monday in October.	N	73	82	
5	1/340	Nov. 12	Motion to send Madison's State of the Union Message to a special committee on the state of the union.	N	91	76	6
	1/341	Nov. 12	Motion to read the documents connected with Madison's State of the Union Message.	N	77	61	

Table I   Continued

Scale Number	Volume and Page (Annals)	Date	Subject	Positive Response	Cohesion Index		Number of Ties
					Rep.	Fed.	
6	2/1632	June 3	Defeat bill declaring war.	N	68	82	1
	2/1634-5	June 4	Second reading of bill to declare war.	Y	69	82	
7	2/1681-2	June 18	Postpone declaration of war to the first Monday in October.	N	69	84	2
	2/1682	June 18	Postpone declaration of war to the first Monday in July.	N	65	84	
8	2/1637	June 4	Final vote for war.	Y	63	83	
9	1/1108	Feb. 27	War Taxes, Resolution 1. Add to duties on imports.	Y	79	82	5
	2/1470-8	May 29	Resolution: Inexpedient to resort to war against Great Britain at this time.	N	75	86	
10	2/1630-1	June 3	Vote to remove secrecy on the bill declaring war.	N	68	88	0
	2/1631-2	June 3	Open the doors of the House to discussion of the bill declaring war.	N	72	89	

11	1/1111-2	Feb. 27	War Taxes, Resolution 3. Add to tax rate on foreign ships per ton.	Y	81	73	7
	1/1148	Mar. 4	War Taxes, Resolution 6. Tax on licenses to retailers of wines, etc.	Y	65	81	
12	1/793-4	Jan. 15	Amendment on bill to raise a volunteer corps.	N	76	84	
13	1/1111	Feb. 27	War Taxes, Resolution 2. Retain 25 per cent of the drawbacks on exports.	Y	73	89	12
	1/1150-1	Mar. 4	War Taxes, Resolution 9. Duties on carriages for transport of persons.	Y	78	89	
14	1/1161	Mar. 6	Resolution to cut funds from maritime defenses.	Y	57	89	

Note: In forming a scale, roll calls of similar subject matter and voting patterns can often be combined to form "contrived items," thereby minimizing the number of absences of legislators in the scale. Items 12 and 14 could not be combined with roll calls of similar content or voting pattern without an excessive number of tied votes occurring (13 dichotomous responses represent about a 10% error). The final vote for war (item 8) stands alone because of its special content. For a discussion of "contrived items," see Anderson et al., *Roll-Call Analysis*, 107.

Table II **Scale of Foreign Policy Roll Calls First Session, Twelfth Congress: House of Representatives**

Representative	Party-State	Scale Type	1	2	3	4	5	6	7	8	9	10	11	12	13	14
Alston	R-NC	14	+	+	+	+	+	+	+	+	+	+	+	+	+	+
Bard	R-Pa	14	+	+	+	+	+	+	+	+	+	+	+	+	+	+
Bibb	R-Ga	14	+	+	+	+	+	+	+	+	+	+	+	+	+	+
Brown	R-Pa	14	+	+	+	+	+	+	+	+	+	+	+	+	+	+
Burwell	R-Va	14	+	+	+	+	+	+	+	+	+	+	+	+	+	+
Butler	R-SC	14	+	+	+	+	+	+	+	+	+	+	+	+	+	+
Calhoun	R-SC	14	+	+	+	+	+	+	+	+	+	+	+	+	+	+
Crawford	R-Pa	14	+	+	+	+	+	+	+	+	+	+	+	+	+	+
Davis	R-Pa	14	+	+	+	+	+	+	+	+	+	+	+	+	+	+
Desha	R-Ky	14	+	+	+	+	+	+	+	+	+	+	+	+	+	+
Earle	R-SC	14	+	+	+	+	+	+	+	+	+	+	+	+	+	+
Hall, O.	R-NH	14	+	+	+	+	+	+	+	+	+	+	+	+	+	+
Harper	R-NH	14	+	+	+	+	+	+	+	+	+	+	+	+	+	+
Kent	F-Md	14	+	+	+	+	+	+	+	+	+	+	+	+	+	+
Lacock	R-Pa	14	+	+	+	+	+	+	+	+	+	+	+	+	+	+
Lyle	R-Pa	14	+	+	+	+	+	+	+	+	+	+	+	+	+	+
Moore	R-SC	14	+	+	+	+	+	+	+	+	+	+	+	+	+	+
McCoy	R-Va	14	+	+	+	+	+	+	+	+	+	+	+	+	+	+
Morrow	R-Oh	14	+	+	+	+	+	+	+	+	+	+	+	+	+	+
Rhea	R-Te	14	+	+	+	+	+	+	+	+	+	+	+	+	+	+
Roane	R-Va	14	+	+	+	+	+	+	+	+	+	+	+	+	+	+
Sage	R-NY	14	+	+	+	+	+	+	+	+	+	+	+	+	+	+
Seaver	R-Ma	14	+	+	+	+	+	+	+	+	+	+	+	+	+	+
Smith, G.	R-Pa	14	+	+	+	+	+	+	+	+	+	+	+	+	+	+
Troup	R-Ga	14	+	+	+	+	+	+	+	+	+	+	+	+	+	+
Findley	R-Pa	14	+	+	+	+	+	+	+	+	+	+	+	+	+	O
Cheves	R-SC	14	+	+	+	+	+	+	+	+	+	+	+	+	+	O
Johnson	R-Ky	14	+	+	+	+	+	+	+	+	+	+	+	+	+	O
Lowndes	R-SC	14	+	+	+	+	+	+	+	+	+	+	+	+	+	O
New	R-Ky	14	+	+	+	+	+	+	+	+	+	+	+	+	+	O
Ormsby	R-Ky	14	+	+	+	+	+	+	+	+	+	+	+	+	+	O
Piper	R-Pa	14	+	+	+	+	+	+	+	+	+	+	+	+	+	O
Cochran	R-NC	14	+	+	+	+	O	+	+	+	+	+	+	+	+	+
Taliaferro	R-Va	14	+	+	+	+	O	+	+	+	+	+	+	+	+	+
Whitehill	R-Pa	14	+	+	O	+	+	+	+	+	+	+	+	+	+	+
Winn	R-SC	14	+	+	+	+	+	+	+	+	+	+	+	+	+	+
Goodwyn	R-Va	14	+	+	O	+	+	+	+	+	+	+	O	+	+	+
Ringgold	R-Md	14	+	+	+	+	O	+	+	+	+	+	+	+	+	O
Dawson	R-Va	14	+	+	+	+	+	+	+	+	+	+	+	O	+	O
Clopton	R-Va	14	+	+	+	+	O	+	+	+	+	O	+	O	O	O
Franklin	R-NC	14	+	+	+	O	+	O	+	O	+	O	+	+	+	+
Clay, M.	R-Va	14	+	+	+	O	+	O	O	O	+	O	+	+	+	+

Table II   **Continued**

Representative	Party-State	Scale Type	1	2	3	4	5	6	7	8	9	10	11	12	13	14
Hall, B.	R-Ga	13	x	+	+	+	+	+	+	+	+	+	+	+	+	+
Pond	R-NY	13	+	+	+	+	+	+	+	+	+	x	+	+	+	+
Smith, J.	R-Va	13	+	+	+	+	+	+	x	+	+	+	+	+	+	+
Dinsmoor	R-NH	13	+	+	+	+	+	+	+	+	+	+	+	+	x	+
Morgan	F-NJ	13	+	+	+	+	+	+	+	+	+	+	+	+	x	+
McKim	R-Md	13	+	+	+	+	+	+	+	+	+	+	+	+	x	+
Seybert	R-Pa	13	x	+	+	+	+	+	+	+	+	+	+	+	+	0
Anderson	R-Pa	13	+	+	+	+	+	+	+	+	+	+	+	+	x	0
Strong	R-Vt	13	+	+	+	+	+	+	+	+	+	+	+	0	x	+
Lefever	R-Pa	13	+	+	+	+	+	+	+	+	+	+	+	x	+	+
Pleasants	R-Va	13	0	+	0	+	x	+	+	+	+	+	+	0	+	+
Blackledge	R-NC	13	+	+	+	+	+	+	+	+	+	+	+	+	+	-
Condict	R-NJ	13	+	+	+	+	+	+	+	+	+	+	+	+	+	-
Green	R-Ma	13	+	+	+	+	+	+	+	+	+	+	+	+	+	-
Little	R-Md	13	+	+	+	+	+	+	+	+	+	+	+	+	+	-
Newton	R-Va	13	+	+	+	+	+	+	+	+	+	+	+	+	+	-
Roberts	R-Pa	13	+	+	+	+	+	+	+	+	+	+	+	+	+	-
Sevier	R-Te	13	+	+	+	+	+	+	+	+	+	+	+	+	+	-
Hyneman	R-Pa	13	+	+	+	+	+	+	+	+	+	+	-	+	+	+
Grundy	R-Te	13	+	+	+	+	+	+	+	+	+	+	-	+	+	+
McKee	R-Ky	13	+	+	+	+	+	+	+	+	+	+	-	+	+	+
Pickens	R-NC	13	+	+	+	+	+	+	+	+	+	+	-	+	+	+
Gholson	R-Va	13	+	+	+	+	0	+	+	+	+	+	+	-	+	+
Shaw	R-Vt	13	+	+	+	+	+	+	+	+	+	+	0	+	~	+
Porter	R-NY	13	+	+	+	+	0	+	0	0	0	+	0	+	-	+
Wright	R-Md	13	+	+	+	+	+	+	+	+	+	+	x	+	+	-
Bacon	R-Ma	13	x	+	+	0	+	0	0	0	+	0	+	-	+	+
Smilie	R-Pa	13	+	+	-	+	+	0	+	+	+	0	+	+	+	+
Turner	R-Ma	12	+	+	+	+	+	+	+	+	x	+	+	+	x	-
Widgery	R-Ma	12	+	+	+	+	+	+	x	+	-	0	+	+	x	+
Archer	R-Md	12	+	+	+	+	+	+	+	+	+	+	+	-	+	-
Bassett	R-Va	12	+	+	+	+	+	+	+	+	-	+	+	+	+	-
Hawes	R-Va	12	+	+	+	+	+	+	+	+	+	-	+	-	+	+
Williams	R-SC	12	+	+	+	+	+	+	+	+	-	+	-	0	+	0
Metcalf	R-NY	12	+	+	+	+	+	-	+	-	+	+	x	+	+	+
Richardson	F-Ma	12	0	+	0	+	0	+	+	+	+	-	+	0	x	-
Fisk	R-Vt	11	x	+	+	+	+	+	+	+	x	+	x	+	-	-
Nelson	R-Va	11	+	+	+	+	x	+	+	+	x	+	+	-	+	-
Macon	R-NC	11	+	x	+	+	x	+	+	+	x	+	+	+	+	+
King	R-NC	11	+	+	+	+	-	+	+	+	+	+	+	-	+	-
Sammons	R-NY	10	+	+	+	-	+	+	0	-	+	+	-	+	+	-
Mitchill	R-NY	9	+	+	+	+	+	x	-	-	+	+	-	+	-	0
Van Courtlandt	R-NY	6	+	+	+	+	+	-	-	-	0	-	-	+	-	0
Sullivan	F-NH	4	+	+	+	-	-	-	-	-	-	-	+	0	0	0
Tracy	R-NY	4	+	+	+	-	+	-	-	-	-	-	-	0	x	-
Stow	F-NY	4	+	+	-	-	+	0	-	-	-	0	x	+	-	-
Rodman	R-Pa	4	+	-	-	-	0	-	-	-	x	-	x	+	x	+

Table II **Continued**

Representative	Party-State	Scale Type	1	2	3	4	5	6	7	8	9	10	11	12	13	14
Reed	F-Ma	3	+	+	+	−	−	−	−	−	−	−	−	−	−	−
Emott	F-NY	3	+	+	+	−	−	−	−	−	−	−	−	O	−	−
Gold	F-NY	3	+	+	+	−	−	−	−	−	O	−	−	−	−	−
Quincy	F-Ma	3	+	+	+	−	−	−	−	−	−	−	−	O	−	O
Bleecker	F-NY	3	+	+	+	−	O	−	−	−	−	−	−	O	−	−
Milnor	F-Pa	3	+	x	+	−	−	−	−	−	−	−	−	O	−	−
McBryde	R-NC	2	+	−	−	−	O	−	−	−	−	−	−	+	−	O
Baker	F-Va	1	+	−	−	−	−	−	−	−	−	−	−	−	−	−
Wilson	F-Va	1	+	−	−	−	−	−	−	−	−	−	−	−	−	−
Breckinridge	F-Va	1	+	−	−	−	−	−	−	−	−	−	−	−	−	−
Ridgely	F-De	1	+	−	O	−	−	−	−	−	−	−	−	−	−	−
Goldsborough	F-Md	1	+	−	O	−	O	−	−	−	−	−	−	O	−	−
Key	F-Md	1	+	−	−	−	−	−	−	−	−	−	−	−	−	O
Randolph	R-Va	1	−	−	−	−	−	−	−	−	−	−	−	+	−	O
Chittenden	F-Vt	1	−	−	−	−	x	−	−	−	−	−	−	−	−	−
Ely	F-Ma	1	−	−	−	−	x	−	−	−	−	−	−	−	−	−
Taggart	F-Ma	1	−	−	−	−	x	−	−	−	−	−	−	−	−	−
Fitch	F-NY	1	x	−	−	−	−	−	−	−	−	−	−	−	−	−
Potter	F-RI	1	−	x	−	−	O	−	−	−	O	−	−	O	−	−
Stanford	R-NC	1	x	−	−	−	−	−	−	−	−	−	−	−	x	−
Jackson	F-RI	0	−	−	−	−	−	−	−	−	−	−	−	−	−	−
Law	F-Ct	0	−	−	−	−	−	−	−	−	−	−	−	−	−	−
Lewis	F-Va	0	−	−	−	−	−	−	−	−	−	−	−	−	−	−
Moseley	F-Ct	0	−	−	−	−	−	−	−	−	−	−	−	−	−	−
Sturges	F-Ct	0	−	−	−	−	−	−	−	−	−	−	−	−	−	−
Wheaton	F-Ma	0	−	−	−	−	−	−	−	−	−	−	−	−	−	−
White	R-Ma	0	−	−	−	−	−	−	−	−	−	−	−	−	−	−
Brigham	F-Ma	0	−	−	−	−	−	−	−	−	−	−	O	−	−	−
Champion	F-Ct	0	−	−	−	−	−	−	−	−	−	−	O	−	−	−
Davenport	F-Ct	0	−	−	−	−	−	−	−	−	−	−	−	−	−	O
Pearson	F-NC	0	−	−	−	−	−	−	−	−	−	−	−	−	−	−
Stuart	F-Md	0	O	−	−	−	−	−	−	−	−	−	−	O	−	−
Tallmadge	F-Ct	0	−	−	−	−	−	−	−	−	−	−	−	O	−	−
Pitkin	F-Ct	0	−	−	−	−	−	−	−	−	−	−	−	−	−	−
Bigelow	F-Ma	0	−	−	−	O	−	O	−	O	−	O	−	−	−	−
Sheffey	F-Va	0	−	−	−	O	−	O	−	O	−	O	−	−	−	−

Total Positive Responses = 96 92 87 80 77 77 77 77 77 74 74 73 70 56
Total Respondents = 125

Notes: + = positive response; − = negative response; × = tied response. Two tied responses per individual raise or lower the scale type one rank. Tied responses were treated as error responses when computing the coefficient of reproducibility (CR = .94). Adam Boyd, Jacob Hufty, George C. Maxwell, and Thomas Newbold (all Republicans from New Jersey) were eliminated because their responses would not scale; other missing legislators did not respond to two-thirds of the scale items.

Table III **Foreign Policy Issue, Attitude Frequency Twelfth Congress, First Session: House of Representatives**

	Scale Type	Number	Percentage
Aggressive	(14-11)	82	65.6
Moderate	(10- 4)	7	5.6
Non-aggressive	(3- 0)	36	28.8
	totals	125	100.0

another diametrically in every section. This opposition appears to have been especially intense in the South and West and Northeast as both factions attained approximately 90 percent cohesion. More diversity was evident in the Middle States, but the party division was virtually the same as in the other two sections. Secondly, the polarization of attitudes evidenced in Table III may be best explained in terms of these partisan divisions. In other words, the attitudinal diversity [i.e., aggressive, moderate, or non-aggressive] is of less importance than the two parties' differing views on the conduct of foreign policy. . . .

A cluster-bloc analysis of the sectional groupings also emphasized a partisan voting pattern rather than factional or geographical ones, especially in the South and West and Northeast where Republicans and Federalists were most heavily concentrated (Figures 3 and 4 in Appendix). In each matrix a near perfect division existed between the two parties. At the 80 percent cohesion level, the diverse Republican blocs are intriguing but at lower levels collapse due to the absence of moderate scale types and the lack of cross-party voting. For example, at the 70 percent cohesion level, the left corner of Figure 3 becomes one bloc. Extensive manuscript research would be necessary before much significance could be assigned to the specific differences between the Republican groups in each section.

One additional observation from the results of the cluster-bloc analysis relates to James Sterling Young's scrutiny of the Washington society of this period. Young discovered that "boarding house fraternities" which developed among the legislators were often more influential in determining political attitudes than partisan or sectional ties. For example, during the Twelfth Congress Abijah Bigelow roomed in Washington with Elijah Brigham and dined with Brigham and William Ely from Massachusetts, Epaphroditus Champion, Jonathan O. Moseley, Lewis B. Sturges, and Lyman Law from Connecticut, Martin Chittenden from Vermont, and Asa Fitch from New York. Figure 4 in the Appendix shows the high voting cohesion of this group (minus Fitch) and would seem to support Young's perceptive insights. The fact that they were all Federalists, however, would also indicate that by the Twelfth Congress party ties had become more important than Young would admit.

. . . Concerning the War Hawk controversy, one may easily distingush from the voting scales a group of representatives who may be classified as "hawks" as well as a

Table IV   Foreign Policy Issue, Sectional Division
Twelfth Con Twelfth Congress, First Session: House of Representatives

Scale Type	South and West		Middle		Northeast	
	No.	Per Cent	No.	Per Cent	No.	Per Cent
Aggressive (14-11)	42	82.4	28	65.1	12	38.7
Moderate (10- 4)	–	–	6	14.0	1	3.2
Non-aggressive (3- 0)	9	17.6	9	20.9	18	58.1
totals	51	100.0	43	100.0	31	100.0

South and West   Virginia, North Carolina, South Carolina, Georgia, Tennessee, Kentucky, and Ohio.

Middle   Pennsylvania, Maryland, New York, New Jersey, and Delaware.

Northeast   Massachusetts, New Hampshire, Vermont, Connecticut, and Rhode Island.

Table V   Foreign Policy Issue Divided by Section and Party Twelfth Congress, First Session: House of Representatives

	Scale Type	Republicans		Federalists	
		No.	Per Cent	No.	Per Cent
South and West					
Aggressive	(14-11)	42	93.3	—	—
Moderate	(10- 4)	—	—	—	—
Non-aggressive	(3- 0)	3	6.7	6	100.0
totals		45	100.0	6	100.0
Middle					
Aggressive	(14-11)	26	83.9	2	16.7
Moderate	(10- 4)	5	16.1	1	8.3
Non-aggressive	(3- 0)	—	—	9	75.0
totals		31	100.0	12	100.0
Northeast					
Aggressive	(14-11)	11	91.7	1	5.3
Moderate	(10- 4)	—	—	1	5.3
Non-aggressive	(3- 0)	1	8.3	17	89.4
totals		12	100.0	19	100.0

group of ''doves.'' And yet, these same divisions may best be labeled Republicans and Federalists as only one Federalist was included in the forty-two legislators in the most aggressive scale type of fourteen, and only one Republican was in the most non-aggressive scale type of zero (Table II). Republican voting became especially cohesive after the war taxes were introduced, but the voting scales indicate that a warlike attitude was present from the beginning of the session. An analysis of the Eleventh Congress and previous Congresses would be necessary to help resolve the larger question of when this party transformation occurred.

In summary, the three statistical techniques—index of cohesion, cluster-bloc analysis, and scaling—although they organized the data differently, each presented overwhelming evidence to support the conclusion that Republican party unity was the determining factor in the decision of the House of Representatives to declare war on Great Britain in June of 1812. This study, therefore, supports Roger H. Brown's contentions, based on the final war vote, that a division of legislators by party explains the voting pattern better than one by geographical blocs or attitudinal considerations. From an analysis of the foreign policy related roll calls over the entire session, however, it is apparent that Brown understated his evidence in support of his major thesis of Republican concerns over their imperiled nation. . . .

When historians debate the conflicting reasons for the declaration of war in the House of Representatives in 1812, they generally minimize the importance of the legislators' partisan motivations. However, a congressman who broke party ties was an exceptional case, and both parties exhibited remarkably strong wills to survive as organizations when confronted with potentially disruptive pressures within or outside their ranks. The victorious Republican faction molded a consensus at the beginning of the session which favored a declaration of war and either adjusted or abandoned positions which threatened to destroy the cohesion necessary to realize its goal. By June the war issue had become so thoroughly entangled with partisan political strategies that the decision for war must be viewed in terms of Republican party unity.

APPENDIX

Figure 1

Republican Party Index of Cohesion Values for Non-unanimous Foreign Policy Roll Calls
Twelfth Congress, First Session: House of Representatives

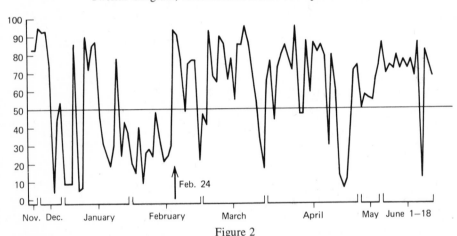

Figure 2

Federalist Party Index of Cohesion Values for Non-unanimous Foreign Policy Roll Calls
Twelfth Congress, First Session: House of Representatives

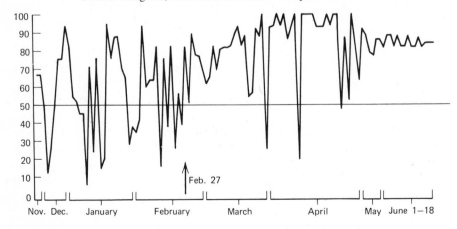

Figure 3
South and West Section Pair-wise Voting Scores on Sixty-three Foreign Policy Roll Calls
Twelfth Congress, First Session: House of Representatives

	Alston, R-NC	Bassett, R-Va	Lowndes, R-SC	Troup, R-Ga	Cheves, R-SC	Calhoun, R-SC	Roane, R-Va	Bibb, R-Ga	Ormsby, R-Ky	Grundy, R-Te	Desha, R-Ky	New, R-Ky	Morrow, R-Oh	Johnson, R-Ky	Butler, R-SC	Hall, R-Ga	Pickens, R-NC	King, R-NC	Gholson, R-Va	McCoy, R-Va	McKee, R-Ky	Moore, R-SC	Franklin, R-NC	Earle, R-SC	Dawson, R-Va	Newton, R-Va	Cochran, R-NC	Sevier, R-Te	Rhea, R-Te	Winn, R-SC	Hawes, R-Va	Blackledge, R-NC	Burwell, R-Va	Smith, R, Va	Clay, R-Va
Alston, R-NC		51		53	50	52	55																	52								51			
Bassett, R-Va	51		57		52	52	53																												
Lowndes, R-SC		57		53	56	54	51																			50									
Troup, R-Ga	53		53		52	52	52		54	54				52									52	51	50										
Cheves, R-SC	50	52	56	52		53	50	51	50			50				50			50																
Calhoun, R-SC	52	52	54	52	53		52	51	50	51				50	50						52											51			
Roane, R-Va	55	53	51	52	50	52		54	55	56	56	53	53		52	54	53	51	53	50		50													
Bibb, R-Ga				51	51	54		54	53	55	52	54	54		53	50		54	50	52											51	50			
Ormsby, R-Ky				50	50	55	54		54	52	53	53	53		52		51																		
Grundy, R-Te			54		51		56	53	54		51	52	50	54	51													51	50						
Desha, R-Ky		54			56	55	52	51		54	52	52	53	53	54	50	50	51	50	50															
New, R-Ky				53	52	53	52	54		51	55	52	50	51		50																			
Morrow, R-Oh			50		53	54	53	50	52	51		51	50		51			53		52		50													
Johnson, R-Ky					54	53	54	52	52	51		54			50	51					51														
Butler, R-SC		52			52			51	53	52	50	54					50	51													50				
Hall, R-Ga					54	53	52		53	50							50	50																	
Pickens, R-NC					50	53	50		54	51	51		50		53	53		51			50														
King, R-NC					50	50	51		51		50				50	53																			
Gholson, R-Va								53				50		50	53														53						
McCoy, R-Va								50				51	50		51																				
McKee, R-Ky								54				50		53					51																
Moore, R-SC								50				50							51								50								
Franklin, R-NC				50		50	52																												
Earle, R-SC	52		52									52													50	51									
Dawson, R-Va		51		52								51													50	50		50							
Newton, R-Va		50	50																						51	50									
Cochran, R-NC												50			50			50												50					
Sevier, R-Te									51																				52						50
Rhea, R-Te									50																			52							
Winn, R-SC																											50								
Hawes, R-Va																	53																		
Blackledge, R-NC	51																																		
Burwell, R-Va											50																								
Smith, R-Va				51																															
Clay, R-Va																											50								

Fringe

ᵃ 80% agreement matrix

Figure 3
Continuation of Original Matrix

	McBryde, R-NC	Pearson, F-NC	Randolph, R-Va	Lewis, F-Va	Wilson, F-Va	Breckinridge, F-Va	Baker, F-Va	Stanford, R-NC	Gray, F-Va	Sheffey, F-Va
McBryde, R-NC		50								
Pearson, F-NC	50			50	50					
Randolph, R-Va				55	52			50		
Lewis, F-Va			55		52	51	52			
Wilson, F-Va	50	52	52			54	55			
Breckinridge, F-Va			51	54			60			
Baker, F-Va		50	52	55	60					
Stanford, R-NC		50								
Gray, F-Va										50
Sheffey, F-Va									50	

305

Figure 3.1
Two Additional Blocs Hidden in the Original Matrix

	Troup, R-Ga	Earle, R-SC	Dawson, R-Va	Newton, R-Va	Grundy, R-Te	Sevier, R-Te	Rhea, R-Te
Troup, R-Ga		52	51	50			
Earle, R-SC	52		50	51			
Dawson, R-Va	51	50		50			
Newton, R-Va	50	51	50				
Grundy, R-Te						51	50
Sevier, R-Te					51		52
Rhea, R-Te					50	52	

Figure 4
rtheast Section Pair-wise Voting Scores on Sixty-Three Foreign Policy Roll Calls Twelfth Congress, First Session: House of Representatives [a]

	Fisk, R-Vt	Shaw, R-Vt	Dinsmoor, R-NH	Green, R-Ma	Hall, R-NH	Seaver, R-Ma	Strong, R-Vt	Harper, R-NH	Turner, R-Ma	Quincy, F-Ma	Reed, F-Ma	White, R-Ma	Brigham, F-Ma	Moseley, F-Ct	Sturges, F-Ct	Bigelow, F-Ma	Champion, F-Ct	Chittenden, F-Vt	Davenport, F-Ct	Ely, F-Ma	Jackson, F-RI	Law, F-Ct	Pitkin, F-Ct	Potter, F-RI	Taggart, F-Ma	Wheaton, F-Ma	Tallmadge, F-Ct
Fisk, R-Vt		52	51																								
Shaw, R-Vt	52		52																								
Dinsmoor, R-NH	51	52		52		52																					
Green, R-Ma			52		55	50			51																		
Hall, R-NH				55		54	50																				
Seaver, R-Ma				50	54		55																				
Strong, R-Vt					50	55																					
Harper, R-NH			52																								
Turner, R-Ma				51																							
Quincy, F-Ma											59																
Reed, F-Ma										59		50	51	51	51												
White, R-Ma											50		60	62	62	53	57	58	60	60	60	60	58	55	59	60	55
Brigham, F-Ma											51	60		61	61	54	58	57	61	59	59	59	59	58	58	59	56
Moseley, F-Ct											51	62	61		63	54	58	59	61	61	61	61	59	56	60	61	54
Sturges, F-Ct											51	62	61	63		54	58	59	61	61	61	61	59	56	60	61	54
Bigelow, F-Ma												53	54	54	54		51	50	52	52	52	52	50	51	51	51	54
Champion, F-Ct												57	58	58	58	51		56	60	56	60	58	56	53	55	58	53
Chittenden, F-Vt												58	57	59	59	50	56		57	61	57	57	59	56	60	59	54
Davenport, F-Ct												60	61	61	61	52	60	57		59	61	61	59	56	58	59	54
Ely, F-Ma												60	59	61	61	52	56	61	59		59	59	61	58	62	59	52
Jackson, F-RI												60	59	61	61	52	60	57	61	59		61	57	54	58	59	52
Law, F-Ct												60	59	61	61	52	58	57	61	59	61		57	54	58	59	54
Pitkin, F-Ct												58	59	59	59	50	56	59	59	61	57	57		58	60	57	52
Potter, F-RI												55	58	56	56	51	53	56	56	58	54	54	58		57	56	51
Taggart, F-Ma												59	58	60	60	51	55	60	58	62	58	58	60	57		58	53
Wheaton, F-Ma												60	59	61	61	54	58	59	59	59	59	59	57	56	58		54
Tallmadge, F-Ct												55	56	54	54	53	54	54	52	52	54	52	52	51	53	54	

[a] 80% agreement matrix

306

chapter nineteen
Cliometrics

Cliometrics, or the New Economic History, stirred up just as much controversy within its corner of the historical profession as any of the other quantitative approaches did in theirs, but the methodological debate was hardly noticed by the remainder of the discipline. Most economic historians who employ quantitative techniques were originally trained in economics, not history, and for that reason the quantitative revolution came earlier to economic history than to political, social, or urban history, and was relatively unnoticed. Ordinary historians tended to ignore the change even if they were aware of it.

Quantification was initially applied to economic history as a simple descriptive technique, using figures to illustrate points of a narrative, explain trends, or demonstrate differences, but this was not really the New Economic History. A more sophisticated level of quantification was introduced when statistical procedures were applied to incomplete or otherwise inadequate data in order to develop series that could be subjected to the application of economic theory. The 1958 publication by Alfred H. Conrad and John R. Meyer of their widely read article on "The Economics of Slavery in the Ante Bellum South" marked the emergence of cliometrics. This article employed capital theory to determine that, on the eve of the Civil War, slavery was profitable throughout the South, meaning that the rate of return was as great as that of other capital investments.[1] In addition, the New Economic History may involve precise, often complex mathematical models pretending to describe some historical situation, and may require gathering data that must be fit into the model. For the traditional historian, these econometric models are the most difficult aspect of the cliometric revolution to accept. By econometric we mean what the last few lines imply—the use of mathematics and statistics for the resolution of economic problems, specifically problems in economic history. But can mathematical models reflect history?

---

[1] Alfred H. Conrad and John R. Meyer, "The Economics of Slavery in the Ante Bellum South," *Journal of Political Economy* 66 (April 1958):96, 121.

One of the reasons for resistance to the cliometric invasion, as to all quantitative history, is that many historians do not realize the extent to which measurement is already involved in their thinking. This is especially so when the nature of the sources requires indirect rather than direct measurement, that is, when the information sought cannot be obtained directly by counting in the most appropriate source, but must instead be inferred from the measurement of some other attribute. Such inference requires that there be a mathematical relationship between what is wanted and what one measures, and this means bringing "equations into a literary discipline." As cliometrician Robert W. Fogel has pointed out, "equations have always been a part of historical literature." Formerly, however, "these equations were implicit, covert, and subliminal."[2]

The primary hallmark of the New Economic History is thus the employment of equations containing explicit assumptions. The significance of this explicitness, and the difference between the "old" and "new" histories, may be illustrated by two articles which appeared in the January, 1975, issue of *Agricultural History*. The first described the growth of wheat production in the Pacific Northwest. In the course of discussion it was suggested that because of the nature of the terrain early tractors were not particularly successful, and that it was not until the coming of the diesel caterpillar tractor in the 1930s that the horse and mule were replaced. This technical innovation was made possible, said the author, because a new tractor cost about $2000, and could replace over thirty horses or mules costing about $200 each. Simple arithmetic helped the farmer make the change.[3] Although the author used statistics to prove the economic advantages of change, he implied—he did not state—a covert equation.

In the second article Robert Higgs attempted to make this somewhat obscure, covert equation more explicit in order to permit broader generalization. His mathematical representation clarified the explanation of a farmer's decision to switch from horses or mules to tractors. Farmers wish to keep costs low, but "whether the shift to a new technique will or will not reduce total costs depends on (1) the technical superiority of the new technique, (2) the relative prices of the capital equipment required to implement the alternative techniques, and (3) the wage rate of labor." Higgs pointed out that when the costs of the two techniques were the same, farmers would be indifferent as to which to use. These principles were then written in the form of an equation:

$$k(dP_h + W) = dP_t + W$$

where k = the ratio of work that a farmer can perform with a tractor compared to that with an animal (measured, for example, in acres plowed)

P_h = price of a horse
P_t = price of a tractor

[2]Robert William Fogel, "The Limits of Quantitative Methods in History," *American Historical Review* 80 (April 1975):338.
[3]James F. Shepherd, "The Development of Wheat Production in the Pacific Northwest," *Agricultural History* 49 (January 1975):267.

d = interest rate plus depreciation rate, "assumed the same for both horses and tractors"

W = wages for labor, "assumed the same for both drivers of horses and drivers of tractors"

In this example the equation represents a state of indifference, when wages plus cost of investment in horses times the proportionally greater amount of work a tractor can do equals wages plus cost of investment in a tractor. If $k = 1$, tractor and horses are equally productive. If a farmer can do twice as much work with a tractor as with animals ($k = 2$), the formula indicates that a state of indifference between production techniques would exist only if tractor costs (depreciation and interest plus drivers' wages) were twice as high as animal costs and animal drivers' wages (i.e., there is then no point in giving up old Dobbin). In this state of indifference, points out Higgs, the farmer would not be motivated to switch from animals to tractors; but change would be rational as the two sides of the equation were no longer in balance, a situation that could be produced by a change in any of the elements of the equation. As tractor prices drop or tractor technology develops to the point where k is greater than 1, the more rational it becomes for a farmer to get a tractor, *given the assumptions of the equation*.[4]

These assumptions may seem unreasonable. Interest rates on horses or mules and tractors may not be the same, for one type of investment may entail more risk than the other. It may be that in an earlier era, when driving a tractor was an unusual skill and driving a horse was not, the tractor driver may have commanded a premium in wages. Furthermore, the farmer could look forward to a return on investment in horses in the form of a natural increase, which would of course be impossible with a tractor. There might also have been differences in maintenance costs (hay versus gasoline, veterinarian versus mechanic), and they too are excluded; but through his mathematical symbols Higgs explicitly stated that he was omitting these costs. The advantage of econometric history is that the historian's theoretical framework is explicit, and in this particular case Higgs acknowledged that the model was oversimplified. "The 'new' economic history," as cliometrician Lance E. Davis remarks, "may not be able to say much, but at least the reader is aware of what has been said."[5]

Despite these assumptions, Higgs' analysis allows far greater room for generalization than the original description of innovation in wheat growing in the Pacific Northwest. Of couse, it would not do to accept these figures as precise indicators of tractor prices or anything else. The econometric model is not a mechanical device to be accepted uncritically, nor should it be taken too literally. But algebraic manipulation of the explicit equation does permit drawing of helpful, if sometimes rough, conclusions. One caveat should be noted, however: empirical estimation of a mathematical model

[4]Robert Higgs, "Tractors or Horses? Some Basic Economics in the Pacific Northwest and Elsewhere," ibid., pp. 281–83.

[5]Lance Davis, "Professor Fogel and the New Economic History," *Economic History Review*, 2d ser. 19 (December 1966):658.

via econometric technique is limited by space and time. To generalize results to other places or periods requires the assumption that no significant changes in the environment would occur that would alter values. In other words, the model is time- and place-bound, unless specifically constructed to include other appropriate variables or altered to meet changed conditions. Due to modifications of work habits or market conditions, current models (i.e., theories) may not fit historical reality. A model that describes conditions in one place and time may not serve to depict similar situations at a later period. One might even say that cliometricians see economic history as a series of models, one following another, and that one of their tasks is to determine why a model that adequately describes one past reality is not capable of explaining a more recent reality and must therefore be replaced by a new one that does.[6]

The effort to achieve mathematical precision and explicit assumption is thus one of the theoretical bases of the New Economic History. A second is the "counterfactual proposition," in which the significance of some phenomenon in the real world is established by constructing a nonexistent world without that phenomenon and then measuring the differences between the two. Robert Fogel, a pioneer in the use of the counterfactual method, used it to construct a hypothetical United States that, in 1890, would have had no railroads. His goal was to determine whether or not railroads were essential to American economic development. In his hypothesis, railroads were replaced by a network of canals, which, supplemented by wagon roads, would supposedly have moved freight almost as efficiently and economically as the railroads did. In fact, concluded Fogel, the social savings of the railroads (total savings in costs to society, thereby releasing resources for other purposes) would only have been about one percent of the Gross National Product. If Fogel's computations were correct, it would appear that railroads were not as important for national development as has been thought.[7] By attempting first to determine the services canals and navigable rivers could have performed in 1890 in the absence of railroads (the counterfactual proposition), Fogel felt able to estimate the true advantage (social savings) that the railroad provided. It is like running an experiment, although obviously much more subjective than a laboratory experience.

The counterfactual proposition has aroused a great deal of debate about the New Economic History. Since, by definition, the counterfactual world never existed, determining its characteristics can be a rather sticky problem, especially for an extended period of time. But Lance E. Davis contends that the method is really not very remarkable at all and that only the explicit use of the counterfactual is new. To say that A caused B, Davis points out, is to imply the counterfactual argument that without A there would be no B; the argument is counterfactual in that A did exist, and in order to examine its consequences one is pretending for the moment that it did not. "In fact,"

[6]Paul A. David, *Technical Choice, Innovation and Economic Growth: Essays on American and British Experience in the Nineteenth Century* (Cambridge: Cambridge University Press, 1975), p. 14.

[7]Robert William Fogel, *Railroads and American Economic Growth: Essays in Econometric History* (Baltimore: The John Hopkins Press, 1964), see especially pp. 79–81, 92, 109–110, 208–219. Fogel's computations did not include nonagricultural products or passengers.

says Davis, there is "no way that cause and effect can be discussed without comparing the observed with the hypothetical."[8] But would not the absence of X in the past alter numerous other variables that would, in domino fashion, change still others? Obviously, the counterfactual technique must be used very carefully lest it become an exercise in futility.

The counterfactual proposition is only one of the vulnerable points of the New Economic History. No matter how elegant the mathematics, it is often quite another thing to find the proper data to substitute into an equation. This may take extended research of a more or less traditional variety, after which the information may often require manipulation to produce the data needed. Of course the data problem gets worse the further back in time one goes. Reliable statistics for the United States generally date from about 1930, and are exceedingly rare for the period prior to the Civil War. Hence the frequent necessity to utilize biased statistics and incomplete series, or to create series from a variety of different sources, adjusting the figures for the biases and omissions of each.

The mathematical simplicity and beauty of the econometric approach rest on some questionable assumptions. One is that human beings are completely rational. If they know how they can make more money, supposedly people will do so. But it would be wrong to infer individual motivation from these models. What may be true for most individuals is not likely to be true for all. Individuals are not always rational (as previous chapters have amply illustrated), and the rational way is not always followed because economic man is not the only man there is. To overemphasize economic man is to forget about the spiritual, intellectual, social, and psychological motivations that may be difficult—or more likely impossible—to measure, but that sometimes play a greater role in motivation than economic rationality. A good widget may be passed over in favor of one that only looks better, or, in the case of tractor versus horse, some farmers may have made the trade when k was less than 1 because manure would no longer get tracked into the house. And surely it would be fruitless to treat slavery only in economic terms, forgetting that it implied a way of life as well as a type of economy. Thus the Conrad and Meyer study of the profitability of slavery does not (and can not) take into account other motivations. Perhaps the major snare to the would-be cliometrician is the temptation to see nothing but the figures and to fail to apply basic historical knowledge. Regardless of their profit, planters and other southerners supported slavery because they thought it the only feasible system of racial accommodation. For those planters and others as well, economics is not the whole measure of the man. "A model is never a piece of history," "old" economic historian Fritz Redlich reminds us, "because it is conjectural or subjunctive or, in Max Weber's language used for all ideal types, a distortion of reality."[9]

---

[8]Lance E. Davis, " 'And It Will Never Be Literature': The New Economic History: A Critique," *Explorations in Entrepreneurial History,* 2d ser. 6 (Fall 1968):83–84.

[9]Fritz Redlich, " 'New' and Traditional Approaches to Economic History and Their Interdependence," *Journal of Economic History* 25 (December 1965):490.

Not only does the cliometric method assume people will always follow the road of economic rationality when given a choice, it also assumes they know when they have this choice and are able to see their own economic interests clearly—an assumption that high-interest loan companies, con men, and slick advertising artists have long managed to disprove for large segments of the population. No historical method illustrates more vividly the dangers of a method that limits the researcher's conclusions. If a variable, economic or otherwise, is not cranked into the equation its explanatory power will automatically be ignored. Thus those variables that cannot be measured are eliminated even though we know them to be powerful determinants of behavior. No study of slavery is complete without some attention being paid to the social outlook of the slaveholder, for example.

On the other hand, one of the major assumptions of any historian is that important events have a multiplicity of causes. The profession rightly looks with skepticism, even hostility, on those who insist on attributing events to the single cause for which they are likely to possess a monomania. One of the most notable characteristics of the cliometricians is that they understand the complex causation that underlies history. If the mathematical models they use become long and involved, it is because they are sensitive to this basic fact and attempt to include within their models as many significant, measurable influences as possible.

The following article, by Robert Higgs, may seem deceptively simple in light of these considerations. But most history students are quite unfamiliar with econometric methods: this article was selected specifically because it would be easy to follow for those whose last mathematics consisted of poorly recalled high school algebra. In a paragraph deleted from this presentation the author indicated this simplified presentation could contribute only partly to an understanding of Populist unrest. Furthermore, he remarked that the indices he developed are not as clear as he would like because appropriate data is not available. True to the precepts of the cliometric approach, Higgs criticizes his own results while his equation indicates the assumptions on which his analysis was based. Whatever the causes of rural discontent, Higgs believes that the cost of freight was one of them, and that economic reality and Populist rhetoric lead to the same conclusion.

In this instance, the symbolic representation of the relationships between the prices farmers received and prices paid at market is used to prove the inadequacy of one class of data that has sometimes been used to indicate farm prices. The proof is that, by the equation, a rise in $\alpha\beta$ biases Pn/t upward as an indicator of Pf/t. That is, an increase distance and tonnage necessarily produces a concomitant rise in prices at the market, even though the price paid to the farmer may have remained constant; price at market is therefore a misleading indicator of the farmers' economic well-being. Far more ade-more adequate, says Higgs, is a determination of prices paid to the farmer, Pf, by the method he suggests.

The reader must determine whether the indices are satisfactory, and whether conclusions based only on wheat, corn, and cotton prices can be considered reliable. Do we have here any more than a hint of the effect of freight rates on tobacco growers, produce farmers, or stockmen? And if Populists were most successful where transport charges were high, how are we to explain their relative lack of success in North Dakota? Transportation was expensive there too; but, contrary to Higgs' indication, Populism had only questionable success in 1892 (in fusion with the Democrats) and none thereafter, declining at the very time its influence was rising nationwide. Is this an example of an inadequate discussion of the historical context?[10]

Railroad Rates and the Populist Uprising
Robert Higgs

A prominent Populist complaint concerned "high" railroad freight rates. During the past two decades, however, economic historians have generally dismissed this complaint as inconsistent with the facts. The historians are apparently unanimous in believing that railroad freight rates fell steeply and steadily throughout the Gilded Age. The purpose of the present paper is to show that this belief, insofar as it concerns farmers, is probably false. The evidence upon which it rests is certainly inadequate, consisting almost exclusively of nominal rates. While these were typically falling, so were prices generally until the late 1890s, when secular deflation finally gave way to secular inflation. Since only the *relative* price of transportation is meaningful, nominal transport rates must be compared with a relevant price index. When this comparison is made, periods of increase as well as periods of decline in *real* freight rates are evident. For the whole period 1867–96 the trend is approximately horizontal; in brief, farmers were not benefiting from lower transportation charges during the three decades before 1897. The amounts of cotton, corn, or wheat exchanged for a ton-mile of railroad transportation were substantially unchanged throughout the Gilded Age. This finding makes the Populist complaint about "high" railroad freight rates a good deal more comprehensible. . . .

Probably the most sophisticated treatment of the issue is H. T. Newcomb's, presented in 1898 [H. T. Newcomb, *Changes in the Rates of Charge for Railway and Other Transportation Services*, USDA, Division of Statistics, Misc. Series, Bull. 15 (Washington, 1898), 78]. Newcomb shows, for the years 1867–96, index numbers of

---

[10]In the first paragraph, the author's reference to nominal rates means published rates as opposed to the actual rates charged, which frequently varied from rate schedules; secular inflation and deflation pertain to long-term changes in purchasing power. On p. 314 the term "least-squares regression line" concerns the regression technique examined in Chapter Sixteen.

Robert Higgs, "Railroad Rates and the Populist Uprising," *Agricultural History*, XLIV (July 1970), 291–297. Copyright © 1970, by Agricultural History Society. Reprinted, with abridgment of text and notes, by permission of the author and publisher.

the freight rate per ton-mile along with index numbers of nine different farm product prices. There is some question about these farm product prices, since no source is given for them; but even if their quality were not contested, the conclusion drawn from them should be. Newcomb says:

> The substantial regularity of the decline in railway rates is especially notable, as is also the fact that for any series of years after the earliest, which may be selected, it is greater than the decline in the price of any crop. Including 1896, the reduction in the price of only one crop, and that of minor importance, is seen to have been greater than that in freight rates, while the decline in the latter has been 23 percent greater than in the price of wheat and 12 percent greater than in that of hay.

The evidence presented, however, will not support these statements. In his comparisons of 1896 with the base period 1867–72 Newcomb falls victim to what statisticians call the regression fallacy: namely, the selection of particular points to draw a conclusion unwarranted by the data considered as a whole. One who wishes to draw an opposing conclusion might note that in 1894 the price of wheat in relation to its price during 1867–72 was lower than an index of railroad rates relative to the same base, and therefore that wheat prices fell faster than railroad rates before 1894; but this conclusion is no more warranted than is Newcomb's. The issue here concerns the direction of a *trend* movement, and *all* the data must be taken into account in determining this trend. This can be done, for example, by fitting a least-squares regression line to the time series.

The figures used here to represent changes in nominal freight rates are taken from Newcomb's compilation for the early years, from the Interstate Commerce Commission after 1889. [For the ICC data, see U.S. Bureau of the Census, *Historical Statistics of the United States, Colonial Times to 1957* (Washington, 1960), series Q–86:431.] The series (represented below by the symbol t) is constructed by dividing total freight revenue by total ton-miles carried; it is an overall index, covering all kinds of goods, movements in all directions, and both short and long hauls. Newcomb correctly comments,

> [this] is an especially desirable measure of changes in freight charges from period to period, because, unlike published schedules of rates, which in earlier years were deviated from so frequently as to render them in many instances of but the slightest value as showing the actual charges, the rate per ton per mile takes account of all concessions from published charges except in those instances, it is impossible to say how frequent, in which rebates were charged as operating expenses.

The data are increasingly comprehensive over time. They are representative in 1867 of 23 percent of total U.S. railroad mileage; after 1872 of more than 50 percent; and after 1888, with the Interstate Commerce Commission in operation, of virtually all. The sample is sufficiently large to allay much doubt that it is representative, except possibly during the very early years when less than half the national mileage is included. For the conclusions drawn here this slight inadequacy is of no consequence. The freight rate index, which Newcomb expressed in terms of gold prices, has been adjusted to reflect the currency premium on gold before 1879.

To determine changes in the position of farmers vis-à-vis the railroads, the prices *received by farmers* for three important crops (wheat, corn, and cotton, each typically shipped substantial distances by railroad) have been examined. These data were collected by field correspondents of the U.S. Department of Agriculture. [USDA, *Agricultural Statistics, 1952* (Washington, 1952), 1–2, 35, 75–76. Prior to 1908 prices are as of 1 December; afterwards they are seasonal averages.] It is important that prices received by farmers rather than prices at a secondary market be used, and, because errors of this sort are frequently encountered, it may be useful, as a digression, to show just what is involved. For example, if the Warren-Pearson index of farm prices were used a misleading impression would be created because that index apparently relies heavily upon the Aldrich Report, which contains prices for farm products only at New York, Cincinnati, and Chicago. [G. F. Warren and F. A. Pearson, *Wholesale Prices for 212 Years, 1720 to 1932,* Cornell University Agricultural Experiment Station, Memoir 142 (Ithaca, 1932), Pt. I, 84–89, 112–15; and Senate Committee on Finances, Report 1394, *Wholesale Prices, Wages, and Transportation,* by Aldrich (Washington, 1893), Pt. II, 2–64.] A few symbols will help to clarify the problem. If Pf is the average price received by farmers, Pn the average price at New York, Cincinnati, and Chicago, α the average tonnage shipped to these markets, β the average distance of a shipment to these markets in miles, and t the transport rate per ton-mile, the Warren-Pearson data allow the calculation of an index of Pn/t, where $Pn/t = (Pf + \alpha\beta t)/t$. What is required is an index of Pf/t. The equation defining Pn/t can also be written $Pn/t = Pf/t + \alpha\beta$. Since $\alpha\beta$ was rising during the 1867–96 period. Pn/t is biased upward as an indication of Pf/t. In plain English, one cannot infer from a rise in the Warren-Pearson index of farm prices relative to an index of railroad rates that farmers were improving their terms of trade with the railroads.

Figure 1 shows the movement over time of wheat prices, corn prices, and cotton prices deflated by the index of railroad freight rates for the 1867–1915 period: that is, indexes of Pf/t for each of the three products. Given the descriptions of recent historians, one would expect that despite year-to-year fluctuations the trends of the curves would move steadily upward. It is evident that they do not. In fact, three aspects of the series stand out: first, they are extremely variable from year to year; [It is a mistake to suppose that this variability can be explained solely by the well-known instability of farm prices. Substantial fluctuations in transport rates, fluctuations not associated with movements of prices generally, did occur.] second, before 1897 the trend is approximately horizontal; and third, real improvement in the farmers' position begins in the late 1890s. Growers of all three crops were put at a particular disadvantage by the depression of the mid- 1890s. Wheat growers in 1894 were at their worst position of

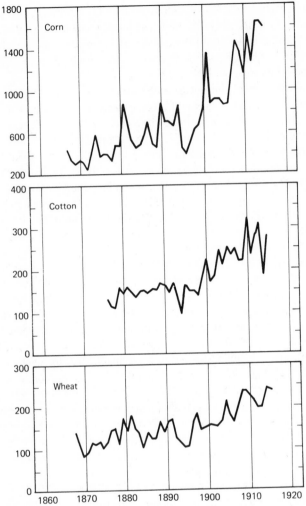

Figure 1. Indices of Farm Price/Railroad Rate Ratios, 1867–1915

the entire period, with the exception of the three years 1869, 1870, and 1874. Corn growers in 1896 had not faced such unfavorable terms of trade since 1878. For cotton, where reliable data are unavailable before 1876, the low mark for the entire period was reached in 1894. It must be emphasized, however, that more is involved here than farmers' suffering from the depression of the 1890s. Even if only the years before 1893 are considered, the data still fail to show any substantial (statistically significant) improvement in the farmers' position.

The indexes in figure 1 are open to criticism. Ideally one would deflate the price of a farm product by an index of the transport rate paid by farmers for shipment of *that product* rather than by a general transport rate index. Unfortunately, since data on total revenue and total ton-miles are not available for individual commodities, it is impossible to construct the appropriate price deflators. One is forced to fall back on published rates with all their defects. Newcomb's compilation presents average rates derived from published schedules for wheat, corn, and cotton shipped over several major routes. As a check on the results obtained above, these rates have been used to deflate the prices received by farmers for the corresponding products. The resulting series, for what they are worth, unanimously corroborate the general patterns shown in figure 1. The trends are appoximately horizontal for the period before 1897, and in almost every case the ratio of farm price to transport rate reaches its minimum point during the depression of 1893–96.

Transport charges were an important part of farmers' costs. In some areas the freight charges incurred in moving crops to a market might absorb as much as half of the crops' value at that market. Under these circumstances the failure of transport rates to decline by more than 10 to 15 percent while farm prices were collapsing by 30 to 50 percent was a genuine economic source of farm distress in the mid-1890s. Where transport charges were a relatively high proportion of farm costs (e.g., Kansas, Nebraska, and the Dakotas) the Populists were most active and successful, while relatively little protest came from areas where transport charges were less important (e.g., Iowa, Missouri, and Illinois). And most important, the experience of the previous twenty-five years gave farmers no reason to expect an imminent improvement. There can be no doubt that farmers themselves perceived their problems as springing *in part* from "high" freight rates. It is difficult to say whether they objected that rates were higher than they "should" have been or whether they considered their position to have been worsening. One thing is clear: they recognized no recent improvement with respect to railroad rates. Notably, the two decades preceding World War I, for which the data show such substantial improvement in the farmers' position (fig. 1), also witnessed the disappearance of agrarian unrest. . . .